STATUS AND GROUPS

RESEARCH ON MANAGING GROUPS AND TEAMS

Series Editors: Elizabeth A. Mannix and
Margaret A. Neale

Volume 1: Composition
Edited by Deborah H. Gruenfeld, 1998

Volume 2: Groups in Context
Edited by Ruth Wageman, 1999

Volume 3: Technology
Edited by Terri L. Griffith, 2000

Volume 4: Toward Phenomenology of Groups and Group Membership
Edited by Harris Sondak, 2002

Volume 5: Identity Issues in Groups
Edited by Jeffrey T. Polzer

Volume 6: Time in Groups
Edited by Sally Blount

RESEARCH ON MANAGING GROUPS AND TEAMS VOLUME 7

STATUS AND GROUPS

EDITED BY

MELISSA C. THOMAS-HUNT
Cornell University, Ithaca, USA

JAI

United Kingdom – North America – Japan – India – Malaysia – China – Australasia

JAI Press is an imprint of Emerald Group Publishing Limited
Howard House, Wagon Lane, Bingley BD16 1WA, UK

First edition 2007

Reprints and permission service
Contact: booksandseries@emeraldinsight.com

British Library Cataloguing in Publication Data
A catalogue record for this book is available from the British Library

ISBN: 978-0-76-231229-0

CONTENTS

LIST OF CONTRIBUTORS

Cameron P. Anderson	Stern School of Business, New York University, USA
Joseph P. Broschak	Department of Business Administration, University of Illinois at Urbana-Champaign, USA
Jonathan M. Bowman	Department of Communication, Boston College, USA
Ya-Ru Chen	Rutgers Business School, Rutgers University, USA
Joshua Correll	Department of Psychology, University of Colorado at Boulder, USA
David De Cremer	Department of Social Psychology, Tilburg University, The Netherlands
P. Christopher Earley	London Business School, UK
Alison R. Fragale	Kenan-Flagler Business School, University of North Carolina at Chapel Hill, USA
Samuel N. Fraidin	University of Southern California Law School, USA
Adam D. Galinsky	Kellogg School of Management, Northwestern University, USA
Martine R. Haas	School of Industrial and Labor Relations, Cornell University, USA
Andrea B. Hollingshead	Department of Communications, University of Illinois at Urbana-Champaign, USA
Edward J. Lawler	School of Industrial and Labor Relations, Cornell University, USA

Lee Chay-Hoon	Nanyang Technical University, Singapore
Paul V. Martorana	McCombs School of Business, University of Texas at Austin, USA
Gregory B. Northcraft	Department of Business Administration, University of Illinois at Urbana-Champaign, USA
Jennifer R. Overbeck	Marshall School of Business, University of Southern California, USA
Bernadette Park	Department of Psychology, University of Colorado at Boulder, USA
Amy E. Randel	Wake Forest University, USA
Hayagreeva Rao	Stanford Graduate School of Business Stanford University, USA
Ashleigh Shelby Rosette	C. T. Bauer College of Business, University of Houston, USA
Sandra E. Spataro	Yale School of Management, Yale University, USA
Leigh Thompson	Kellogg School of Management, Northwestern University, USA
Tom R. Tyler	Department of Psychology, New York University, USA
Heather C. Vough	Department of Business Administration, University of Illinois at Urbana-Champaign, USA
Gwen M. Wittenbaum	Department of Communication, Michigan State University, USA

PREFACE

> An organized social group is always a stratified social body. There has not been and does not exist any permanent social group which is 'flat' and in which all members are equal.—Pitirim Sorokin (1927)

This seventh volume of *Research on Managing Groups and Teams* contains the work of scholars who gathered in May, 2003, at a conference held at Cornell University. When I was invited by the series editors to coordinate the conference and select a theme, I immediately suggested that of "Status and Groups" to which they agreed. At that time, my choice of status as a conference theme reflected my own interest in the effects of groups' status hierarchies on group member interactions and group effectiveness. Realizing that group functioning is inextricably linked to group and member status and that status is so often derived from membership in groups, we decided to adopt a broad construal of status and invited submissions from a wide array of researchers. As a result, we include works by some authors who have not been traditionally categorized as status and/or groups researchers, but whose work fundamentally lies at the intersection of the study of groups and status.

At the most basic level, status describes the rank of individuals or groups within a specified context. It refers to the prestige hierarchy which determines which individuals are afforded honor, respect, and opportunities to influence outcomes. Status is inherently relative in that it can only be assessed in comparison to that of other individuals or groups. Early notions of status are derived from the sociological writings of Marx, Weber and Homans who argued that status emerges because groups within society are inherently unequal. More recently, other researchers, Bales, Berger and colleagues, Lawler, Ridgeway and their students have specifically focused on the emergence of status within groups. Their investigations have largely been confined to considerations of the characteristics that give rise to expectations of performance and, hence convey status within groups. Similarly, more social psychological treatments of status primarily focus on the effects of status on group identification and individuals' distribution of effort within and across groups.

Our investigations consider both the role of status within groups and how the status of groups within their larger context affects their members and their effectiveness. Consequently, the works presented here cut across levels, examining the relationship between individuals and groups, the treatment they receive, and their participation within their immediate environment; the link between exhibited behaviors and status conferral; and the emergence and effects of status rivalries within and across groups.

The works in this volume, contributed by members of the next generation of researchers on status and groups, draw upon impressive earlier literatures, build bridges between domains that had previously remained theoretically distinct, and give more nuanced attention to the age-old questions "Which groups and group members are afforded status?" "How is status acquired?" "How is status used?" and "How do individuals and groups experience and react to and against their own and others' status?" While the questions raised, at the surface, are not new, the application of a status lens will enable readers to emerge from this volume with a more informed understanding of group functioning.

Melissa C. Thomas-Hunt
Volume Editor

A MATTER OF INTRAGROUP STATUS: THE IMPORTANCE OF RESPECT FOR THE VIABILITY OF GROUPS

David De Cremer and Tom R. Tyler

ABSTRACT

Respect is an important indicator of intragroup status, and it can influence within-group behavior. Being respected by other group members indicates a positive standing within the group that is relevant to two important identity concerns: belongingness and social reputation. Belongingness refers to the extent to which a person feels included in the group, and social reputation refers to how other in-group members evaluate a person. We review a series of studies that show that respect indeed communicates information relevant to these identity concerns, and as such influences a person's sense of affiliation, self-esteem, and cooperation (all variables considered to be important for the viability of groups). In addition, we also discuss whether the source of respect (i.e., peers vs. authority), culture, and group size matter in influencing these group-related variables. Finally, some implications for research on groups are discussed.

Status and Groups
Research on Managing Groups and Teams, Volume 7, 1–21

ISSN: 1534-0856/doi:10.1016/S1534-0856(05)07001-5

In contemporary society, one of the aims of many organizations is to achieve a high status, relative to other organizations. Status derived from interorganizational comparisons provides a company with economic benefits (i.e., having a competitive edge) and social benefits (i.e., being a proud organization). Consequently, a great deal of research has been devoted to understanding the role of group status for group members. For example, social identity theory (Tajfel & Turner, 1986) states that people use their group memberships to define their social identity, as such implying that people prefer to derive their sense of worth and identity from high-status groups. Individual employees prefer to belong to high-status and prestigious organizations in which they can bask in reflected glory (cf., Cialdini et al., 1976).

Of course, the striving for high-status group memberships may complicate how members of different groups and organizations interact. For example, the issue of intergroup-based status plays an important role in several industries that rely heavily on employees from both their own company, but, in addition, also from employees of other more marginal businesses (e.g., hotels, retail establishments). In these situations, employees from the main and high-status company (in-group) are more or less "forced" to work together with employees from related, but, more marginal businesses (out-group). Research on such in-group vs. out-group interactions shows convincingly that status differences between such companies negatively influence working relationships and collaborative behavior between them (Stamper & Masterson, 2002).

However, in the present chapter we wish to argue that employees do not only derive a sense of their personal status from intergroup relations, but also attend to their status within the group, and that such intragroup status has important consequences for group behavior. Surprisingly, social psychology and management research has devoted little attention to the relation between intragroup status, and the viability of groups and organizations. In fact, assessing the impact of how people perceive their status (how they are perceived by themselves and others) within groups and organizations has only recently attracted the attention of social scientists (e.g., Kramer, 2001; Tyler, 1999; Tyler & Blader, 2000).

THE IMPORTANCE OF INTRAGROUP STATUS

The recent interest in the issue of intragroup status emerges largely from several lines of inquiry examining how newcomers in groups and organizations attend to social information. For example, Kramer (2001, p. 173) observed that newcomers in organizations are very motivated to engage in the process of sense-making "to reduce uncertainty about standing." For these purposes, newcomers assign significant weight to relational information, which communicates how others perceive their intragroup status. Thus, concerns about intragroup status could be expected to strongly influence newcomers' actions and attitudes, more so than those of old-timers in organizations. Such a perspective is indeed supported by recent research conceptualizing the newcomer as an active participant in the socialization process, in which he or she actively seeks information to define his or her role in a clear and stable way (e.g., Bauer & Green, 1994; Ashford & Black, 1996).

What social psychological motives underlie people's search for intragroup status information? In the present chapter, we argue that information about one's status within the group or organization influences one's relational self, or, in other words, that aspect of their identity which is based on the quality of their interactions with others (Tyler & Smith, 1999). One's relational self is based on personalized relationships with particular others and these relationships include friendships, relationships with colleagues, and with supervisors (Sedikides & Brewer, 2001). This type of self relies on the process of reflected appraisal, and this level of appraisal is, in turn, associated with how people evaluate interpersonal relatedness, intimacy, and interdependence within the relationship (see Baumeister & Leary, 1995).

Thus, one's relational self is constructed within the context of intragroup relationships and can be assessed by means of one's status within the group. Following from such a focus on the relational self, we reason that knowing one's intragroup status provides information about two identity concerns: (1) whether one belongs or not (i.e., inclusion) and (2) whether one is evaluated positively by others (i.e., social reputation). Obtaining such diagnostic social information reduces uncertainty about one's social self (see cf., Van den Bos & Lind, 2002; De Cremer & Sedikides, 2005). In line with this assumption, several lines of inquiry have indeed indicated that the attempt to define one's relational self raises questions, such as: (a) "Can I define myself in terms of my relationships with others in the group?" (i.e., "Do I belong to this group?") and (b) "Am I evaluated positively by the others (i.e., social reputation)?" Moreover, research on procedural fairness has also defined the concept of intragroup status by referring to the process of inclusion (Lind, 2001), and the process of social evaluation of one's position within the group (Tyler, 1989): processes similar to the two identity concerns of belongingness and social reputation.

In the following sections, we will focus more closely on the meaning and importance of both identity concerns, and will operationalize intragroup status by using the concept of received respect.

Belongingness and Reputation as Identity Concerns

Owing to our focus on the relational self, we will examine both the identity concerns at the interpersonal level. Why? First, the *need to belong* implies that people wish to form positive and potentially continuous social relationships, and, therefore, they focus strongly on what happens at the interpersonal level (Baumeister & Leary, 1995; De Cremer & Leonardelli, 2003). Second, evidence exists that particularly within *interpersonal relationships* people seek social approval and wish to convey favorable images of themselves through others (Baumeister, 1982; Leary & Kowalski, 1990). We will explore the implications of these two identity concerns at the interpersonal level.

With respect to belongingness needs, several lines of research point to the conclusion that people are social beings in that they use their relationships with other individuals or groups to define their social self (Aron & Aron, 1986; Tajfel & Turner, 1986). A crucial aspect in this process is that people thus pursue a sense of inclusion for self-definitional purposes, a tendency that is believed to be inherent in human beings in general (Kurzban & Leary, 2001).

Research on the need to belong (e.g., Baumeister & Leary, 1995; Gardner, Pickett, & Brewer, 2000b; Twenge, Baumeister, Tice, & Stucke, 2001; Twenge, Catanese, & Baumeister, 2002), indeed demonstrates that people are fundamentally motivated to belong to groups and relationships considered to be important to the self. As a result, people are very attentive toward any type of relational information communicated by others, but particularly so when their need to belong is unfulfilled. The importance and pervasiveness of this need to belong has been shown by research demonstrating that a lack of positive social relationships has detrimental effects on the physical, cognitive, and behavioral level (Baumeister & Leary, 1995; Reis, Collins, & Berscheid, 2000). For example, not feeling accepted by others influences well-being negatively, reinforces selective memory for socially relevant information and undermines intrinsic motivation (e.g., Berscheid & Reis, 1998; Deci & Ryan, 2000; Gardner, Gabriel, & Diekman, 2000a; Gardner et al., 2000b), whereas fulfilling the need to belong positively influences cooperative behavior within groups (De Cremer & Leonardelli, 2003).

We are also interested in social reputation. As early as the writings of James (1890), researchers acknowledge that one's social self is, at least partly, determined by one's social reputation. Indeed, because social evaluation is an important element in the process of constructing the self (cf., Tice, 1992), people are, by their very nature, motivated to obtain a positive image or reputation (e.g., the extensive literature on people's public self-presentation skills; Baumeister, 1982; Leary, 2001). In fact, social reputations largely determine how one's behaviors are recognized and rewarded (e.g., Johnson, Erez, Kiker, & Motowidlo, 2002). As a result, one's social self clearly entails a concern about social evaluation and consequently a concern about one's reputation within the group. The powerful effects of social reputation in groups has, for example, been demonstrated by recent research showing that people exhibit more cooperative behavior when their reputation is threatened, help others more easily when they have a positive image, and are more likely to develop positive and enjoyable relationships with others if they possess a positive reputation (e.g., Gächter & Fehr, 1999; De Cremer, & DeWitte, 2001; Milinski, Semmann, & Krambeck, 2002).

Of course, we acknowledge that due to their connection to identity issues, concerns about inclusion and about social reputation are strongly related to one another. In fact, research suggests that belongingness needs and concern for reputation share a common ground. That is, a lack of social connections (e.g., being abandoned by others, being a peripheral member of society, etc.) and feelings of having a deprived status (i.e., a low social reputation), often seem to go hand in hand in negatively influencing a person's mental well-being, emotions, cognitions, and actions (e.g., Baumeister, 1991; Baumeister & Leary, 1995). For example, youth lacking social bonds frequently join gangs to feel included, just as they join them to get a positive social reputation from those gangs (Jankowski, 1991). All of these suggest that a lack of belongingness and a low social reputation, or deprived social status are often linked, with both making people focus more on relational information, such as their intragroup standing (e.g., Forsyth, 1991) or how they are treated by others (Tyler & Smith, 1999). Although they may be related at some conceptual level, it is important to note that the aim of the present chapter is not to outline which factor determines the other, but to stress that information about both belongingness and reputation is communicated by information about one's intragroup status.

Respect as an Indicator of Intragroup Status

What type of intragroup information is related to these identity concerns? One specific type of information that indicates one's position and status within the group, and as such influences one's self-definition, is whether one feels *respected* by the other group members. In the present chapter, respect is seen as social information including one's relational value within the group, which is communicated by others via the way they treat the person in question (see also Tyler & Smith, 1999). Why should respect be particularly relevant to intragroup status?

In the present chapter, we start from the assumption that people attend to cues about their relationships within their group to derive information about their social self and self-regard (see Tyler & Smith, 1999; De Cremer, 2002b). Following relational models of justice (Lind & Tyler, 1988; Tyler & Lind, 1992), one important type of information that provides us with such cues is the fairness of procedures enacted by the group and its members. Research on procedural fairness has indeed shown that the use of fair procedures positively influences people's self-regard and identity (e.g., Koper, van Knippenberg, Bouhuijs, Vermunt, & Wilke, 1993). The reason for this is that fair procedures communicate to people that they are perceived as having a respected position within the group. Thus, in these relational models, respect is seen as an important indicator of intragroup status. In line with this proposition, research indeed shows that people's judgments about their standing within the group, and their associated feelings of self-regard, are enhanced when they receive respectful treatment by the group and its authorities (Tyler, Degoey, & Smith, 1996; Boeckman & Tyler, 2002). As such, we consider respect not as something that people simply intuit by themselves, but rather as a judgment that emerges from the treatment they receive from others.

Thus, Tyler and colleagues (e.g., Tyler & Smith, 1999; Tyler, 2001) argue that whether people feel that others treat them with respect shape their judgments about their acceptance within their group (inclusion) and about their status within the group (reputation). Based on this, we predict that the respect given by in-group members can be seen as an important means to tell people whether: (a) they belong to the relationships within their group and (b) they have a positive social reputation within those relationships. Therefore, we perceive respect as an indicator of intragroup status communicating identity-relevant information, which, in turn, will influence important group outcomes (see Fig. 1).

The implication of these predictions, as derived from our respect model, is that once people's need for belongingness and positive social reputation are satisfied, they will care less strongly about issues of respect. However, we hasten to say that this latter assumption only implies that people will be less likely to use information about respect to satisfy the above-mentioned

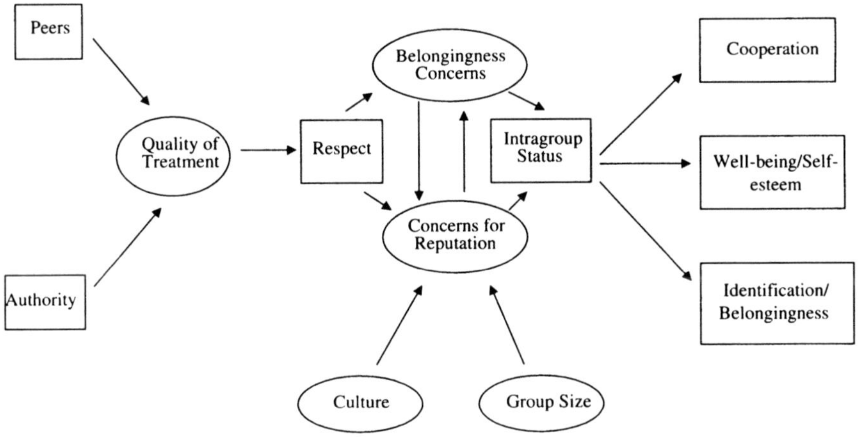

Fig. 1. Respect as Intragroup Status Model.

identity needs. They may still be strongly motivated to use respect for other purposes associated with their high(er) intragroup status. For example, Chen, Brockner, and Greenberg (2003) showed that both high- and low-status members of work organizations (in terms of their management position) valued relational information like procedural fairness, but for different purposes. Those high in status were interested in affirming existing power differences. Thus, this data suggests that those with high intragroup status positions may still value and process respect information, but we argue that they will do so for reasons that have less to do with identity concerns, but rather for reasons associated with power and legitimacy (e.g., Jost & Major, 2001).

RESPECT AND THE VIABILITY OF GROUPS

What behavioral, cognitive, and affective outcomes does respect influence by addressing identity concerns, and why is respect important for the viability of groups? In the present chapter, we will focus on three such outcomes that are of relevance toward the group and its members – cooperation, feelings of affiliation, and members' self-esteem (see Fig. 1).

Groups fare well if their members are willing to devote extra time, energy, and effort to interdependent tasks and actions that benefit the group or organization. This contribution of individual effort, time, and resources to collective projects is referred to as *cooperation* (e.g., cf., Katz, 1964; Smith, Carroll, & Ashford, 1995; Van Vugt, Snyder, Tyler, & Biel, 2000). For a variety of reasons, cooperation has long been deemed necessary to the survival of groups. For example, cooperation by the group members leads to improved coordination of activities and interdependent tasks, a factor considered important to the success of groups in reaching their goals (e.g., Smith et al., 1995; Wagner II, 1995). Further, promoting cooperation reduces non-cooperative tendencies like free riding and social loafing (e.g., Olson, 1965; Kerr & Bruun, 1983).

Further, for groups to remain viable and long lasting, their members also have to identify with the group and feel that they are part of it. If no sense of *affiliation* exists, group members are likely to leave, leading to the group's demise. In addition, the nature of work (e.g., role definition, organizational goals) can change rapidly, and only group members who feel a strong sense of affiliation may be intrinsically motivated to adapt to these changes. Indeed, having affiliations with others is a fundamental psychological need, and as Deci and Ryan (2000, p. 233) argue "intrinsic motivation will be facilitated by conditions that conduce toward psychological need satisfaction." Moreover, expressing strong group identification is also believed to motivate people to pursue the group goals, sacrifice own interests, and to express loyalty to the group (e.g., De Cremer & Van Vugt, 1999; De Cremer & Van Dijk, 2002).

Finally, because of changing business conditions, which have been characterized by an increasing trend toward employee involvement in decision making, group research has begun to devote more attention to the role that members' *self-esteem* plays in terms of group functioning (e.g., Pfeffer, 1998; McAllister & Bigley, 2002). More precisely, in the last decade it has become increasingly clear that self-esteem is not only an important psychological need, but also an important economic need (Branden, 1998). That is, self-esteem plays a role in how people evaluate themselves and how efficacious they feel. These feelings, in turn, are of major importance in the process of how employees, at different levels in the organization, reason, decide, and regulate action (e.g., Wiesenfeld, Brockner, & Thibault, 2000). Moreover, research has also demonstrated that individuals with high and low self-esteem react differently toward conflict situations and task interdependence, and perceive relationships with others in the group as serving different functions (Brockner, 1988; Duffy, Shaw, & Stark, 2000; Leary & Baumeister, 2000).

In the following section, we will review our research on the extent to which belongingness needs and concerns for reputation account for the effect of respect on the above-mentioned group outcomes.

EMPIRICAL EVIDENCE

To examine whether concerns for belongingness and reputation explain why group members attend carefully to respect information, we conducted several experimental and field studies. These studies used a moderator approach to examine more closely whether respect indeed communicates information relevant to belongingness and social reputation. That is, in our line of research, we assessed whether respect influences a person's affect, cognition, and behavior more strongly when concerns for belongingness and social reputation were high rather than low. Finding this type of evidence would indicate that respect communicates information relevant to both identity concerns. Thus, a moderator approach informs us about the processes underlying both the hypothesized moderator (i.e., identity concerns) and the relevant social domain (i.e., respect information) (Snyder & Cantor, 1998; De Cremer, 2002a). Below, we will provide an overview of some of these studies. More precisely, evidence will be presented that the interactive effect between respect and belongingness needs influences cooperation, and that the interactive effect between respect and social reputation influences affiliation and reports of self-esteem.

Belongingness as Moderator

In order to examine the interactive effect of belongingness needs and respect on cooperation experimentally, we conducted a study in which we employed the public good paradigm (De Cremer, 2002b). Public good dilemmas represent the conflict between personal and collective interests (as often observed in-group and organizational settings), and as such provide a useful tool to assess the degree of cooperation group members are willing to engage in. More precisely, in this paradigm group members are asked to contribute toward the establishment of a public good (e.g., contributing time and effort to a team project, investing departmental money to achieve a higher outcome for the company, etc.). Provision of the good provides each group member with a (monetary) bonus. Once the public good is provided, however, every group member can benefit, regardless of his or her contributions. This *impossibility of exclusion* (Olson, 1965) leads individuals to think about whether it is possible to consume the good even without contributing substantially to its provision. It is thus in one's personal interest not to contribute (Dawes, 1980). However, if all people adopt such a self-interest perspective, nobody will contribute, and the public good will not be provided. In other words, the emergence of cooperation may be problematic, because the pursuit of personal self-interest may lead to non-cooperation.

Participants took part in this study in groups of three. Before starting with this study, participants were required to fill out a questionnaire assessing different personality types, referred to as Type O or P personality. Then, the structure of the dilemma game was explained. Each participant received an endowment of 300 cents (Dutch) (approximately U.S. $1.20) and was free to choose any amount they wanted to contribute (ranging from 0 to 300 cents). The total amount contributed by the group would be multiplied by two and then divided equally amongst all group members, regardless of their contribution. The amount one decided not to contribute would accrue totally to oneself.

Thereafter, participants were told that the members in their group were all classified as personality P types. The Type P personality was made relatively *attractive* (compared to the Type O personality) by pointing out the positive traits that are usually exhibited by those with a P personality. This was done because it is assumed that people are more motivated to gain acceptance by desired groups. Then, the manipulation of need to belong was introduced. In the *peripheral* membership condition (i.e., high need to belong; see Noel, Wann, & Branscombe, 1995), participants were told that their questionnaire responses placed them just inside the Type P category. If they had responded slightly different, they would not have been a Type P personality but an O personality. Participants in the *core* membership condition (i.e., low need to belong) were told that their responses were clear examples of a core member of the Type P category. That is, they could be considered as a near-perfect example of a person with a Type P personality.

Thereafter, participants received a message from the other two group members expressing their opinion about the group and its members. This was the respect manipulation. Respect was operationalized by using self-identified criteria in the interactional justice scale of Moorman (1991). More specifically, based on this scale the summarizing message included a reference to the extent that: (a) the group would accept feedback or not about group decisions and its implications; (b) the viewpoint of others would be considered or not; and (c) others would be treated in a friendly and kind way or not. In the respect condition, participants were informed that the other group members would appreciate the opinions of others, would be willing to discuss important issues, and pay respect to what others say. In the disrespect condition, the message said exactly the opposite.

The most important result was a significant interaction, showing that the respect manipulation influenced cooperation among peripheral group members (respect vs. disrespect: *Ms* = 145.23 cents vs. 83.00 cents), but not among core members (respect vs. disrespect: *Ms* = 128.05 cents vs. 119.95 cents). These results clearly point out that peripheral group members contributed the most when they received respect (although this level of cooperation was not significantly different from the levels reported by core group members), and contributed the least when disrespect was shown. Thus, levels of cooperation were only a function of respect when the need to belong was high. If the need to belong was low, respect did not matter.

In addition, we also found the same interaction pattern in a public good dilemma study (see De Cremer & Tyler, in press) in which the desire to belong was not manipulated, but directly assessed by means of the individual difference scale of need to belong (see Leary, Kelly, Cottrell, & Schreindorfer, 2001 for the use of this scale). In this study (dis)respect was also communicated by the other in-group members. Finally, in a field study including employees working with chemicals (in a German company), again we found that respect from coworkers was significantly and positively correlated with organizational citizenship behavior (OCB) among employees high in need to belong, but not among employees low in need to belong. We considered OCB to be an example of the organizational cooperative behavior Katz (1964) and others alluded to (Organ, 1988).

To summarize, within groups, respect information influenced decisions about cooperating. This effect, however, only occurred when group members had a strong need to belong. As such, this moderating approach provides evidence that respect communicates information relevant to people's identity concern of belongingness, and in this process influences cooperation within groups.

Social Reputation as Moderator

To examine whether people's concern about their social reputation moderated the effect of respect, we first conducted several studies assessing individual differences in the extent to which people cared about their reputation (De Cremer & Tyler, in press). These studies showed that respect influenced affective reactions and feelings of affiliation when people's concerns about reputation were high, relative to low. In addition, we also attempted to manipulate people's concern about their social reputation.

To manipulate concern for social reputation, it was reasoned that if the way you are evaluated or how you act is identifiable to others, people become concerned about conforming to normative social influences (Deutsch &

Gerard, 1955), and as a consequence are concerned about their social reputation. For example, if people are evaluated negatively and others are aware of this, those under scrutiny will fear for their social reputation. Therefore, concern for reputation was operationalized by means of identifiability of evaluations or actions (see also Sedikides, Herbst, Hardin, & Dardis, 2002).

In this study, participants were given a scenario that asked them to imagine that they were part of a workforce at their university, and that they would defend their own proposal to the university council. Then, the manipulation of respect was introduced. In the *disrespect* condition, participants read that the university council did not respect their proposal and the presentation of it, whereas in the respect condition the university council did respect all of these. Thereafter, the identifiability manipulation was introduced. In the identifiability condition, participants were told that the outcome of their meeting with the university council would be communicated to the rest of the university community, whereas this would not be the case in the no identifiability condition.

With respect to the affiliation data, the results revealed a significant interaction showing that feelings of affiliation were more strongly influenced by our respect manipulation when their actions were identifiable (respect vs. disrespect: $Ms = 5.30$ vs. 2.85) than when they were not identifiable (respect vs. disrespect: $Ms = 3.84$ vs. 2.75). With respect to the self-esteem data, a similar interaction pattern was found. Participants' self-esteem in the identifiability condition (respect vs. disrespect: $Ms = 5.37$ vs. 2.67) was more strongly influenced than in the no identifiability condition (respect vs. disrespect: $Ms = 4.15$ vs. 2.79).

To summarize, variations in respect influenced group members' sense of affiliation and self-esteem, but particularly so when they were concerned about their social reputation. Thus, these data support our assertion that respect (as an indicator of intragroup status) exerts significant influence because it communicates information relevant to group members' social reputation.

Does It Matter Who Respects? Authority or Peers as Source

To date, most research on respect and the importance of intragroup status was motivated by assumptions derived from the relational model of authority (Tyler & Lind, 1992). As a consequence, the impact of this group variable has been examined mostly in hierarchical relationships. However, authorities are not the only group members serving as the source for respect. Indeed, recent research has demonstrated that one's peers or own group members can also be seen as the source that communicates this type of relational information (see e.g., Branscombe, Spears, Ellemers, & Doosje, 2002; De Cremer, 2002b; Simon & Stürmer, 2003). For example, the earlier reported studies by De Cremer (2002b) showed that respect from the other in-group members or coworkers significantly influenced cooperation within groups.

In fact, this non-hierarchical perspective on respect fits well with recent suggestions by social justice researchers. For example, Smith and Tyler (1997, p. 157) reasoned that "respect is an important aspect of group membership even when there is no clear authority structure." More recently, Lind (2001, p. 222), in discussing the importance of feelings of inclusiveness and belongingness in fair process effects, mentioned that "The … threat of exclusion (i.e., not belonging) manifests itself very starkly in hierarchical contexts … but it can be just as strong in close equal-power relations." In line with these recent suggestions, Tyler and Blader (2003) suggested that respect from both authorities and others in the group are relevant to one's identity. Future research, however, is urgently needed to examine this proposition in greater detail.

Thus, both authorities and in-group members may function as a source of respect. The question, of course, is which relational aspect people evaluate to conclude whether they are respected or not? We suggest that both sources communicate respect via the quality of how they treat others. In other words, the quality of treatment people receive is considered to be a main communication channel of respect (Tyler & Blader, 2000). This perspective suggests that people not only evaluate authorities and in-group members in terms of the quality of the decisions they make (e.g., "Formal rules have been followed, so I should be happy about my group membership."), but also in terms of how they are treated when making these decisions (e.g., "When following formal procedures, I also felt that I was really being valued and treated well.").

These arguments suggest that quality of treatment is linked to the specific type of information that signals how one is perceived and evaluated in terms of his or her dealings, and relationships with the group, and as such, closely resembles our treatment of respect as an indicator of intragroup status. Thus, the concept of quality of treatment has no association with the outcomes that people receive, but more with the quality of treatment that accompanies the communication of outcomes. For example, if employees have to be fired because of economic reasons, a respectful and fair treatment is beneficial when communicating the bad personal outcome of being fired because it mitigates the negative interpersonal message. Indeed, being treated with respect and dignity signals to the fired employee that he or she is not excluded from the group due to judgments about them as a person. To be fired due to external problems that a company is having does not necessarily reflect on a person. To be fired due to perceived incompetence does reflect on the person. To conclude, based on our studies, it appears to be the case that group members will assign more weight to quality of treatment when they are in need of belongingness and social reputation information.

SITUATIONAL MODERATORS OF THE RELATIONSHIP RESPECT IDENTITY: CULTURE AND GROUP SIZE

Of course, treating respect as a major impetus to the identity concerns of belongingness and social reputation also invites suggestions as to when this relationship will be the strongest. Two situational features that have received considerable attention in the literature on groups, teams, and organizations are the influence of culture and the size of the group one operates in (Thomas & Fink, 1963; Steiner, 1972; Hofstede, 1980; Kim, Park, & Suzuki, 1990). In a similar vein, we think that these two situational influences will also matter in determining the extent to which respect satisfies belongingness and social reputation concerns. To the degree that this is true, these situational influences need to be included in future research examining the impact of respect in group settings.

Regarding the influence of culture, it could be the case that respect from others, as a function of cultural differences, is more or less relevant to identity. That is, an interesting finding emerging from cross-cultural research is that the importance of one's interaction partner for one's self-definition varies with cultural values (Markus & Kitayama, 1991; Markus, Kitayama, & Heiman, 1996). Findings have shown that people in collectivistic cultures are more likely to use the social norms adopted by the members of their groups to shape their behavior, self-esteem, and personal attitudes (e.g., Abrams, Ando, & Hinkle, 1998). People in individualistic cultures, however, tend to think of themselves as autonomous individuals and as such do not use their interdependent relationships as input for their attitudes, self-esteem, and feelings (Markus & Kitayama, 1991). Consequently, recent procedural fairness research has suggested that differences in terms of the collectivistic–individualistic dimension will determine whether much attention is devoted to relational information (Brockner, De Cremer, Van den Bos, & Chen, 2005). Following from these findings, we suggest that cultural differences in terms of individualism vs. collectivism may moderate the extent to which respect satisfies belongingness and social reputation needs (see Fig. 1).

Another cultural difference variable that may impact the influence of respect on identity concerns is whether one lives in a high-power vs. low-power society, or, also referred to as masculine vs. feminine cultures, respectively (Hofstede, 1980). Hofstede (1991, p. 93) argued that "Organizations in a masculine society stress results and want to reward on the basis of equity, organizations in a feminine society, however, are more likely to reward people on the basis of equality." Thus, in contrast to masculine cultures, feminine cultures stress the importance of solidarity and equality. As a result, feminine cultures, or low-power societies, may regard respect as more important than masculine or high-power societies, because due to its identity potential of communication belongingness information, people in those cultures will regard respect as more important of the viability of their groups, organizations, and societies. Similarly, Tyler, Lind, and Huo (2000) found that people in high-power distance cultures were less strongly influenced by relational information than were those in low-power distance cultures.

Another important situational feature that may moderate the relationship between respect and identity is how the group or organization is structured, or, in other words, are you a member of a small or large group? Research, for example, has shown that group size has a significant influence on potential productivity and on process loss (Steiner, 1972). Also, cooperation mostly decreases in groups because social constraints like identifiability, a strong sense of social responsibility, and so forth are not present anymore. For these reasons, De Cremer and Leonardelli (2003) argued that when such social constraints that promote cooperation are absent (or at least present to a lesser degree), cooperation might depend on psychological needs, such as the need to belong. In line with this prediction, they found that group members high in the need to belong were more cooperative than those low in the need to belong, but only in large groups. In small groups, no such difference was found. Deriving from this finding, one could suggest that the need to belong may be a more salient motive in larger groups, and as such, respect can be expected to have a stronger influence in larger groups than in smaller groups where the need to belong is not so strongly activated (see Fig. 1).

CONCLUDING REMARKS

Several researchers have noted that throughout our society (e.g., organizations, teams, close relationships, customer relationships, etc.) there is an increasing demand for respect (Tyler & Lind, 1992; Hill Jr., 2000; O'Connell, 2000), leading people to constantly worry about whether such respect has been granted. Our present chapter suggests that one important reason for this concern is that respect can be considered an indicator of one's intragroup status, and as such, communicates information about two important identity concerns. As a result, contributing positively to these identity concerns by means of respectful treatment leads to outcomes that are relevant to group productivity and the well-being of its members – cooperation, affiliation, and self-esteem. For these reasons, it is essential that contemporary organizations, societies, and groups recognize that success does not solely depend on how well one performs relative to economic competitors (Dosi, 1995), but also on the extent to which one devotes attention to how the quality and trustworthiness of relationships are developed and maintained.

On a final note, it is interesting to acknowledge that from the perspective of the group, this demand for respect (to infer one's intragroup status) and its related outcomes is not easy to understand, because it is generally assumed that the group and its norms influence the behavior of its members. However, our studies show that group members actively seek individual attention before they engage in group-promoting activities. As such, this observation signals a certain rise of individualism in group settings. That is, group members seem to be active participants that contribute to group life and productivity as a function of how they have been treated by the group (see also Simon & Stürmer, 2003). In a similar vein, Heuer, Penrod, Hafer, and Cohn (2002) also noted that "People care about respect, because of what it conveys about others evaluation of their worth as individuals rather than its group-based connotations."

All these observations align well with the recent debate in the literature on self and identity; that is, whether the personal self or the self derived from the collective or group is primary in determining people's actions in social settings. A recent meta-analysis by Gaertner, Sedikides, Vevea, and Luzzini (2002) demonstrates that the personal self seems most primary, suggesting that indeed the individual needs and motives of group members may dictate group outcomes to a large extent.

ACKNOWLEDGMENT

Preparation of this chapter was supported by a fellowship of the Netherlands Organization for Scientific Research (NWO, Grant No. 016.005.019) awarded to the first author.

REFERENCES

Abrams, D., Ando, K., & Hinkle, S. (1998). Psychological attachment to groups: Cross-cultural differences in organizational identification and subjective norms as predictors of workers' turnovers intentions. *Personality and Social Psychology Bulletin, 24*, 1027–1039.

Aron, A., & Aron, N. E. (1986). *Love as the expansion of self: Understanding attraction and satisfaction*. New York: Hemisphere.

Ashford, S. J., & Black, J. S. (1996). Proactivity during organizational entry: The role of desire for control. *Journal of Applied Psychology, 81*, 199–214.

Bauer, T. N., & Green, S. G. (1994). Effect of newcomer involvement in work-related activities: A longitudinal study of socialization. *Journal of Applied Psychology, 79*, 211–223.

Baumeister, R. F. (1982). A self-presentational view of social phenomena. *Psychological Bulletin, 91*, 3–26.

Baumeister, R. F. (1991). *Meanings of life*. New York: Guilford Press.

Baumeister, R. F., & Leary, M. R. (1995). The need to belong: Desire for interpersonal attachments as a fundamental human motivation. *Psychological Bulletin, 117*, 497–529.

Berscheid, E., & Reis, H. T. (1998). Attraction and close relationships. In: D. T. Gilbert, S. T. Fiske & G. Lindzey (Eds), *The handbook of social psychology*, (4th ed., Vol. 2, pp. 193–281). New York: McGraw-Hill.

Boeckman, R. J., & Tyler, T. R. (2002). Trust, respect, and the psychology of political engagement. *Journal of Applied Social Psychology, 32*, 2067–2088.

Branden, N. (1998). *Self-esteem at work*. San Francisco: Jossey-Bass Publishers.

Branscombe, N. R., Spears, R., Ellemers, N., & Doosje, B. (2002). Intragroup and intergroup evaluation effects on group behavior. *Personality and Social Psychology Bulletin, 28*, 744–753.

Brockner, J. (1988). *Self-esteem at work*. Lexington, MA: Lexington Books.

Brockner, J., De Cremer, D., Van den Bos, K., & Chen, Y. (2005). The influence of interdependent self-construal on procedural fairness effects. *Organizational Behavior and Human Decision Processes, 96*, 155–167.

Chen, Y., Brockner, J., & Greenberg, J. (2003). When is it "a pleasure to do business with you?"The effects of relative status, outcome favorability, and procedural fairness. *Organizational Behavior and Human Decision Processes, 92*, 1–21.

Cialdini, R. B., Borden, R. J., Thorne, A., Walker, M. R., Freeman, S., & Sloan, L. R. (1976). Basking in reflected glory: Three (football) field studies. *Journal of Personality and Social Psychology, 34*, 366–375.

Dawes, R. M. (1980). Social dilemmas. *Annual Review of Psychology, 31*, 169–193.

Deci, E. L., & Ryan, R. M. (2000). The what and why of goal pursuits: Human needs and the self-determination of behaviour. *Psychological Inquiry, 11*, 227–268.

De Cremer, D. (2002a). Exploring the instrumental versus non-instrumental aspects of procedural fairness: The usefulness of a person x situation approach. In: F. Columbus (Ed.), *Advances in psychology research*, (Vol. 15, pp. 157–172). New York: NOVA Science Publishers.

De Cremer, D. (2002b). Respect and cooperation in social dilemmas: The importance of feeling included. *Personality and Social Psychology Bulletin, 28*, 1335–1341.

De Cremer, D., & Leonardelli, G. (2003). Individual differences in need to belong and cooperation in social dilemmas: The moderating effect of group size. *Group Dynamics: Theory, Research, and Practice, 7*, 168–174.

De Cremer, D., & Sedikides, C. (2005). Self-uncertainty and responsiveness to procedural justice. *Journal of Experimental Social Psychology*, *41*, 157–173.
De Cremer, D., & Tyler, T. R. (in press). Am I respected or not? Inclusion and reputation as issues in group membership. *Social Justice Research*.
De Cremer, D., & Van Dijk, E. (2002). Reactions to group success and failure as a function of identification level: A test of the goal-transformation hypothesis in social dilemmas. *Journal of Experimental Social Psychology*, *38*, 435–442.
De Cremer, D., & Van Vugt, M. (1999). Social identification effects in social dilemmas: A transformation of motives. *European Journal of Social Psychology*, *29*, 871–893.
De Cremer, S., & De Witte (2001). The less I trust, the less I contribute (or not?): The effects of trust, accountability, and self-monitoring in social dilemmas. *European Journal of Social Psychology*, *31*, 93–107.
Deutsch, M., & Gerard, H. B. (1955). A study of normative and informational social influences upon individual judgment. *Journal of Abnormal and Social Psychology*, *51*, 629–636.
Dosi, G. (1995). Hierarchies, markets, and power: Some foundational issues on the nature of contemporary economic organization. *Industrial and Corporate Change*, *4*, 1–19.
Duffy, M. K., Shaw, J. D., & Stark, E. M. (2000). Performance and satisfaction in conflicted interdependent groups: When and how does self-esteem make a difference. *Academy of Management Journal*, *43*, 772–782.
Forsyth, D. R. (1991). Change in therapeutic groups. In: C. R. Snyder & D. R. Forsyth (Eds), *Handbook of social and clinical psychology* (pp. 664–680). New York: Pergamon Press.
Gächter, S., & Fehr, E. (1999). Collective action as a social exchange. *Journal of Economic Behavior and Organization*, *39*, 341–369.
Gaertner, L., Sedikides, C., Vevea, J. L., & Luzzini, J. (2002). The "I," the "We," and the "When": A meta-analysis of motivational primacy in self-definition. *Journal of Personality and Social Psychology*, *83*, 574–591.
Gardner, W. L., Gabriel, S., & Diekman, A. (2000a). Interpersonal processes. In: L. Tassinary, J. Cacioppo & G. Berntson (Eds), *The Handbook of psychophysiology* (pp. 643–664). Cambridge, MA: Cambridge Press.
Gardner, W. L., Pickett, C. L., & Brewer, M. B. (2000b). Social exclusion and selective memory: How the need to belong influences memory for social events. *Personality and Social Psychology Bulletin*, *26*, 486–496.
Heuer, L., Penrod, S., Hafer, C. L., & Cohn, I. (2002). The role of resource and relational concerns for procedural justice. *Personality and Social Psychology Bulletin*, *28*, 1468–1482.
Hill, T. E., Jr. (2000). *Respect, pluralism, and justice*. Oxford: Oxford University Press.
Hofstede, G. (1980). *Culture's consequences: International differences in work-related values*. Beverly Hills, CA: Sage.
Hofstede, G. (1991). *Culture and organizations: Software of the mind*. London: McGraw-Hill.
James, W. (1890). *The principles of psychology*. New York, NY: Holt.
Jankowski, M. S. (1991). *Islands in the street: Gangs and American urban society*. Berkeley: University of California Press.
Johnson, D. E., Erez, A., Kiker, D. S., & Motowidlo, S. J. (2002). Liking and attributions of motives as mediators of the relationships between individuals' reputations, helpful behaviors, and raters' reward decisions. *Journal of Applied Psychology*, *87*, 808–815.
Jost, J. T., & Major, B. (2001). *The psychology of legitimacy*. Cambridge, UK: Cambridge University Press.

Katz, D. (1964). The motivational basis of organizational behavior. *Behavioral Science, 9*, 131–146.
Kerr, N. L., & Bruun, S. E. (1983). Dispensability of member effort and group motivation losses: Free-rider effects. *Journal of Personality and Social Psychology, 44*, 78–94.
Kim, K. I., Park, H. J., & Suzuki, N. (1990). Reward allocations in the United States, Japan, and Korea: A comparison of individualistic and collectivistic cultures. *Academy of Management Journal, 33*, 188–198.
Koper, G., van Knippenberg, D., Bouhuijs, F., Vermunt, R., & Wilke, H. (1993). Procedural fairness and self-esteem. *European Journal of Social Psychology, 23*, 313–325.
Kramer, R. M. (2001). Identity and trust in organizations: One anatomy of a productive but problematic relationship. In: M. A. Hogg & D. J. Terry (Eds), *Social identity processes in organizational contexts* (pp. 167–180). Philadelphia, PA: Psychology Press.
Kurzban, R., & Leary, M. R. (2001). Evolutionary origins of stigmatization: The functions of social exclusion. *Psychological Bulletin, 127*, 187–208.
Leary, M. (2001). The self as a source of relational difficulties. *Self and Identity, 1*, 137–142.
Leary, M. R., & Baumeister, R. F. (2000). The nature and function of self-esteem: Sociometer theory. *Advances in Experimental Social Psychology, 32*, 1–62.
Leary, M. R., & Kowalski, R. M. (1990). Impression management: A literature review and two-factor model. *Psychological Bulletin, 107*, 34–47.
Leary, M. R., Kelly, K. M., Cottrell, C. A., & Schreindorfer, L. S. (2001). Individual differences in the need to belong. Unpublished manuscript, Wake Forest University, Winston-Salem, NC.
Lind, E. A. (2001). Thinking critical about justice judgments. *Journal of Vocational Behavior, 58*, 220–226.
Lind, E. A., & Tyler, T. R. (1988). *The social psychology of procedural justice*. New York: Plenum Press.
Markus, H., & Kitayama, S. (1991). Culture and the self: Implications for cognition, emotion, and involvement. *Psychological Review, 98*, 224–253.
Markus, H., Kitayama, S., & Heiman, R. J. (1996). Culture and the basic psychological principles. In: E. T. Higgins & A. W. Kruglanski (Eds), *Social psychology: Handbook of basic principles*. New York: The Guilford Press.
McAllister, D. J., & Bigley, G. A. (2002). Work context and the definition of self: How organizational care influences organization-based self-esteem. *Academy of Management Journal, 45*, 894–904.
Milinski, M., Semmann, D., & Krambeck, H. J. (2002). Reputation helps solve the "tragedy of commons". *Nature, 415*, 424–426.
Moorman, R. H. (1991). Relationship between organizational justice and organizational citizenship behaviors: Do fairness perceptions influence employee citizenship? *Journal of Applied Psychology, 76*, 845–855.
Noel, J. G., Wann, B. L., & Branscombe, N. R. (1995). Peripheral ingroup membership status and public negativity toward outgroups. *Journal of Personality and Social Psychology, 68*, 127–137.
O'Connell, L. J. (2000). The worlds of religion and psychiatry: Bioethics as arbiter of mutual respect. In: J. K. Boehnlein (Ed.), *Psychiatry and religion: The convergence of mind and spirit* (pp. 145–157). Washington, DC: American Psychiatric Press, Inc.
Olson, M. (1965). *The logic of collective action*. Cambridge, MA: Harvard University Press.

Organ, D. W. (1988). *Organizational citizenship behavior: The good soldier syndrome*. Lexington, MA: Lexington Books.

Pfeffer, J. (1998). Understanding organizations: Concepts and controversies. In: D. Gilbert, S. Fiske & G. Lindzey (Eds), *The handbook of social psychology*, (4th ed.) (pp. 733–777). New York: Oxford University Press.

Reis, H. T., Collins, W. A., & Berscheid, E. (2000). The relationship context of human behavior and development. *Psychological Bulletin, 126*, 844–872.

Sedikides, C., & Brewer, M. B. (2001). *Individual self, relational self, collective self.* Philadelphia, PA: Psychology Press.

Sedikides, C., Herbst, K. C., Hardin, D. P., & Dardis, G. J. (2002). Accountability as a deterrent to self-enhancement: The search for mechanisms. *Journal of Personality and Social Psychology, 83*, 592–605.

Simon, B., & Stürmer, S. (2003). Respect for group members: Intragroup determinants of collective identification and group-serving behavior. *Personality and Social Psychology Bulletin, 29*, 183–193.

Smith, H. J., & Tyler, T. R. (1997). Choosing the right pond: The impact of group membership on self-esteem and group-oriented behavior. *Journal of Experimental Social Psychology, 33*, 146–170.

Smith, K. G., Carroll, S. J., & Ashford, S. J. (1995). Intra- and interorganizational cooperation: Toward a research agenda. *Academy of Management Journal, 38*, 7–23.

Snyder, M., & Cantor, N. (1998). Understanding personality and social behavior: A functionalist strategy. In: D. Gilbert, S. Fiske & G. Lindzey (Eds), *Handbook of social psychology*, (Vol. 1, pp. 635–679). New York: McGraw-Hill.

Stamper, C. L., & Masterson, S. S. (2002). Insider or outsider? How employee perceptions of insider status affect their work behavior. *Journal of Organizational Behavior, 23*, 875–894.

Steiner, I. D. (1972). *Group process and productivity*. New York: Academic Press.

Tajfel, H., & Turner, J. (1986). The social identity theory of intergroup behavior. In: S. Worchel (Ed.), *Psychology of intergroup relations*. Chicago: Nelson Hall.

Tice, D. M. (1992). Self-presentation and self-concept change: The looking glass self as magnifying glass. *Journal of Personality and Social Psychology, 63*, 435–451.

Thomas, E. J., & Fink, C. F. (1963). Effects of group size. *Psychological Bulletin, 60*, 371–384.

Twenge, J. M., Baumeister, R. F., Tice, D. M., & Stucke, T. S. (2001). If you can't join them, beat them: Effects of social exclusion on aggressive behavior. *Journal of Personality and Social Psychology, 81*, 1058–1069.

Twenge, J. M., Catanese, K. R., & Baumeister, R. F. (2002). Social exclusion and self-defeating behavior. *Journal of Personality and Social Psychology, 83*, 606–615.

Tyler, T. R. (1989). The psychology of procedural justice: A test of the group value model. *Journal of Personality and Social Psychology, 57*, 333–344.

Tyler, T. R. (1999). Why people cooperate with organizations: An identity-based perspective. *Research in Organizational Behavior, 21*, 201–246.

Tyler, T. R. (2001). Cooperation in organizations: A social identity perspective. In: M. A. Hogg & D. J. Terry (Eds), *Social identity processes in organizational contexts* (pp. 149–166). Philadelphia, PA: Psychology Press.

Tyler, T. R., & Blader, S. (2000). *Cooperation in groups: Procedural justice, social identity, and behavioral engagement*. Philadelphia: Taylor & Francis.

Tyler, T. R., & Blader, S. (2003). Procedural justice, social identity, and cooperative behavior. *Personality and Social Psychology Review*, *7*, 349–361.

Tyler, T. R., & Lind, E. A. (1992). A relational model of authority in groups. In: M. Zanna (Ed.), *Advances in experimental social psychology*, (Vol. 25, pp. 115–191). New York: Academic Press.

Tyler, T. R., & Smith, H. J. (1999). Justice, social identity, and group processes. In: T. R. Tyler, R. M. Kramer & O. P. John (Eds), *The psychology of the social self* (pp. 223–264). Mahwah, NJ: Lawrence Erlbaum Associates, Inc.

Tyler, T. R., Degoey, P., & Smith, H. (1996). Understanding why the justice of group procedures matter: A test of the psychological dynamics of the group-value model. *Journal of Personality and Social Psychology*, *70*, 913–930.

Tyler, T. R., Lind, E. A., & Huo, Y. J. (2000). Cultural values and authority relations. *Psychology, Public Policy, and Law*, *6*, 1138–1163.

Van den Bos, K., & Lind, E. A. (2002). Uncertainty management by means of fairness judgments. In: M. P. Zanna (Ed.), *Advances in experimental social psychology*, (Vol. 34, pp. 1–60). San Diego, CA: Academic Press.

Van Vugt, M., Snyder, M., Tyler, T. R., & Biel, A. (2000). *Cooperation in modern society: Dilemmas and solutions*. London: Routledge.

Wagner, J. A., II (1995). Studies of individualism–collectivism: Effects on cooperation in groups. *Academy of Management Journal*, *38*, 152–172.

Wiesenfeld, B. M., Brockner, J., & Thibault, V. (2000). Procedural fairness, managers' self-esteem and managerial behaviors following a layoff. *Organizational Behavior and Human Decision Processes*, *83*, 1–32.

IT'S NOT JUST ABOUT DIFFERENCES: AN INTEGRATION OF ROLE IDENTITY THEORY AND STATUS CHARACTERISTICS THEORY

Amy E. Randel, Lee Chay-Hoon and P. Christopher Earley

ABSTRACT

This chapter examines how individuals' perceptions of others' task competence, treatment of other group members, tendency to conform, and work group identification depend on both status and identity commitment. We integrate tenets of both role identity theory and status characteristics theory in formulating propositions concerning which of multiple status attributes are utilized when assessing others' task competence and treating other group members, when a solo low-status group member is less likely to conform with the group, and when a solo high-status group member has low identification with his or her group. Our theory development highlights the value of integrating these theories in understanding group phenomenon for both research and practice.

Status and Groups
Research on Managing Groups and Teams, Volume 7, 23–42

ISSN: 1534-0856/doi:10.1016/S1534-0856(05)07002-7

INTRODUCTION

The usage of work groups has proliferated with intense pressures to compete in a global marketplace (Earley & Gibson, 2002; Garten, 1998; Mohrman, Cohen, & Mohrman, 1995). In addition, work group members today often differ from one another in terms of such characteristics as age, race, gender, and nationality (Guzzo, Salas, & Associates, 1995; Snow, Snell, Davison, & Hambrick, 1996). Concurrent with these workplace trends, researchers have considered the effect of demographic differences on outcomes, such as group cooperation (Chatman & Flynn, 2001), individual advancement (Riordan & Shore, 1997), organization-level turnover (Alexander, Nuchols, Bloom, & Lee, 1995), and individual (Tsui & O'Reilly, 1989) or group (Pelled, Eisenhardt, & Xin, 1999) performance. When demographic characteristics are considered in such research, the focus has been on the effects of similarity and differences through theoretical perspectives, such as social identity theory (Tajfel, 1982; Turner, 1987) and the similarity-attraction paradigm (Byrne, 1971). In this chapter, we look to additional theoretical perspectives (status characteristics theory and role identity theory), in considering how status and identity commitment are integral to better understanding assessments of other group members' task competence, treatment of other group members, conformity, and work group identification in diverse work groups.

Currently, specifying the effects of multiple group memberships at the individual level of analysis is an empirical and a conceptual challenge for researchers (Lau & Murnighan, 1998; Randel, 2000). When individuals have multiple group memberships, it can be problematic to assess which of those memberships are most important to the individual and to outcomes of interest. By considering the status associated with a characteristic and the extent to which the individual's relationships depend on that characteristic, we propose a framework for understanding which multiple group memberships influence interaction and work group identification within a work group context, and how both status and identity commitment relate to work group identification.

STATUS CHARACTERISTICS WITHIN A WORK GROUP

Status characteristics theory was developed as part of a research program on expectation states to explain group member differences in participation and influence (Berger, Cohen, & Zelditch, 1972; Berger, Fisek, Norman, & Zelditch, 1977; Wagner & Berger, 1993). According to this theory, a status characteristic is defined as any personal attribute that can be used to assess the status of others relative to oneself (Berger et al., 1972; Cohen & Zhou, 1991). Status characteristics can be specific (limited to a particular situation or task) or diffuse (applying to a wide range of situations). Specific characteristics might include mathematical ability for a finance class or oral presentation skills at a school debate. Examples of diffuse characteristics are gender, race, and age that are derived from outside of the immediate task situation but are perceived at the societal level to be associated with expectations regarding competence. For example, older employees may be perceived as being less skilled in technically oriented tasks (e.g., those involving advanced computer skills) than younger employees.

Within a work group, members depend on status characteristics as a basis for interaction and to form expectations of how others in the group will perform. Status characteristics theory posits that high-status group members are considered to be more competent at a task than low-status group members (Berger et al., 1972, 1977). As a result of being perceived as more competent, higher-status individuals interact more frequently with others in the group and are more influential. This tenet of status characteristics theory goes beyond the emphasis in demographic research on similarity and differences to address the valence associated with those differences (e.g., whether differences hold positive or negative connotations), as well as the implications for interaction associated with such differences (Kalkhoff & Barnum, 2000). Status characteristics theory allows for predictions about the extent to which work group members will consider differences to be advantageous (or detrimental) to the work group and, as a result, how they will interact with these work group members. In support of the status characteristics theory argument that status is used as a basis for interaction, high-status group members have been shown to exhibit a high level of directive behavior (e.g., Johnson, Clay-Warner, & Funk, 1996; Johnson, Funk, & Clay-Warner, 1998), a propensity to interrupt (e.g., Robinson & Reis, 1989; Smith-Lovin & Brody, 1989), and frequent questioning of his suggestions (e.g., Stewart, 1988).

Such interactions among group members of differing status are reflective of the effects of status on individuals' influence within work groups. Research has demonstrated that the exertion of influence is a key behavior that affects group processes and outcomes (e.g., Asch, 1955; Hollander, 1960; Moscovici, 1976). When group members differ with respect to status, influence bears a pronounced mark on group processes. High-status group members have stronger influence over low-status group members unless additional performance attributes that contradict status expectations are introduced (e.g., Earley, 1999; Freese & Cohen, 1973). When status expectations have been confirmed, such as when group leaders have demonstrated task competence, these group leaders have continued influence even after demonstrating nonconforming behavior (Hollander, 1960; Wahrman & Pugh, 1972).

Status characteristics theory suggests that when individuals within a work group differ with respect to certain attributes, those attributes become activated as determinations of status among work group members (Cohen & Zhou, 1991). For example, if a work group consists of members who differ with respect to gender, age, and nationality, these characteristics can be used to estimate the relative status of various group members. While some work group members may be high- or low-status members across all three characteristics, often group members will possess both high- and low-status characteristics. That is, if we assume that older people have higher status than younger people and males have higher status than females, then a young man and an older woman would both have a combination of high- and low-status characteristics. However, it is not merely the possession of particular status characteristics that determines a group member's self and other evaluations. To predict the particular high- or low-status characteristics taking precedence, we require a determination of the value associated with each status characteristic. To do so, we turn to role identity theory. We consider how role identity theory complements and extends status characteristics theory when examining outcomes pertinent to diverse work groups.

IDENTITY COMMITMENT

Identity commitment is a construct that is derived from role identity theory (Stryker, 1980, 1987, 2000; Stryker & Serpe, 1982). Identity commitment refers to the degree to which relationships with others depend on that identity and how extensive and deep those relationships are (Stryker, 1980). Drawing upon the work of James (1890/1950) and Mead (1934), role identity theory posits that individuals are comprised of multiple selves or identities, such as being an African–American, a family member, and an employee. These identities are organized in a hierarchical fashion such that identities that are higher in the hierarchy are valued more and affect behavior more than identities at lower levels (McCall & Simmons, 1978; Stryker, 1980).

Role identity theory posits that individuals construct their identities based on investments in social relationships rather than, as demographic research suggests, on the social categories to which they could claim membership. The relationships individuals hold based on their identities reflect the relevance of each identity. However, it is important to note that identity commitment refers to involvement in relationships that depend on the individual having a particular identity. Thus, identity commitment differs from personal identity, in that identity commitment refers to relationship investments while personal identity relies on the importance that an individual places on an identity (Brewer & Gardner, 1996; Brickson, 2000).

The identities held by an individual are ordered in a hierarchy with identities associated with strong valence more likely to be evoked in response to a given situation (Stryker, 1980). The valence or salience of an identity is based on an individual's level of commitment to his or her social networks and not the mere possession of a characteristic. Thus, it is not necessarily critical that a person belongs to a particular group based on a characteristic possessed (e.g., Anglo–European); however, it is critical to recognize those identities to which a person is committed. Situations for which responses from multiple salient identities conflict become problematic, and the individual then responds with the identity that holds a stronger commitment (Stryker, 1987; Burke & Reitzes, 1991). For example, if two individuals are more committed to their identities as managers than to their ethnic identities, they would be able to temper what otherwise might be hostility towards one another based on being members of quarreling ethnic groups. Next we propose to examine how role identity theory applies to interactions with work group members and work group identification, as we further integrate role identity theory with status characteristics theory.

PROPOSITIONS BUILDING UPON STATUS CHARACTERISTICS THEORY AND ROLE IDENTITY THEORY

Status characteristics theory suggests that the characteristics on which work group members differ activate determinations of status. However, status characteristics theory does not provide guidance about which identity(ies) takes precedence in determining interactions with fellow work group members. Returning to our earlier example, it is not clear whether the low- or high-status characteristics for a young man (with a low/high-status combination of attributes) or an older woman (with a high/low-status combination) are invoked in a work group interaction.

Based on role identity theory, status characteristics are activated depending on identity commitment. The higher an individual's identity commitment associated with a particular status characteristic, the more likely that individual is to rely on that status characteristic when making assessments of fellow work group members' task competence. In our example, assume that the man identifies more positively with age than gender while the woman identifies more positively with gender than age. We would predict that each one will view and treat the other as a high-status group member. What appears to be a potentially conflicting collage of attributes is fully compatible.

Role identity theory suggests that the greater the commitment to an identity, the higher that identity is placed within that individual's salience hierarchy. As a result of achieving high placement within the salience hierarchy, an individual relies on an identity more often than less important ones. However, the focus of role identity theory is on an individual's own perceptions and behavior rather than on an individual's interaction with, and perceptions of, other work group members based on particular characteristics. We propose to extend role identity theory's focus on an individual's behavior in our examination of what identities are involved in interactions with other work group members. If an individual places importance on a certain identity (e.g., age), we suggest that she relies on that identity both for her own behavior as well as when perceiving other people. For example, a person approaching retirement and for whom age is an important identity will base perceptions of others in part by comparing other group members' ages to her own. At the same time, we seek to extend status characteristics theory by understanding which of the numerous possible status characteristics is involved within a work group context. Status characteristics theory suggests that although any characteristic that can be used to distinguish the status of individuals may be activated, the more relevant a status characteristic is to a particular situation, the more likely that characteristic will be activated and thus utilized in determining how to behave in social situations. This is an important point of departure between status characteristics theory and role identity theory, since identity commitment is anchored in social networks and relationships rather than in the task context per se.

If an individual relies on a particular status characteristic because of its placement in the salience hierarchy, then that identity is accessed frequently and is cognitively prominent (McCall & Simmons, 1978; Stryker, 1980).

A status characteristic that is cognitively prominent is likely to be utilized in interactions across situations and tasks. This is because, as attributional research has demonstrated, information that is cognitively prominent is automatically accessed more often than information requiring more conscious processing (Pyszczynski & Greenberg, 1981). Characteristics that, by function of being associated with a high level of identity commitment, are used to evaluate or define the self also are used in evaluating others.

People often categorize others with whom they interact because they desire to make sense of their environment (Fiske & Neuberg, 1990; Weick, 1979). Categorizing others often occurs before much information is available about these others. Lacking information and constrained by natural cognitive limitations, people tend to rely on the same characteristics that are important to them in their assessments of others. Since status characteristics provide information about task competence (among other things), an individual makes an assessment of others' competence via the status characteristics that are most important to him or her (e.g., the status characteristic with the highest level of identity commitment). For example, if gender is salient to an individual, gender status beliefs shape the expectations that an individual forms of the competence of others in the work group.

In summary, we propose that an identity an individual is committed to is one that influences personal action, as well as determines status about other work group members. Since a status characteristic that a person is most committed to is cognitively prominent, it is used as a basis for other interactions. In particular, it is used when individuals attempt to categorize their work group members and make assessments of their competence on the job. Stated formally:

> **Proposition 1.** The higher an individual's identity commitment associated with a particular status characteristic, the more likely the individual relies on that characteristic in making determinations of the task competence of fellow work group members.

We next further consider how role identity can be used to explain which of several possible status characteristics is most relevant in how an individual treats others within the group. For example, if a female group member is of higher status than a younger male member due to being older, but is lower status than him due to being a female, it is possible to predict whether her treatment of him will reflect being of lower or higher status depending on which of these identities have a higher level of identity commitment associated with it.

Continuing with our example, suppose that the female group member has higher identity commitment linked to her age than to her gender. We can predict that her treatment of the younger male group member will reflect her higher status with respect to age because an individual's behavior is shaped by the identity on which he or she places a high level of importance (Shamir, 1990; Stryker, 1980). Despite being of lower status than the younger male group member on the dimension of gender, her stronger identity commitment regarding age overpowers the effect of being lower status on another dimension. The status she possesses as a result of her gender has less of an effect than her status due to age, not because it is more beneficial to her in this particular situation, but rather because her social relationships depend more on her age than her gender, resulting in higher identity commitment for age. Her age identity is accessed more frequently than other identities for which she has less commitment and thus it is her age identity that influences her interactions with others (Stryker, 1980). In this instance, we would expect the female group member to treat the younger male group member such that her behavior reflects her higher status relative to him. This suggests:

Proposition 2. The higher an individual's identity commitment associated with a particular status characteristic, the more likely the individual relies on that characteristic in his or her treatment of other group members.

In the remainder of our discussion, we offer propositions that concern solo group members of either high or low status. We do so in order to avoid consideration of situations in which sharing status with others within the group affects attachment to that group. Next, we consider how identity commitment influences a solo low-status group member's propensity to conform within the group.

A solo low-status group member experiences the sense of being low status in the extreme since everyone else in the group is of higher status. As a result of being in a context in which there are no others like himself or herself, a solo low-status group member becomes especially aware of being of lower status than other group members (Swan & Wyer, 1997). Others see solo low-status group members as highly visible and scrutinize their work (Kanter, 1977). The tendency of low-status group members to conform to the opinions of their fellow group members (Montgomery, 1971; Nemeth, 1988) may be particularly problematic for solo low-status group members. As previously mentioned, influence is a key behavior that affects group processes and outcomes, and conformity on the part of solo low-status group members can result from influence exertion within status differentiated groups.

By considering both status characteristics theory and role identity theory, it is possible to better understand a condition under which a solo low-status group member is less likely to conform within a work group setting. Work groups can realize their potential effectively when group members air their perspectives and express their true opinions. In groups in which there are status differences, however, low-status group members often conform to the majority group opinion, resulting in less-effective group outcomes (e.g., Janis, 1972). This problem is similarly noted in the literature on diverse work groups (e.g., Milliken & Martins, 1996; Riordan, 2000; Williams & O'Reilly, 1998) with researchers and managers alike expressing frustration over the tendency for diverse groups not to perform as well as promised due to problems related to conformity.

In groups in which status differences exist, there is strong evidence that low-status group members tend to conform to high-status group members' opinions (cf., Cohen & Zhou, 1991). Just as newcomers attempt to fit in with their organizations in order to experience increased acceptance, low-status group members similarly attempt to conform to the opinions of their group members (Katz, 1985; Louis, 1990; Van Maanen & Schein, 1979; Wanous, 1980). Low-status individuals also conform because they determine that they do not have the influence to alter the direction of group opinion (Maas & Clark, 1984). High-status group members hold the power of being revered by others due to their high-status position. High-status group members often do not have to be particularly persuasive to convince low-status group members to conform; their high status frequently is enough to convince low-status group members to go along with the momentum of the group initiated by high-status group members.

While there are strong influences that may lead low-status group members to conform to the group, there are also reasons why low-status group members may opt not to conform. Group members may fear that they will be thought not to have contributed sufficiently to the group if they conform (Asch, 1955). In addition, a low-status group member may be compelled not to conform with the group as a whole when another member of the immediate work group vocalizes support of his or her position (McGrath, 1984). While a low-status group member in the minority might be expected to conform in general as a result of not having the social support of another individual, role identity theory points to a condition under which a solo low-status group member might be inclined not to conform.

A solo low-status group member who has a high level of identity commitment to the characteristic on which he or she is low status may be less likely to conform to the majority group opinion. The solo low-status group member may not be able to turn to any other members of the immediate group for social support, but by having a high level of identity commitment, he or she has relationships with others based on the low-status characteristic and may feel a sense of empowerment based on those relationships that provide the strength not to conform. The solo low-status member's social relationships outside of the group reinforce his or her sense of self-worth, thereby providing the individual with increased confidence not to conform with the overall group (cf. Ethier & Deaux, 1990).

For example, a junior person on a product development team may have reservations about a new product that the organization is about to introduce. As the other members of the product development team have much more tenure within the organization and industry in general and thus have accrued high status, a junior person with low identity commitment associated with being relatively new within the organization would be inclined to conform to the group's opinion. However, a junior person who has built strong relationships with other relatively new individuals within the organization and whose identity depends on being a part of a new direction envisioned by these relatively new organizational members would be more likely to resist conformity. The identity commitment the individual has based on being a junior person within the organization, is what makes the difference for a low-status individual between conformity and having the courage to follow his or her convictions. Thus, we posit:

Proposition 3. Identity commitment will moderate the relationship between being a solo member of a group with a low-status characteristic and an individual who conforms within the group suggesting that a solo low-status group member will conform less with the group when his or her identity commitment to the associated status characteristic is high.

Not only do status characteristics theory and role identity theory hold implications for a group member's propensity to conform within the group, they also impact an individual's work group identification. Individuals form attachments to their work group based on whether they assess the group as being a forum where self-esteem can be attained effectively (e.g., Hogg & Terry, 2000). An individual's status relative to others' status in the group and identity commitment to his or her status characteristics determine whether the individual depends on the work group for self-worth or looks outside the group for self-validation.

We argue that a solo high-status group member that has high identity commitment associated with his or her high-status characteristic will have lower work group identification than a solo high-status group member with low identity commitment. When individuals have high identity commitment associated with the characteristic that provides them with high status, they can rely on other individuals besides other work group members to provide them with validation and self-esteem in support of the characteristic. Recall that role identity theory posits that an individual's identity commitment is derived from broad, social networks and relationships that extend beyond the boundaries of any given work group. Since others within the work group are of lower status and, according to status characteristics theory, lower status individuals are perceived as possessing lower task competence, it is advantageous for a high-status member to place less emphasis on identifying with work group members than on those who can provide the same validation of one's identity without being associated with low-competence individuals (Berger et al., 1972, 1977).

We believe that this is a very important qualification using our integration of these two theories. Although one might expect high-status members to have stronger attachments to their group (I am admired by my group so I feel attached to them), we are arguing that their attachments are weaker (If I do not respect the competence of my group's members then their evaluations of me are inconsequential and I will seek affirmation with my own social networks). While experiencing the respect of others within a group comprised of lower-status individuals may be rewarding at that moment, the solo high-status individual experiences threat to his or her reputation by identifying strongly with others who are thought to have lower-task competence (as a result of their lower status). A high-status group member with high identity commitment has relationships outside of the work group that are defined by his or her high-status characteristics and thus does not depend on work group members for validation of that aspect of his or herself. In order to maintain his or her high status in relationships in general, a solo high-status group member with high identity commitment does not identify strongly with a group comprised of lower-status group members.

However, for high-status individuals with low identity commitment, high status is derived from within the work group. Low identity commitment indicates that individuals are less invested in the identity in question and thus are more likely to attribute the respect received in the group to their effort or performance. Individuals prefer to believe that they are respected due to their own efforts rather than to characteristics outside of their control (Bem, 1972; Miller, Brickman, & Bolen, 1975). Receiving respect and being influential within the group, based on merit rather than merely because they possess a high-status characteristic, increases the work group's attractiveness to the individual. The status afforded to individuals based on their efforts is desirable and so they feel attachment towards their work group.

To further explore the effect we posit for high-status individuals with high identity commitment, first consider the example of an individual that has been newly promoted to a top-level position; however, few people think of her in these terms and she has not yet had the chance to build high identity commitment associated with the position. This individual has high status as a result of attaining a top-level position, but low identity commitment associated with being a top-level manager. As part of her new job, she has joined a recently formed work/family committee group comprised entirely of employees at lower levels in the organizational hierarchy. The top-level manager wants to develop relationships pertinent to her new position (relationships on which her identity as a top-level manager depend). The work/family committee group provides a setting in which she is looked upon as the highest status member and this increases her affinity towards the group and her propensity to identify with this group. We would expect this individual to have higher work group identification than another individual in a group with similar composition (with group members who are all of lower status) who has long been in a top-level position, has established social networks associated with this position, and thus has high identity commitment related to being in a top-level position. Both individuals are assumed to have been members of their groups for the same length of time since tenure has been found to be related to identification (e.g., Dulebohn & Martocchio, 1998; Mael & Ashforth, 1992). However, the individual with high identity commitment does not identify as strongly with her group because she has established social relationships outside of the group that provide reinforcement of her identity as a top-level manager. She prefers to validate her identity as a top manager through these relationships outside of the group, rather than within the group comprised of individuals assumed to be of lower-task competence. Thus, we propose:

Proposition 4. Identity commitment will moderate the relationship between being a solo member of a group with a high-status characteristic and work group identification, such that the higher the solo high-status group member's identity commitment, the lower his or her work group identification.

CONCLUSION

We have proposed that both individuals' status characteristics and identity commitment are important factors in influencing how group members interact and identify with their work group. Status characteristics theory suggests that it is not just being different that influences group dynamics, but it is the relative status among group members that shapes interaction and work group identification. Identity commitment complements status characteristics theory by indicating which of numerous possible status characteristics are most important to an individual and to the nature of interaction with others in a work group context. In this chapter, we have considered how identity commitment associated with status characteristics relates to determinations of the task competence of work group members, treatment of other group members, solo low-status group members' conformity within the group, and solo high-group members' work group identification.

Status characteristics theory, social identity theory, self-categorization theory, and the demography paradigm – perspectives most often used to examine differences within a work group context – share in common a lack of consideration of which characteristics might be most relevant to a particular situation. Status characteristics theory suggests that any characteristic on which group members differ is relevant (since all reflect status to varying extents) while social identity theorists (e.g., Oakes, 1987) argue that a characteristic is relevant if it is cognitively accessible and maximizes similarities with in-group members and differences from out-group members. By using role identity theory to inform which of multiple status characteristics were relevant, we were able to increase the precision with which we theoretically examined the effects of status characteristics on perceptions of task competence, treatment of other group members, conformity, and work group identification.

An advantage of considering both status characteristics theory and role identity theory is that it allows a broader range of outcomes related to differences to be examined using traditional approaches, such as demography. Demography focuses on being different and what the implications of merely being different are, whether those differences involve being of higher or lower status. Demography research is based on the premise that the more different individuals are from their fellow work group members the more difficulty they will have integrating into the work group and therefore will tend to have a low level of identification with such a work group (e.g., Chatman & Flynn, 2001; Mehra, Kilduff, & Brass, 1998). Other outcomes considered within the demography literature include turnover, absenteeism, satisfaction, conflict, and group cohesiveness (e.g., Jehn, Northcraft, & Neale, 1999; Keller, 2001; O'Reilly, Caldwell, & Barnett, 1989; Pelled et al., 1999; Tsui, Egan, & O'Reilly, 1992). With the juxtaposition of status characteristics theory and role identity theory, it is possible to expand the range of study to focus on other outcomes, such as perceptions of other group members' task competence and how individuals treat other group members. As we have proposed, status characteristics theory allows researchers to add the dimension of relative status to research questions involving differences among group members while role identity theory provides a means of honing in on which of several status characteristics is most relevant to an individual.

Practical Implications

For managers, our proposition that a status characteristic is likely to be used as basis for assessing the task competence of fellow group members, when high identity commitment is associated with that status characteristic, points to the importance of understanding the level of individuals' identity commitment. Supervisors responsible for performance appraisals or individuals involved in providing 360-degree performance feedback to their group members may be particularly biased in assessing the performance of individuals who are of low status on attributes on which the rater has a high level of identity commitment.

Our theoretical discussion leads us to several suggestions for managers regarding group composition. Our proposition that individuals will rely on a status characteristic for which they have high identity commitment in their treatment of lower-status group members suggests that managers should consider composing groups so that status differences exist on characteristics for which high-status group members do not have high identity commitment. By doing so, it may be possible to minimize the poor treatment that high-status group members may exhibit towards lower-status group members. Another group composition suggestion for managers is that when only one individual with a low-status characteristic is assigned to a work group, it may be possible to minimize that individual's tendency to conform to the group by selecting an individual with high identity commitment to the low-status characteristic. Efforts also may be taken to encourage identity commitment development for low-status individuals with low to moderate identity commitment, such as providing opportunities and encouragement to develop relationships that reinforce the low-status identity.

Lastly, managers may want to avoid assigning high-status individuals with high identity commitment to a work group. When this scenario is necessary, it may be possible to attenuate the potential for low-work group identification for such individuals by pointing out the importance of their efforts in this group, or even to base a portion of their pay on their performance in the group. In addition, adding more than one high-status individual to the group may increase the work group identification of these high-status group members, since higher-status individuals are associated with higher task competence.

Future Research Directions

Future research should explore how status information derived from multiple demographic attributes is considered. Lau and Murnighan (1998) proposed a method for empirically capturing the multiple demographic attributes present in a group. They discussed the role of status as it relates to subgroup size and subgroup power disparities, but further research is needed that integrates status derived from group composition with other sources of status information.

Another relevant issue is the valence of status characteristics. Most research (including this chapter) presumes that the key status markers are those derived from task or social networks and are of a positive nature. That is, we largely ignore the relevance of highly salient, but negative, characteristics. For example, Hughes (1971) suggested that the significance to social evaluation of primary status-determining traits (those valued within a society) may be moderated by secondary ones. For example, a positive status marker such as being a physician (in a society valuing doctors) may be interpreted negatively if an additional secondary status marker such as race (in a society differentiating people based on race) is present. This discussion suggests that it is important for future research to focus on individuals' positive and negative identities (identities with positive or negative connotations of worthiness), as long as there is high commitment to these identities. One might imagine a situation for which a very strong and committed, but negative, role identity may overwhelm other more positive features.

Future research also could explore the effects of individuals who have high identity commitment across the many identities that comprise their self-definition. Research on individual-collective primacy (e.g., Chen, Brockner, & Chen, 2002; Chen, Brockner, & Katz, 1998) and on collective self-esteem (e.g., Crocker & Luhtanen, 1990) has found that there are individuals for whom groups (both in-groups and out-groups) are positively rated. Empirical research efforts could examine how high identity commitment across multiple identities impacts outcomes associated with status. It may be, for instance, that high identity commitment across multiple identities attenuates the effects of status in some instances. It may be wise to consider individuals' identity commitment across multiple identities as an additional variable in future empirical work on the effects of identity commitment in work groups.

Another avenue for future research is to explore how the status of the group relative to other groups within an organization, affects the interplay of within-group status and identity commitment. When an individual has low status within the group, but is of high status within the organization due to being a part of a high-status group, and has high identity commitment associated with this high-status attribute, the individual's behavior within the group may be less reflective of the low within-group status position of the individual (i.e., the individual may exhibit less conformity and more participation than would be expected otherwise). Further, status characteristics theory focuses on assessments of individuals' status, but assessments are made of the group, relative to other organizational groups based on characteristics that may not relate to the status of the individuals comprising the group, such as support extended to the group by top management or the size of the group. Consideration of these factors is warranted in future research.

We have suggested that status characteristics theory and role identity theory complement each other as well as complement traditional demographic approaches to work group member differences. We encourage researchers to consider other questions concerning identity commitment associated with status characteristics, such as those related to perceptions of others in the group and flexibility towards team role changes. For instance, when an individual has identity commitment associated with a status characteristic, it would be expected that the individual would have a greater propensity to perceive others in the group in terms of that same status characteristic. In addition, a possible advantage of having low commitment to a status characteristic is flexibility in accepting different roles within a group and a high level of acceptance of the roles taken on by other group members.

We believe that research on the effect of group member differences on group outcomes may benefit from an approach that integrates status characteristics theory and identity commitment. Further theoretical and empirical research in this area would greatly enhance our understanding of status characteristics influences on group processes and may lead to important intervention strategies to help reduce ineffectiveness in work groups.

ACKNOWLEDGEMENTS

We would like to thank Melissa Thomas-Hunt, Greg Northcraft, and Ya-Ru Chen for their comments and suggestions on an earlier draft of this chapter. We also acknowledge the contributions of the participants of the Seventh Annual Conference on Research on Groups and Teams to the development of the ideas included in this chapter.

REFERENCES

Alexander, J., Nuchols, B., Bloom, J., & Lee, S. (1995). Organizational demography and turnover: An examination of multiform and nonlinear heterogeneity. *Human Relations*, *48*, 1455–1480.

Asch, S. E. (1955). Opinions and social pressure. *Scientific American*, *193*, 31–35.

Bem, D. (1972). Self-perception theory. In: L. Berkowitz (Ed.), *Advances in experimental social psychology* (Vol. 6). New York: Academic Press.

Berger, J., Cohen, B. P., & Zelditch, M. (1972). Status characteristics and social interaction. *American Sociological Review*, *37*, 241–255.

Berger, J., Fisek, M. H., Norman, R. Z., & Zelditch, M. (1977). *Status characteristics and social interaction: An expectation states approach*. New York: Elsevier.

Brewer, M. B., & Gardner, W. (1996). Who is this "we"? Levels of collective identity and self representations. *Journal of Personality and Social Psychology*, *71*(1), 83–87.

Brickson, S. (2000). The impact of identity orientation on individual and organizational outcomes in demographically diverse settings. *Academy of Management Review*, *25*, 82–101.

Burke, P. J., & Reitzes, D. C. (1991). An identity theory approach to commitment. *Social Psychology Quarterly*, *54*, 239–251.

Byrne, D. E. (1971). *The attraction paradigm*. New York: Academic Press.

Chatman, J. A., & Flynn, F. J. (2001). The influence of demographic heterogeneity on the emergence and consequences of cooperative norms in work teams. *Academy of Management Journal*, *44*(5), 956–974.

Chen, Y., Brockner, J., & Katz, T. (1998). Toward an explanation of cultural differences in in-group favoritism: The role of individual versus collective primacy. *Journal of Personality and Social Psychology*, *75*(6), 1490–1593.

Chen, Y., Brockner, J., & Chen, X. (2002). Individual-collective primacy and in-group favoritism: Enhancement and protection effects. *Journal of Experimental Social Psychology*, *38*(5), 482–491.

Cohen, B. P., & Zhou, X. (1991). Status processes in enduring work groups. *American Sociological Review*, *56*, 179–188.

Crocker, J., & Luhtanen, R. (1990). Collective self-esteem and in-group bias. *Journal of Personality and Social Psychology*, *39*, 406–415.

Dulebohn, J. H., & Martocchio, J. J. (1998). Employee perceptions of the fairness of work group incentive pay plans. *Journal of Management*, *24*(4), 469–488.

Earley, P. C. (1999). Playing follow the leader: Status-determining traits in relation to collective efficacy across cultures. *Organizational Behavior and Human Decision Processes*, *80*, 1–21.

Earley, P. C., & Gibson, C. B. (2002). *Multinational work teams: A new perspective.* Mahwah, New Jersey: Lawrence Erlbaum.

Ethier, K. A., & Deaux, K. (1990). Hispanics in ivy: Assessing identity and perceived threat. *Sex Roles, 22*(7–8), 427–440.

Fiske, S. T., & Neuberg, S. L. (1990). A continuum of impression formation from category-based to individuating processes: Influences of information and motivation on attention and interpretation. *Advances in Experimental Social Psychology, 23*, 1–74.

Freese, L., & Cohen, B. P. (1973). Eliminating status generalization. *Sociometry, 36*(2), 177–193.

Garten, J.E. (1998). Why the global economy is here to stay. *Business Week*, March 23, 21.

Guzzo, R.A., Salas, E., & Associates. (1995). *Team effectiveness and decision making in organizations.* San Francisco, CA: Jossey-Bass.

Hogg, M. A., & Terry, D. J. (2000). Social identity and self-categorization processes in organizational contexts. *Academy of Management Review, 25*(1), 121–140.

Hollander, E. P. (1960). Competence and conformity in the acceptance of influence. *Journal of Abnormal and Social Psychology, 61*, 365–369.

Hughes, E. C. (1971). *The sociological eye: Selected papers.* Chicago, OH: Aldine-Atherton, Inc.

James, W. (1890/1950). *The principles of psychology* (3rd ed.). Dover Publications, Inc.

Janis, I. L. (1972). *Victims of groupthink* (2nd ed.). Boston, MA: Houghton Mifflin.

Jehn, K. A., Northcraft, G. B., & Neale, M. A. (1999). Why differences make a difference: A field study of diversity, conflict, and performance in work groups. *Administrative Science Quarterly, 44*, 741–763.

Johnson, C., Clay-Warner, J., & Funk, S. J. (1996). Effects of authority structures and gender on interaction in same-sex task groups. *Social Psychology Quarterly, 59*(3), 221–236.

Johnson, C., Funk, S. J., & Clay-Warner, J. (1998). Organizational contexts and conversational patterns. *Social Psychology Quarterly, 61*(4), 361–371.

Kalkhoff, W., & Barnum, C. (2000). The effects of status-organizing and social identity processes on patterns of social influence. *Social Psychology Quarterly, 63*(2), 95–115.

Kanter, R. M. (1977). *Men and women of the corporation.* New York: Basic Books.

Katz, R. (1985). Organizational stress and early socialization experiences. In: T.A. Beehr & R.S. Bhagat (Eds), *Human stress and cognition in organizations* (pp. 117–139).

Keller, R. T. (2001). Cross-functional project groups in research and new product development: Diversity, communications, job stress, and outcomes. *Academy of Management Journal, 44*(3), 547–555.

Lau, D. C., & Murnighan, J. K. (1998). Demographic diversity and faultlines: The compositional dynamics of organizational groups. *Academy of Management Review, 23*(2), 325–340.

Louis, M. R. (1990). Acculturation in the workplace: Newcomers as lay ethnographers. In: B. Schenider (Ed.), *Organizational climates and cultures* (pp. 85–127). San Francisco: Jossey-Bass.

Maas, A., & Clark, R. D. (1984). Hidden impact of minorities: Fifteen years of minority influence research. *Psychological Bulletin, 95*(3), 428–450.

Mael, F., & Ashforth, B. E. (1992). Alumni and their alma mater: A partial test of the reformulated model of organizational identification. *Journal of Organization Behavior, 13*, 103–123.

McCall, G. J., & Simmons, J. L. (1978). *Identities and interactions: An examination of human associations in everyday life* (Revised edition). New York: The Free Press.

McGrath, J. (1984). *Groups: Interaction and performance*. Englewood Cliffs, NJ: Prentice-Hall.

Mead, G. (1934). *Mind, self, and society*. Chicago: University of Chicago Press.

Mehra, A., Kilduff, M., & Brass, D. J. (1998). At the margins: A distinctiveness approach to the social identity and social networks of underrepresented groups. *Academy of Management Journal*, *41*(4), 441–453.

Miller, R., Brickman, P., & Bolen, D. (1975). Attribution versus persuasion as a means of modifying behavior. *Journal of Personality and Social Psychology*, *31*, 430–441.

Milliken, F., & Martins, L. (1996). Searching for common threads: Understanding the multiple effects of diversity in organizational groups. *Academy of Management Review*, *21*, 402–433.

Mohrman, S. A., Cohen, S. G., & Mohrman, A. M. (1995). *Designing team-based organizations: New forms for knowledge work*. San Francisco, CA: Jossey-Bass.

Montgomery, R. L. (1971). Status, conformity, and resistance to compliance in natural groups. *Journal of Social Psychology*, *84*(2), 197–206.

Moscovici, S. (1976). *Social influence and social change*. London: Academic Press.

Nemeth, C. J. (1988). Style without status expectations: The special contributions of minorities. In: M. Webster Jr. & M. Foschi (Eds), *Status generalization: New theory and research* (pp. 281–290). Palo Alto, CA: Stanford University Press.

Oakes, P. J. (1987). The salience of social categories. In: J. C. Turner, M. A. Hogg, J. P. Oakes, S. D. Reicher & M. Wetherell (Eds), *Rediscovering the social group: A self-categorization theory* (pp. 117–141). New York: Basil Blackwell.

O'Reilly, C. A., Caldwell, D. F., & Barnett, W. P. (1989). Work group demography, social integration, and turnover. *Administrative Science Quarterly*, *34*, 21–37.

Pelled, L. H., Eisenhardt, K. M., & Xin, K. R. (1999). Exploring the black box: An analysis of team diversity, conflict, and performance. *Administrative Science Quarterly*, *44*(1), 1–28.

Pyszczynski, T. A., & Greenberg, J. (1981). Role of disconfirmed expectancies in the instigation of attributional processing. *Journal of Personality and Social Psychology*, *40*(1), 31–38.

Randel, A.E. (2000). How do members of groups diverse on multiple dimensions conceptualize one another? Social contextual triggers and work group conflict implications of identity salience. *Academy of Management Proceedings*.

Riordan, C. M. (2000). Relational demography within groups: Past developments, contradictions, and new directions. *Research in Personnel and Human Resources Management*, *19*, 131–173.

Riordan, C. M., & Shore, L. M. (1997). Demographic diversity and employee attitudes: An empirical examination of relational demography within work units. *Journal of Applied Psychology*, *82*(3), 342–358.

Robinson, L. F., & Reis, H. T. (1989). The effects of interruption, gender, and status on interpersonal perceptions. *Journal of Nonverbal Behavior*, *13*(3), 141–153.

Shamir, B. (1990). Calculations, values, and identities: The sources of collectivistic work motivation. *Human Relations*, *43*(4), 313–332.

Smith-Lovin, L., & Brody, C. (1989). Interruptions in group discussions: The effects of gender and group composition. *American Sociological Review*, *54*(3), 424–435.

Snow, C. C., Snell, S. A., Davison, S. C., & Hambrick, D. C. (1996). Use transnational teams to globalize your company. *Organizational Dynamics*, *32*, 20–32.

Stewart, P. (1988). Women and men in groups: A status characteristics approach to interaction. In: M. Webster Jr. & M. Foschi (Eds), *Status generalization: New theory and research* (pp. 69–85). Palo Alto, CA: Stanford University Press.

Stryker, S. (1980). *Symbolic interactionism: A social structural version.* Menlo Park, CA: The Benjamin/Cummings Publishing Company.

Stryker, S. (1987). Identity theory: Developments and extensions. In: K. Yardley & T. Honess (Eds), *Self and identity: Psychosocial perspectives* (pp. 89–103). London: Wiley.

Stryker, S. (2000). *Symbolic interaction theory. Encyclopedia of psychology.* Washington, DC and New York: American Psychological Association and Oxford Press.

Stryker, S., & Serpe, R. C. (1982). Commitment, identity salience, and role behavior: Theory and research examples. In: W. Ickes & E. Knowles (Eds), *Personality, roles, and social behavior* (pp. 199–218). New York: Springer-Verlag.

Swan, S., & Wyer, R. S. (1997). Gender stereotypes and social identity: How being in the minority affects judgment of self and others. *Personality and Social Psychology Bulletin, 23*, 1265–1276.

Tajfel, H. (1982). Social psychology of intergroup relations. *Annual Review of Psychology, 33*, 1–39.

Tsui, A., & O'Reilly, C. (1989). Beyond simple demographic effects: The importance of relational demography in superior-subordinate dyads. *Academy of Management Journal, 32*, 402–423.

Tsui, A. S., Egan, T. D., & O'Reilly, C. A. (1992). Being different: Relational demography and organizational attachment. *Administrative Science Quarterly, 37*, 549–579.

Turner, J. C. (1987). *Rediscovering the social group: A self-categorization theory.* Oxford, England: Basil Blackwell.

Van Maanen, J., & Schein, E.H. (1979). Toward a theory of organizational socialization. In: B.M. Staw (Ed.), *Research in organizational behavior* (Vol. 1, pp. 209–264). Greenwich, CT: JAI Press.

Wagner, D. G., & Berger, J. (1993). Status characteristics theory: The growth of a program. In: J. Berger & M. Zelditch (Eds), *Theoretical research programs: Studies in the growth of theory.* Stanford, CA: Stanford University Press.

Wahrman, R., & Pugh, M. D. (1972). Competence and conformity: Another look at Hollander's study. *Sociometry, 35*(3), 376–386.

Wanous, J. P. (1980). *Organizational entry: Recruitment, selection, and socialization of newcomers.* Reading, MA: Addison-Wesley.

Weick, K. E. (1979). *The social psychology of organizing.* Reading, MA: Addison-Wesley.

Williams, K.Y., & O'Reilly, C. (1998). Demography and diversity in organizations: A review of 40 years of research. In: B. Staw, & R. Sutton (Eds), *Research in organizational behavior* (Vol. 20). Greenwich, CT: JAI Press.

A BIG FISH IN A SMALL POND OR A SMALL FISH IN A BIG POND? IMPORTANCE OF INTRA- VERSUS INTERGROUP STATUS ACROSS CULTURES

Ya-Ru Chen

ABSTRACT

This chapter examines the underlying concerns people have for relative status within their group (i.e., intragroup status) and their group's relative status to that of other groups (i.e., intergroup status). I adopt a deductive approach using arguments and evidence in the cross-cultural research and literature. I begin by reviewing the basic findings in social psychology and organizational behavior literatures, which suggest that both intragroup status and intergroup status will have positive impact on important group outcomes such as people's evaluation of, and commitment to, the group. Moreover, consistent with the notion of the fishpond phenomenon, past findings also suggest that those with high-intragroup status and low-intergroup status show more group-oriented reactions than those with low-intragroup status and high-intergroup status (i.e., people prefer to be a big fish in a small pond than a small fish in a big pond). Next, I provide both psychological and structural reasoning to argue that

Status and Groups
Research on Managing Groups and Teams, Volume 7, 43–68

ISSN: 1534-0856/doi:10.1016/S1534-0856(05)07003-9

the fishpond phenomenon will be less likely to emerge in collectivistic than individualistic cultures. I close by considering the implications from the cross-cultural analysis to the broader conceptual understanding of mechanisms underlying people's concerns for intragroup status vs. intergroup status in work groups and organizations.

One of the ways in which individuals strive to assert their importance, or *status*, in the world around them is to affiliate with groups that compare favorably with other groups (e.g., Tajfel & Turner, 1986). For this reason, there are many people willing to exert great effort and pay outrageous membership fees to be a part of exclusive social clubs, such as the Metropolitan Club in New York City. Similarly, within work organizations, employees often compete to be included in prestigious project teams or departments.

In addition to achieving status through favorable comparisons at the intergroup level, individuals' quest for status also exists within their work groups (e.g., Frank, 1985; Ridgeway, 1997; Chen, Blount, & Sanchez-Burks, 2004; Chen, Brockner, & Greenberg, 2003). For example, to gain status, people build strong connections with powerful authorities in the organization in which their group is embedded (Pfeffer, 1992; Kramer & Neale, 1998). Or, they may gain status by exhibiting competence critical to the attainment of group goals (Bales, 1950; Homans, 1950; Berger, Rosenholtz, & Zelditch Jr., 1980; Ridgeway, 1984, 1987). Finally, they may achieve high status based on socially desirable behavioral or physical attributes they possess, such as being attractive, tall, and articulate (Mazur, 1985).

Past research has shown that both intergroup status (i.e., the status of one's group in relation to other groups) and intragroup status (i.e., the status of an individual in relation to other members within his/her group) have positive impact on how people evaluate themselves and their groups (e.g., Davis, 1966; Marsh, 1987; McFarland & Buehler, 1995; Chen, Brockner, & Katz, 1998; Chen, Brockner, & Chen, 2002; Gardner, Gabriel, & Hochschild, 2002). Clearly, the most satisfying result for self-evaluation and group evaluation is being a high-status member in a highly prestigious group, that is, a big fish in a big pond (Davis, 1966; Marsh, 1987; McFarland & Buehler, 1995). However, the combination of favorable intergroup status and favorable intragroup status is not always possible. Unfavorable intragroup status can dampen the luster of being in a big pond. Conversely, unfavorable intergroup status can mitigate the benefits associated with being a big fish.

It is well established in social psychological literature that people in general prefer to be a big fish in a small pond rather than a small fish in a big pond, that is, the fishpond phenomenon, or the frog-pond effect (e.g., Davis, 1966; Marsh, 1987; Seta & Seta, 1992; Taylor & Moghaddam, 1994; McFarland & Beuhler, 1995; Seta & Seta, 1996; Ellemers, Spears, & Doosje, 1999; Gardner et al., 2002). The implication of this set of findings obviously poses a great challenge to effective functioning of work groups and organizations. For example, achievement of group goals requires cooperation and commitment not only from high-status members, but also low-status members. If low-status members (even when they are part of a prestigious group) are not satisfied with their group memberships, they are likely to be uncooperative toward achieving the group goals. Moreover, cohesion within the group can only be established when both high-status members and low-status members of the group work well with one another. Given that status ordering naturally emerges in all social groups (Homans, 1950; Goffman, 1957; Blau, 1986; Chen et al., 2003) and there are inevitably a significant number of members in low-status positions in every work group and organization, it is both theoretically and practically important that organization researchers help to delineate the mechanisms underlying such a phenomenon.

With this goal in mind for the current chapter, I will contend that the fishpond phenomenon or the frog-pond effect is not universal. Specifically, I posit that this phenomenon is less likely to emerge in collectivistic cultures than in individualistic cultures. In collectivistic cultures, people's group-oriented behaviors and attitudes will be similarly high when they are either a small fish in a big pond, or a big fish in a small pond: An ideal result for effective organization and work group functioning.

I begin by reviewing the basic findings in the existing literatures, which have shown positive main effects of intragroup status vs. intergroup status, and an interaction effect between the two on important group outcomes, such as people's evaluations of their group. Next, I provide both psychological and structural reasoning to argue how these effects might vary across individualistic and collectivistic cultures. I then present preliminary findings based on a sample from the U.S. and a sample from the People's Republic of China (the PRC) to support my arguments. I close by discussing the implications of my cross-cultural analysis to the broader understanding of mechanisms underlying people's concerns for intra group status vs. intergroup status in work groups and organizations.

PREVIOUS RESEARCH ON INTRAGROUP VS. INTERGROUP STATUS

Status refers to the relative rank or position that a person or a group has in a hierarchy of social esteem and respect in the eyes of others (Ridgeway, 1997). Many scholars in social psychology and sociology have long noted that when individuals or groups gather, status orderings among them naturally emerge: Some individuals or groups gain higher status than others (Homans, 1950; Goffman, 1957; Frank, 1985; Blau, 1986; Earley, 1997; Brewer & Brown, 1998; Sidanius & Pratto, 1999; Chen et al., 2003). Theoretically speaking, status ordering can emerge at the interpersonal level, at the intragroup level, or at the intergroup level. The current chapter focuses on the effects of intragroup status and intergroup status, and how these two combined affect people's group-oriented behaviors and attitudes, such as their collectivistic self-esteem (Crocker & Luthanen, 1990), or effort they are willing to exert on behalf of their group (Dutton, Dukerich, & Harquail, 1994).

The Role of Intergroup Status

According to social identity theory, individuals' social identity is defined as "that part of an individual's self-concept which derives from his knowledge of his membership in a social group (or groups) together with the value or emotional significance attached to that membership" (Tajfel, 1978, p. 63). Based on this perspective, the motivation underlying individuals' association with their groups is to accomplish "a relatively positive self-evaluation that endows the individual with a sense of well-being, enhanced self-worth, and self-esteem" (Hogg & Abrams, 1988, p. 23). When people can easily join or leave a group, those in low-status groups will leave their groups to seek membership in groups of high status (Ellemers et al., 1999). When mobility across groups is not possible, however, members of low-status groups are expected to downplay the importance of comparison dimensions that are unfavorable to their social position, whereas members of high-status groups will stress intergroup differences in ways that maximize their favorable positions (Elsbach & Kramer, 1996).

The predictions based on social identity theory have received strong support in both social psychological, and organizational behavior studies (e.g., Schneider, Hall, & Nygren, 1971; Hall & Schneider, 1972; Ashforth & Mael,

1989; Brewer, 1991; Mullen, Brown, & Smith, 1992; Taylor & Moghaddam, 1994; Elsbach & Kramer, 1996). For example, research in BIRG, that is, basking in reflected glory (e.g., Cialdini et al., 1976), showed that people stressed affiliation with their sports team when the team won, but distanced themselves from the team when it lost the game. Moreover, it has also been illustrated that employees in high-status groups tend to have stronger group identification and expend greater effort on behalf of their groups than those in low-status groups (e.g., Ashforth & Mael, 1989).

The Role of Intragroup Status

Relative to intergroup status, past social psychological research has paid much less attention to the role of intragroup status in people's group-oriented behaviors and attitudes. According to social identity theory, intragroup status becomes a concern to members only when leaving a lower-status group is not possible or when lower-status group members do not see other possible strategies to alter their present intergroup positions (Taylor & Moghaddam, 1994). An individual may compare him/herself with other group members to minimize the implication of being in a low-status group, but intragroup status should not influence a person's social identity or his/her group evaluations or behaviors.

For the above reason, past research in the social identity tradition rarely examines the causal relationship between intragroup status and group evaluations (without investigating the role of intergroup status). However, as discussed earlier, status hierarchy exists not only between groups, but also within groups (e.g., Ridgeway, 1997; Chen et al., 2003). Moreover, if self-esteem need is the motivational driver for people's affiliation with groups, then where people stand in the social status hierarchy within their groups should also exert similar impact on how they evaluate their groups. Ultimately, the causal relationship is between self-esteem and group-oriented outcomes, based on the assertion in social identity theory. It is quite likely that intragroup status also positively affects one's sense of self-worth, which in turn influences how one evaluates his/her group (Tyler & Blader, 2000).

Evidence in other existing literatures supports my reasoning. For example, research on collectivistic self-esteem by Jennifer Crocker et al. (Crocker & Luhtanen, 1990; Luhtanen & Crocker, 1992) shows a strong positive correlation (around 0.45) between private collectivistic self-esteem (i.e., how favorably people evaluate their groups), and membership collectivistic self-esteem (i.e., people's intragroup status). Further, as discussed by De Cremer and Tyler in Chapter 1 of the current volume, organizational justice research, in particular, the relational models of procedural justice (e.g., Tyler & Lind, 1992; Smith & Tyler, 1997; Tyler & Badler, 2000) also suggests a positive relationship between intragroup status and group-oriented behaviors and attitudes. As Tyler (1999) argues, employees use procedural justice information to make inferences about their standing within their group (such as their work group or organization), which subsequently influences their group-oriented reactions.

The Fishpond Phenomenon: Joint Effects of Intergroup Status Vs. Intragroup Status

My discussion thus far suggests that the optimal status combination is when one attains high status within a high-status group (i.e., being a big fish in a big pond). Such ideal positions in the social respect hierarchy, however, are few and often limited (Frank, 1985). Most people are likely to occupy other types of positions: Being a big fish in a small pond, a small fish in a big pond, or even a small fish in a small pond.

Since sociologist Davis (1966) formally presented an analysis of the fishpond phenomenon or the frog-pond effect, many scholars have examined the joint effects of intragroup status and intergroup status on people's self-evaluation and group evaluation. The conclusion is that people are neither satisfied about being in a highly prestigious group if they are not accorded high status in their group, nor are people dissatisfied about being in a less-prestigious group if they are conferred high status by their group members. When faced between the two, past research has consistently shown that people show more positive reactions toward the latter than the former (e.g., Davis, 1966; Marsh, 1987; McFarland & Buehler, 1995; Chen et al., 1998; Gardner et al., 2002). Therefore, it is not entirely true that intergroup status is the only predominant factor in people's evaluations of their groups, as social identity theory initially suggested (Tajfel & Turner, 1986). What is just as important is people's intragroup status. After all, the relevance and immediacy of intragroup status to one's sense of self-worth and esteem are likely to be strong and salient to people in most of their social and organizational lives.

Is intra- vis-à-vis intergroup status always simultaneously salient and impactful on how people relate to their groups and organizations? Moreover, is the fishpond phenomenon more likely to appear among certain individuals and in some social contexts than others? In the remaining portion of this chapter, I will adopt a deductive approach beginning with arguments and evidence in the cross-cultural research and literature. My objective is to arrive at a preliminary conceptual understanding of the key determinants underlying variations of people's concerns for intragroup status vs. intergroup status in work groups and organizations.

CULTURE AND INTRAGROUP STATUS VS. INTERGROUP STATUS

In this section, I will present arguments for the proposition that the salience and the impact of these two status concerns vary across national cultures. Specifically, I will argue that certain psychological emphasis and structural features make intragroup status more of an esteem enhancing and/or threatening concern for people in individualistic cultures, whereas a different set of psychological and structural mechanisms make intergroup status more of an esteem enhancing and/or threatening concern for their counterparts in collectivistic cultures.

It is worth noting that I recognize that there are wide distributions along most psychological and structural dimensions within any given national culture (Chen et al., 1998; Vandello & Cohen, 1999; Chen et al., 2002; Chen, Mannix, & Okumura, 2003). For the sake of making compelling conceptual assertions, however, I will make stereotypical accounts and comparisons about these cultures. Evidence in support of my motivational reasoning will be presented following these arguments.

Individualistic vs. Collectivistic Cultures

National cultures can differ in various dimensions (Kluckhohn & Strodtbeck, 1961; Hofstede, 1980, 1991; Erez & Earley, 1993; Triandis, 1995; Trompenarrs, 1998). One dimension that has received most attention in past research and is very relevant to the focus of the current chapter is the individualism/collectivism cultural dimension (see Oyserman, Coon, & Kemmelmeier, 2002 for a recent review). According to this line of research, cultures vary in the degree to which individual identities vs. collective identities are emphasized. Collectivistic cultures, such as the PRC, are characterized by a social pattern consisting of closely linked individuals who see themselves as parts of one or more collectives and groups. In contrast, individualistic cultures, such as the U.S., are characterized by a social pattern comprising loosely linked individuals who view themselves as autonomous entities, independent of collectives and groups. Such difference in the emphasis between individual and collective identities results in important psychological and within-group structural consequences that bear great implications to my current discussion of intragroup status and intergroup status.

Psychological Differences across Cultures and Concerns for Intragroup Status vs. Intergroup Status

Previous research on individualism and collectivism has shown important cognitive and motivational differences between people in individualistic and collectivistic cultures (e.g., Earley, 1989, 1993; Triandis, 1989; Markus & Kitayama, 1991; Oyserman et al., 2002). I will reason how these differences may influence the salience and importance of intragroup status and intergroup status to people in these cultures.

Cognitive Differences in Individual vs. Group Level Processing

Research has shown that the more salient and predominant unit of analysis in people's social cognition and perception is the individual in individualistic cultures, and the group in collectivistic cultures (Earley, 1989; Triandis, 1989, 1995; Markus & Kitayama, 1991; Trafimow, Triandis, & Goto, 1991; Erez & Earley, 1993). For example, Menon, Morris, Chiu, and Hong (1999) found that participants from Hong Kong, a collectivistic culture, tend to make group or collectivistic level attributions for target actors, while participants from the U.S., an individualistic culture, made individual level attributions. When presented information about a rogue trader, Hong Kong participants discussed the incident in terms of the company's traits, citing problems with the organization's policies, norms, etc. In contrast, U.S. participants described the incident in terms of the dispositional qualities of the individual trader. Similar results also appeared in the study by Trafimow et al. (1991). Using the Kuhn and McPartland (1954) self-attitudes instrument, which requires subjects completing 20 sentences beginning with "I am," they found that subjects from individualistic cultures retrieved more cognition about the individual self, and less about the collectivistic self, than their counterparts from collectivistic cultures.

Given the stronger focus on the collectivistic level cognition in collectivistic cultures, and the stronger focus on the individual level cognition in individualistic cultures, it stands to reason that the comparison at the intergroup level will be particularly more salient to people in collectivistic cultures. To people in individualistic cultures, however, the more salient comparison is likely to be at the interpersonal level within their groups.

Motivational Difference in Individual vs. Group Relationship

How an individual *should* relate to his/her group, particularly when faced with the dilemma between self-interests and the interests of the group, is perhaps one of the most important differences between individualistic and collectivistic cultures (Earley, 1989; Triandis, 1989, 1995; Erez & Earley, 1993). I coined the notion with the term "individual–collectivistic primacy," defined as the extent to which an individual will be willing to sacrifice his/her own personal interests to achieve the interests of the group when there is a conflict between the two (Chen et al., 1998, 2002). Based on the essence of this notion, people in cultures where collectivistic primacy is emphasized are likely to attach emotional and psychological significance to their groups, thus being more affected by the relative status between their groups and other groups than people in cultures where individual primacy is stressed. In contrast, people in cultures where individual primacy is stressed should attach great importance to their personal standing and benefits, thus being more affected by their intragroup status than their counterparts in collectivistic cultures.

This motivational reasoning is consistent with the basic tenet in social categorization theory (Turner, 1985). As Turner posits, the most central mediating factor in many group-oriented behaviors and attitudes is the *depersonalized* transformation, that is, seeing self and others within the group no longer represented as individuals with unique attributes and differences but, rather, as embodiments of a common shared group entity (Hogg & Terry, 2000). Similarly, when people, such as those high on collectivistic primacy, no longer differentiate between their own interests and the group interests, and by association, the interests of other members within the group, then intragroup status or comparison becomes less esteem enhancing or threatening. For this reason, the well-established fishpond phenomenon or the frog-pond effect will also be less likely to emerge in collectivistic cultures, particularly those high on collectivistic primacy. Recent research using similar conceptualizations on the individual/group relationship (e.g., the self-expansion concept by Gardner et al., 2002) supports my motivational reasoning arguments here. Those with a stronger bond toward their group are less affected by their intragroup status and, therefore, less likely to display the fishpond reaction pattern toward the combined information of intragroup status and intergroup status.

In summary, past cross-cultural findings in the individualism/collectivism domain noted that people in individualistic cultures tend to see the individual as the unit of analysis in their information processing (Earley, 1989; Triandis, 1989; Menon et al., 1999). When it comes to the relationship with their group, those in individualistic cultures also tend to place primacy on their own individual interests as opposed to those of their group (Chen et al., 1998, 2002). In contrast, people in collectivistic cultures have been shown to view the group as a more salient unit of analysis in the way they process social information and form social perception (Earley, 1989; Triandis, 1989; Menon et al., 1999). Moreover, those in collectivistic cultures tend to place the group's interests first when faced with the dilemma between self and group interest (Chen et al., 1998, 2002).

Similar inferences can be derived from sociological perspectives, in particular, Stryker's role identity theory (1980, 1987, 2000). Role identity theory holds that behavioral response patterns that are unique to situations involving group memberships are organized as identities, so that a person has separate identities as a student, a family member, or a member of a work group. Based on this theory, separate identities are ordered in a salient hierarchy in which highly salient identities are more likely to be evoked in response to a relevant situation. Role identity configuration in this theory, therefore, might suggest that people in the collectivistic cultures are more likely to subjugate personal status to the group using a unified role identity of the self and the group, while people in individualistic cultures may seek to maintain a conglomeration of role identities, since group status is only one facet of individual identity; that is, one of several roles that one adopts to determine individual identity (Earley & Laubach, 2001).

The above discussion suggests differential salience and the importance people may attach to intragroup status and intergroup status across cultures and individuals. Hence, although intragroup status and intergroup status are important to all people across cultures, relative to those in collectivistic cultures, intragroup status may be a more prominent and essential concern to those in individualistic cultures. Those in collectivistic cultures, on the other hand, are likely to show more group enhancing reactions when their group's status is high, but display more group-protecting reactions when their group's status is low, compared to their counterparts in individualistic cultures. Furthermore, past literature also suggests a lower likelihood of observing the fishpond phenomenon in collectivistic cultures.

Empirical Evidence in Support of Psychological Reasoning

Using the unpublished portion of the data in Chen et al. (2002), I was able to provide a preliminary test of the motivational reasoning for the effects of culture, intragroup status, and intergroup status on group evaluations, in particular, people's sense of collectivistic self-esteem (Crocker & Luhtanen, 1990; Luthanen & Crocker, 1992). As reasoned above, the mediating factor underlying the effect of national culture is the extent to which people attach importance to the collectivistic aspect of their self-identity. Here, I focused on participants' responses to the measure of individual–collectivistic primacy (Chen et al., 1998, 2002).

Another measure of my focus in this analysis is Luhtanen and Crockner's (1992) collectivistic self-esteem scale. Three sub-measures of this scale assess people's chronic levels of intragroup status (membership collectivistic self-esteem), intergroup status (public collectivistic self-esteem), and collectivistic self-esteem (private collectivistic self-esteem; i.e., the extent to which people evaluate their social groups favorably). Culture, individual–collectivistic primacy, membership collectivistic self-esteem, and public collectivistic self-esteem were treated as independent variables and private collectivistic self-esteem, the dependent variable in my regression analysis.

It is worth noting that participants completed these measures at the very beginning of the experimental sessions in Chen et al.'s study, so they were not influenced at all by the subsequent experimental manipulations. Samples included 203 undergraduate students from Indiana University in the U.S. and 396 undergraduate students from Peking University in the PRC. I tested three specific hypotheses in the analysis.

Hypothesis 1. The PRC participants will show a higher level of private collectivistic self-esteem than their U.S. counterparts when their public collectivistic self-esteem (the proxy for intergroup status) was high. However, when their public collectivistic self-esteem was low, the PRC participants' private collectivistic self-esteem level would not be as low as that displayed by the U.S. participants.

Hypothesis 2. The U.S. participants' private collectivistic self-esteem level would be more strongly associated with their membership collectivistic self-esteem than their PRC counterparts.

Hypothesis 3. The fishpond attitudinal reactions, that is, higher private collectivistic self-esteem when membership collectivistic self-esteem is high and public collectivistic self-esteem is low, than when membership collectivistic self-esteem is low and public collectivistic self-esteem is high, will emerge among the U.S. participants, but not the PRC participants.

As I mentioned above, of greatest importance to my central arguments is whether I can observe the expected differences between collectivistic primacy and individual primacy participants across cultures. Participants' cultural background was used as the proxy for the individual–collectivistic primacy orientation. Ultimately, it is the moderating roles of individual–collectivistic primacy (instead of culture) I need to examine in order to test the validity of my reasoning.

Similar to what was reported in Chen et al. (2002), I did not observe any cultural difference in my analysis. As Chen et al. explained, although the difference in individual–collectivistic primacy between the two cultural samples was significant, it was markedly smaller than what had been found in a prior study (Chen et al., 1998). In fact, the difference between cultures in this study was actually smaller than the within-culture difference between the U.S. samples in the prior study and this one.

Of greatest importance, I did observe the significant effects of my theoretical interest: A two-way interaction between membership collectivistic self-esteem and individual–collectivistic primacy; a two-way interaction between public collectivistic self-esteem and individual–collectivistic primacy; a two-way interaction between membership collectivistic self-esteem and public collectivistic self-esteem; and a triple interaction between membership collectivistic self-esteem, public collectivistic self-esteem, and individual–collectivistic primacy.

In support of Hypothesis 1, those high on collectivistic primacy had higher private collectivistic self-esteem than those high on individual primacy when their public collectivistic self-esteem was high, and still maintained a relatively high-level of private collective self-esteem compared to their individual primacy counterparts when their public collectivistic self-esteem was low. My second hypothesis also received support. The private collectivistic self-esteem of those high on individual primacy was more strongly associated with membership collectivistic self-esteem than that of those high on collectivistic primacy.

The two-way interaction between membership collectivistic self-esteem and public collectivistic self-esteem illustrated the typical fishpond pattern: Participants' private collectivistic self-esteem level was higher when their membership collectivistic self-esteem was high and public collectivistic self-esteem was low, compared to when their membership collectivistic self-esteem was low and public collectivistic self-esteem was high. This pattern was qualified by the triple interaction between membership collective self-esteem, public collective self-esteem, and individual–collectivistic primacy. The nature of this interaction shows that the fishpond pattern did not emerge among those high on collectivistic primacy, but did appear among those high on individual primacy.

The overall results of this analysis lend support for the motivational reasoning regarding the differential impact of intragroup status and intergroup status on people whose identity is more individual vs. collective based. Moreover, as stated earlier, my conceptual reasoning regarding differences across cultures was based on stereotypical accounts and arguments about national cultures. My results echoed the importance of directly testing the theoretical construct underlying the effect culture, rather than relying on the crude measure of culture for the analysis (Chen et al., 1998, 2002, 2003).

Structural Differences within Groups Across Cultures and Intragroup Status Concern

Most research that has examined the effects of intragroup status and intergroup status mainly focuses on psychological explanations for why they affect people's group-oriented behaviors and attitudes (e.g., Davis, 1966; Seta, & Seta 1996; Ellemers et al., 1999; Gardner et al., 2002). Just as important, however, as I will delineate below, are the structural features that give rise to people's concerns for status, in particular their status within groups.

In essence, I argue that different social practices, such as resource allocation principles (Leung & Bond, 1984; Leung, 1987; Chen & Church, 1993), and cultural beliefs, such as cooperation vs. competition-based status relationships (Chen, 2003), raise different degrees of uncertainty concerns regarding one's perceived membership value within a group. Two types of uncertainty are relevant and noteworthy. One is the degree of instability of intragroup status hierarchy (Ravlin, Thomas, & Ilsev 2000; Chen, 2003). The more frequently members' relative status gets reorganized, the more uncertainty they should experience. The second type of uncertainty arises from the distribution of perceived membership value an individual may receive from interactions with other group members. The wider the distribution, the greater uncertainty members should feel about their membership value. My central thesis is that compared to those in collective cultures, social practices in individualistic cultures create much greater instability of intragroup status hierarchy, as well as a much wider distribution of status differential among members within a group, or organization. These two structural features in individualistic cultures in turn heighten frequent concerns about why one member deserves more than another member, providing esteem enhancing or threatening information to all members involved. Conversely, in collective cultures intragroup status hierarchy is relatively stable, and a much smaller distribution of perceived membership values can be noted among group members.

The following ideological and incentive factors help explain why the instability and the distribution of intragroup status might be greater and wider in individualistic than in collectivistic cultures. The list is not meant to be exhaustive. My objective is to call attention to the potentially important role the overall "system" and interactions among members within the group might also play in affecting the significance people attached to intragroup status, in addition to the psychological factors past research has mainly focused on.

Vigilant vs. Complacent Practice of Individual Evaluation

It has long been noted that the evaluation systems across all domains in the socialization process in individualistic cultures, such as the U.S. are often elaborate and intensive (Markus & Kitayama, 1991; Balch, 2003), ranging from weight/height percentile charts for newborns, standardized admission tests at all education stages starting from preschool, to psychological batteries for promotion and placement, and quarterly performance evaluations in work organizations. Such social and organizational practices are conducted not only with high frequency, but with great precision, rendering constant concern for one's standing in relation to others, thus yielding great ease with which individuals can be compared and ranked with one another.

Social psychologists have long noted that individual evaluation results, often presented in comparative forms, add clarity to the individual understanding of his or her skills and attributes (Festinger, 1954; Markus & Kitayama, 1991). However, concomitant to such information is the heightened awareness of one's relative values to that of comparable others, exerting esteem pressure and concerns. Further, individualistic cultural beliefs in the causal link between individual performance results and internal abilities (as opposed to less stable factors such as effort, or external attribution factors) add fuel to people's concern for inferences others might make about their value from their individual performance (Brockner & Chen, 1996).

In such a vigilant individual evaluation system, there is little wonder that people in the individualistic cultures will react strongly to their individual standing, even when they are part of a work group where members are expected to support and assist one another. While the desire to keep up with the Joneses is probably universal, people in collectivistic cultures show much less concern for their individual performance, particularly when they are in group settings (Earley, 1989, 1993, 1994). Instead of stressing individual uniqueness and providing comparative information, social and organizational practices in collectivistic cultures emphasize similarity and harmony among members within a group. Moreover, even when individual performance information is given, the cultural attribution tendency of using external factors, such as group members' support as the main explanatory factor for success, and less threatening factors, such as efforts to explain failure, further reduce esteem enhancement or threat to individual members in work group contexts.

Individual vs. Group-Based Resource Allocation Principles
Another important social and organizational practice that might help explain why people in individualistic and collectivistic cultures react to intragroup status information differently is reward allocation practices. Previous research has found that when allocating rewards or resources to work group members, people in individualistic cultures prefer the equity principle – (i.e., allocation based on the individual input/output ratio), whereas people in collectivistic cultures prefer the equality or the need principles – (i.e., allocation of rewards equally among all members regardless of the input from each or based on each individual's need) (Leung & Bond, 1984; Leung, 1987; Erez & Earley, 1993). Clearly, an equity-based incentive system promotes differentiation among members within the group, providing information about differential membership value among individual group members. An equality-based incentive system, on the other hand, emphasizes similarity in membership value among members.

Note that within every culture, there should always be allocation differences across various ranks. For example, the manager on a consulting project team is likely to receive greater resources than an associate. Such allocation difference is likely to be viewed as a legitimate external factor, not causing threat or enhancement opportunities to members of a group. Where the use of resource allocation will evoke status concerns is the allocation differential among people of the same rank. It is quite common in the individualistic culture, such as the U.S. that employees of the same rank working on similar tasks receive differential pay rewards. In collective cultures, however, no such difference in reward allocations among employees of the same rank will be observed (and socially accepted). Differences in reward allocation practice between individualistic and collectivistic cultures are in synch with the performance evaluation concerns discussed above. Both supports the assertion that the distribution of intragroup status in work groups in individualistic cultures is likely to be wider than that in collectivistic cultures.

Competitive vs. Cooperative Assumptions in Status Relationships

Another structural feature and belief that makes intragroup status more of an esteem concern to people in individualistic cultures is the shared assumption of a competitive relationship between people in various status positions (Frank, 1985; Fiske, 1993; Sidanius & Pratto, 1999; Jost & Burgess, 2000; Owens & Sutton, 2001; Chen, 2003). Individualistic cultures promote tight couplings among performance, status, and membership value. Performance results tend to be interpreted as indicative of a member's individual worth and ability (Brockner, 1988; Blaine & Crocker, 1994; Fiske, Kitayama, Markus, & Nisbett, 1998). Those endowed with high status feel a sense of superiority to those in low status, whereas those in low status feel esteem threats when interacting with high-status members (Frank, 1985; Fiske, 1993; Sidanius & Pratto, 1999; Jost & Burgess, 2000). Under such a social system, high-status and low-status members essentially view each other more as out-group rather than in-group members, even though they presumably belong to the same group (Kramer, 1996). Moreover, status positions within the group are often associated with the distinction between core vs. peripheral group memberships (De Cremer, 2002; De Cremer & Tyler, Chapter 1 of this volume), arousing esteem concerns among those occupying different status positions.

In collectivistic cultures, however, performance results and status are not tightly associated with perceived differences in members' "worthiness." The cultural norm stresses equal value in each member's contribution to the maintenance of group integrity and the attainment of group goals. All members are stressed to share similar values of group membership regardless of their functional roles or performance (Lunyu, 1991; Yang, 1993; Mao, 1994). Both those in high- and low-functional positions bear mutual accountability toward each other and the group, and they are expected to work cooperatively with one another. Those in leadership roles (e.g., project manager) work to ensure that they carry critical responsibilities for attaining group goals, but they are also expected to take care of other members' needs (Confucius, 1997; Chen, Lee-Chai, & Bargh, 2001). Those in less critical functional roles, in turn, work to ensure that they assist the efforts of those members in leadership roles by showing deference for the guidance from them (Lunyu, 1991). Logically, the notion and concern of intragroup status become inconsequential under such a cooperative social system in which high mutual respect is displayed between all members in the group.

One analogy that might help illustrate the above point is the status difference between an engine and a screw on an airplane. Clearly, like any other systems, there exist differences in status and importance between a large engine and a small screw on a plane. However, to achieve the overall effectiveness of plane functioning, the values of the engine and the screw are equally important. It is this ideology that stresses group integrity and goal attainment that alleviates members' esteem concerns in collectivistic cultures. Given this ideological emphasis and the necessary concomitant features of high mutual accountability and respect between high-and low-status members (for such ideology to exist and prevail), low status members' acceptance of the status (or power) discrepancy with high-status members is naturally high. This relationship perhaps explains the nature of the power distance cultural notion (Hofstede, 1980), and the high correlation (around 0.70) between collectivism and power distance at the national level.

My prior discussion on the differences in ideologies, norms, and incentives between individualistic and collectivistic cultures supports the assertion that the instability and distribution of membership value within work groups is likely to be greater and wider in individualistic than in collectivistic cultures, hence making intragroup status more of a concern to people in individualistic cultures. I am not suggesting, however, that there is no hierarchy within work groups in collectivistic cultures, as made clear in the engine/screw analogy. Instead, what I am suggesting is greater stability and more narrow distribution of perceived membership value within work groups in collectivistic cultures. Note that such distribution is decoupled from the performance hierarchy or the functional hierarchy all groups need to have in order to perform effectively and efficiently (Leavitt, 2003).

Structural Differences between Groups and Intergroup Status Concern

Uncertainty concerns of status hierarchy instability and perceived value distribution should also apply at the intergroup level (Hogg & Abrams, 1988). That is, people's concern and reaction about their relative intergroup status will be more salient, and therefore more impactful, if there is greater instability of the status hierarchy, and a wider distribution of perceived value among all groups in their given culture or social system. There is relatively little research and knowledge regarding the difference in the distribution of perceived value at the group level in individualistic and collectivistic cultures. Triandis's (1995) argument that there is a great competition between groups in collectivistic cultures, but greater competition between individuals in individualistic cultures is consistent with the possibility that there might be wider distribution of perceived value among groups in collectivistic than in individualistic cultures. However, ample research in the domain of intergroup relations, in particular social dominance literature, suggests that the distribution of perceived value among groups in individualistic cultures might be the same or wider than in collectivistic cultures (Brewer & Brown, 1998; Sidanius & Pratto, 1999; Jost & Burgess, 2000).

Following the same logical flow I used when discussing perceived membership value distribution within groups, I note no obvious difference in the frequency and availability of comparative group evaluations across individualistic and collectivistic cultures. Second, resource allocation principles at the group level in individualistic and collectivistic cultures both seem to be based on equity, as opposed to equality, or need. Third, tight coupling between performance hierarchy and group value appears to exist at the intergroup level across cultures. For example, there is a clear relationship between performance of academic institutions and social value of these institutions in both the U.S. (an individualistic culture) and the PRC (a collectivistic culture). In other words, value distribution in academic institutions in both of these cultures seems to be wide to a similar extent. Finally, competition, rather than cooperation, characterizes relationships between high-status and low-status work groups across cultures (Hinkle & Brown, 1990).

Thus, while I suggest the structural features of status hierarchy stability and perceived value distribution as two theoretical facets of concerns for why intragroup status is more of a worry to people in individualistic cultures, I do not see the same role it plays in accounting for cultural differences in people's concern for intergroup status. The basic thesis, however, should still hold: When people perceive that there is greater instability and a wide distribution in perceived value or "worthiness" members within groups or groups in their social system receive, they will show great concern for their intragroup status or intergroup status. In the instance of examining people's concern for intergroup status, it appears that motivational differences between individualistic and collectivistic cultures better explain the differences in intergroup status across cultures. As I previously reasoned, people in collectivistic cultures are socialized to place primacy in their collectivistic identities. For this reason, the information of their group being higher status than other groups elicits group enhancement reactions from them, and the information of their group being lower status than other groups results in their strong group protection reactions (Chen et al., 2002).

CONCLUSION

People across all cultures share the need to know and assert their importance in the world around them (James, 1890; Tajfel & Turner, 1986; Brockner, 1988; Taylor & Brown, 1988; Swann Jr., 1996). For this reason, in the group settings, they often exert great effort to join prestigious groups that compare favorably with other groups, and to attain high standing within the groups to which they belong. Theoretically, people may assert their status at the interpersonal, intergroup, or intragroup levels. The focus of this chapter has been on the latter two, and the interaction between the two.

I proposed that the concerns for intragroup status vs. intergroup status vary across individualistic and collectivistic cultures. In particular, the concern for intragroup status will be stronger in individualistic cultures, whereas the concern for intergroup status will be stronger in collectivistic cultures. These hypotheses were substantiated by the cognitive and motivational differences in the self-collective relationship across cultures. Specifically, I suggested that people in individualistic cultures tend to view the individual as the basic unit of analysis in information processing and attach great importance to their own individual interests; hence, they are likely to react strongly to their personal standing in relations to others, including intragroup status. In contrast, those in collectivistic cultures tend to view the group as the salient unit in their cognition and have a strong bond with their group; thus, they are likely to respond in group enhancing or protecting manners to the status information between their group and other groups.

I further introduced the structural notions of status hierarchy instability and perceived membership value distribution as additional potential reasons for why intragroup status might have a stronger effect in individualistic than collectivistic cultures. I suggested that ideological and incentive practices in individualistic cultures stimulate people's frequent concerns about why one group member deserves more than another member, providing esteem enhancing or threatening information to all members involved. In contrast, intragroup status hierarchy is relatively stable in collective cultures, and there also exists a much smaller distribution of perceived membership values.

In summary, I call attention to the roles of both psychological and structural factors in affecting people's concerns for status across cultures. My analysis using the angle of national culture offers the following broad conceptual conclusion. When the unit of analysis (an individual or a group) is salient, either evoked by individuals' psychological orientations or by the surrounding social system, and attached with strong psychological significance, people show strong esteem reactions to the implication of the comparison between that unit and its comparable others. Moreover, people would show greater concern and react more strongly to their relative status at both intragroup and intergroup levels if there was greater instability of the status hierarchy and a wide distribution of perceived individual or group worthiness in their given social system.

Implications to Work Groups and Organizations

Several organizational factors can potentially influence the salience of intergroup vs. intragroup status. First, where people are, in the functional structure of the group or the organization, should influence the salience and impact of intergroup status and intragroup status. People in the leadership positions or boundary spanning roles are more likely to act on behalf of their groups, hence will pay greater attention to and be more affected by intergroup status than others in positions that are more internally focused (Bartel, 2001). In contrast, those in lower-level functional positions within the group or the organization would be more likely to have more frequent interactions with other members and, thus might show greater interest in their intragroup status. Indeed, a recent study by Schminke, Cropanzano, and Rupp (2002) showed that people at the lower levels of the organizational hierarchy were more affected by procedural justice than their counterparts at the top.

Second, an external threat outside of the group or the organization should also reduce people's concern for their intragroup status, and eliminate their tendency to show the fish-pond effect (Sherif, 1961; Brewer, 1979). Following my logic above, it is quite likely that under such circumstances, the need to be united against the common threat makes people more willing to emphasize the importance of each group member, hence reducing the overall distribution of perceived group membership value. Third, the nature of the group task might also influence the salience and impact of intragroup status. It is more likely that intragroup status will be more of a concern when the group task is characterized by pooled, rather than sequential or reciprocal, interdependence. Clearly, compared to sequential or reciprocal interdependent tasks, a pooled interdependent task is more likely to be accompanied by individual-based evaluation and reward setup, hence providing more individual relevant information and comparisons. Finally, changes and uncertainty occurring in the broader context of the organization or the market might heighten people's intergroup status concern, whereas internal structural, leadership, or cultural changes might increase people's intragroup status concern (O'Reilly & Tushman, 2002).

My application of the principles derived from the cultural analysis above is a preliminary step toward a broader understanding of when and why people in work groups and organizations care about, and react to the implications of their intragroup and intergroup status. As noted above, in addition to examining psychological factors underlying people's reactions to intragroup status vs. intergroup status information, I also suggested the importance of considering the overall structural features of the environment within which work groups and organizations are embedded. I hope that this additional angle expands the current thinking of status and highlights the ultimate goal people in all cultures strive to achieve a clear sense of personal worthiness and importance.

REFERENCES

Balch, K. S. (2003). Testing ... testing: The IQ, the SAT, & SJG. *Odyssey, 12*, 28–30.

Bales, R. (1950). *Interaction process analysis.* Reading, MA: Addison Wesley.

Bartel, C. A. (2001). Social comparisons in boundary-spanning work: Effects of community outreach on members' organizational identity and identification. *Administrative Science Quarterly, 46*, 379–413.

Berger, J., Rosenholtz, S. J., & Zelditch, M., Jr. (1980). Status organizing processes. *Annual Review of Sociology, 6*, 479–508.

Blaine, B., & Crocker, J. (1994). Self-esteem and self-serving biases in reactions to positive and negative events: An integrative review. In: R. F. Baumeister (Ed.), *Self-esteem: The puzzle of low self-regard.* New York: Plenum Press.

Blau, P. (1986). *Exchange and power in social life.* New Brunswick, NJ: Transaction Publishers.

Brewer, M. B. (1979). Ingroup bias in the minimal intergroup situation: A cognitive motivational analysis. *Psychological Bulletin, 86*, 307–324.

Brewer, M. B. (1991). The social self: On being the same and different at the same time. *Personality and Social Psychology Bulletin, 17*, 475–482.

Brewer, M. B., & Brown, R. J. (1998). Intergroup relations. In: D. T. Gilbert, S. T. Fiske & G. Lindzey (Eds), *The handbook of social psychology* (4th ed., Vol. 2, pp. 554–594). New York: Oxford University Press.

Brockner, J. (1988). *Self-esteem at work.* Boston: Lexington.

Brockner, J., & Chen, Y. (1996). The moderating roles of self-esteem and self-construal in reaction to a threat to the self: Evidence from the People's Republic of China and the United States. *Journal of Personality and Social Psychology, 71*, 603–615.

Chen, Y. (2003). How one experiences and uses status depends upon how one gets it: Differences in the effects of status in cooperative vs. competitive social systems. Working paper.

Chen, Y., Blount, S., & Sanchez-Burks, J. (2004). Status in group synchronization. In: M. Neale & E. A. Mannix (Eds), *Research on managing groups and teams*, Vol. 6. Greenwich, CT: JAI Press.

Chen, Y., Brockner, J., & Chen, X. (2002). Individual–collectivistic primacy and ingroup favoritism: Enhancement and protection effects. *Journal of Experimental Social Psychology, 38*, 482–491.

Chen, Y., Brockner, J., & Greenberg, J. (2003). When is it "a pleasure to do business with you?" The effects of relative status, outcome favorability, and procedural fairness." Organizational Behavior and Human Decision Processes.

Chen, Y., Brockner, J., & Katz, T. (1998). Toward an explanation of cultural differences in ingroup favoritism: The role of individual versus collectivistic primacy. *Journal of Personality and Social Psychology, 75*, 1490–1502.

Chen, Y., & Church, A. (1993). Reward allocation preferences in groups and organizations. *International Journal of Conflict Management, 4*, 25–59.

Chen, S., Lee-Chai, A. Y., & Bargh, J. A. (2001). Relational orientation as a moderator of the effects of social power. *Journal of Personality and Social Psychology, 80*, 173–187.

Chen, Y., Mannix, E. A., & Okumura, T. (2003). The importance of who you meet: Effects of self- vs. other-concerns among negotiators in the United States, the People's Republic of China, and Japan. *Journal of Experimental Social Psychology, 39*, 1–15.

Cialdini, R. B., Borden, R. J., Thorne, A., Walker, M. R., Freeman, S., & Sloan, L. R. (1976). Basking in reflected glory: Three (football) field studies. *Journal of Personality and Social Psychology, 34*, 366–375.

Confucius. (1997). *The analects of Confucius* (S. Leys, Trans.). New York: Norton.

Crocker, J., & Luhtanen, R. (1990). Collectivistic self-esteem and in-group bias. *Journal of Personality and Social Psychology, 58*, 60–67.

Davis, J. A. (1966). The campus as a frog pond: An application of the theory of relative deprivation to career decisions of college men. *American Journal of Sociology, 72*, 17–31.

De Cremer, D. (2002). Respect and cooperation in social dilemmas: The importance of feeling included. *Personality and Social Psychology Bulletin, 28*, 1335–1341.

De Cremer, D., & Tyler, T. R. (this volume). A matter of intragroup status: The importance of respect for the viability of groups. In: E. A. Mannix, M. Neale & M. C. Thomas-Hunt (Eds), *Research on managing groups and teams* (Vol. 7). Greenwich, CT: JAI Press.

Dutton, J. E., Dukerich, J. M., & Harquail, C. V. (1994). Organizational images and member identification. *Administrative Science Quarterly, 39*, 239–263.

Earley, P. C. (1989). Social loafing and collectivism: A comparison of the United States and the People's Republic of China. *Administrative Science Quarterly, 34*, 565–581.

Earley, P. C. (1993). East meets west meets mideast: Further exploration of collectivistic and individualistic work groups. *Academy of Management Journal, 36*, 319–348.

Earley, P. C. (1994). Self or group? Cultural effects of training on self-efficacy and performance. *Administrative Science Quarterly, 39*, 89–117.

Earley, P. C. (1997). *Face, harmony and social structure: Analysis of organizational behavior across cultures*. New York: Oxford University Press.
Earley, P. C., & Laubach, M. (2001). Structural identity theory and the dynamics of cross-cultural work groups. In: M. L. Gannon & K. Newman (Eds), *Handbook of cross-cultural management*. Malden, MA: Blackwell.
Ellemers, N., Spears, R., & Doosje, B. (1999). *Social identity: Context, commitment, content*. Malden, MA: Blackwell.
Elsbach, K., & Kramer, R. M. (1996). Members' responses to organizational identity threats: Encountering and countering the Business Week rankings. *Administrative Science Quarterly, 41*, 442–476.
Erez, M., & Earley, P. C. (1993). *Culture, self-identity, and work*. New York: Oxford University Press.
Festinger, L. (1954). A theory of social comparison processes. *Human Relations, 7*, 117–140.
Fiske, S. T. (1993). Controlling other people: The impact of power on stereotyping. *American Psychologists, 48*, 621–628.
Fiske, A. P., Kitayama, S., Markus, H. R., & Nisbett, R. E. (1998). The cultural matrix of social psychology. In: D. T. Gilbert, S. T. Fiske & G. Lindzey (Eds), *The handbook of social psychology*, (4th ed) (pp. 315–394). New York: Oxford University Press.
Frank, R. H. (1985). *Choosing the right pond: Human behavior and the quest for status*. New York: Oxford University Press.
Gardner, W. L., Gabriel, S., & Hochschild, L. (2002). When you and I are "we," you are not threatening: The role of self-expansion in social comparison. *Journal of Personality and Social Psychology, 82*, 239–251.
Goffman, I. W. (1957). Status consistency and preference for change in power distribution. *American Sociological Review, 22*, 275–288.
Hall, D. T., & Schneider, B. (1972). Correlates of organizational identification as a function of career pattern and organizational type. *Administrative Science Quarterly, 17*, 340–350.
Hinkle, S., & Brown, R. (1990). Intergroup comparisons and social identity: Some links and lacunae. In: D. Abrams & M. Hogg (Eds), *Social identity theory: Constructive and critical advances* (pp. 48–70). London: Harvester Wheatsheaf.
Hofstede, G. (1980). *Culture's Consequences*. Beverly Hills, CA: Sage.
Hofstede, G. (1991). *Cultures and Organizations*. London: McGraw-Hill.
Hogg, M. A., & Abrams, D. (1988). *Social identifications: A social psychology of intergroup relations and group processes*. London: Routledge.
Hogg, M. A., & Terry, D. J. (2000). Social identity and self-categorization processes in organizational contexts. *Academy of Management Review, 25*, 121–140.
Homans, G. C. (1950). *The human group*. New York: Harcourt, Brace & World.
James, W. (1890). *The principles of psychology*. Reprint. New York: Dover.
Jost, J. T., & Burgess, D. (2000). Attitudinal ambivalence and the conflict between group and system justification motives in low status groups. *Personality and Social Psychology Bulletin, 26*, 293–305.
Kluckhohn, F., & Strodtbeck, F. (1961). *Variations in value orientations*. Evanston, IL: Row, Peterson.
Kramer, R. M. (1996). Divergent realities and convergent disappointments in the hierarchic relation: Trust and the intuitive auditor at work. In: R. M. Kramer & T. R. Tyler (Eds), *Trust in organizations: Frontiers of theory and research* (pp. 216–245). Thousand Oaks, CA: Sage.

Kramer, R. M., & Neale, M. A. (1998). *Power and influence in organizations*. Thousand Oaks, CA: Sage.
Kuhn, M. H., & McPartland, T. S. (1954). An empirical investigation of self-attitudes. *American Sociological Review*, *19*, 68–76.
Leavit, H. (2003). Why hierarchies thrive. *Harvard Business Review*, March 2003.
Leung, K. (1987). Some determinants of reactions to procedural models for conflict resolution: A cross-national study. *Journal of Personality and Social Psychology*, *53*, 898–908.
Leung, K., & Bond, M. H. (1984). The impact of cultural collectivism on reward allocation. *Journal of Personality and Social psychology*, *47*, 793–804.
Luhtanen, R., & Crocker, J. (1992). A collectivistic self-esteem scale: Self-evaluation of ones' social identity. *Personality and Social Psychology Bulletin*, *18*, 302–318.
Lunyu. (1991). *New interpretations of Lunyu*. Taipei: Sa Ming Book Company.
Mao, L. R. (1994). Beyond politeness theory: "Face" revisited and renewed. *Journal of Pragmatics*, *21*, 451–486.
Markus, H., & Kitayama, S. (1991). Culture and the self: Implications for cognition, emotion, and motivation. *Psychological Review*, *98*, 224–253.
Marsh, H. W. (1987). The big frog little pond effect on academic self-concept. *Journal of Educational Psychology*, *79*, 280–295.
Mazur, A. (1985). A biosocial model of status in face-to-face primate groups. *Social Forces*, *64*, 377–402.
McFarland, C., & Buehler, R. (1995). Collectivistic self-esteem as a moderator of the frog-pond effect in reactions to performance feedback. *Journal of Personality and Social Psychology*, *68*, 1055–1070.
Menon, T., Morris, M. W., Chiu, C., & Hong, Y. (1999). Culture and construal of agency: Attribution to individual versus group dispositions. *Journal of Personality and Social Psychology*, *76*, 701–717.
Mullen, B., Brown, R., & Smith, C. (1992). Ingroup bias as a function of salience, relevance, and status: An integration. *European Journal of Social Psychology*, *22*, 103–122.
O'Reilly, C. A., & Tushman, M. L. (2002). *Winning through Innovation: A practical guide to leading organizational change and renewal*. Cambridge, MA: Harvard Business School Press.
Owens, D. A., & Sutton, R. I. (2001). Status contests in meetings: Negotiating the informal order. In: M. E. Turner (Ed.), *Groups at work: Theory and research* (pp. 120–135). Mahwah, NJ: Lawrence Erlbaum.
Oyserman, D., Coon, H. M., & Kemmelmeier, M. (2002). Rethinking individualism and collectivism: Evaluation of theoretical assumptions and meta-analyses. *Psychological Bulletin*, *128*, 3–72.
Pfeffer, J. (1992). *Managing with power: Politics and influence in organizations*. Boston, MA: Harvard Business School Press.
Ravlin, E. C., Thomas, D. C., & Ilsev, A. (2000). Beliefs about values, status, and legitimacy in multicultural groups: Influence on intragroup conflict. In: P. C. Earley & H. Singh (Eds), *Innovations in international and cross-cultural management*. Thousand Oaks, CA: Sage.
Ridgeway, C. L. (1984). Dominance, performance, and status in groups. In: E. J. Lawler (Ed.), *Advances in group processes*, (Vol. 1, pp. 59–93). Greenwich, CT: JAI.
Ridgeway, C. L. (1987). Nonverbal behavior, dominance, and the basis of status in task groups. *American Sociological Review*, *52*, 683–694.

Ridgeway, C. L. (1997). Where do status value beliefs come from? New developments. In: J. Szmatka, J. Skvoretz & J. Berger (Eds), *Status, network, and structure* (pp. 137–158). Stanford, CA: Stanford University Press.

Schminke, M., Cropanzano, R., & Rupp, D. E. (2002). Organization structure and fairness perceptions: The moderating effects of organizational level. *Organizational Behavior and Human Decision Processes*, *89*, 881–905.

Schneider, B., Hall, D. T., & Nygren, H. T. (1971). Self-image and job characteristics as correlates of changing organizational identification. *Human Relations*, *24*, 397–416.

Seta, C. E., & Seta, J. J. (1992). Observers and participants in an intergroup setting. *Journal of Personality and Social Psychology*, *63*, 629–643.

Seta, J. J., & Seta, C. E. (1996). Big fish in small ponds: A social hierarchical analysis of intergroup bias. *Journal of Personality and Social Psychology*, *71*, 1210–1221.

Sherif, C. W. (1961). *Intergroup conflict and cooperation: The robber's cave experiment*. Norman, OK: University of Oklahoma Press.

Sidanius, J., & Pratto, F. (1999). *Social dominance theory: An intergroup theory of social hierarchy and oppression*. New York: Cambridge University Press.

Smith, H. J., & Tyler, T. R. (1997). Choosing the right pond: The impact of group membership on self-esteem and group-oriented behavior. *Journal of Experimental Social Psychology*, *33*, 146–170.

Stryker, S. (1980). *Symbolic interactionism: A social structural version*. Menlo Park: CA: Benjamin/Cummings.

Stryker, S. (1987). Identity theory: Developments and extensions. In: K. Yardley & T. Honess (Eds), *Self and identity: Psychosocial perspectives* (pp. 89–103). London: Wiley.

Stryker, S. (2000). *Symbolic interaction theory: Encyclopedia of Psychology*. Washington, D.C. and New York: American Psychological Association and Oxford University Press.

Swann, W. B., Jr. (1996). *Self-traps: The elusive quest for higher self-esteem*. New York: W.H. Freeman.

Tajfel, H. (1978). *Differentiation between social groups: Studies in the social psychology of intergroup relations*. London: Academic Press.

Tajfel, H., & Turner, J. C. (1986). The social identity theory of intergroup behavior. In: S. Worchel & W. G. Austin (Eds), *Psychology of intergroup relations*, (Vol. 2, pp. 7–24). Chicago: Nelson-Hall.

Taylor, S. E., & Brown, J. (1988). Illusion and well-being: Some social psychological contributions to a theory of mental health. *Psychological Bulletin*, *103*, 193–210.

Taylor, D. M., & Moghaddam, F. M. (1994). *Theories of intergroup relations: International social psychological perspectives*. Westport, CT: Praeger.

Trafimow, D., Triandis, H. C., & Goto, S. G. (1991). Some tests of the distinction between the private self and the collectivistic self. *Journal of Personality and Social Psychology*, *60*, 645–655.

Triandis, H. C. (1989). The self and social behavior in differing cultural contexts. *Psychological Review*, *96*, 506–520.

Triandis, H. C. (1995). *Individualism and collectivism*. Boulder, CO: Westview Press.

Trompenarrs, F. (1998). *Riding the waves of culture: Understanding diversity in global business*. New York: Irwin.

Turner, J. C. (1985). Social categorization and the self-concept: A social cognitive theory of group behavior. *Advances in Group Processes*, *2*, 77–121.

Tyler, T. R. (1999). Why people cooperate with organizations. *Research in Organizational Behavior, 21*, 201–246.

Tyler, T. R., & Blader, S. (2000). *Cooperation in groups: Procedural justice, social identity, and behavioral engagement*. Philadelphia, PA: Psychological Press.

Tyler, T. R., & Lind, E. A. (1992). A relational model of authority in groups. *Advances in Experimental Social Psychology, 25*, 115–191.

Vandello, J. A., & Cohen, D. (1999). Patterns of individualism and collectivism across the United States. *Journal of Personality and Social Psychology, 77*, 279–292.

Yang, K. S. (1993). Chinese social orientations: An integrative analysis. In: L. Y. Cheng, F. M. C. Cheung & Char-Nie (Eds), *Psychotherapy for the Chinese: Selected papers from the first international conference* (pp. 19–56). The Chinese University of Hong Kong.

MISPERCEIVING YOUR PLACE: HUMILITY AND HUBRIS IN SOCIAL HIERARCHIES

Cameron P. Anderson and Sandra E. Spataro

ABSTRACT

In the current chapter, we examine people's perceptions of their place in hierarchies. We explore the complexity of these self-perceptions and show how they are susceptible to inaccuracy and bias. We examine how such inaccuracies, however, can lead to negative social consequences: Overestimating one's place can lead to collective punishment by other group members, and underestimating one's place can lead to underutilizing levers of influence, and ultimately, to losing one's social standing.

Understanding the political landscape is critical to success in any social arena. Individuals who seek to satisfy their demands, or to initiate change, must first identify the key political actors who control valued resources and make decisions for the group and those who have the ability to mobilize and coordinate the collective efforts of others. They must understand the network of interpersonal ties throughout the group, how and where information flows, and where loyalties exist among group members, which helps

Status and Groups
Research on Managing Groups and Teams, Volume 7, 69–92

ISSN: 1534-0856/doi:10.1016/S1534-0856(05)07004-0

identify where potential pockets of resistance or support might emerge for their agenda.

Part of understanding the political landscape, however, is also having an accurate perception of one's own place in it. Accurately perceiving one's own place in a group allows individuals to behave in ways appropriate to their position and thus helps them avoid missteps that can damage their interpersonal relationships and broader reputation. Moreover, accurate self-perceptions of one's "place" help individuals identify and deploy their levers of control, which allows them to fully utilize the tactics of influence they have at their disposal.

While we have begun to make strides in understanding the way people perceive the hierarchies and the social networks in which they are embedded (Krackhardt, 1990; Pettigrew, 1973; Pfeffer & Salancik, 1977), we still understand little about the way people perceive their own place in a social group. How are self-perceptions of place constructed? How accurate do they tend to be? What are the consequences of inaccurate self-perceptions of place? In the current chapter, we aim to fill this lacuna by addressing these fundamental questions. We integrate work in psychology, sociology, and organizational behavior, and draw on recent findings in each of these areas, as well as from our own studies of intragroup hierarchies.

DEFINITIONS

To understand self-perceptions of "place," it is important to first offer some definitional clarity. The two primary dimensions of hierarchical differentiation in social groups are power and status. Power is defined as the capacity to influence others (Emerson, 1962; Fiske, 1993; French & Raven, 1959; Keltner, Gruenfeld, & Anderson, 2003; Lewin, 1951). It is a context-specific variable, such that a person's power can only be understood with reference to a particular relationship or group (Emerson, 1962; Thibaut & Kelley, 1959). On the other hand, status is defined as individuals' prominence and respect in their social group (Anderson, John, Keltner, & Kring, 2001). People who have higher status are more prominent, visible, and well-known, and they are more respected and held in higher regard (Barkow, 1975; Chance, 1967; Eibl-Eibesfeldt, 1989; Fiske, 1993; Goldhammer & Shils, 1939). Thus, power and status are often closely related. When individuals have high status they are better able to influence others because other people seek to identify with them (French & Raven, 1959). Moreover, when individuals have control over resources and occupy a position of power, they are often afforded a great deal of prominence and respect (Ridgeway & Balkwell, 1997).[1]

In the current chapter, we will focus primarily on power and self-perceptions of power. However, the arguments we present will hold for both power and status, and thus, the terms "power" and "status" will often be interchangeable in our theoretical framework. This is not to say that power and status are conceptually isomorphic, but rather, that many of the same consequences will befall people who inaccurately view their power or their status in groups.

How Are Self-Perceptions of Power Constructed?

Individuals' power, or their capacity to influence others, is dependent on a myriad of factors. We will use Fig. 1 to unpack these factors, referring to the

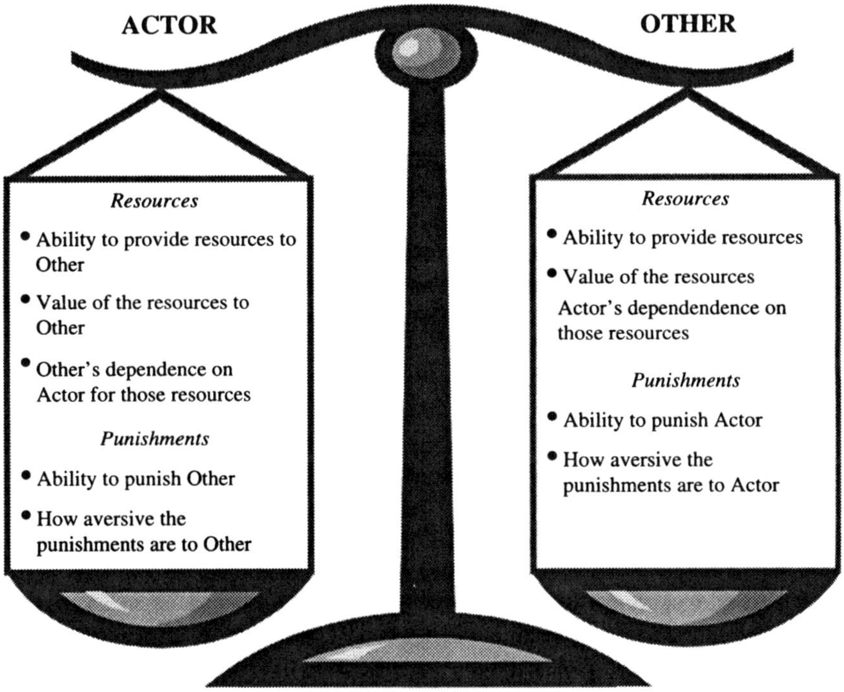

Fig. 1. The Balance of Power.

individual whose power is under consideration as "Actor," and to the other party in the relationship as "Other." Therefore, we will focus on an individual's power within one specific relational context (for similar discussions, see Bacharach & Lawler, 1976; Emerson, 1962; Kim, Pinkley, & Fragale, in press). It is important to note that "Other" can refer to a single individual, as when considering a person's power in a dyadic relationship, or it can refer to a collection of individuals, as when considering an individual's power in relation to a group.

The first major component of Actor's power in relation to Other involves the ability to *provide resources* to Other (French & Raven, 1959). This ability depends not only on whether Actor has control over resources, but also on how valuable Actor's resources are to Other (How badly does Other want those resources?) and on Other's ability to obtain those resources from other parties (Can Other easily get those resources from someone else?). Second, Actor's power is a function of his or her ability to *administer punishments* to Other (French & Raven, 1959). This ability depends both on Actor's capacity to punish Other and on how aversive those punishments are to Other (Does Other fear those punishments?). Finally, Actor's power is a function of *Other's control* over resources and punishments that are important to Actor (Emerson, 1962). For example, the more Other controls resources that are highly valuable to Actor, the less power Actor has over Other. In sum, therefore, Actor's power is best construed as the net balance between Actor's ability to administer resources and punishments, and Other's ability to administer resources and punishments.

Self-perceptions of power are thus individuals' perception of their ability to influence others. It is individuals' assessment of the net balance between their control over resources and punishments, and the other party's control over resources and punishments.

How Can Self-Perceptions of Power Be Inaccurate?

Given the complexity of factors that determine a person's power, and the ambiguity in many criteria used to assess power, it is easy to see that self-perceptions of power are very susceptible to inaccuracy and bias. There are many ways individuals can form a distorted perception of their power, either believing they have a higher capacity to influence others than they actually do, or alternatively, failing to recognize the influence they could exert on others.

In terms of overestimation, one way people can overestimate their power is by being overly optimistic of their ability to punish others. This often occurs in conflict situations, wherein disputing parties overestimate their ability to inflict damage on their opponent through arbitration or litigation (Bazerman & Neale, 1992; Brett, 2000), or during wars, when national leaders overestimate their country's military prowess (Friedman, 1995). It can also occur when individuals are more powerful in some contexts than others; people often presume a carryover of their power from a group in which they are at the top of the hierarchy to a group in which they are not (e.g., Spataro, 2005). Finally, people might overestimate their power by underestimating their dependence on others. For example, it has been argued that former President Clinton overestimated his power in his early years in office because he underestimated his dependence on allies in Congress (Gergen, 2000).

In terms of underestimation, one way people can underestimate their power is by having a skewed perception of the resources that others provide them. Dissatisfied employees often stay with their company because they believe there are few attractive alternatives (Cotton & Tuttle, 1986), an often incorrect perception. Similarly, in abusive relationships, one reason why victims of abuse remain with their partner is that they underestimate their ability to find a better, alternative relationship (Smuts, 1996).

Above and beyond over- or underestimating different elements of the power balance, individuals might also simply focus their attention too narrowly on certain aspects of the power balance and ignore others. They might focus on the resources they control and ignore their dependence on others, for example, or they might focus more on how they can punish their opponent and less on how their opponent can punish them. This narrowing of attention seems to occur among individuals who have a high need for power but do not possess it (Winter & Stewart, 1978). These individuals commonly engage in profligate behaviors, such as gambling or drinking, because such behavior temporarily makes them feel powerful; it focuses their attention on the freedoms they do have and distracts them from the power they lack.

How Accurate Do Self-Perceptions of Power Tend to Be?

The issue of accuracy in self-perceptions of power is important for two reasons. First, as a practical concern, accurate perceptions of power helps individuals successfully navigate their social environments. Second, as a theoretical concern, this question speaks to how accurately people perceive themselves and their environment more broadly, an issue of considerable interest among behavioral scientists (e.g., Colvin & Block, 1994; John & Robins, 1994; Taylor & Brown, 1988).

In a series of studies on peer groups, organizations, ad hoc teams, and competitive negotiations, Anderson and colleagues have assessed the correspondence between individuals' self-perceptions of power and external indices of their power (Anderson & Berdahl, 2002; Anderson, John, & Keltner, 2005; Anderson, Srivastava, Beer, Spataro, & Chatman, 2005). While the findings from these studies do not conclusively assess perceptual accuracy per se (Who is to know whether external indices are perfect measures of individuals' actual power?), these findings at least provide some suggestive evidence of how accurately people perceive their power in specific social contexts.

In each of these studies, people's self-perceptions of power were measured by asking individuals how much they agree with statements such as, "I think I have a great deal of power," "If I want to, I get to make the decisions," and "I can get others to do what I want," in relation to the context under consideration (e.g., in their ad hoc team). The external index used to assess power depended on the study. In a study of organizations, individuals' formal position in the hierarchy was measured. In a study of cooperative dyads working on decision-making tasks (Anderson & Berdahl, 2002), power was randomly assigned by placing one member of the dyad in the position of "leader." This individual was given ostensive control over a resource highly valued by his or her "subordinate," namely, how many extra credit points the subordinate would receive for their introductory business course. In studies of sororities, dormitories, and ad hoc teams, individuals' referent power was measured by asking peers to report how much prominence, respect, and influence individuals had in the group (French & Raven, 1959). In a study of negotiations, individuals were randomly assigned to either a position of high power, which gave them an alternative to the negotiation (i.e., as job candidates, they were told they could take an alternative job offer, or as job recruiters, they were told they could hire an equally attractive job applicant), or to a position of low power, which gave their opponent an alternative to the negotiation. By manipulating negotiators' alternatives, individuals' power was affected by making them more or less dependent on their negotiation opponent (Emerson, 1962).

As shown in Table 1, the correlations between self-perceptions and external indices of power ranged from 0.32 to 0.46. This is suggestive, at least, that self-perceptions of power are somewhat accurate, but not highly accurate. That is, people's perceptions of their power are not wholly

Table 1. Correlations between Self-Perceptions of Power and External Indices of Power.

External Index	Correlation with Self-Perceived Power
Formal position in an organization	0.31**
Leader vs. subordinate position in a dyad	0.43**
Referent power in an ad hoc team	0.46**
Positional power in a negotiation	0.34*
Peer rated power in a sorority	0.37**
Peer rated power in a dormitory	0.32**

Note: Self-perceived power was measured with respect to the context under consideration. For example, participants were asked in the study of organizations to rate their power in their organization.
*$P<0.05$.
**$P<0.01$.

disconnected from reality, but there is still much room for improvement. Again, strong caution must be used in drawing inferences from these correlations. First, single external indices of individuals' socio-structural power might not be adequate in measuring their actual power. A person's power in an organization, for example, might depend on their position in an informal social network, in addition to their formal position in the organizational hierarchy (Brass, 1984). Second, some of the external indices of power used might be systematically biased; for example, peer ratings of prominence and influence might be confounded with others' liking for them. However, the consistency of the correlations obtained, even when using such a diverse array of measures, provides some confidence that these correlations provide a decent indicator of accuracy.

THE PRIMACY OF SELF-PERCEPTIONS OF POWER IN DIRECTING THOUGHT, FEELING, AND ACTION

Lewin (1951) probably best articulated the idea that individuals' "psychological ecology" determines their thoughts and behavior more strongly than their physical or social ecology, but that idea in different forms has been supported in various lines of research. For example, the body of work on positive illusions has shown that individuals' overly optimistic perceptions of their abilities facilitate positive moods, higher self-esteem, and greater persistence in the face of obstacles, even though these self-perceptions of ability are commonly misguided (Taylor, Lerner, Sherman, Sage, & McDowell, 2003). Similarly, individuals' often inaccurate rosy perceptions of their romantic partners can help maintain relationship longevity and stability (Murray & Holmes, 1999).

In terms of power perceptions more specifically, anecdotal evidence suggests that the primacy of perceptions in shaping behavior extends to power perceptions as well. Accounts of Lyndon Johnson's presidency describe how in his latter days in office, Johnson developed an overwhelming feeling of powerlessness. He believed that he was surrounded by political enemies who posed a constant threat (that communists had taken control over the major television networks and outlets of communication) and that "the communist way of thinking" had infected everyone around him (Dallek, 1998). Thus, even though he occupied an incredibly powerful position, he began to show many of the signs of powerlessness, including depression, wide moods swings, and a suspiciousness of others that verged on paranoia. While it is true that Johnson's actual power in the White House was in fact decreasing, it was his exaggerated feelings of powerlessness that lead to his declining mental state and to his inability to govern.

Bugental's pioneering work provides more direct empirical evidence for the primacy of power perceptions in shaping behavior. In studying parent–child relationships, she has found that some parents feel powerless in their relationship with their children, even though they occupy a nominally higher power position (Bugental, Blue, & Cruzcosa, 1989; Bugental, Lyon, Krantz, & Cortez, 1997). Importantly, these "powerless" parents behave as though they actually have lower power vis-à-vis their children, they use passive–aggressive and indirect influence tactics (e.g., the silent treatment), they show submissiveness in their communication patterns, and they exhibit nonverbal behaviors aimed at appeasing their children (Bugental & Lewis, 1999).

Approach and Inhibition Tendencies

Recent studies of the Approach/Inhibition Theory of power (Keltner et al., 2003) also support the idea that people's behavior is tied more to their self-perceived power than to their actual power. The Approach/Inhibition Theory posits two broad hypotheses. First, having power triggers the behavioral approach system, which produces more positive emotion, enhances sensitivity to rewards, and elicits more approach-oriented behavior. Second, lacking power triggers the behavioral inhibition system, which produces more negative emotion, enhances sensitivity to threats, and evokes more behavioral inhibition. While studies have found consistent support for these hypotheses, they have also shown that individuals' approach- and inhibition-related tendencies are more strongly tied to their perceptions of their power than to their socio-structural positions.

For example, in the aforementioned study of dyads that worked together on a decision-making task, dyad members were randomly assigned to be either the "leader" or the "subordinate" (Anderson & Berdahl, 2002). After working together, participants were asked to report how much power they thought they had in the dyad, how much positive and negative emotion they felt, how much their partner felt threatening emotions toward them, such as anger and contempt, and how much they expressed vs. suppressed the expression of their ideas and opinions. While the manipulation of positional power produced the expected approach- and inhibition-related behaviors, most of these effects were mediated by individuals' perceptions of their power. Thus, some people in the leadership position actually perceived themselves to have lower power in the dyad, and these leaders behaved like followers: they felt more negative emotion, overestimated how much anger and contempt their partner felt toward them, and were more inhibited in expressing their opinions. Further, some people in the subordinate position actually perceived themselves as higher in power, and these subordinates behaved like leaders: they felt more positive emotion, overestimated how much their partner liked them, and more freely expressed their thoughts and ideas.

In the study of negotiations mentioned above, in addition to manipulating individuals' positional power and assessing their self-perceived power following the negotiation, Anderson et al. (2003a) asked participants to rate how much they felt positive and negative emotion during the negotiation, whether they perceived their opponents as trustworthy and respectful, and how much they assertively pursued resources in the negotiation. Table 2 displays the beta coefficients for both self-perceived power and external index of their power, entered simultaneously in multiple regression equations. As shown, individuals' thoughts, feelings, and behaviors were more strongly related to their self-perceived power than to their positional power. Self-perceived power was more strongly related to (a) higher levels of positive emotion and lower levels of negative emotion; (b) more optimistic perceptions of their opponent; and (c) a more assertive approach to the negotiation, which entailed working harder to reach a deal that benefited themselves, as well as their opponents.

Table 2. The Primacy of Self-Perceptions of Power in Predicting Behavior.

Behavioral Outcome	Beta Coefficients in Simultaneous Regression	
	Self-Perceived Power	External Index of Power
In a negotiation		
Positive emotional experience	0.41**	0.02
Negative emotional experience	−0.23*	0.10
Perceptions of opponents' trustworthiness, respectfulness	0.25*	−0.05
Assertive pursuit of outcomes	0.44**	−0.06
In a peer group		
Positive emotional experience	0.21*	0.09
Negative emotional experience	−0.21*	−0.13
Perceptions of environment as more predictable and certain	0.26*	0.06
Emotional expressiveness		
Self-reported	0.20*	0.11
Expert-coded from videotape	0.21*	0.11
Self-esteem	0.64**	0.20*
Subjective well-being	0.49**	0.11

*$P<0.05$.
**$P<0.01$.

Moreover, in the study of peer groups mentioned above (Anderson et al., 2003a), in addition to assessing their self-perceived and peer rated referent power, individuals were asked how often they experienced various positive and negative emotions in their peer group; if they perceive their environment as predictable and certain; and to express their emotions. In addition, during a laboratory exercise in which participants watched short film clips, participants' facial displays of emotion were coded by experts. Specifically, three emotion-inducing films were employed, each of which had been used in previous research on emotional elicitation (Gross & Levenson, 1995). Each film was 2–⟨k30⟩3⟨k0⟩ min long: The first film, used to measure baseline mood, shows flowers in a park; the second film, a clip from the movie *The Champ*, shows a boy crying after the death of his father, and it elicits negative emotion; and the third film shows a comedy routine by Robin Williams, and it elicits positive emotion. Independent coders rated participants' facial expressions of positive and negative emotion during each film on a 7-point scale with 1 = "no expressions" and 7 = "frequent expressions." For example, a participant who showed "Duchenne" (i.e., genuine) smiles and laughter 11 times or more would be assigned a score of 7 for positive emotional expression.

Again, as shown in Table 2, self-perceptions of power were more strongly related to all of these behavioral outcomes than were external indices of power. Compared to positional power, self-perceptions of power were more strongly associated with their positive and negative emotional experiences, perceptions of the environment, and behavioral expressiveness. Importantly, these findings involved self-reported outcomes, as well as objectively measured outcomes, such as expert-coded facial displays of emotion. Therefore, the higher predictive ability of self-perceived power cannot be attributed solely to shared method variance. It is also worth noting that the findings were consistent across people in the high and low power positions.

Self-Esteem and Subjective Well-Being

Individuals' more global feelings of self-esteem and well-being have been shown to be highly correlated with their power (Barkow, 1975; Hamilton, 1971; Heaven, 1986; Raskin, Novacek, & Hogan, 1991), and there have been various theoretical accounts for this correlation. According to Barkow's dominance theory, for example, self-esteem evolved as a psychological system that monitors how much power individuals have in their relationships; thus, when their power increases or decreases, so does their self-esteem (Barkow, 1975; see also Leary, Cottrell, & Phillips, 2001). However, as we have argued, people's thoughts, feelings, and behaviors will be more closely tied to their perceptions of their power than to their actual power. Thus, we expect people's self-perceived power to drive their self-esteem and subjective well-being more than their actual power.

Consistent with this argument, research has shown that sometimes people do not need to change their actual power in order to boost their self-esteem, as long as they change their sense of power. David Winter and other researchers have shown that people with a high need for power behave in profligate ways, such as drinking alcohol, taking risks, and taking on physical challenges, because these behaviors make individuals temporarily feel powerful (McClelland & Teague, 1975; McClelland & Watson, 1973; Winter, 1973). These behaviors allow individuals to focus on the resources and freedoms they do have, and it distracts them from the constraints placed on their behavior; thus, bolstering their well-being.

Anderson and colleagues (2003a) also found evidence for the primacy of self-perceptions of power in predicting self-esteem and well-being in the study of peer groups previously described. Specifically, they found individuals' self-perceived power predicted their self-esteem (as measured with Rosenberg's Self-Esteem Scale; Rosenberg, 1965) and subjective well-being (as measured with the Satisfaction with Life Scale; Diener, Sandvik, Seidlitz, & Diener, 1993), much more strongly than did their referent power in the peer group (these beta coefficients are shown in Table 2).

What might be most interesting about these results is that they seem to contradict the null correlation often found between individuals' socio-economic status and their subjective well-being (e.g., Diener et al., 1993). People higher in socio-economic status have more access to, and control over, financial resources (Ellis, 1993). Thus one might expect wealthier people to be happier, yet they are not. The explanation commonly given for this null effect is that people habituate to their incomes so that wealth has little effect on their happiness in the long run. However, as our findings suggest, while people might habituate to their financial resources, they seem not to habituate to their social resources. Feeling powerful, or perceiving oneself as influential, seems to be continually rewarding, bolstering people's thoughts of themselves and of the world.

Summary

So what does this all mean? The evidence we presented suggests that individuals' thoughts, feelings, and behaviors are more strongly shaped by their perceptions of their power than by their actual power. This evidence, therefore, suggests that people in high power positions can sometimes behave as though they are powerless and that people in low power positions can behave at times as though they are more powerful. Building from this discussion, we now turn to interpersonal implications by addressing how inaccuracies in the sense of power affect one's interpersonal relationships and broader social standing.

THE CONSEQUENCES OF MISPERCEPTION: WHAT HAPPENS WHEN PEOPLE OVER- OR UNDERESTIMATE THEIR POWER

What are the interpersonal consequences of inaccurate power perceptions? Misperceiving one's place would seem to affect not only inner psychological processes such as emotional experiences, self-esteem, and well-being, as we have discussed. Rather, it would likely shape the dynamics of individuals' relationships because it would influence how individuals deal with and relate to others. By misperceiving their power, individuals would likely affect how others evaluate them, which in turn should affect their actual social standing.

To explore the social consequences of misperceiving one's power, we will use the 2 × 2 matrix shown in Fig. 2. In the figure, the horizontal axis is self-perceived power, broken down into "low" and "high" (i.e., the person either sees his or her power as being low or high), and the vertical axis is actual power, also broken down into "low" and "high" (i.e., whether the person actually has low or high power). Of course, we recognize that both perceived and actual power are continuous variables and not dichotomous, but only characterize them as such for the sake of simplicity.

		Self-Perceived Power	
		Low	**High**
Actual Power	**Low**	***DEFERENCE*** • Show appeasement, deference to other • Promote stability of current hierarchy • Maintain one's inclusion in the group	***HUBRIS*** • Violate socially imposed boundaries on behavior • Provoke intragroup conflict • Receive social punishment, ostracism
	High	***UNDERUTILIZATION*** • Fail to pursue resources • Lack of influence over others • Ineffective leadership	***RESOURCE LEVERAGING*** • Recognize and capitalize on opportunities • Effectively influence others • Lead, coordinate group action effectively, efficiently

Fig. 2. The Power × Perceived Power Matrix.

Overestimating One's Power: Deference Vs. Hubris

Hierarchies are the primary way by which group activity is organized (Bernstein, 1981; Ellis, 1993; Keltner & Haidt, 2001; Levine & Moreland, 1999). Hierarchies outline, implicitly or explicitly, a host of behavioral prescriptions for people at the top and bottom of the order; in a sense, hierarchies provide a set of "power rules" for group members' behavior. To name just a few examples, people at the top of the hierarchy get to make decisions, give out orders, speak more in social interactions, express anger, interrupt others, offer their opinions, and have more control over group processes (Keltner et al., 2003). People at the bottom of the hierarchy, on the other hand, are not allowed to engage in these behaviors, but instead are expected to look to others to make decisions, defer to others in conversation, follow the lead of those higher in power, and keep their ideas and opinions to themselves.

When individuals lower in power accurately view their disadvantaged position, therefore, they will likely follow the socially prescribed boundaries placed on their behavior (e.g., Jost & Banaji, 1994). In essence, they will follow the rules imposed upon them. In contrast, when people overestimate their power and act as though they have higher power, their behavior will violate those rules. For example, overestimators will attempt to make decisions for the group, impose their opinions on others, or claim a more favorable allocation of resources and labor.

One should expect, therefore, that groups would react quite differently to individuals with lower power who perceive their position accurately compared to individuals who believe they have higher power. Groups should look very kindly on individuals who view their place accurately, because those individuals would be showing appropriate deference; they would be seen as accepting the norms and constraints placed upon their behavior. In contrast, groups should look quite harshly upon low power individuals who think they have higher power, because those individuals would be seen as exhibiting hubris, behaving in ways the group sees as illegitimate and out of bounds.

Anecdotally, the idea that people react harshly to individuals who overestimate their power seems to hold water. When President Reagan was shot in 1981, Secretary of State Alexander Haig called a press conference to explain that the government was continuing to operate without interruption. During the conference he stated that he was "in control," implying he had assumed the duties of the presidency while President Reagan was incapacitated. Haig was mistaken, of course, he was actually fourth in line to the presidency, behind the Vice President, the Speaker of the House, and the President pro tempore of the Senate, and his misreading of the chain of command turned out to be a major blunder. People reacted severely to what they saw as Haig's illegitimate grab for power, and after much ridicule from the media and public embarrassment, Haig resigned after only a year and a half on the job.

Our research also provides empirical support for this idea (Anderson et al., 2003a). We examined 108 four-person ad hoc teams who worked together on problems from the Graduate Management Aptitude Test. After groups worked together on these problems, each member rated their own power in the group, in terms of how much influence they had in the group, how much they led the group's activities, and how much respect they received from other group members (each item was rated on a 1–7 scale). Other group members also rated each participant's power, using the same items. To assess the consequences of overestimating one's power, we asked group members to rate how much they liked each participant; we expected individuals who overestimated their power in the group would be liked less.

As shown in Fig. 3, we found that overestimators (i.e., those whose self-perceptions of power were higher than their peer rated power) were liked less by other group members, suggesting they were being punished for overestimating their power.[2] In the figure, we broke this finding down by gender, to illustrate that both men and women were punished for

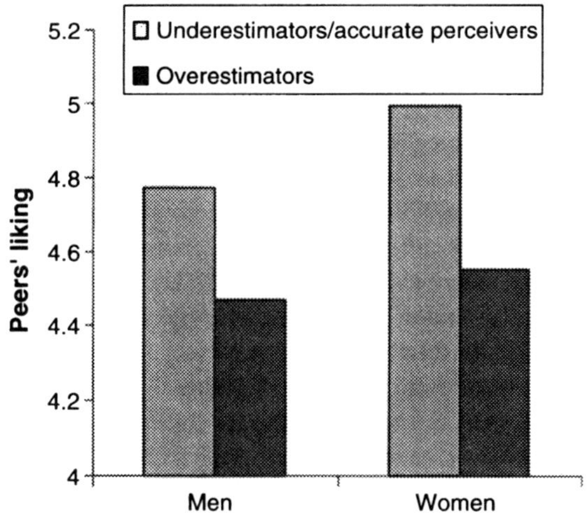

Fig. 3. The Social Consequences of Overestimating One's Power in Ad hoc Groups.

overestimating their power. These findings suggest, therefore, that both men and women who overestimated their power behaved in ways that others viewed as illegitimate. They might have given out orders, spoken more, or imposed their views on the group much more than others felt was appropriate. As we did not measure group members' perceptions of participants' behavior directly, this is only speculation, and thus it is therefore important that future research empirically document this mediating path.

Underestimating One's Power: Resource Leveraging Vs. Underutilization

Whereas overestimating one's power has adverse consequences for the individual and the group, so too should underestimating one's power. When people have high power, but fail to recognize it, we believe three things should happen: First, they will be too focused on the threats that surround them, and thus fail to recognize opportunities for resource gains. Second, they will fail to leverage the resources at their disposal, which will decrease their ability to influence others. Third, as a consequence of their lower influence over others, they will be less effective in leading their group, and unable to coordinate and mobilize group members into collective action toward its shared goals.

Failure to Capitalize on Opportunities

According to the Approach/Inhibition Theory of power, lacking power activates the behavioral inhibition system at the same time it dampens the behavioral approach system (Keltner et al., 2003). Thus, we argue when people perceive themselves to be lower in power, regardless of the power they actually possess, they will be less sensitive to opportunities and rewards in the environment and less active in pursuing those opportunities, because they are focused more on potential threats. This implies, therefore, that individuals who actually have high levels of power, but who feel powerless, will be in an ironic and somewhat tragic position. They will have multiple opportunities for resource gain in front of them, by virtue of their power, but they will be ineffective in capitalizing on them, as they would be less attentive to them and less assertive in pursuing them.

A few of the findings mentioned above lend support for this argument. In the study of negotiations previously described (Anderson et al., 2003a), those in the higher power position who had a low perception of their power were less focused on what they could gain from the interaction, worked less hard to maximize their slice of the pie, and put less effort into reaching an agreement than those with a higher perception of their power. Thus, they were not focused enough on reaching their "aspiration point," or the best possible outcome they could attain in the negotiation. Moreover, this failure to pursue resources affected how much of the resource pie they actually obtained in the negotiation. Individuals' outcomes were quantified into a point system, wherein people could obtain anywhere from −13,200 points to 13,200 points; individuals in the higher power position with a lower perception of their power ended up with worse outcomes in the negotiations ($\underline{M} = 6,480$) than those with a higher perception of their power in the same position ($\underline{M} = 6,862$).

Failure to Influence Others

Research on influence strategies has shown that powerful people use more "direct" influence tactics, such as directly asking someone to do something, or making verbal commands (tactics that end up being quite effective in getting others to comply). In contrast, people with less power tend to use more "indirect" tactics that are less effective, such as hinting at a desired outcome, using the silent treatment, or appealing to another person's generosity or kindness (Bugental & Lewis, 1999; Falbo & Peplau, 1980; Kipnis, Schmidt, & Wilkinson, 1980). As we have argued, people in powerful positions who perceive themselves as powerless are more likely to behave as though they actually have low power. This suggests, therefore, that powerful people with a low perception of their power will use less effective indirect tactics, instead of more effective direct tactics. As a result, powerful people who see themselves as powerless should lose their ability to influence others.

Bugental's research on power in parent–child relationships provides empirical support for this idea. In her studies, "powerless" parents were the ones who underestimated their power, they attributed their child as being a stronger causal agent than themselves, even though they were in a nominally higher power position (Bugental & Lewis, 1999). Consistent with the notion that underestimating one's power diminishes one's influence, she finds that these "powerless" individuals are in fact ineffectual parents. They use ineffective influence strategies and exhibit non-fluent speech patterns that diminish their control over their child's behavior (Bugental & Lewis, 1999).

Support for this argument was also found in the previously mentioned study of decision making in dyads (Anderson & Berdahl, 2002). In that study, participants were first given a decision-making task to do alone, in which they allocated bonuses to four employees of a hypothetical company. After they made their decisions, they were paired with another participant, and dyads were asked to come to agreement on the same bonus decisions. Therefore, one could measure how much leaders were able to influence their subordinates' decisions by assessing how much subordinates' decisions changed from their original opinions. As expected, leaders with a lower perception of their power had less influence over their subordinates' decisions, suggesting they used less effective influence strategies. Specifically, leaders with a low perception of their power changed their subordinates' bonus allocation decisions by an average of \$570 (SD = \$436.29), whereas leaders with a higher perception of their power changed their subordinates' allocation decisions by an average of \$837 (SD = \$474.71).

Failure to Effectively Lead

The old saying, "with power comes responsibility," appropriately implies that powerful individuals are often responsible for more than just their own outcomes and behavior. They are often given the charge of leading their group toward its goals. In occupying positions of leadership, powerful individuals must find ways to "persuade other people to set aside for a period of time their individual concerns and to pursue a common goal that is important for the responsibilities and welfare of a group" (Hogan, Curphy, & Hogan, 1994, p. 493). This duty generally requires that they exert a great deal of influence over the attitudes, motivation, and behavior of individual group members in ways that enable them to work together efficiently and effectively.

As we have just discussed, however, underestimating one's power can have detrimental effects on one's ability to influence others. Thus, when individuals with power fail to utilize the levers of control at their disposal (i.e., the carrots and sticks that they can use to change the thoughts and behaviors of others), they will be less able to lead their groups effectively. In short, we propose that effective leadership requires that individuals accurately assess their ability to influence others. Lyndon Johnson's paranoia during the declining years of his presidency offers an illustration of this point. His failures in leadership stemmed partly from failing to recognize the control he could exert over others by virtue of his position (Dallek, 1998).

Final Thoughts and Further Questions

In the current chapter, we examined how individuals' perceptions of their power can differ from the power they actually possess, and how it can be a stronger determinant of their behavior. We examined the consequences of inaccurate self-perceptions of power, arguing that overestimating one's power can bring social punishment and ostracism, whereas underestimating one's power can lead to failures in resource utilization. Although we might have made some preliminary strides in addressing these issues, it is clear that further research should examine them more closely, as well as examine many additional questions.

Determinants

One important issue concerns the determinants of self-perceptions of power (Bacharach & Lawler, 1976). If people's perceptions of their power are only moderately correlated with their actual power, what individual difference variables or contextual factors distort a person's perception of their power? What factors make some people feel more powerful than others, given that they possess the same level of actual power? In terms of individual differences, a few variables seem relevant. First, research has shown that individuals high in narcissism (John & Robins, 1994) and self-esteem (Taylor & Brown, 1988) have overly optimistic views of themselves in general, suggesting that these two variables will contribute to higher perceptions of power. Second, the need for power (nPower) might make people predisposed to perceive themselves as high in power; with a stronger need to feel powerful, those high in the power motive might be more likely to distort their perceptions of their place in hierarchies (Winter & Stewart, 1978). Third, in many contexts, men might be more inclined to have higher perceptions of their power than women, as is suggested by the finding that men sometimes show higher levels of narcissism (e.g., John & Robins, 1994).

In terms of contextual factors, we have already discussed how people can temporarily feel powerful by engaging in profligate behaviors such as drinking, gambling, or excessive risk taking (Winter & Stewart, 1978). Recent work also suggests that for some individuals, engaging in aggressive and even violent acts can restore their damaged feelings of power and superiority (Baumeister, Smart, & Boden, 1996). In either case, the temporary spike in individuals' perceptions of their power seems to stem from focusing their attention on the freedoms and powers they do have, and distracting them from the powers they lack. Thus, future research should examine how behaving in certain ways leads to short-term boosts in perceptions of power.

Plasticity

Another important issue regarding self-perceptions of power is their plasticity across contexts and time. One quality of self-perceptions of power that make them so different from structural power, and so interesting, is that they are more dynamic than static. A person's perception of his or her power should be flexible from context to context, and even across time within the same context. Yet how plastic are self-perceptions of power? If a person feels powerful in one context and moves to another (if a person meets with a supervisor immediately following a meeting with a subordinate) how much do self-perceptions of power change, and how much do they carry over into new contexts? Are there any residual effects from previous contexts in which individuals were powerful or powerless (Spataro, 2005)? Moreover, even within the same context, when a person realizes that the power balance is slightly different than he or she had previously perceived, how quickly can perceptions of power be changed?

Reducing inaccuracy

Yet another important concern is how people might go about reducing discrepancies between their perceptions of their power and their actual power. As we have discussed, the complexity of factors that contribute to power balances and the ambiguity of criteria used to assess power make it sometimes highly difficult to accurately assess one's place. To mitigate perceptual inaccuracy, we can think of at least two approaches to take. One would be to reduce the ambiguity inherent on a systemic level, by spelling out clearly who is high and who is low in the hierarchical order; this approach is commonly attempted in corporations or military organizations. Another approach would be to train people to assess their own and other party's resources more thoroughly. For example, students of negotiation classes are often taught to conduct a "pre-negotiation diagnosis," in which they write down their sources of power, as well as the other party's sources of power. These exercises often make students recognize sources of power they hadn't thought of earlier, and thus realize the influence they could exert over the other party (of course, it also causes many students to recognize the bases of power the other party likely has, and thus realize they are in a power disadvantage). These exercises illustrate that simply having individuals assess what they "bring to the table" can provide more accurate assessments of their place.

Boundary conditions

Finally, it is important to point out that having an inaccurate perception of one's power is not always going to be harmful. On the contrary, overestimating one's power might actually be beneficial for the individual at times, as it might lead to positive changes in their impact on the group, and thus their actual power. For example, research on minority influence has shown how people in nominally lower power roles can have a profound impact on the thoughts and behaviors of others higher in power (e.g., Nemeth, 1986). People in low power positions, therefore, might sometimes be better off believing they have higher power, because they will be more likely to assert themselves; if they were to accurately view their lower position, they might suppress the expression of opinions and ideas (Anderson & Berdahl, 2002). In a sense, having an inaccurately high perception of one's power might sometimes be self-fulfilling, leading to increases in one's actual power.

NOTES

1. Two other conceptual and definitional issues are worth noting. First, the perception of one's ability to influence others is conceptually distinct from the willingness to use that ability. For example, individuals might believe they are highly capable of influencing another individual, but may not wish to take advantage of that ability. Indeed, recent studies have shown that individuals' perceived capacity to influence others and their willingness to use that influence are not highly correlated (Anderson et al., 2005). Second, in French and Raven's framework (1959), we view expert power as very similar to status or referent power; when people perceive someone as an expert, they tend to voluntarily comply with that person's advice or suggestions. We view legitimate power, as when a person occupies a position of authority, as implying the ability to reward and punish, which fits well within our framework.
2. Given the problems inherent in using difference scores in correlational analyses (Cronbach, 1955; Edwards, 1994; Gonzalez & Griffin, 1997), we tested the significance of this difference using regression techniques suggested by Edwards (1994).

REFERENCES

Anderson, C., & Berdahl, J. L. (2002). The experience of power: Examining the effects of power on approach and inhibition tendencies. *Journal of Personality and Social Psychology*, *83*, 1362–1377.

Anderson, C., John, O. P., & Keltner, D. (2003a). Defining and measuring the subjective sense of power. Manuscript in preparation.

Anderson, C., John, O. P., & Keltner, D. (2005). The sense of power: Its structure and antecedents. Manuscript in preparation.

Anderson, C., John, O. P., Keltner, D., & Kring, A. M. (2001). Who attains social status? Effects of personality traits and physical attractiveness in social groups. *Journal of Personality and Social Psychology, 81*, 116–132.

Anderson, C., Srivastava, S., Beer, J. S., Spatara, S. E., & Chatman, J. A. (2005). Knowing your place: Self-perceptions of status in social groups. Manuscript submitted for publication.

Bacharach, S. B., & Lawler, E. J. (1976). The perception of power. *Social Forces, 55*, 123–134.

Barkow, J. H. (1975). Prestige and culture: A biosocial interpretation. *Current Anthropology, 16*, 553–572.

Baumeister, R. F., Smart, L., & Boden, J. M. (1996). Relation of threatened egotism to violence and aggression: The dark side of high self-esteem. *Psychological Review, 103*, 5–33.

Bazerman, M. H., & Neale, M. A. (1992). *Negotiating rationally*. New York: Free Press.

Bernstein, I. S. (1981). Dominance: The baby and the bathwater. *Behavioral and Brain Sciences, 4*, 419–457.

Brass, D. J. (1984). Being in the right place: A structural analysis of individual influence in an organization. *Administrative Science Quarterly, 29*, 518–539.

Brett, J. M. (2000). *Negotiating globally*. San Francisco, CA: Jossey-Bass.

Bugental, D. B., & Lewis, J. C. (1999). The paradoxical misuse of power by those who see themselves as powerless: How does it happen? *Journal of Social Issues, 55*, 51–64.

Bugental, D. B., Blue, J., & Cruzcosa, M. (1989). Perceived control over caregiving outcomes: Implications for child abuse. *Developmental Psychology, 25*, 532–539.

Bugental, D. B., Lyon, J. E., Krantz, J., & Cortez, V. (1997). Who's the boss? Differential accessibility of dominance ideation in parent–child relationships. *Journal of Personality and Social Psychology, 72*, 1297–1309.

Chance, M. R. A. (1967). Attention structure as the basis of primate rank order. *Man, 2*, 503–518.

Colvin, C. R., & Block, J. (1994). Do positive illusions foster mental health? An examination of the Taylor and Brown formulation. *Psychological Bulletin, 116*, 3–20.

Cotton, J. L., & Tuttle, J. M. (1986). Employee turnover: A meta-analysis and review with implications for research. *Academy of Management Review, 11*, 55–70.

Cronbach, L. J. (1955). Processes affecting scores on "understanding of others" and "assumed similarity". *Psychological Bulletin, 52*, 177–193.

Dallek, R. (1998). *Flawed giant: Lyndon B. Johnson, 1960–1973*. New York: Oxford University Press.

Diener, E., Sandvik, E., Seidlitz, L., & Diener, M. (1993). The relationship between income and subjective well-being: Relative or absolute? *Social Indicators Research, 28*, 195–223.

Edwards, J. R. (1994). The study of congruence in organizational behavior research: Critique and a proposed alternative. *Organizational Behavior and Human Decision Processes, 58*, 51–100.

Eibl-Eibesfeldt, I. (1989). *Human ethology*. New York: Aldine De Gruyter.

Ellis, L. (1993). Conceptually defining social stratification in human and nonhuman animals. In: L. Ellis (Ed.), *Social stratification and socioeconomic inequality*. Vol. 1: A comparative biosocial analysis (pp. 1–14). Westport, CT: Praeger Publishers/Greenwood Publishing Group.

Emerson, R. M. (1962). Power dependence relations. *American Sociological Review, 27*, 31–41.

Falbo, T., & Peplau, L. A. (1980). Power strategies in intimate relationships. *Journal of Personality and Social Psychology, 38*, 618–628.

Fiske, S. T. (1993). Controlling other people: The impact of power on stereotyping. *American Psychologist, 48*, 621–628.

French, J., & Raven, B. (1959). The bases of social power. In: D. Cartwright (Ed.), *Studies in social power* (pp. 150–167). Ann Arbor, MI: Institute for Social Research.

Friedman, T. L. (1995). *From Beirut to Jerusalem*. New York: Anchor Books.

Gergen, D. (2000). *Eyewitness to power: The essence of leadership*. New York: Touchstone.

Goldhammer, H., & Shils, E. A. (1939). Types of power and status. *American Journal of Sociology, 45*, 171–182.

Gonzalez, R., & Griffin, D. (1997). On the statistics of interdependence: Treating dyadic data with respect. In: S. Duck (Ed.), *Handbook of Personal Relationships*. New York: John Wiley & Sons.

Gross, J. J., & Levenson, R. W. (1995). Emotion elicitation using films. *Cognition and Emotion, 9*, 87–108.

Hamilton, D. L. (1971). A comparative study of five methods of assessing self-esteem, dominance, and dogmatism. *Educational and Psychological Measurement, 31*, 441–452.

Heaven, P. C. (1986). Authoritarianism, directiveness, and self-esteem revisited: A cross-cultural analysis. *Personality and Individual Differences, 7*, 225–228.

Hogan, R., Curphy, G. J., & Hogan, J. (1994). What we know about leadership: Effectiveness and personality. *American Psychologist, 49*, 493–504.

John, O. P., & Robins, R. W. (1994). Accuracy and bias in self-perception: Individual differences in self-enhancement and the role of narcissism. *Journal of Personality and Social Psychology, 66*, 206–219.

Jost, J. T., & Banaji, M. R. (1994). The role of stereotyping in system-justification and the production of false consciousness. *British Journal of Social Psychology, 33*, 1–27.

Keltner, D., Gruenfeld, D. H., & Anderson, C. (2003). Power, approach, and inhibition. *Psychological Review, 110*, 265–284.

Keltner, D., & Haidt, J. (2001). Social functions of emotions. In: T. J. Mayne & G. A. Bonanno (Eds), *Emotions: Current issues and future directions*. New York: Guilford.

Kim, P. H., Pinkley, R., & Fragale, A. (in press). Power dynamics in negotiation. *Academy of Management Review*.

Kipnis, D., Schmidt, S. M., & Wilkinson, I. (1980). Intraorganizational influence tactics: Explorations in getting one's way. *Journal of Applied Psychology, 65*, 440–452.

Krackhardt, D. (1990). Assessing the political landscape: Structure, cognition, and power in organizations. *Administrative Science Quarterly, 35*, 342–369.

Leary, M. R., Cottrell, C. A., & Phillips, M. (2001). Deconfounding the effects of dominance and social acceptance on self-esteem. *Journal of Personality and Social Psychology, 81*, 898–909.

Levine, J. M., & Moreland, R. L. (1999). Small groups. In: D. T. Gilbert & S. T. Fiske (Eds), *The handbook of social psychology*, (Vol. 2, pp. 415–469). New York, NY: McGraw-Hill.

Lewin, K. (1951). *Field theory in social science: Selected theoretical papers*. Chicago: Harper & Brothers.

McClelland, D. C., & Teague, G. (1975). Predicting risk preferences among power related tasks. *Journal of Personality, 43*, 266–285.

McClelland, D. C., & Watson, R. I. (1973). Power motivation and risk-taking behavior. *Journal of Personality, 41*, 121–139.
Murray, S. L., & Holmes, J. G. (1999). The (mental) ties that bind: Cognitive structures that predict relationship resilience. *Journal of Personality and Social Psychology, 77*, 1228–1244.
Nemeth, C. J. (1986). Differential contributions of majority and minority influence. *Psychological Review, 93*, 23–32.
Pettigrew, A. M. (1973). *Politics of organizational decision-making*. London: Tavistock.
Pfeffer, J., & Salancik, G. (1977). Administrator effectiveness: The effects of advocacy and information on resource allocations. *Human Relations, 30*, 641–656.
Raskin, R., Novacek, J., & Hogan, R. (1991). Narcissistic self-esteem management. *Journal of Personality and Social Psychology, 60*, 911–918.
Ridgeway, C. L., & Balkwell, J. W. (1997). Group processes and the diffusion of status beliefs. *Social Psychology Quarterly, 60*, 14–31.
Rosenberg, M. (1965). *Society and the adolescent self-image*. Princeton, NJ: Princeton University Press.
Smuts, B. (1996). Male aggression against women: An evolutionary perspective. In: D. M. Buss & N. M. Malamuth (Eds), *Sex, power, conflict*. New York: Oxford University Press.
Spataro, S. (2005). Divergent hierarchies: Organizational demography and formal versus informal status in organizations. Manuscript in preparation.
Taylor, S. E., & Brown, J. D. (1988). Illusion and well-being: A social psychological perspective on mental health. *Psychological Bulletin, 103*, 193–210.
Taylor, S. E., Lerner, J. S., Sherman, D. K., Sage, R. M., & McDowell, N. K. (2003). Portrait of the self-enhancer: Well-adjusted and well-liked or maladjusted and friendless? *Journal of Personality and Social Psychology, 84*, 165–176.
Thibaut, J. W., & Kelley, H. H. (1959). *The social psychology of groups*. New York: Wiley.
Winter, D. G. (1973). *The power motive*. New York: Free Press.
Winter, D. G., & Stewart, A. J. (1978). The power motive. In: H. London & J. E. Exner Jr (Eds), *Dimensions of personality* (pp. 391–447). New York: Wiley.

TO BE SMART OR TO BE SOCIAL? THE CONTEXT-DEPENDENT EFFECTS OF COMMUNICATION STYLES ON STATUS CONFERRAL IN TASK GROUPS

Alison R. Fragale

ABSTRACT

The verbal and nonverbal behaviors that individuals display (i.e., their communication styles) influence the status positions they attain in their task groups. Prior research has generally concluded that communication behaviors that convey agency (i.e., characteristics denoting intelligence, ambition, and dominance) are more effective for obtaining a high-status position in a task group than communication behaviors that convey communality (i.e., characteristics denoting warmth, sincerity, and agreeableness). The message from these prior studies is that it is more status enhancing to be smart than to be social. The objective of this chapter is to challenge this assertion and argue that in some task groups it may be more status enhancing to be social rather than to be smart. I suggest that the status benefits of particular communication styles depend on the characteristics of the group to which an individual belongs to. Thus, in contrast to prior research in this area, I argue for a more contextual

Status and Groups
Research on Managing Groups and Teams, Volume 7, 93–119

ISSN: 1534-0856/doi:10.1016/S1534-0856(05)07005-2

approach to the study of communication styles and status conferral, focusing on how structural and process differences between groups influence how the group members' words and actions are evaluated.

For most individuals, participation in task groups is a frequent and familiar aspect of both work and non-work life. For example, in the course of a single day, an individual may meet with coworkers to discuss their responsibilities for a new marketing project, work with fellow parents to organize a school bake sale, and talk with neighbors about establishing a neighborhood watch group. In such task groups, *status* (i.e., the value and social worth that others ascribe to an individual; Ridgeway, 2001) is often distributed unequally among group members (Bales, 1999). Some group members may be viewed as high status: They have prestige and the respect of fellow group members, influence group decisions, and may hold formal positions. Other individuals may be seen as low status in the group: They may take direction from high-status members and exert little influence over others. This unequal distribution of status in many task groups raises an interesting question: How do groups decide which individuals should be leaders and which should be followers? In other words, how is status conferred to various members of a group?

In this chapter, I focus on one important factor that has been shown to influence the status that individuals attain in their task groups, i.e., *communication style*. Communication style is a term used to encompass a wide array of both vocal and verbal attributes (such as pitch, volume, and word choice), and nonverbal attributes (such as gestures and facial expressions). Communication behaviors provide an interesting domain to study status conferral because these behaviors are often quite subtle, yet they frequently exert substantial influences on individuals' status positions. For example, an individual's speech style (Erickson, Lind, Johnson, & O'Barr, 1978), emotional expressions (Tiedens, 2001), and even subtle patterns of eye contact (Rosa & Mazur, 1979), to name a few, can affect how the individual is perceived by fellow group members, and hence the individual's status position within the group. Thus, to develop a complete understanding of how status is conferred in task groups, it is necessary to investigate how specific communication behaviors influence individuals' status positions. For example, what are the status consequences of speaking loudly? Putting one's feet on the desk? If one hopes to gain status in a group, should one interrupt others, or wait quietly for a turn to speak?

Providing answers to these questions is complicated, however, by the fact that task groups vary enormously along many dimensions, including their structures, the tasks they undertake, and the composition of their memberships. These group differences are likely to have implications for the types of communication behaviors that influence status conferral in different groups. However, despite this variability across different task groups, there has been, to date, little systematic study of how these contextual factors may influence the relationship between an actor's communication style and the actor's awarded status position in a group. Rather, prior research has often focused on categorizing communication behaviors into one of two broad classes, namely *high-status* behaviors (which are associated with high-status individuals and are *effective* for increasing an individual's status) and *low-status* behaviors (which are associated with low-status individuals and are *ineffective* for enhancing an individual's status position). A multitude of studies have demonstrated that individuals gain more status in task groups by displaying high-status communication behaviors, such as assertive speech or expansive body postures, than low-status communication behaviors, such as unassertive speech or constricted body postures (e.g., Erickson et al., 1978; Ridgeway, 1987). In contrast to these prior approaches, I argue for a more contextualized approach to the study of status conferral in task groups that accounts for differences in group goals, processes, and structure. I suggest that the status benefits of a high-status communication style, relative to a low-status style, may not be absolute and that, in many cases, individuals may gain *more* status from displaying low-status behaviors that have generally been deemed "ineffective" for enhancing one's status position than by displaying the high-status behaviors that have traditionally been linked to status attainment. In this sense, what constitutes a high-status or low-status communication style is not static, but context dependent.

I suggest that these contextual differences in status conferral emerge because both types of communication styles can convey positive, socially desirable qualities about the individual displaying them. Behaviors characterized as high status in prior research generally convey that the actor displaying the behaviors is highly *agentic* (i.e., intelligent, ambitious, and dominant), whereas behaviors characterized as low status convey that the actor is very *communal* (i.e., affiliative, selfless, and warm; Bakan, 1966). As a result, the status enhancing benefits of these communication behaviors may depend on the extent to which the qualities of agency and communality are seen as valuable and worthy qualities in particular groups. In groups that place a high value on agency, group members are likely to award more status to those individuals who display traditional high-status behaviors (which convey high agency) than to those who display low-status behaviors (which convey high communality). However, in groups that place a greater value on communality, the reverse may be true and individuals may award more status to those individuals who display the behaviors that have been, to date, classified as low status.

The objective of this chapter is to explore *why* group differences may affect the characteristics, i.e., agency and communality, and hence the communication styles, that are most status enhancing in different groups, and to identify the particular group characteristics that affect this relationship. I begin by reviewing prior research on communication styles and status attainment, and discussing the relationship between communication styles, and perceptions of agency and communality. I then discuss different theoretical frameworks that make predictions about the status enhancing benefits of agency relative to communality. Finally, I explore two group characteristics, the level of interdependence in the task group and difficulty of detecting social loafing (i.e., free-riding on the efforts of others; e.g., Jackson & Williams, 1985; Karau & Williams, 1993; Latane, Williams, & Harkins, 1979), which may affect the characteristics, and thus the communication styles, that are most effective for attaining status in a task group.

COMMUNICATION STYLES

The Components of Communication Styles

An actor's communication style refers to all aspects of an actor's behavior that he or she displays while communicating or interacting with others. An actor's communication style includes both the messages and signals that are deliberately conveyed by the actor (e.g., conveying to others that one is persuasive by choosing specific language to craft a convincing argument), and also those behaviors that the actor may display unintentionally (e.g., conveying to others that one is nervous by biting one's nails). Furthermore, communication styles include both the content of an actor's message (e.g., nodding one's head in agreement conveys a different message than shaking one's head in disagreement), as well as the manner in which this content is delivered (e.g., shaking one's head slowly versus rapidly).

For the most part, prior research on communication styles and status conferral has generally focused on the manner of message delivery, rather than the content (for an exception see Tiedens, 2001, which investigates the status consequences resulting from the content of emotional expressions).

Many of these studies have focused on nonverbal communication behaviors. For example, some studies have examined displays of eye contact, including both the duration of eye contact with others (Rosa & Mazur, 1979), as well as specific patterns of eye contact, such as individuals' visual dominance ratios (defined as the ratio of making eye contact while speaking, to making eye contact while listening; Exline, Ellyson, & Long, 1975). Other research on nonverbal behavior has focused on individuals' postures and gestures. In particular, research has demonstrated that individuals often change their level of postural expansion (i.e., the amount of physical space they consume) during their interactions with others (Tiedens & Fragale, 2003). Additionally, individuals often communicate, usually unintentionally, through gestures. For example, gestures such as hand-wringing or grooming behavior (e.g., touching one's hair or face) often convey nervousness on the part of the actor (Mazur, 1985), whereas intrusive gestures, such as pointing, convey dominance (Ridgeway, 1987). Finally, nonverbal behaviors also include vocal attributes, or voice characteristics, such as one's speaking volume, tone of voice (e.g., a confident voice tone or an uncertain voice tone), and rate of speech (i.e., speaking fast or slow; Ridgeway, 1987).

Although they have not been as frequently studied, studies of status conferral have also examined verbal communication behaviors. In particular, these studies have generally investigated verbal markers of speech assertiveness, or the confidence and assuredness of one's speech (e.g., Erickson et al., 1978; Carli, 1990). Unassertive speech is defined as a tentative, or uncertain, manner of speaking often characterized by the use of hesitations (e.g., "Well ...," "Um ..."), tag questions (e.g., "Don't you think?"), hedges (e.g., "Kinda ...," "Sort of ..."), disclaimers (e.g., "This may be a bad idea, but ..."), and formal addresses (e.g., "Yes, Sir"), whereas assertive speech is an assured, confident manner of speaking usually marked by the absence of these characteristics (Hewitt & Stokes, 1975; Lakoff, 1975; Erickson et al., 1978).

The Effects of Communication Styles on Status Positions

Communication behaviors may come to influence status positions because individuals often adjust their communication styles based on the status positions they currently occupy (see Berger, Webster, Ridgeway, & Rosenholtz, 1986, for a review). For example, status positions affect patterns of eye contact such that low-status individuals have a lower visual dominance ratio (i.e., they make more frequent eye contact when listening to others than when speaking to others) than high-status individuals (who make more frequent eye contact while speaking than while listening; Exline et al., 1975; Ellyson, Dovidio, Corson, & Vinicur, 1980; Ridgeway, Berger, & Smith, 1985). Similarly, status positions affect vocal and verbal behaviors, with high-status individuals speaking more quickly (Ridgeway et al., 1985) and assertively (Carli, 1990) than low-status individuals. As a result of these frequently observed differences, observers may learn to associate particular communication behaviors with high-status and low-status individuals, so that, over time, these communication behaviors may become indicators of status in their own right. Individuals often make inferences about actors' likely and deserved status positions based solely on the communication behaviors that these individuals display. For example, prior research has demonstrated that actors gain more status when they speak quickly rather than slowly (Brown, Strong, & Rencher, 1973; Smith, Brown, Strong, & Rencher, 1975), use a confident voice tone as opposed to a hesitant voice tone (Ridgeway, 1987), sustain eye contact rather than break it (Washburn & Hakel, 1973; Wexley, Fugita, & Malone, 1975; Hamada & Hakel, 1977), and express anger rather than sadness (Tiedens, 2001), which are all behaviors that are displayed more frequently by high-status than low-status individuals. (see Ridgeway, 1987 for a discussion.) Thus, prior research on communication styles and status conferral has generally distinguished between a high-status communication style, which is associated with high-status individuals and results in a high level of status for an actor, and a low-status style, which is associated with low-status individuals and results in lower status for an actor.[1]

Communication Styles as Signals of Agency and Communality

In addition to serving as signals for an actor's likely or deserved status position, communication behaviors also serve as signals for an actor's underlying abilities and traits. In particular, communication behaviors generally convey information about two types of traits, *agency* (i.e., how intelligent, ambitious, and dominant an actor is) and *communality* (i.e., how affiliative, selfless, and concerned with others an individual is; Bakan, 1966), which are considered to be the two fundamental dimensions of person perception (e.g., Asch, 1946; Bakan, 1966; Wiggins, 1979; Fiske, Cuddy, Glick, & Xu, 2002).[2] These trait inferences develop because individuals associate different traits with different status positions. Individuals in high-status positions are assumed to be highly agentic, but not particularly communal, whereas individuals in low-status positions are perceived to be highly communal, but not particularly agentic (Conway, Pizzamiglio, & Mount, 1996; Glick & Fiske, 2001; Fiske et al., 2002). As a result, individuals learn to associate the traits of high-status and low-status individuals with the behaviors they display. Over time, communication behaviors become signals of agency and communality in their own right, with high-status communication behaviors signaling a high degree of agency, but a lesser amount of communality, and low-status communication behaviors signaling high communality, but relatively low agency. For example, emotions associated with high-status positions, such as anger and pride (Tiedens, Ellsworth, & Mesquita, 2000; Tiedens, 2001), and high-status speech styles, such as a direct and assertive style (Erickson et al., 1978), convey the impression that an individual is highly agentic, but not particularly communal. In contrast, low-status emotions such as sadness and appreciation (Tiedens et al., 2000; Tiedens, 2001), or an unassertive speech style (Erickson et al., 1978), convey a lower level of agency, but a higher level of communality.

Thus, both high-status and low-status communication styles are each associated with one socially desirable trait (agency and communality, respectively; Glick & Fiske, 2001). The objective of this chapter is to explore the circumstances under which one of these traits, and hence communication styles, may be more status enhancing than the other. As a result, I focus on situations in which an individual is perceived, as a function of his or her communication style, to be either highly agentic or highly communal, but not both, and explore the consequences of these trait attributions for status conferral. Of course, both empirical evidence and our own everyday experiences suggest that individuals can be perceived as *both* agentic and communal, or *neither* agentic nor communal. Although this is undoubtedly true, in this chapter I focus on the relative, rather than independent, effects of these two traits. I do this for two reasons. First, the goal of this chapter is to compare two communication styles, the high-status style and the low-status style, that have been widely discussed in the status conferral literature. As discussed above, these two styles are each associated with a high rating on one of the two trait dimensions, and a lower rating on the other trait dimension. Thus, to compare the relative effectiveness of these two styles requires that one compare a situation in which an individual is perceived to have high agency (i.e., a high-status communication style) to a situation in which an individual is perceived to have high communality (i.e., a low-status communication style). Second, although there is a general consensus in the literature that agency and communality are separate dimensions of person perception, in the sense that it is *possible* for an individual to be rated as either high or low on both dimensions, evidence from several perspectives suggests that it is most common for individuals to be classified as higher on one dimension than the other (e.g., Bales, 1958; Fiske, Xu, Cuddy, & Glick 1999; Glick & Fiske, 2001; Fiske et al., 2002). Although this evidence is not incompatible with the notion that agency and communality are separate dimensions, it suggests that the most frequently observed person categorizations are those in which there is a negative relationship between perceived agency and communality. Thus, by focusing on situations in which one is perceived as either highly agentic or highly communal, but not both, I am examining the two person categorizations that are likely to be most frequently occurring in everyday life.

Given that both agency and communality are viewed as positive attributes, it seems likely that both agency and communality should be socially valued (i.e., high-status) qualities and that, in some cases, displays of communality may be viewed as even higher status than displays of agency. However, little is known about the circumstances, if any, in which this might be the case. Although communality has been shown to be an important predictor of status positions in social groups (Anderson, John, Keltner, & Kring, 2001), there has been little systematic study of if, or when, communality may positively influence individuals' status positions in task groups. In fact, to date, the benefits of displaying communality through low-status communication behaviors have been discussed only in the context of low-status group members. Research investigating the effects of the communication behaviors of both women (Kleinke & Kahn, 1980; Carli, 1990; Eagly, Makhijani, & Klonsky, 1992; Carli, LaFleur, & Loeber, 1995; Rudman, 1998) and racial minorities (Katz & Cohen, 1962) has demonstrated that individuals in these demographic categories are sometimes evaluated negatively when they use a high-status communication style, since these behaviors are considered counter-stereotypical for these social groups, and therefore may be granted higher status when they display the lower-status behaviors that are considered normative for their roles. Thus, this research suggests that individuals in low-status positions may gain more status from displaying low-status, rather than high-status, communication behaviors. However, given that these studies have focused only on members of low-status demographic groups, it is not yet clear if these effects generalize to a larger population, and if they do, what structural or situational factors are necessary to produce these results.

Although there have been few empirical investigations of the status enhancing benefits of communality, several theoretical perspectives have touched upon this issue. These perspectives differ in their views about the potential for communality to be a status enhancing trait, and the circumstances, if any, in which communality may actually be more beneficial for an individual's status position than agency. Three theoretical frameworks, theories of group stereotyping (Fiske et al., 1999, 2002; Glick & Fiske, 2001), theories of emergent leadership in groups (Bales, 1950, 1970), and theories of status generalization (Berger, Cohen, & Zelditch, 1972; Berger, Conner, & Fisek, 1974), all make somewhat different predictions about whether and when displays of communality may be beneficial for enhancing individual status in task groups. Each of these perspectives is discussed below.

AGENCY AND COMMUNALITY AS BASES OF SOCIAL STATUS

Group Stereotypes

Research on stereotype content has generally focused on the status positions of groups within society (Fiske et al., 1999, 2002; Glick & Fiske, 2001). However, this perspective is useful for thinking about status attainment at the individual level, since group membership (e.g., one's gender or racial group) is often an important determinant of an individual's status position (Webster & Driskell, 1978). This research has demonstrated that a social group's status in society is commensurate with their perceived level of agency: High-status groups (e.g., business professionals, wealthy people) are perceived as highly agentic (e.g., intelligent, ambitious, dominant, confident), whereas low-status groups (e.g., housewives, elderly people) are perceived as less agentic. Furthermore, low-status groups are generally viewed as more communal (i.e., likeable, agreeable, sincere, tolerant) than high-status groups, but these researchers argue that these attributions of communality are essentially a consolation prize for those individuals deemed unworthy of high status. Attributing characteristics of communality to individuals or groups is characterized as "throwing the bone ... to subordinates" (Glick & Fiske, 2001, p. 287), aimed at both "stifling resentment" among low-status group members (because they can feel good about the positive traits attributed to them) and "promoting deference" to the high-status group members (because the stereotype provides a prescription that low-status individuals *ought* to behave in a communal and friendly way). Thus, research on stereotype content conceptualizes communality as a "socially desirable, though, subordinating" trait (Fiske et al., 2002) that serves only to pacify low-status individuals. This suggests, consistent with the research on minority groups and communication styles (Katz & Cohen, 1962; Kleinke & Kahn, 1980; Carli, 1990; Carli et al., 1995), that communality only has the potential to be status enhancing in groups that are viewed as low status in society. Since displays of communality are normative for these groups (i.e., part of the group stereotype), individuals who conform to behavioral expectations may be valued more (i.e., seen as higher status) than those who violate such norms by displaying counter-stereotypical high agency behaviors.

Emergent Leadership

Research on small group interaction and emergent leadership provides a somewhat more optimistic view about the status enhancing benefits of communality, arguing that perceptions of communality are associated with certain types of leadership (i.e., high-status roles), but that communality is still viewed as a lower-status trait than agency. Much of the research in this area stems from Bales's (1950) distinction between task and social leaders in groups. According to this perspective, group members that are perceived as communal are more likely to be viewed as social leaders (i.e., those who manage the socio-emotional problems arising between group members) by the group, whereas those members perceived as agentic are more likely to emerge as task leaders (i.e., those who help the group complete the task at hand; Bales & Slater, 1955; Slater, 1955; Bales, 1958; Eagly & Karau, 1991). Although both types of leaders are seen as necessary for group functioning, and both are generally considered to be high-status group members, task leaders (who display agency) are ultimately rated as higher status than social leaders (who display communality; Bales & Slater, 1955; Slater, 1955; Bales, 1958). In further support of this assertion, related research has demonstrated that, when choosing only *one* overall leader, group members are more likely to nominate a leader that displays characteristics of agency than a leader that displays characteristics of communality (Moss & Kent, 1996). These researchers argue that this occurs because one's status position is a function of one's task contribution, and thus task leaders, who directly enhance the group's performance, contribute more to the task than social leaders, who enhance task performance only indirectly, by fostering harmonious interpersonal relations (Bales, 1950, 1999). As a result, although little explicit discussion is devoted to this topic in the theory, these researchers suggest that communality should be valued more than agency only in situations where the socio-emotional problems of the groups are more urgent and important than the task problems (i.e., in "dysfunctional" groups; Bales, 1950; Slater, 1955).

Status Generalization

The effects of agency and communality on status conferral are also discussed by expectation states theory (Berger et al., 1972, 1974), a prominent sociological theory developed to explain the creation and maintenance of status differences in task groups. This theory suggests that status is conferred to an actor based on others' assessments of the actor's expected performance in the group. Thus, similar to Bales's research on group interaction (1950, 1970), this perspective asserts that the traits and behaviors that result in the highest status for an individual within a group will be those that are perceived to be the most valuable for helping the group complete the task at hand (Berger et al., 1972; Webster & Driskell, 1978). However, unlike the group interaction perspective, expectation states theory does not make an explicit distinction between task and social behaviors, or limit the role of communality to facilitating harmonious interpersonal relations. According to this theory, *any* characteristic that is associated with a high level of expected performance in a group should result in increased status for those individuals possessing that characteristic. In both discussions of the theory (e.g., Ridgeway et al., 1985) and in empirical tests of the theory (e.g., Ridgeway, 1987), these researchers often claim that agency should be the biggest predictor of an individual's performance, and hence status, in a task group. Those individuals who are intelligent and ambitious should be able to perform better on most tasks than those that are not. Thus, similar to both research on group stereotyping and research on emergent leadership, expectation states theory has generally been used, to date, to argue that agency should be, and is, a bigger predictor of one's status position than any other quality (including communality). However, by defining status in terms of expected performance, the theoretical framework is broader than the way it is often discussed, and does allow for the possibility that traits other than agency (i.e., communality) may be status enhancing in circumstances where these characteristics are seen as important for facilitating task performance. Thus, according to this perspective, displays of communality should be more status enhancing for an individual than displays of agency in any situation where group members perceive communality to be more relevant for high task performance than agency.

In sum, these three theoretical frameworks make different predictions about if, or when, communality may be an important predictor of one's status position, and whether communality may ever be a more status enhancing trait than agency. Both research on stereotype content and research on emergent leadership contend that although displays of communality are functional for the group, they are not necessarily functional for the individual. Although these two literatures focus on different sources of individuals' status positions – status arising from one's group membership versus status arising from one's task roles – they both share the notion that communality is generally viewed as a lower-status trait than agency. The group stereotype perspective suggests that communality should never be a status enhancing trait, except, perhaps, in groups that are generally devalued in society (i.e., low-status groups), since displays of communality are stereotypical and normative in such groups (Fiske et al., 2002). Taking a slightly different approach, the emergent leadership perspective maintains that communality is an important characteristic for social leaders, who are generally seen as high-status group members, but not quite so high status as the high agency task leaders, except in situations where the group's interpersonal relations are so dysfunctional as to impede effective task performance (Bales, 1950; Slater, 1955). However, expectation states theory stands somewhat in contrast to these two perspectives, allowing for the possibility that communality may be status enhancing, and even more status enhancing than agency, in situations where communality is important for facilitating task performance. Thus, of all the perspectives, expectation states theory is the most open to the possibility that attributions of communality may improve an individual's status position, and is also the most specific about the circumstances under which this might be the case.

Consistent with expectation states theory, I argue that the relative importance of agency versus communality depends on the perceived importance of these two characteristics for facilitating task performance. Furthermore, I suggest that certain group features alter the extent to which one of these characteristics is perceived to be more important for task performance than the other. In particular, I focus on two group characteristics, the level of interdependence in the task group and the difficulty of detecting social loafing (i.e., shirking one's share of the workload), that may influence the extent to which group members perceive agency and communality as important for task performance, and hence affect the communication styles that are most effective for status conferral.

It is important to note that in addition to elucidating the criteria for status conferral in different situations, identifying the factors that moderate the relationship between communication styles and status conferral should also help to determine which of the three theoretical frameworks discussed above most adequately captures what the status is and why it is awarded to others. All three frameworks make similar predictions about the role of agency in the status conferral process, but make different predictions about the role of communality. Thus, exploring situations in which communality may be important for status advancement should help to differentiate these perspectives and provide a more thorough understanding of the process of status conferral in task groups.

TASK INTERDEPENDENCE

The level of *task interdependence* in a group is the extent to which group members collaborate, coordinate, or simply interact with others to complete their work (Thompson, 1967; Johnson & Johnson, 1989; Wageman, 1995). Although all task groups, by definition, necessitate some degree of interdependence among members (Bales, 1950), there is substantial variation among groups in level of interdependence required for task completion; in some groups, group members work relatively independently and rarely interact with others, whereas in other groups, group members interact and work with others on a constant basis (Wageman, 1995). The level of task interdependence influences the amount of interaction, collaboration, and cooperation that occurs within a group (Thomas, 1957; Thompson, 1967; Spilerman, 1971; Crawford & Haaland, 1972; Johnson, 1973; Susman, 1976; Galbraith, 1977; Slocum & Sims, 1980). In general, the higher the level of interdependence in a group, the greater the need for, and expectation of, collective effort and coordination among group members (March & Simon, 1958; Thompson, 1967; Perrow, 1970; Galbraith, 1977).

I argue that the level of task interdependence in a group affects the importance of agency and communality for facilitating group performance, and hence the weights that groups place on these two characteristics when making status conferral decisions. Collaboration and interaction among group members should be more efficient and productive when the group members working together are friendly, nurturing, and concerned with others (i.e., when they have high communality) than when they are not. Thus, in highly interdependent groups, where collaboration and collective effort is necessary for task completion, displays of communality should be more important for task performance than in less interdependent groups, which do not require as much interpersonal interaction. At the same time, the agency of individual group members may be relatively less important in highly interdependent groups because the collaborative nature of these groups implies that members can pool their collective talents and rely more on the abilities of the group as a whole rather than on the efforts of any one member. However, an individual's agency may be more critical for performance in groups with a low level of task interdependence, where individuals will need to rely primarily on their own capabilities to complete tasks. Individuals that are highly agentic are, by definition, very ambitious, confident, and independent, which are all qualities that should facilitate successful performance when one is working alone. Thus, the relative importance of agency versus communality for task performance in a given group is likely to depend on the amount of interdependence in the group. In highly interdependent groups, task performance may be based more on communality, which facilitates collaboration and interaction, than on agency, which fosters independent work. However, in groups with low interdependence, we should see the pattern that has been demonstrated in prior research: Performance assessments may be based more on agency than on communality. This suggests the following hypotheses:

Proposition 1A. In groups with a low level of interdependence, individuals will view agency as more important for task performance than communality.

Proposition 1B. In groups with a high level of interdependence, individuals will view communality as more important for task performance than agency.

Proposition 2A. In groups with a low level of interdependence, an individual's status position should be based primarily on assessments of the individual's agency.

Proposition 2B. In groups with a high level of interdependence, an individual's status position should be based primarily on assessments of the individual's communality.

If the relative importance of agency and communality for task performance is affected by the level of interdependence in a group, this implies that the communication behaviors that are most effective for status conferral should also depend on the level of interdependence in the group in question. In groups with a low level of interdependence, we should see the familiar pattern that has been demonstrated in prior research: Individuals should gain more status when displaying traditional high-status communication behaviors that convey high agency than when displaying the low-status communication behaviors that convey high communality. However, in highly interdependent groups, the opposite pattern may emerge and individuals may attain more status from displaying the communality-indicating behaviors that have previously been associated with low-status individuals.

Proposition 3A. In groups with a low level of interdependence, individuals should gain more status from displaying high-status communication behaviors (which convey agency) than from low-status communication behaviors (which convey communality).

Proposition 3B. In groups with a high level of interdependence, individuals should gain more status from displaying low-status communication behaviors (which convey communality) than from high-status communication behaviors (which convey agency).

The level of task interdependence in a group can be affected by many factors, such as norms or rules about the process that group members should use to complete the task, the type of task in question, and the degree to which information and resources necessary to complete the task are distributed among group members (Wageman, 1995, 1999). Below I discuss and provide empirical examples of two sources of interdependence, group culture and task type, that affect the traits, and hence the communication styles, that are most effective for enhancing an individual's status position within a group.

Interdependence Arising from Group Culture

One reason that groups may vary in their level of interdependence is because they differ in the processes used to accomplish their tasks. These procedural differences can stem from the culture of an organization, which establishes norms about how work should be accomplished. One cultural distinction that was originally made at the national level, and then extended to the organizational level, is the distinction between individualistic and collectivistic cultures (Earley, 1993; Chatman & Barsade, 1995; Chatman, Polzer, Barsade, & Neale, 1998). Individualistic cultures emphasize individual effort and achievement, whereas collectivistic cultures focus on collective goals and collaborative action (Chatman & Barsade, 1995). Evidence suggests that these cultural distinctions influence the level of interdependence in an organization, with members of collectivistic cultures interacting and collaborating more frequently than members of individualistic cultures (Chatman et al., 1998). Based on the predictions above, this suggests that in collectivistic cultures individuals should perceive displays of communality as more important for task performance than displays of agency, and thus award more status to an individual who conveys communality through their communication behaviors than an individual who conveys agency through their behaviors. Conversely, in individualistic cultures, the reverse should be true: An individual should gain more status from displaying agency-indicating communication behaviors than communality-indicating communication behaviors.

Recently, I conducted a study that found support for these predictions (Fragale, 2003). In this study, participants read a description of an organization described as either collectivistic or individualistic (adapted from Chatman & Barsade, 1995). In the collectivistic condition, the organization (named Alliance Partners) was described as valuing cooperation and team effort, whereas the individualistic organization (named Solo Ventures) was described as valuing independent work and individual effort. After reading these descriptions, participants read a transcript of a phone conversation allegedly made by a male employee (Robert) of the organization. Participants read either an assertive (high-status) or unassertive (low-status) version of this transcript (adapted from Holtgraves, Srull, & Socall, 1989). Although, the content of Robert's speech was identical in both the versions of the transcript, the versions differed in the style in which the content was delivered. In the unassertive version, Robert used hedges (e.g., "Kinda ..." "Sort of ..."), hesitations (e.g., "Well ..." "Um ..."), disclaimers (e.g., "This may be a bad idea, but ..."), formal addresses (e.g., "Yes, Sir ..."), and tag questions (e.g., "Don't you think?"), whereas the assertive version of the interview did not contain these tentative speech patterns.

The main question of interest in this study was the amount of status that participants would award to Robert based on his speech style and the culture of the organization. After reading the transcript, participants completed a questionnaire in which they answered several questions. Participants were informed that Robert, who had just completed the training phase of his employment, was interested in a permanent position in the company, and their responsibility was to make decisions about his future status in the company. Participants rated how likely they would be to offer Robert a permanent position in the organization, how much social status he should have if he were to have a permanent position in the organization, and the extent to which they thought Robert would be a success in the organization. These questions were averaged to create a composite measure of status conferral. Participants also indicated their impressions of Robert's disposition, by rating him on several traits relating to the dimensions of agency and communality. Finally, to rule out the possibility that any differences in the patterns of status conferral across the two cultures were due to perceived status differences between individualistic and collectivistic cultures, participants indicated the extent to which they thought the organization in question was a high-status or low-status organization within its industry.

The results of this study supported my predictions: Robert was perceived as more agentic when displaying a traditionally high-status behavior, assertive speech, than when displaying a lower-status behavior, unassertive speech. Conversely, Robert was perceived as more communal when using an unassertive speech style than when using an assertive speech style. These perceived trait differences affected the amount of status that was awarded to Robert in the two organizational cultures. In the individualistic culture, the traditional relationship between communication style and status conferral emerged: Participants awarded more status to Robert when he displayed a high-status communication behavior, assertive speech, than when he displayed a low-status behavior, unassertive speech. However, this pattern reversed in the collectivistic culture: Robert was awarded more status when speaking in an unassertive manner, a style traditionally viewed as relatively ineffective for enhancing an individual's status position, than when speaking in an assertive manner. Furthermore, mediation analyses revealed that these results emerged because individuals valued agency and communality differently in the two cultures. In the individualistic culture, participants used assessments of the actor's agency, but not his communality, as the basis for status conferral judgments. However, in the collectivistic culture, participants did the opposite: Only perceptions of the actor's communality, and not perceptions of his agency, affected the amount of status that was awarded to the actor. Finally, this study revealed no status differences between the two cultures, ruling out the alternative that communality is only a status enhancing characteristic in low-status groups where displays of communality may be considered expected and normative (Fiske et al., 2002).

Interdependence Arising from Task Type

In addition to process differences, differences in the level of interdependence among groups can also arise from the types of tasks that groups are trying to accomplish (Thompson, 1967). As Wageman (1999) discusses, some tasks, such as dancing the tango, require interdependence by definition (since one cannot complete the dance without the cooperation of a partner), whereas other tasks, such as writing a computer program, limit interdependence (since only one person can work on a computer at a time). Various researchers have attempted to classify the myriad of tasks that groups undertake according to defining features (e.g., Hackman, 1968; Steiner, 1972; Laughlin, 1980; Shaw, 1981), and the level of interdependence necessitated by the task is often a feature that is discussed in these typologies. McGrath (1984) developed a task typology that synthesized the task distinctions proposed by these earlier researchers, and organized tasks according to two "fundamental" dimensions, a cognitive–behavioral dimension and a cooperative–conflictual dimension. This latter dimension has been discussed in terms of interdependence (e.g., Strauss, 1999), with the cooperative end of the dimension corresponding to relatively low interdependence tasks and the conflictual end of the dimension corresponding to relatively high interdependence tasks. At the low interdependence (i.e., cooperative) end of the spectrum are what McGrath (1984) refers to as "generate" tasks, or tasks, such as creativity and brainstorming tasks, that require idea generation. As each member can independently contribute ideas to the task, and as the group is not required to decide on a single best idea or decision in these tasks, generate tasks are considered to be low interdependence tasks; little coordination or consensus is required for generate tasks to be completed (Strauss, 1999). Compared to generate tasks, "choose" and "execute" tasks, which are located near the midpoint of McGrath's (1984) cooperative–conflictual dimension, require a higher level of coordination among group members. Choose tasks are intellective or judgment tasks that require group members to reach a decision or a consensus on a problem or issue. Execute tasks are those that require physical movement or coordination, such as athletic competitions. As group members are working toward a group decision or outcome, choose and execute tasks require more collaboration and interaction among members (i.e., higher interdependence) than generate tasks. Finally, at the conflictual end of the spectrum are "negotiate" tasks, which are tasks that require members to resolve conflicting viewpoints and arrive at a joint decision. Negotiate tasks, because they inherently involve conflicting interests, require a high level of coordination and interaction if a consensus or resolution is to be reached. Thus, of all the task types discussed in McGrath's (1984) task circumplex, negotiate tasks require the highest level of interdependence among group members.

If, as I have argued, the relative importance of agency and communality for task performance is affected by the level of interdependence in the group in question, this suggests that, in addition to differences in group culture, differences in the type of tasks that groups are trying to accomplish should also affect the traits and communication styles that are most beneficial for status conferral. In groups with low interdependence tasks, such as "generate" tasks in McGrath's (1984) circumplex, communication styles that convey agency should be more effective for enhancing an individual's status than communication styles that convey communality. However, as the level of interdependence necessitated by the group task increases (e.g., to "choose" and "execute", and then to "negotiate" tasks), the communication styles associated with status advancement may change, with communality-indicating communication behaviors resulting in more status than agency-indicating communication behaviors in highly interdependent tasks.

The effects of task type on group status conferral processes were examined in another study by Fragale (2003). In this study, participants evaluated an actor in terms of his deserved status in two organizational departments, finance and human resources, which differed in the level of interdependence necessitated by the departmental task. Tasks of a finance department are generally intellective or judgment tasks (tasks in the "choose" quadrant of McGrath's (1984) circumflex), which require a lower level of interdependence than the tasks of a human resources department, which are often judgment or negotiation tasks (tasks in the "choose" or "negotiate" quadrants of the circumplex). A pretest revealed that participants did perceive the tasks of human resources departments to be inherently more interdependent than the tasks of finance departments. Thus, finance and human resources were chosen as two organizational departments that differed in their level of task interdependence.

As in the study described above, participants first read a transcript of a conversation between an actor and a target, two employees of a large international company, in which the actor used either an assertive or unassertive speech style. Subsequently, for each of the two departments, finance and human resources, participants rated how successful the actor would be in that department, and how much status he should have if he did work in that department (combined to create a composite measure of status conferral). The results indicated that the status consequences of the low-status unassertive speech style, relative to the high-status assertive style, depended on the organizational department in question. In the finance department, which was rated as having low interdependence, the actor was predicted to be more successful and deserving of more status when he used a high-status assertive speech style than when he used the low-status unassertive speech style. However, in the human resources department, which was rated as a high interdependence department, the actor was seen as more successful and deserving of higher status when he used the low-status communication style than when he used the high-status communication style. Furthermore, mediation analyses revealed that participants used different criteria in the two organizational departments to make status conferral decisions. In the finance department, participants based their status conferral decisions primarily on their perceptions of the actor's agency, whereas in the human resources department, participants based their status conferral decisions on their perceptions of the actor's communality. Thus, this study demonstrated that the benefit of a high-status, relative to low-status, communication style was moderated by the group's overall task.

THE DIFFICULTY OF DETECTING SOCIAL LOAFING

In addition to facilitating interdependent work, perceptions of an individual's communality may also be important for determining the individual's expected task contribution because communality may serve as a signal of the individual's likely level of commitment to act in the best interests of the group. Recall that the expectation states model (Berger et al., 1972, 1974) predicts that the greatest status in a group will be awarded to those who are expected to contribute the most to the fulfillment of the group's objectives. However, performance expectations are likely to be affected not only by how *able* one is to contribute, but also by how *likely* one is to use their abilities for the benefit of the group. Regardless of an individual's level of ability, the individual will not contribute much to the group task unless he or she is willing to put forth the effort to apply those abilities to the task. As discussed above, communality is a construct capturing an individual's affiliation with and concern for others.[3] Prior research has demonstrated individuals who care about the other members of their group (i.e., have high communality) are more likely to act in the best interests of the group and often exert more effort on group tasks than those individuals that do not (Karau & Williams, 1993). Thus, individuals who display characteristics of communality may be perceived as more likely to contribute to the task at hand, since displays of communality signal that these individuals care about the other group members and will therefore work hard to contribute to the collective goal.

Relying on perceptions of a group member's communality as a cue for the group member's likelihood of performance should be highly probable in situations in which it is difficult to tell who is contributing to the task and who is not. One concern in task groups is that individuals will engage in *social loafing*, or the tendency to expend less effort when working as part of a group than when working alone (e.g., Latane et al., 1979; Jackson & Williams, 1985; Karau & Williams, 1993). Social loafing is a particularly distressing problem for task groups because it reduces the group's ability to complete the task at hand efficiently. If individual group members do not put forth their share of the effort, and instead rely on other group members to carry the load, the main advantage of the task group, the ability to pool individual resources, is greatly diminished (Latane et al., 1979). As a result, task groups have an incentive to know which individuals are shirking their share of the workload and which are pulling their weight. However, it is often difficult to determine which group members are engaging in social loafing and which are not, because the exact situations in which individuals are most prone to shirk their share of the work are exactly those situations in which it is difficult to detect (Karau & Williams, 1993). Thus, in situations in which social loafing is difficult to determine objectively, group members may need to look for other signals to determine which individuals are most likely to contribute to the group, and hence should be awarded high status. In such situations, group members may use perceptions of an individual's communality as a cue that the individual will put forth a high level of task performance, even when it is possible to avoid doing so. Individuals who display a high level of communality should be perceived as having higher task performance (due to their lower tendency to engage in social loafing and hence their increased likelihood of contributing to the group), and therefore awarded higher status, than individuals who do not display such communality. Furthermore, in such groups, displays of agency may be relatively less important for assessing an individual's expected performance. Even in situations where agency is a signal of an individual's ability to perform well on the task (e.g., in low task interdependence groups), this ability will not translate into a high level of task performance if the individual does not use these abilities to contribute to the group (i.e., if he or she engages in social loafing). However, in groups where social loafing is easy to determine objectively (and therefore less likely to occur), group members will not need to look for other signals to make inferences about task performance, and therefore are unlikely to award more status to those individuals who display a high level of communality.

Proposition 4. The greater the difficulty of detecting social loafing in a task group, the more the groups will weigh perceptions of an individual's communality (relative to perceptions of the individual's agency) in determining the individual's expected performance, and hence status, in a task group.

This suggests that low-status communication behaviors, which convey a higher level of communality than high-status communication behaviors, should be more status enhancing as the difficulty of detecting social loafing in a group increases.

> **Proposition 5.** The greater the difficulty of detecting social loafing in a task group, the more the low-status communication behaviors will be effective for increasing an individual's status position in a group.

There are many group characteristics that may affect the ease or difficulty of detecting social loafing in a task group. The amount of input redundancy in group members' contributions may influence members' abilities to disentangle individual contributions (Karau & Williams, 1993). For example, in a group brainstorming session, each group member may be responsible for generating ideas for a unique product (low redundancy), or all group members may collectively suggest ideas for all of the products (high redundancy). In general, the more redundancy between group members' contributions, the more difficult it may be to disentangle individual inputs. Another reason that groups may not be able to assess individual contributions is because no contributions have yet been made. In a group that is newly formed, it may be beneficial to determine who is likely to contribute the most to the group before assigning particular group members to tasks. Communality may be an important signal of likely future contributions when no prior evidence of contributions is available. This suggests that the importance of communality for assessing expected performance may be sensitive to the group's life cycle stage. Communality may be a bigger predictor of status conferral in more nascent groups, and less of a predictor in older, more established groups that can rely on past performance to assess an individual's group commitment. One direction for future research is to examine how these and other factors that affect the ease of identifying social loafing influence the relative importance of communality versus agency in the status conferral process.

CONCLUSION

The objective of this chapter is to propose the idea that being perceived as agentic may not always be the most status enhancing perception in task groups. Prior research has often tried to classify particular communication styles as either effective or ineffective for gaining status in task groups: High-status communication behaviors that convey high agency increase one's status, whereas low-status communication behaviors that convey high communality do not. In contrast to this prior research, I have argued for a more contextual approach to understanding how communication styles influence status conferral in task groups. The results of the preliminary evidence presented in this chapter demonstrate that the effects of individuals' words and actions on their status positions are unlikely to be absolute, but rather dependent on the specific situation. Thus, both high-status and low-status communication behaviors have the potential to positively influence an individual's status, depending on the particular characteristics of the group in question.

I have argued that two factors, the level of interdependence in a group and the difficulty of detecting social loafing in the group, may influence the relative effectiveness of particular communication behaviors for status conferral. Although preliminary evidence supports the notion that these group characteristics influence the traits, and hence the communication styles that are the most important for status conferral in different groups, a great deal of future research is necessary to determine the extent to which these results are robust and to identify other group characteristics, beyond the ones discussed in this chapter, that may affect the particular qualities that individuals value in high-status group members. Thus, rather than providing answers, this chapter aims to raise new questions about how individuals' words and actions influence their status positions, with the hopes of directing future research toward developing a more complex understanding of how individuals' behaviors influence their status attainment in task groups.

NOTES

1. High status and low status communication styles, are equivalent to the high task and low task communication styles, respectively, that have been discussed in status conferral literature (e.g., see Berger et al., 1986; Ridgeway, 1987). For the purposes of the current discussion, however, I use the labels of high status and low status to designate these two styles. I do so because I feel that the high task and low task labels for these dimensions are somewhat misleading in that they suggest that one set of behaviors is more beneficial for task performance than the other, which I later argue is not necessarily the case.

2. Although specific theories differ in the names for these dimensions and the exact traits that comprise each dimension, there is a general consensus across perspectives that traits can be organized into two dimensions: One that captures traits associated with ambition, materialism, and intelligence and the other that captures traits associated with one's affiliation and concern for others. For example, Asch's (1946) early work on impression formation demonstrated that individuals evaluate an actor based on assessments of both the actor's intelligence and the actor's warmth.

Subsequently, interpersonal circumplex theories (Leary, 1957; Carson, 1969; Wiggins, 1979, 1982; Kiesler, 1983) have organized interpersonal traits along a control dimension (anchored by dominant/submissive) and an affiliation dimension (anchored by warm/cold). Similarly, a distinction has been made between agentic traits (those associated with self-assertion and mastery of one's environment) and communal traits (those associated with selflessness and nurturance; Bakan, 1966). Most recently, research on group stereotyping has demonstrated that individuals evaluate out-groups along the dimensions of competence and warmth (Fiske et al., 1999, 2002; Glick & Fiske, 2001). For the purposes of the current discussion, I will adopt Bakan's (1966) nomenclature and refer to these two dimensions as agency and communality.

3. Ibid. note 2.

ACKNOWLEDGMENTS

I would like to thank Alex Abell, Adam Galinsky, Margaret Neale, Melissa Thomas-Hunt, and Gwen Wittenbaum for their helpful suggestions on earlier drafts of this chapter.

REFERENCES

Anderson, C., John, O. P., Keltner, D., & Kring, A. M. (2001). Who attains social status? Effects of personality and physical attractiveness in social groups. *Journal of Personality and Social Psychology*, *81*, 116–132.

Asch, S. E. (1946). Forming impressions of personality. *Journal of Abnormal and Social Psychology*, *41*, 1230–1240.

Bakan, D. (1966). *The duality of human existence: An essay on psychology and religion*. Oxford: Rand McNally.

Bales, R. F. (1950). *Interaction process analysis: A method for the study of small groups*. Cambridge, MA: Addison-Wesley.

Bales, R. F. (1958). Task roles and social roles in problem-solving groups. In: E. Maccoby, T. Newcomb & E. Hartley (Eds), *Readings in social psychology* (pp. 437–447). New York: Henry Holt.

Bales, R. F. (1970). *Personality and interpersonal behavior*. New York: Holt, Rinehart, & Winston.

Bales, R. F. (1999). *Social interaction systems: Theory and measurement*. New Brunswick, NJ: Transaction.

Bales, R. F., & Slater, P. E. (1955). Role differentiation. In: T. Parsons & R. F. Bales (Eds), *The family, socialization, and interaction process*. Glencoe, IL: Free Press.

Berger, J., Cohen, B. P., & Zelditch, M., Jr. (1972). Status characteristics and social interaction. *American Sociological Review*, *37*, 241–255.

Berger, J., Conner, T. L., & Fisek, M. H. (1974). *Expectation states theory: A theoretical research program*. Cambridge, MA: Winthrop.

Berger, J., Webster, M., Jr., Ridgeway, C. L., & Rosenholtz, S. J. (1986). Status cues, expectations, and behaviors. In: E. J. Lawler (Ed.), *Advances in group processes*, (Vol. 3, pp. 1–22). Greenwich, CT: JAI Press.

Brown, B. L., Strong, W. J., & Rencher, A. C. (1973). Perceptions of personality from speech: Effects of manipulation of acoustical parameters. *Journal of Acoustical Society of America, 54*, 29–35.

Carli, L. L. (1990). Gender, language, and influence. *Journal of Personality and Social Psychology, 59*, 941–951.

Carli, L. L., LaFleur, S. J., & Loeber, C. C. (1995). Nonverbal behavior, gender, and influence. *Journal of Personality and Social Psychology, 68*, 1030–1041.

Carson, R. C. (1969). *Interaction concepts of personality*. Chicago: Aldine.

Chatman, J. A., & Barsade, S. G. (1995). Personality, organizational culture, and cooperation: Evidence from a business simulation. *Administrative Science Quarterly, 40*, 423–443.

Chatman, J. A., Polzer, J. T., Barsade, S. G., & Neale, M. A. (1998). Being different yet feeling similar: The influence of demographic composition and organizational culture on work processes and outcomes. *Administrative Science Quarterly, 43*, 749–780.

Conway, M., Pizzamiglio, M. T., & Mount, L. (1996). Status, communality, and agency: Implications for stereotypes of gender and other groups. *Journal of Personality and Social Psychology, 71*, 25–38.

Crawford, J. L., & Haaland, G. A. (1972). Predecisional information-seeking and subsequent conformity in the social influence process. *Journal of Personality and Social Psychology, 23*, 112–119.

Eagly, A. H., & Karau, S. J. (1991). Gender and the emergence of leaders: A meta-analysis. *Journal of Personality and Social Psychology, 60*, 685–710.

Eagly, A. H., Makhijani, M. G., & Klonsky, B. G. (1992). Gender and the evaluation of leaders: A meta-analysis. *Psychological Bulletin, 111*, 3–22.

Earley, P. C. (1993). East meets west meets mideast: Further explorations of collectivistic and individualistic work groups. *Academy of Management Journal, 36*, 319–348.

Ellyson, S. L., Dovidio, J. F., Corson, R. L., & Vinicur, D. L. (1980). Visual dominance behavior in female dyads: Situational and personality factors. *Social Psychology Quarterly, 43*, 328–336.

Erickson, B., Lind, E. A., Johnson, B. C., & O'Barr, W. M. (1978). Speech style and impression formation in a court setting: The effects of "powerful" and "powerless" speech. *Journal of Experimental Social Psychology, 14*, 266–279.

Exline, R. V., Ellyson, S. L., & Long, B. (1975). Visual behavior as an aspect of power role relationships. In: P. Pliner, L. Krames & T. Alloway (Eds), *Nonverbal communication of aggression* (pp. 21–52). New York: Plenum Press.

Fiske, S. E., Xu, J., Cuddy, A. C., & Glick, P. (1999). (Dis)respecting versus (dis)liking: Status and interdependence predict ambivalent stereotypes of competence and warmth. *Journal of Social Issues, 55*, 473–489.

Fiske, S. E., Cuddy, A. C., Glick, P., & Xu, J. (2002). A model of (often mixed) stereotype content: Competence and warmth respectively follow from perceived status and competition. *Journal of Personality and Social Psychology, 82*, 878–902.

Fragale, A.R. (2003). *The power of powerless speech: The effects of speech style and task interdependence on status conferral.*

Galbraith, J. R. (1977). *Organization design*. Reading, MA: Addison-Wesley.

Glick, P., & Fiske, S. T. (2001). Ambivalent stereotypes as legitimating ideologies: Differentiating paternalistic and envious prejudice. In: J. T. Jost & B. Major (Eds), *The psychology of legitimacy* (pp. 278–306). New York: Cambridge.

Hackman, J. R. (1968). Effects of task characteristics on group products. *Journal of Experimental Social Psychology, 4*, 162–187.
Hamada, A. S., & Hakel, M. D. (1977). Influence of nonverbal communication and rater proximity on impressions and decisions in simulated employment interviews. *Journal of Applied Psychology, 62*, 295–300.
Hewitt, J. P., & Stokes, R. (1975). Disclaimers. *American Sociological Review, 40*, 1–11.
Holtgraves, T., Srull, T. K., & Socall, D. (1989). Conversation memory: The effects of speaker status on memory for the assertiveness of conversation remarks. *Journal of Personality and Social Psychology, 56*, 149–160.
Jackson, J. M., & Williams, K. D. (1985). Social loafing on difficult tasks: Working collectively can improve performance. *Journal of Personality and Social Psychology, 49*, 937–942.
Johnson, D. W. (1973). Communication in conflict situations: A critical review of the research. *International Journal of Group Tensions, 3*, 46–67.
Johnson, D. W., & Johnson, R. T. (1989). *Cooperation and competition: Theory and research*. Edina, MN: Interaction.
Karau, S. J., & Williams, K. D. (1993). Social loafing: A meta-analytic review and theoretical integration. *Journal of Personality and Social Psychology, 65*, 681–706.
Katz, I., & Cohen, M. (1962). The effects of training negroes upon cooperative problem solving in biracial teams. *Journal of Abnormal and Social Psychology, 64*, 319–325.
Kiesler, D. J. (1983). The 1982 interpersonal circle: A taxonomy for complementarity in human transactions. *Psychological Review, 90*, 185–214.
Kleinke, C. L., & Kahn, M. L. (1980). Perceptions of self-disclosers: Effects of sex and physical attractiveness. *Journal of Personality, 48*, 190–205.
Lakoff, R. (1975). *Language and woman's place*. New York: Harper & Row.
Latane, B., Williams, K., & Harkins, S. (1979). Many hands make light the work: The causes and consequences of social loafing. *Journal of Personality and Social Psychology, 37*, 822–832.
Laughlin, P. R. (1980). Social combination processes on cooperative, problem-solving groups as verbal intellective tasks. In: M. Fishbein (Ed.), *Progress in social psychology* (pp. 127–155). Hillsdale, NJ: Lawrence Erlbaum.
Leary, T. (1957). *Interpersonal diagnosis of personality*. New York: Ronald Press.
March, J. G., & Simon, H. A. (1958). *Organizations*. New York: Wiley.
Mazur, A. (1985). A biosocial model of status in face-to-face primate groups. *Social Forces, 64*, 377–402.
McGrath, J. E. (1984). *Groups: Interaction and performance*. Englewood Cliffs, NJ: Prentice Hall.
Moss, S. E., & Kent, R. L. (1996). Gender and gender-role categorization of emergent leaders: A critical review and comprehensive analysis. *Sex Roles, 35*, 79–96.
Perrow, C. (1970). *Organizational analysis: A sociological view*. Belmont, CA: Wadsworth.
Ridgeway, C. L. (1987). Nonverbal behavior, dominance, and the basis of status in task groups. *American Sociological Review, 52*, 683–694.
Ridgeway, C. L. (2001). The emergence of status beliefs: From structural inequality to legitimizing ideology. In: J. T. Jost & B. Major (Eds), *The psychology of legitimacy* (pp. 257–277). New York: Cambridge.
Ridgeway, C. L., Berger, J., & Smith, L. (1985). Nonverbal cues and status: An expectation states approach. *American Journal of Sociology, 90*, 955–978.
Rosa, E., & Mazur, A. (1979). Incipient status in groups. *Social Forces, 58*, 18–37.

Rudman, L. A. (1998). Self-promotion as a risk factor for women: The costs and benefits of counterstereotypical impression management. *Journal of Personality and Social Psychology, 74*, 629–645.

Shaw, M. (1981). *Group dynamics: The psychology of small groups*. New York: McGraw-Hill.

Slater, P. E. (1955). Role differentiation in small groups. *American Sociological Review, 20*, 300–310.

Slocum, J. W., & Sims, H. (1980). A typology for integrating technology, organization, and job design. *Human Relations, 33*, 193–212.

Smith, B. L., Brown, B. L., Strong, W. J., & Rencher, A. C. (1975). Effects of speech rate on personality perception. *Language and Speech, 18*, 145–152.

Spilerman, S. (1971). Raising academic motivation in lower class adolescents: A convergence of two research traditions. *Sociology of Education, 44*, 101–108.

Steiner, I. D. (1972). *Group process and productivity*. New York: Academic Press.

Strauss, S. G. (1999). Testing a typology of tasks: An empirical validation of McGrath's (1984) group task circumplex. *Small Group Research, 30*, 166–187.

Susman, G. (1976). *Autonomy at work: A sociotechnical analysis of participative management*. New York: Praeger.

Thomas, E. J. (1957). Effects of facilitative role interdependence on group functioning. *Human Relations, 10*, 347–366.

Thompson, J. D. (1967). *Organizations in action*. New York: McGraw-Hill.

Tiedens, L. Z. (2001). Anger and advancement versus sadness and subjugation: The effect of negative emotion expressions on social status conferral. *Journal of Personality and Social Psychology, 80*, 86–94.

Tiedens, L. Z., & Fragale, A. R. (2003). Power moves: Complementarity in dominant and submissive nonverbal behavior. *Journal of Personality and Social Psychology, 84*, 558–568.

Tiedens, L. Z., Ellsworth, P. C., & Mesquita, B. (2000). Stereotypes about sentiments and status: Emotional expectations for high- and low-status group members. *Personality and Social Psychology Bulletin, 26*, 560–574.

Wageman, R. (1995). Interdependence and group effectiveness. *Administrative Science Quarterly, 40*, 145–180.

Wageman, R. (1999). Task design, outcome interdependence, and individual differences: Their joint effects on effort in task-performing teams. *Group Dynamics: Theory, Research, and Practice, 3*, 132–137.

Washburn, P. V., & Hakel, M. D. (1973). Visual cues and verbal content as influences of impressions formed after simulated employment interviews. *Journal of Applied Psychology, 58*, 137–141.

Webster, M., Jr., & Driskell, J. E., Jr. (1978). Status generalization: A review and some data. *American Sociological Review, 43*, 220–236.

Wexley, K. N., Fugita, S. S., & Malone, M. P. (1975). Applicants' nonverbal behavior and student-evaluators' judgments in a structured interview setting. *Psychological Reports, 36*, 391–394.

Wiggins, J. S. (1979). A psychological taxonomy of trait-descriptive terms: The interpersonal domain. *Journal of Personality and Social Psychology, 37*, 395–412.

Wiggins, J. S. (1982). Circumplex models of interpersonal behavior in clinical psychology. In: P. C. Kendall & J. N. Butcher (Eds), *Handbook of research methods in clinical psychology*. New York: John Wiley and Sons.

"I KNOW WHAT I'M DOING": THE IMPACT OF GENDER STEREOTYPES ABOUT EXPERTISE ON TASK ASSIGNMENTS IN GROUPS

Samuel N. Fraidin and Andrea B. Hollingshead

ABSTRACT

This chapter investigates the effects of gender stereotypes on expectations about expertise and task assignments. We present a theoretical model that predicts and explains the pervasive and self-reinforcing effects of gender-based stereotypes on expected knowledge and task assignments in groups. In the model, stereotypes influence expertise recognition, which influences tasks assignments. Task assignments provide group members with task experience and expertise. Expertise influences expertise recognition, making the model cyclical. Expertise gained from task experience also affects stereotypes, creating a cycle that reinforces stereotypes. We describe findings from a program of research designed to examine ways of breaking this self-reinforcing cycle, which investigates the effectiveness of various types of expertise claims made by people with expertise, that is inconsistent with stereotypical expectations. We consider the implications

Status and Groups
Research on Managing Groups and Teams, Volume 7, 121–141

ISSN: 1534-0856/doi:10.1016/S1534-0856(05)07006-4

of our theory and data for effects of status on evaluation of expertise claims in work groups.

"I know what I'm doing." Sometimes this type of statement, an explicit claim about expertise, is met with a skeptical response ("Are you sure you know how to operate that machine?"), and other times it is accepted at face value. Claims about expertise are quite common; they are made explicitly when people apply for jobs, and somewhat more implicitly when new employees are given titles such as "forklift operator." A significant amount of research shows that identifying expertise and assigning tasks to those with relevant expertise can enhance group performance. Thus, group performance may hinge on the extent to which groups can accurately evaluate the expertise claims of their members.

Research indicates that group members form initial expectations about one another's expertise and possible contributions to the task based on demographic characteristics such as gender (Oldmeadow, Platow, Foddy, & Anderson, 2003; Berger, Rosenholtz, & Zelditch Jr., 1980). For example, in the absence of other information, a burly male wearing a plaid shirt is likely to be judged to know a lot more about operating a forklift and a lot less about party planning than a matronly looking woman in her forties. These inferences about expertise are likely to affect task assignments in groups: The male may be assigned to operate a forklift and the older woman may be assigned to plan the supervisor's retirement party with little discussion by group members. When members' knowledge on different topics is consistent with stereotypes, assigning tasks based on those stereotypes can lead to effective group performance.

However, members may have expertise that is not consistent with their stereotype. For example, the matronly woman in her forties may in fact be an expert forklift operator and know little about party planning. In this case, assigning tasks based on stereotypes may lead to less effective group performance, at least in the short term, and could cause the woman who would rather operate a forklift than plan a retirement party to feel resentment toward the group.

This chapter investigates the effects of gender stereotypes on expectations about expertise and task assignments within groups. Although gender is just one of many social categories that invoke stereotypes about what people know, the persistent domination of gender over race, age, and other cues as the basis for categorization across a variety of contexts (for a review see

Zemore, Fiske, & Kim, 2000) prompts us to focus on gender in this chapter. We will present a theoretical model that predicts and explains the pervasive and self-reinforcing effects of gender-based stereotypes on expected knowledge and task assignments in groups, and we will present data from a program of research designed to examine ways to break this self-reinforcing cycle. This program of research builds on previous work on transactive memory, impression formation, stereotypes, status characteristics theory, and gender roles.

TRANSACTIVE MEMORY AND COORDINATING KNOWLEDGE RESPONSIBILITIES IN GROUPS

Transactive memory is the shared division of cognitive labor in relationships involving the encoding, storage, retrieval, and communication of information from different domains (Wegner, 1987). The basic idea is that people who are interdependent often develop an implicit plan for dividing knowledge responsibilities and assigning tasks based on their shared conception of one another's expertise. Each individual becomes a specialist in some domains but not others, and individuals rely on one another to access information across domains. Over time, knowledge in transactive memory systems becomes more specialized or "differentiated" among members as a result of the delegation of knowledge responsibilities to different members (Wegner, 1987; Wegner, Guiliano, & Hertel, 1985). This division of labor means that members are responsible for less information individually, yet have access to more information collectively. Transactive memory occurs in interpersonal relationships as well as work groups. As individuals become aware of the expertise of other group members, responsibility for information related to expertise is implicitly or explicitly assigned to the most expert member (Anand, Manz, & Glick, 1998; Hollingshead, 1998a, 2000; Moreland, 1999). The specialized roles and responsibilities assigned to members often continue through the life of the group. When group members are aware of one another's areas of expertise, they can coordinate storage and retrieval of information, and allocate tasks to the member who will perform them best.

Transactive memory systems are more likely to develop when members are interdependent and have convergent expectations about who will learn what (Hollingshead, 2001). An important determinant of convergent expectations is whether group members have shared beliefs about how their own knowledge differs from that of others in the group (Hollingshead, 2001). Convergent expectations can affect how group members tacitly coordinate who will learn what (cf., Wittenbaum, Vaughan, & Stasser, 1998). In newly formed mixed-sex groups, people use gender stereotypes to infer the relative knowledge of others, and stereotypes guide the development of convergent expectations about responsibilities for knowledge in transactive memory systems (Driskell & Mullen, 1990; Foddy & Smithson, 1999; Hollingshead & Fraidin, 2003; Wood & Karten, 1986). Gender stereotypes affect not only how people make judgments about relative knowledge, but also how they assign knowledge categories to themselves and to other group members.

THE EFFECTS OF STEREOTYPING ON JUDGMENTS OF EXPERTISE AND STATUS WITHIN GROUPS

When individuals have "expected" knowledge for a given task, that is, knowledge consistent with gender-based stereotypes, they are likely to have high status with respect to that task. When we refer to status in this chapter we mean the degree to which a person is respected and has influence when the group makes decisions about a particular task, such as deciding which member will be assigned to perform it (see Webster Jr. & Driskell Jr., 1978). Members who are not expected to have knowledge in task-relevant areas may have low status on those tasks initially (Oldmeadow et al., 2003; Ridgeway & Berger, 1986; Ridgeway, Boyle, Kuipers, & Robinson, 1998). Groups may perform a variety of tasks, and it is possible for members to have high and low status with respect to different tasks depending on their expected level of knowledge relevant to each task.

Status is not always an accurate indicator of knowledge (Hollingshead, 1996). We refer to individuals who have knowledge that is not consistent with gender-based stereotypes (e.g., women who know about cars) as having "unexpected" knowledge. In a situation in which high and low status individuals both claim to have expertise on a particular topic, the low status individuals may have to provide more evidence to be accepted as an expert (Foschi, 2000). There are situations in which a low status individual may be more competent or have more task-related knowledge than a high status individual. In these situations, there is a risk that tasks will not be assigned to the individual with the highest level of relevant expertise (Hollingshead, 1996).

Expertise recognition involves making an inference about stable personal characteristics based on evidence. Delegation of knowledge responsibilities in transactive memory systems is dependent on converging judgments of relative expertise across group members. In new groups or with new members of ongoing groups, the lack of a performance history means that members are likely to make inferences about one anothers' expertise on the basis of indirect cues (Berger et al., 1980; Oldmeadow et al., 2003). One such cue may be members' category memberships and the stereotypes associated with them. Research on the effects of stereotypes on impression formation can help us understand the effects of stereotypes on expertise recognition.

People may rely on stereotypes based on demographic characteristics (such as gender) to infer others' knowledge in particular domains (Clark & Marshall, 1981; Krauss & Fussell, 1991; Wegner, 1987). In these situations, stereotypes can help people make predictions about what others know and what others might contribute to a group effort (Plaks & Higgins, 2000). When stereotypes accurately reflect individuals' expertise (e.g., Fussell & Krauss, 1992) they can increase the speed with which information can be processed (Macrae, Milne, & Bodenhausen, 1994), hastening the recognition of expertise.

However, stereotypes can lead people to make incorrect attributions about individuals' skills and abilities. In particular, gender stereotypes may guide impressions of women and men's knowledge on particular tasks (Berger et al., 1980; Foschi, 2000; Oldmeadow et al., 2003). Individuals involved in tasks that are inconsistent with gender stereotypes (e.g., a woman operating a fork-lift) may have low status because they are expected to lack knowledge of those topics.

AN EXPERIMENTAL PARADIGM TO INVESTIGATE STEREOTYPES AND TASK ASSIGNMENTS

To investigate how gender-based stereotypes affect task assignments under different conditions, we developed a computer-based laboratory paradigm that involved expertise recognition and task assignments. In this paradigm, participants were told that they would be working with another person in the study to learn as much information as possible in different knowledge categories without interacting or meeting. First, participants rated their own knowledge relative to the typical male and female in their peer group (undergraduate students at the University of Illinois) on six topics on a 1–7 scale (with 1 indicating, "I know much less than the average undergraduate," and 7 indicating, "I know much more than the average undergraduate"). We also asked participants to briefly describe their previous experiences with each topic.

Afterward, they were "assigned" a partner, ostensibly another participant in the study who was sitting at a different computer. Participants were not in fact assigned partners; they were only given an assumed partner's name (which indicated the partner's gender) and we varied the amount of other information given about the partner across studies. Participants were told that they would memorize six lists of words with their partner, and that the pairs that remembered the most words would receive cash prizes. The six lists included two that were consistent with male stereotypes, two that were consistent with female stereotypes, and two neutral lists.[1] These categories were the same ones on which they rated their own knowledge at the beginning of the study.

Our goal in the first study (Hollingshead & Fraidin, 2003) was to demonstrate the powerful effects of gender-based stereotypes on task assignments in the absence of other information about members. In this study, the only information that we provided about participants' partners was their names – whether they were female (Amanda or Jennifer) or male (Patrick or Scott). We expected that participants would be more likely to assign word lists based on their partner's gender when their partner was of the opposite sex than when they were of the same sex, as a result of convergent expectations of relative expertise based on gender stereotypes.

As expected, we found that participants with opposite-sex partners assigned stereotypically female lists to female partners and stereotypically male lists to male partners regardless of their self-reported knowledge on those topics. In contrast, participants with same-sex partners divided both categories of stereotype-associated word lists much more evenly between themselves and their assumed partner. Assignments were clearly influenced by the partner's gender. This study demonstrated that stereotypes can influence task assignments (see also Biernat & Vescio, 2002).

Moreover, the participants' task assignments led to a fairly strict division of labor along gender lines in mixed-sex pairs. Male participants tended to assign themselves stereotypically male word lists; female participants tended to assign themselves stereotypically female word lists. In mixed-sex pairs, most of the words participants memorized were consistent with their gender stereotype. Had the participants' partners been real, they would have learned information from stereotype-consistent word lists as well. In contrast, participants in same-sex pairs may have relied more on assessments of their own knowledge in each of the categories than on their partner's gender to assign lists.

SELF-REINFORCING EFFECTS OF STEREOTYPES

The division of labor along gender lines among mixed-sex pairs observed in the study described above is significant because it indicates that not only can expectations of knowledge (derived from gender stereotypes in our study) influence task assignments, but that task assignments can affect the knowledge a person acquires – participants who memorized stereotype-consistent word lists learned stereotype-consistent information. This almost certainly made them better candidates for the same task if future rounds of assignments had been made.

The mutual influence among expectations of knowledge, task assignments, and task experience can give rise to a self-reinforcing cycle. Stereotypes begin the cycle by influencing expectations of knowledge. The expectations lead to stereotypical task assignments (Hollingshead & Fraidin, 2003), and the assignments cause men and women to gain stereotypical knowledge. That improvement in stereotypical knowledge could justify future stereotypical task assignments. This cycle is depicted in Fig. 1.

For example, men in a workplace may be expected to be knowledgeable about stereotypically male tasks such as working with computers. As a result, they may be assigned such tasks on a regular basis, even if they actually have little prior knowledge. This will cause them to gain experience working with computers. The task experience will increase their knowledge

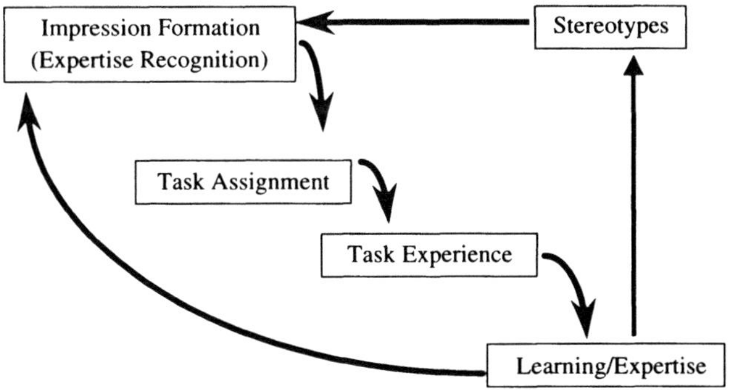

Fig. 1. The Self-Reinforcing Effect of Stereotypes.

and skill (Littlepage, Robison, & Reddington, 1997), and this improved ability will make them more suitable for these stereotypical assignments in the future.

Ideally, to maximize performance, group members will be assigned tasks in their actual domains of expertise (if they have expertise); this will increase their specialized knowledge. This cycle can be beneficial to the extent that it leads groups to assign the same individuals to the same tasks on repeated occasions. Individuals can increase their expertise as their experience grows. The cycle also leads group members to have relatively stable roles: If a person has done a task before, there may be little reason to switch him or her to a new one unless they have performed poorly. Stability can promote coordination and teamwork (cf., Arrow & McGrath, 1993).

The cycle can have costs as well. When stereotypes drive expertise recognition, groups may fail to assign tasks to those who will perform them best. The self-reinforcing cycle reduces the likelihood that task assignments will be changed to correct the initial assignment error. A significant fact about this cycle is that the person's initial level of skill or knowledge may not play an important role. A person may be assigned a task regardless of his or her initial expertise on that task; the experience gained from performing the task will make the person better suited for it over time. Thus, stereotypes can determine the skills and abilities that individuals possess (Eagly, 1987); initial expertise, interests, and an individual's intentions may not guide the individual's development. In addition to the effects on the individuals who are assigned tasks and the group as a whole, this cycle can have broader effects on society by increasing the division of knowledge and skills between the sexes in a way that strengthens gender stereotypes (Eagly, 1987). Another cost is that individuals may be assigned tasks that they do not want to perform and they may develop skills in areas in which they are not interested.

EXPERTISE CLAIMS AND BREAKING THE SELF-REINFORCING CYCLE

How does one get out of this cycle, or avoid entering it in the first place? We investigated expertise claims as a way to counteract the effects of stereotypes on task assignments. People can be a source of information about their own skills and knowledge, and their assertions about their knowledge (i.e., expertise claims) may counteract the expectations raised by stereotypes. For example, in Hollingshead (1998b), partners who were allowed to communicate prior to learning categorized lists of words tended to discuss their areas of expertise and were more likely to assign tasks based on expertise than were partners who were not allowed to communicate.

A claim of expertise can function as individuating information that contradicts a stereotype. A person may claim to have counter-stereotypical (i.e., unexpected) knowledge. Observers must weigh the claim of expertise against stereotypical expectations. A credible claim should change beliefs about a person's knowledge.

However, a significant amount of research has examined the effects of counter-stereotypical individuating information on impression formation, and the findings are not particularly encouraging. It is quite difficult to counteract the effects of stereotypes on impressions (Borgida, Rudman, & Manteufel, 1995). When individuating information is minimal or ambiguous, it may fail to overcome effects of stereotypes because it can be interpreted in ways that preserve stereotype-driven inferences (Borgida et al., 1995; Darley & Gross, 1983). Stereotypes can influence decisions even when there is base-rate evidence suggesting that they are unlikely to be an accurate guide for the decision at hand (Nelson, Biernat, & Manis, 1990; Tversky & Kahneman, 1974). Forming impressions using stereotypes requires less effort than does paying careful attention to individuating information (Macrae et al., 1994). Group members may still fail to recognize expertise accurately if expertise claims fail to overcome stereotype-driven inferences.

On the other hand, there is research that suggests that there may be circumstances under which stereotypes may be less likely to thwart expertise recognition. The outcomes and rewards of those who make task assignments are often dependent on the performance of group members in their assigned roles, and this dependence could motivate task assigners to think carefully about the abilities of the group members and give weight to individuating information. According to this reasoning, expertise claims should generally be considered carefully by other group members. This argument is supported by Neuberg and Fiske (1987), who found that outcome interdependence increased participants' motivation to form accurate impressions. When participants in their study were told that they would have to work on a task with a schizophrenic partner, individuating information influenced their impressions of the partner more than when their outcomes were not dependent on the schizophrenic person's behavior. The expectation of working with the schizophrenic partner motivated participants to rethink negative inferences driven by stereotypes of mentally ill people. This research suggests that people working in groups should give great weight to individuating information (when it is available), and stereotypes should play little role in task assignments among interdependent individuals.

Expectations states theory (Berger et al., 1980) says that group members aggregate direct indicators of competence (such as experience, and perhaps expertise claims) and characteristics interpreted as indirect indicators of competence (such as social category memberships) to form an expectation about one another's competence. Group members who are motivated to conduct a thorough evaluation of one anothers' expertise might consider more cues, or restrict their evaluations to highly relevant cues and ignore indirect cues such as stereotypes. Group members whose tasks are interdependent may learn more about one another and therefore have access to cues that are more direct than category memberships.

EVALUATION OF EXPERTISE CLAIMS

However, there are two reasons why Neuberg and Fiske's result and the expectation states argument outlined above may not apply to the effects of expertise claims on task assignments. First, although expertise claims can function like individuating information, the two concepts are not identical. Expertise claims are a type of social influence attempt, because they are intended to shape an individual's view of the person making the claim. Claims made to an individual who is about to make task assignments could be construed as an effort to influence the task assignments.

Status is relevant when people try to influence one another, and the source of an influence attempt can be critical (Latané, 1981). Research on Status Characteristics Theory (Berger et al., 1980; Oldmeadow et al., 2003) indicates that expectations can determine a group member's influence on the group:

> [P]articipation rates and social influence in task groups are a function of the expectations that group members hold for themselves and for others about their relative ability on the task ... Those who are expected to be more competent at the group's task participate more and exert more influence over group decisions than those who are expected to be less competent (Oldmeadow et al., 2003).

Low expected knowledge (based on stereotypical expectations) can lead to low task-related status and, as a result, low expected knowledge can be associated with an inability to influence group decisions. This relation is depicted in Fig. 2.

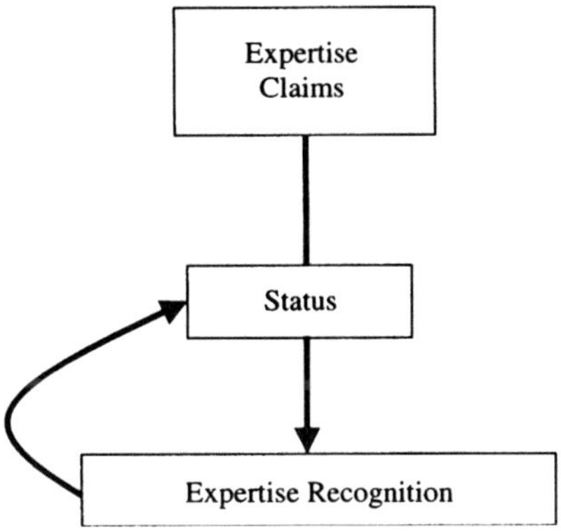

Fig. 2. Status Moderates the Effects of Expertise Claims on Expertise Recognition.

Group members may feel that a person who has little knowledge can be ignored because he or she does not contribute much to group outcomes. Group members may resist being influenced by a low status person's claims of expertise (cf., Hollingshead, 1996; Ridgeway & Berger, 1986). Lower expectations can also lead to more critical evaluations of evidence of competence (Foschi, 2000).

Second, the shifting standards model (Biernat & Fuegen, 2001; Biernat & Vescio, 2002) holds that subjective ratings (such as "good" and "expert") are typically interpreted as comparisons within the target's category. For example, if a woman claims to be an "expert," this may be interpreted as meaning that the woman is more knowledgeable about a particular topic than other women. However, if women in general are seen as having little knowledge about a topic, a woman who knows more than most women may still be expected to know less than the average man. As a result, men may still be seen as more knowledgeable than a woman who claims to have unexpected expertise. The shifting standards model suggests that even if people take claims of expertise into account, they may interpret them in ways that fail to reduce the effects of stereotypes.

In a second study, using a slight variation of the laboratory paradigm described above, we examined the extent to which participants accepted others' counter-stereotypical expertise claims.

In this study (Hollingshead & Fraidin, in preparation), participants were assigned the role of manager (referred to as the "boss") and, on each of a set of trials, were given one word list topic to assign to one of two people (referred to as "employees") who were (falsely) identified as other participants in the study. Each employee's name was presented (conveying gender information) with the employee's self-rated expertise on the topic on a 1–7 scale (with 1 indicating, "I know much less than the average undergraduate," and 7 indicating, "I know much more than the average undergraduate"). We varied whether the two employees were same- or mixed-sex, the stereotypicality of the knowledge topic (male, female, or neutral), whether the expertise claims by the employees were expected (e.g., a male employee reporting higher self-rated expertise on cars than a female employee) or unexpected (e.g., a female employee reporting higher self-rated expertise on cars than a male employee), and the extremity of the claims (e.g., 7 out of 7 is more extreme than 5 out of 7).

We found that, in mixed-sex pairs of employees, participants virtually always accepted expected expertise claims (e.g., a man claiming to be an expert on sports) and claims regarding neutral topics (e.g., a woman claiming to be an expert on world geography). In contrast, participants accepted unexpected claims of expertise less frequently (e.g., a woman claiming to be an expert on sports). However, when unexpected claims were extreme (e.g., a woman rating her knowledge of sports as 7 out of 7), they were more likely to be accepted than when they were moderate (e.g., a woman rating her knowledge of sports as 5 out of 7). In this study, expertise claims influenced task assignments, but gender also played a role when the claims conflicted with stereotypes.

SUPPORTING EXPERTISE CLAIMS

As suggested earlier, people with stereotypical expertise may have high task-related status, whereas people with unexpected expertise may have low task-related status. As demonstrated above, people with stereotypical expertise have their expertise claims accepted (and tasks assigned to them) with little supporting evidence. People with unexpected expertise may have to provide more evidence to convince group members to accept a claim that they are an expert and assign them tasks. In our view, gender affects task-related status through its effects on expectations of knowledge, and task-related status affects the acceptance of expertise claims.

The finding that expected contributions to the group influence member status (Webster Jr. & Driskell Jr., 1978), coupled with the acceptance of expected expertise claims, suggests that objective indicators of ability could provide validation for expertise claims and cause them to be accepted. Group members may initially expect few contributions from a member if that member is assigned to a counter-stereotypical task, but that expectation might change if the person could provide persuasive evidence of their expertise. This would change the member's task-relevant status at the same time it changes the member's expected knowledge. We investigated this premise in a third study using a similar experimental paradigm as the previous two studies.

In this study, we examined whether participants would be more likely to accept a partner's unexpected expertise claim if it was supported by a description of the partner's relevant experience. We found that this was indeed the case. When the partner's expertise was counter-stereotypical, his or her expertise claims were consistently accepted when they were supported by a description of the person's relevant experience. For example, a woman who claimed to be an expert on cars was consistently assigned to memorize words related to cars when participants were given her statement that her father owns a car repair shop and she used to work there every summer. Similarly, a man who claimed to be an expert on cosmetics was consistently assigned to memorize words related to cosmetics when participants were given his statement that he worked as an intern at a cosmetics company the previous summer. These relatively objective indicators of knowledge appear to have provided sufficient support for the unexpected knowledge claim to be accepted by participants.

By "relatively objective," we mean that the evidence (such as doing an internship at a cosmetics company) can be interpreted without regard to the knowledge level of the person making the claim. In addition, unlike subjective terms such as "good" and "skilled" which are typically interpreted relative to a within-category comparison group (Biernat & Vescio, 2002), the facts about the assumed partner's experience used in this study do not lend themselves to being interpreted relative to typical abilities of other members of the target's gender. In contrast, a statement such as, "I know more than most people about cosmetics," must be interpreted in light of the speaker's knowledge of how much "most people" know about cosmetics. A person who knows very little may have an inaccurate perception of what most people know (Kruger & Dunning, 1999), and, as a result, counter-stereotypical expertise claims alone (e.g., "I know more than most people do about cosmetics") may be ineffective.

In summary, the results of our studies suggest that people making unexpected expertise claims must supply more supporting evidence than people claiming to have expected expertise. Tasks were assigned to those who were expected to have expertise whether expertise claims were made or not. Tasks were routinely assigned to those with unexpected expertise only when the claims were extreme or were supported by additional, relatively objective, information.

DISCUSSION

This chapter presented a model of the self-reinforcing effects of stereotypes on task assignments and learning in diverse groups. The data from our program of research designed to identify what needs to be done to break the cycle, as described in this chapter, are supportive of the model. Members of groups must provide objective evidence of their counter-stereotypical expertise before their claims are accepted by the group. Simply claiming high levels of unexpected knowledge is not enough unless a person claims to have an extremely high level of knowledge.

Our discussion of the self-reinforcing effects of stereotypes focused on gender, but gender is only one cue that members may use to infer the relative knowledge of other members. Other cues can influence status and expectations of knowledge such as race, nationality, organizational role, or age. Each of these social categories has associated stereotypes and expectations of knowledge. We expect the self-reinforcing model to predict and explain the effects of stereotypes based on these other social categories on task assignments and learning as well. However, it is important to note that in some Internet communities such as newsgroups and support groups, the only information that members may have about other members is their name or "handle," which may or may not convey information about gender.

This model applies only to diverse groups. When the characteristics on which members vary are readily apparent, it is easy for members to develop convergent expectations about relative expertise and to use those convergent expectations to make task assignments (Ridgeway & Berger, 1986; Ridgeway & Smith-Lovin, 1999). Members of homogeneous groups may need to engage in discussion to come to shared agreement about who knows what and who will do what (cf., Brandon & Hollingshead, in press). Members who are of solo status (the only female or male in a group) may be more likely to be assigned tasks based on stereotypes, and it may be especially difficult for solos with counter-stereotypical knowledge to convince the group to assign them tasks based on their unexpected knowledge. We also expect that the pervasive effects of stereotypes we observed in dyads will be even more prevalent in larger groups. As group size increases, the cognitive burden of evaluating the relative expertise of members increases. Using stereotypes to infer knowledge can greatly reduce this cognitive burden.

This model considers only the cognitive antecedents and consequences of task assignments in groups. It does not consider the affective, social, and motivational factors that can influence and result from employing stereotypes to make task assignments in groups. For example, members who have unexpected expertise and are unable to convince the group of that expertise may become resentful of other group members and lessen their commitment to the group. This may reduce their motivation to perform the tasks that they are assigned; they may also lose interest in the topics that are not socially reinforced by the group. In contrast, members who are able to convince the group to rely on their unexpected expertise may feel more pressure to succeed and may in fact be under more scrutiny from group members (Foschi, 2000). If the unexpected experts do not perform the task effectively, it is unlikely that they will be assigned that task again.

It is important to note that individuals in groups may also rely on information other than cues based on physical appearance to infer the expertise of other members in the initial stages of group development. For example, individuals can consult or be instructed by third parties about members' expertise or their reputation. Reputation is one of the most important sources of information on which people rely to infer the competence of coworkers (Yoon, Gupta, Hollingshead, & Hinkle, 2003). In work settings, people can learn about the expertise and job responsibilities of coworkers from other coworkers, managers, or office handbooks. Conversations and shared experiences with others can provide more accurate information about what others know (Hollingshead, 1998b; Moreland, 1999; Wegner, Erber, & Raymond, 1991). All of these sources of information can impact the development of expectations of expertise.

This chapter primarily concerns counter-stereotypical expertise but it is also possible that people may have counter-stereotypical ignorance. Unexpected ignorance occurs when people do not have expertise in areas consistent with gender-based stereotypes (e.g., a woman not knowing about cosmetics or planning social events). Under what conditions will individuals admit unexpected ignorance? And if an individual claims not to know about an area consistent with a gender-based stereotype, will that claim be accepted or discounted by the group? A claim of ignorance could cause a person who is expected to be knowledgeable to have low status (cf., Ridgeway & Berger, 1986). A woman who claimed to know little about cosmetics, for example, might have little input on group decisions related to cosmetics as a result. This would support our belief that status derives directly from knowledge level and ability to contribute to the group. Alternatively, it is possible that a person who knows little would nevertheless be able to influence task assignments, and that would suggest that status is not necessarily tied to a person's level of knowledge. Instead, status might derive directly from stereotypes. For example, even women who are not knowledgeable might have high status when groups consider a stereotypically female topic, such as cosmetics. This result would conflict with the idea that a person's influence on group decisions is related to the person's contributions to the group. Future research should address this topic.

IMPLICATIONS FOR WORK GROUPS IN ORGANIZATIONAL SETTINGS

What are some practical guidelines regarding how to break the cycle in organizational settings? Performance feedback might seem like a simple solution for breaking the self-reinforcing cycle described in this chapter. However, some preliminary evidence from our research program supports the notion that the relations between performance feedback and expertise recognition are complex, and that tests that do not lead to expected results (e.g., a woman scores higher than a man on sports knowledge) are discounted or viewed as invalid. This result is consistent with Expectation States Theory (Berger et al., 1980), which says that member status influences the interpretation of members' work. A low status member's work will be evaluated less positively than identical work done by a high status group member. When members work on tasks with which other members expect them to do poorly, good performance may be reinterpreted as poor performance (cf., Borgida et al., 1995).

On the other hand, a person who exhibits good performance on a stereotype-consistent task seems likely to be given the same assignment again. This is what our model of the self-reinforcing effects of stereotypes predicts. This also hints at a potential strategy: Unexpected experts may be able to use their positive performance on stereotype-consistent tasks to their advantage. Group members are likely to respect the input of a person who contributes significantly to the group, and such a person may therefore be able to ask (or demand) reassignment to a different (and perhaps counter-stereotypical) task. In other words, high status, derived from contributions to the group, may help break the cycle. However, for this to happen, another person would have to be available to step in to perform the stereotype-consistent tasks abandoned by the unexpected expert. If enough time has elapsed, such that specialized roles have developed in the group, it is unlikely that there would be a substitute available.

In a similar vein, the idea that expected contributions to the group drive acceptance of expertise claims suggests that expertise claims would be accepted from members who are expected to contribute to their group, even if the contribution is unrelated to the expertise claim. For example, group members might accept a female member's counter-stereotypical claim that she is a computer expert if she has a powerful social network that helps the group obtain needed resources. Her contribution to the group (her social network) would give her high status, and members would be concerned about keeping her happy and a member of the group. As a result, they would pay close attention to her unexpected claim. In contrast, if a member who contributes little to the group made an unexpected claim, group members would rely on stereotypes to evaluate it, and would arrive at a quick conclusion that the claim is unlikely to be valid.

Making managers accountable is another potential method of preventing the self-reinforcing cycle from occurring. Managers who are required to explain their task assignment decisions might refrain from relying on status and stereotypes and instead take expertise claims into account to a greater degree. Lerner and Tetlock (1999) reviewed research on accountability and argued that accountability can have positive effects as a result of increased effort and attention to decision-making processes. This might mean that managers who are required to explain their task assignment decisions would be motivated to make accurate decisions. In terms of our model, this would mean that, instead of relying on stereotypes, they might take expertise claims into account to a greater degree. The fear of being second-guessed might motivate them to carefully investigate expertise claims even when made by low status group members.

However, other effects of accountability make it unclear how frequently these benefits will occur. For example, Siegel-Jacobs and Yates (1996) suggested that outcome accountability can cause stress, which narrows one's information search. This effect could lead task assigners to focus on stereotypes and also evaluate expertise claims heuristically by relying more heavily on the status of the group member claiming to have expertise. Hattrup and Yates (1996) found that accountability increased the use of occupational stereotypes in laboratory decisions about individuals' suitability for membership on a committee. They suggested that the complexity of making decisions about several individuals (such as might occur in a group) can overwhelm decision makers who attempt to take individuating information into account; instead, decision makers might make decisions quickly and use new information only to bolster and defend their choices.

Another reason accountability might not help groups recognize member expertise is that the members might consider stereotypes an accurate source of information about what individuals know, and therefore rely on them even when they know they will have to justify their decisions. In our studies, participants were asked to describe how they made their task assignment decisions, and a number of participants said that some of their task assignments were "random." Truly random assignments are unlikely to be optimal. However, we suspect that "random" assignments were not actually random, but are in fact influenced by stereotypes, and participants were unaware or were uncomfortable saying so. In either case, managers who are required to explain their task assignment decisions may view random choice, status, and stereotypes as invalid bases for rejecting expertise claims. Thus, accountability could give expertise claims greater effect.

It should be noted that many effects of stereotypes are relatively automatic, and stereotypes can determine which decision is the default. This suggests that the self-reinforcing cycle described here may be relevant even when managers are accountable. In any case, future studies should investigate the effects of accountability on assignments to stereotypical tasks.

NOTES

1. These topics were chosen based on pilot testing which measured students' beliefs about their own knowledge of each topic and their expectations of how much other men and women would know. Our pilot testing indicated that the average male undergraduate was expected to know more about cars and sports than the average female undergraduate. The average female undergraduate was expected to know more than the average male undergraduate about soap operas and cosmetics. No differences in men's and women's knowledge of geography or US history were expected by pilot test participants. These results were the same for male and female pilot test subjects, and they were consistent with the pilot test participants' self-ratings of their own knowledge (cf., Fussell & Krauss, 1992). The expected knowledge differences were strongest for the stereotypically female topics, soap operas and cosmetics.

ACKNOWLEDGEMENT

We thank Jen Overbeck, Melissa C. Thomas-Hunt, and an anonymous reviewer for their helpful comments on an earlier draft.

REFERENCES

Anand, V., Manz, C. C., & Glick, W. H. (1998). An organizational memory approach to information management. *Academy of Management Review, 23*, 796–809.

Arrow, H., & McGrath, J. E. (1993). Membership matters: How member change and continuity affect small group structure, process, and performance. *Small Group Research, 24*, 334–361.

Berger, J., Rosenholtz, S. J., & Zelditch, M., Jr. (1980). Status organizing processes. *Annual Review of Sociology, 6*, 479–508.

Biernat, M., & Fuegen, K. (2001). Shifting standards and the evaluation of competence: Complexity in gender-based judgment and decision making. *Journal of Social Issues, 57*, 707–724.

Biernat, M., & Vescio, T. K. (2002). She swings, she hits, she's great, she's benched: Implications of gender-based shifting standards for judgment and behavior. *Personality and Social Psychology Bulletin, 28*, 66–77.

Borgida, E., Rudman, L. A., & Manteufel, L. L. (1995). On the courtroom use and misuse of gender stereotyping research. *Journal of Social Issues, 51*, 181–192.

Brandon, D. P., & Hollingshead, A. B. (2004). Transactive memory systems in organizations: Matching tasks, expertise and people. *Organization Science, 15*(6), 633–645.

Clark, H. H., & Marshall, C. (1981). Definite reference and mutual knowledge. In: A. Joshi, I. Sag & B. Webber (Eds), *Elements of discourse understanding* (pp. 10–63). Cambridge: Cambridge University Press.

Darley, J. M., & Gross, P. H. (1983). A hypothesis-confirming bias in labeling effects. *Journal of Personality and Social Psychology, 44*, 20–33.

Driskell, J., & Mullen, B. (1990). Status, expectations, and behavior: A meta-analytic review and test of the theory. *Personality and Social Psychology Bulletin, 16*, 541–553.

Eagly, A. H. (1987). *Sex differences in social behavior: A social role approach*. Mahwah, NJ: Lawrence Erlbaum Associates.

Foddy, M., & Smithson, M. (1999). Can gender inequalities be eliminated? *Social Psychology Quarterly, 62*, 307–324.

Foschi, M. (2000). Double standards for competence: Theory and research. *Annual Review of Sociology, 26*, 21–42.

Fussell, S. R., & Krauss, R. M. (1992). Coordination of knowledge in communication: Effects of speakers' assumptions about what others know. *Journal of Personality and Social Psychology, 62*, 378–391.

Hattrup, K., & Yates, J. F. (1996). Effects of procedural and outcome accountability on judgment quality. *Organizational Behavior and Human Division Processes, 65*, 1–17.

Hollingshead, A. B. (1996). Information suppression and status persistence in group decision making: The effects of communication media. *Human Communication Research, 23*(2), 193–219.

Hollingshead, A. B. (1998a). Retrieval processes in transactive memory systems. *Journal of Personality and Social Psychology, 74*, 659–671.

Hollingshead, A. B. (1998b). Communication, learning, and retrieval in transactive memory systems. *Journal of Experimental Social Psychology, 34*, 423–442.

Hollingshead, A. B. (2000). Perceptions of expertise and transactive memory in work relationships. *Group Processes and Intergroup Relations, 3*, 257–267.

Hollingshead, A. B. (2001). Cognitive interdependence and convergent expectations in transactive memory. *Journal of Personality and Social Psychology, 81*, 1080–1089.

Hollingshead, A. B., & Fraidin, S. N. (2003). Gender stereotypes and assumptions about expertise in transactive memory. *Journal of Experimental Social Psychology, 39*, 355–363.

Hollingshead, A.B., & Fraidin, S.N. (in preparation). Acceptance of expertise claims: Amount and type of supporting information.

Krauss, R. M., & Fussell, S. R. (1991). Constructing shared communicative environments. In: L. B. Resnick, J. M. Levine & S. D. Teasley (Eds), *Perspectives on socially shared cognition* (pp. 172–200). Washington, DC: American Psychological Association.

Kruger, J., & Dunning, D. (1999). Unskilled and unaware of it: How difficulties in recognizing one's own incompetence lead to inflated self-assessments. *Journal of Personality and Social Psychology, 77*, 1121–1134.

Latané, B. (1981). The psychology of social impact. *American Psychologist, 36*, 343–356.

Lerner, J., & Tetlock, P. E. (1999). Accounting for the effects of accountability. *Psychological Bulletin, 125*, 255–275.

Littlepage, G., Robison, W., & Reddington, K. (1997). Effects of task experience and group experience on group performance, member ability, and recognition of expertise. *Organizational Behavior and Human Decision Processes, 69*, 133–147.

Macrae, N. C., Milne, A. B., & Bodenhausen, G. V. (1994). Stereotypes as energy-saving devices: A peek inside the cognitive toolbox. *Journal of Personality and Social Psychology, 66*, 37–47.

Moreland, R. L. (1999). Transactive memory: Learning who knows what in work groups and organizations. In: L. Thompson, D. Messick & J. Levine (Eds), *Sharing knowledge in organizations*. Mahwah, NJ: Lawrence Erlbaum Associates.

Nelson, T. E., Biernat, M. R., & Manis, M. (1990). Everyday base rates (sex stereotypes): Potent and resilient. *Journal of Personality and Social Psychology, 59*, 664–675.

Neuberg, S. L., & Fiske, S. T. (1987). Motivational influences on impression formation: Outcome dependency, accuracy-driven attention, and individuating processes. *Journal of Personality and Social Psychology, 53*, 431–444.

Oldmeadow, J. A., Platow, M. J., Foddy, M., & Anderson, D. (2003). Self-categorization, status, and social influence. *Social Psychology Quarterly, 66*, 138–152.

Plaks, J. E., & Higgins, E. T. (2000). Pragmatic use of stereotyping in teamwork: Social loafing and compensation as a function of inferred partner-situation fit. *Journal of Personality and Social Psychology, 79*, 962–974.

Ridgeway, C. L., & Berger, J. (1986). Expectations, legitimation, and dominance behavior in task groups. *American Sociological Review, 51*, 603–617.

Ridgeway, C. L., & Smith-Lovin, L. (1999). The gender system and interaction. *Annual Review of Sociology, 25*, 191–216.

Ridgeway, C. L., Boyle, E. H., Kuipers, K. J., & Robinson, D. T. (1998). How do status beliefs develop? The role of resources and interactional experience. *American Sociological Review, 63*, 331–350.

Siegel-Jacobs, K., & Yates, J. F. (1996). Effects of procedural and outcome accountability on judgement quality. *Organizational Behavior and Human Decision Processes, 65*, 1–17.

Tversky, A., & Kahneman, D. (1974). Judgment under uncertainty: Heuristics and biases. *Science, 185*, 1124–1131.

Webster, M., Jr., & Driskell, J. E., Jr. (1978). Status generalization: A review and some new data. *American Sociological Review, 43*, 220–236.

Wegner, D. M. (1987). Transactive memory: A contemporary analysis of the group mind. In: B. Mullen & G. R. Goethals (Eds), *Theories of group behavior* (pp. 185–208). New York: Springer-Verlag.

Wegner, D. M., Guiliano, T., & Hertel, P. T. (1985). Cognitive interdependence in close relationships. In: W. J. Ickes (Ed.), *Compatible and incompatible relationships* (pp. 253–276). New York: Springer-Verlag.

Wegner, D. M., Erber, R., & Raymond, P. (1991). Transactive memory in close relationships. *Journal of Personality and Social Psychology, 61*, 923–929.

Wittenbaum, G. M., Vaughan, S. I., & Stasser, G. (1998). Coordination in task-performing groups. In: R. S. Tindale, et al. (Eds), *Theory and research on small groups* (pp. 177–204). New York: Plenum Press.

Wood, W., & Karten, S. J. (1986). Sex differences in interaction style as a product of perceived sex differences in competence. *Journal of Personality and Social Psychology, 50*, 341–347.

Yoon, K., Gupta, N., Hollingshead, A.B., & Hinkle, A. (2003). Judging competence in the workplace: A comparison of information sharing methods. Paper presented at the *International communication association meeting*, San Diego (May).

Zemore, S. E., Fiske, S. T., & Kim, H. (2000). Gender stereotypes and the dynamics of social interaction. In: T. Eckes & H. M. Trautner (Eds), *The developmental social psychology of gender* (pp. 207–242). Mahwah, NJ: Lawrence Erlbaum Associates.

MEMBER STATUS AND INFORMATION EXCHANGE IN DECISION-MAKING GROUPS

Gwen M. Wittenbaum and Jonathan M. Bowman

ABSTRACT

Two decades of research have identified a robust effect: Members of decision-making groups mention and repeat shared information that all members know more so than unshared information that a single member knows. This chapter explores the idea that processes related to member status both affect and explain information exchange in decision-making groups. First, we offer five propositions that identify information sharing patterns and their implications for high- and low-status group members. Second, we highlight three theoretical explanations for the group preference for shared information and examine how well each theory accounts for the proposed member status processes.

Organizations increasingly are entrusting important decisions to small groups (Devine, Clayton, Philips, Dunford, & Melner, 1999). Such a trend may benefit the organization if group members effectively pool their unique knowledge and expertise. The sharing of novel information in decision-making groups can potentially lead to better decisions by groups than by

Status and Groups
Research on Managing Groups and Teams, Volume 7, 143–168

ISSN: 1534-0856/doi:10.1016/S1534-0856(05)07007-6

individuals. Research, however, suggests that group members inadequately exchange information. Discussions tend to focus on *shared information* that all members know rather than *unshared information* that a single member knows (Christensen, Abbot, & Franz, 1998; Cruz, Boster, & Rodriguez, 1997; Dennis, 1996a, b; Devine, 1999; Franz & Larson Jr., 2002; Kelly & Karau, 1999; Lam & Schaubroeck, 2000; Larson Jr., Christensen, Abbot, & Franz, 1996; Larson Jr., Christensen, Abbot, & Franz, 1998a; Larson Jr., Foster-Fishman, & Franz, 1998b; Larson Jr., Foster-Fishman, & Keys, 1994; Lavery, Franz, Winquist, & Larson Jr., 1999; Parks & Cowlin, 1995; Savadori, Van Swol, & Sniezek, 2001; Schittekatte & Van Hiel, 1996; Stasser, Taylor, & Hanna, 1989; Stasser & Titus, 1987; Stasser, Vaughan, & Stewart, 2000; Stewart & Stasser, 1995; Van Hiel & Schittekatte, 1998; Winquist & Larson, 1998; Wittenbaum, 1998; Wittenbaum, 2000). Members not only favor mentioning more shared than unshared information, but they also prefer to repeat shared over unshared information once it has already been mentioned (Larson Jr. et al., 1996; Larson Jr. et al., 1994; Larson Jr. et al., 1998a; Parks & Cowlin, 1995; Savadori et al., 2001; Schittekatte & Van Hiel, 1996; Stasser et al., 1989; Winquist & Larson, 1998). Although most of the research has been conducted on college student samples, other research has demonstrated the preference for shared information in medical decision-making teams (e.g., Larson Jr. et al., 1996, 1998a) and in groups of mid-level managers (Lam & Schaubroeck, 2000). The conclusion from two decades of research is clear: Groups are not the reliable conduits for information exchange that we may expect.

Poor information exchange in groups would not be a problem if decision quality remained unaffected. Unfortunately, failure to discuss unshared information will hurt the quality of the group's decision, if it is critical for determining the optimal decision alternative. Such is the case when information is distributed among members as a *hidden profile* (e.g., Stasser et al., 1989; Stasser & Titus, 1987). In a hidden profile, the shared information largely supports a suboptimal decision alternative, whereas the unshared information supports the optimal decision alternative. For such tasks, group members enter discussion preferring a suboptimal alternative and only discover the best alternative by thoroughly discussing their unshared knowledge (Winquist & Larson, 1998). Therefore, the concern about groups neglecting unshared information during discussion is legitimate: In doing so, group decision quality will suffer if the information is distributed as a hidden profile. Although some have questioned the pervasiveness of hidden profiles in applied settings (e.g., Winquist & Larson Jr., 1998; Wittenbaum, Hollingshead, & Botero, 2004), this research area raises the concern that work group decisions suffer as a result of ineffective information exchange.

Group problems with information exchange may be exacerbated by differences among group members in *status*, the prestige and perceived task competence accorded to members. In all likelihood, natural work groups contain members who differ in their status. Even in initially status-undifferentiated groups, status differences emerge quickly and automatically (e.g., Berger, Fisek, Norman, & Zelditch Jr., 1977). Members higher in status are considered to be more task competent than lower-status members and are afforded luxuries, such as additional speaking time and influence over the group decision (e.g., Berger, Rosenholtz, & Zelditch Jr., 1980; Dovidio, Brown, Heltman, Ellyson, & Keating, 1988; Kirchler & Davis, 1986). As a consequence, what may be the fate of unshared information held by low-status members? Members of low status may hold valuable expert knowledge, but if their opportunities to communicate such knowledge are limited, then group decision quality likely will suffer. If decision-making groups are to function effectively, high-status members must welcome the unshared information of low-status members.

This chapter explores the role of member status in the collective information sharing process, offering five propositions about the role of group member status in information exchange. Existing theory and research provide support for these propositions. In addition, we identify three theoretical explanations for the collective preference for shared information and highlight the ability of each to account for status effects. Finally, we describe remaining questions that beg future research.

PROPOSITIONS AND FINDINGS

A decade after Stasser and Titus (1985) published their first information sharing study, researchers began asking how members within a group differ in their sharing of information (for a review, see Wittenbaum & Stasser, 1996). Some researchers varied member status within groups as *diffuse status characteristics* that were indirectly or not related to the group task, such as member sex (e.g., Propp, 1995; Wittenbaum, 1996). Other researchers varied *specific status characteristics* that were directly task related, such as leader status (e.g., Larson Jr. et al., 1994), member task experience (e.g., Wittenbaum, 1998), expertise (e.g., Franz & Larson Jr., 2002), and cognitive centrality (e.g., Kameda, Ohtsubo, & Takezawa, 1997). Also helpful in understanding the role of status in information sharing are studies examining the effects of group status composition (e.g., Hollingshead, 1996). The findings of these and other studies will be reviewed and used to develop five propositions about status processes and information exchange in decision-making groups.

The propositions identified herein synthesize and integrate existing literature rather than introduce new findings or theories. Based on this prior literature, we conclude that (a) high-status members communicate more total information than low-status members; (b) high-status members show less discussion bias toward shared information compared to low-status members; (c) unshared information communicated by a high-status member is more likely repeated and remembered by others than that of low-status members; (d) communicating much-shared knowledge increases a group member's status; and (e) members may deliberately communicate more shared than unshared information to gain status. The research used to develop these propositions has examined member status under conditions that likely constrain the occurrence of the proposed effects. For example, in most of the reviewed studies, members were unfamiliar with each other and the group's task, they did not know which items of information were shared and which were unshared, and member status often was not related to task-related expertise. Under these conditions, shared information may be particularly important and influential because it can validate members' knowledge when they feel uncertain and inexperienced. Our purpose is not to generate universal propositions that hold for all decision-making groups. Rather, we wish to summarize current knowledge about member status and information exchange in newly formed and short-lived decision-making groups of strangers. We suggest some factors that may moderate the proposed effects throughout and in the concluding section.

The Amount of Information Shared

In heterogeneous status groups, high-status members tend to dominate the conversation by talking and initiating communication more often than low-status members (e.g., Berger et al., 1977; Berger et al., 1980; Silver, Cohen, & Crutchfield, 1994). It seems natural to expect that when communication largely requires information exchange, high-status group members will contribute more information than those with low status. Research on collective information sharing largely supports this idea.

Propp (1995) examined the effects of member sex on information exchange and found support for the notion that high-status members share more information. Member sex can be used as a status characteristic when other, more task relevant cues are absent in the situation (Berger et al., 1980; Ridgeway & Diekema, 1992). Generally, men are presumed to be more task competent and are given more opportunities to guide the group as compared to women. The empirical literature shows that women in mixed-sex interactions talk less and have less influence than men (e.g., Dovidio et al., 1988; Eagly, 1983; Kelly, Wildman, & Urey, 1982). As such, Propp predicted that men would share more information in mixed-sex groups compared to women. She composed four-person groups of two women and two men, and randomly assigned group members to one of three levels of information redundancy. In the common condition, all members read the same information about the decision alternatives. In the shared-by-half condition, members shared half of the information in common, and in the unshared condition, each group member held unique information. Results showed that men mentioned more information than women, and this effect was strongest in the unshared condition. This finding supports the idea that high-status members dominated discussion by sharing more information than low-status members.

Interestingly, this sex difference was not replicated by Wittenbaum (1996). Like Propp (1995), she assigned two men and two women to four-person, mixed-sex groups. Members read information about two hypothetical job candidates and decided as a group which one to hire. All group members read some shared and unshared information. Overall, men did not mention more information about the job candidates than women did. However, men did repeat more information than women. Therefore, the greater information contributions of men may lie largely in their repetition of information, a behavior that may indicate a member's desire to emphasize information because of its presumed importance. Propp did not distinguish information repeated from information mentioned. So, it is difficult to determine whether the higher rate of mentioning information by men in her study was driven by their tendency to repeat information after it had been mentioned at least once. Even though returning to a previously mentioned piece of information may signal-added attention to it, relative to information mentioned just once, both mentioning and repeating information are indications of greater talk in the group, something expected for high-status group members.

Franz and Larson Jr. (2002) examined the effect of member expertise as a status characteristic. They composed three-person groups of men who read information about two college running backs and chose one to play on a National Football League team. Each group was composed of one expert who held more knowledge about football than the other two non-expert members. Members either knew or did not know which one was the expert in the group. Results revealed the expected expertise effect: Expert members mentioned more of their information than non-expert members, especially when the experts were known by others. A similar finding was reported by Thomas-Hunt, Ogden, and Neale (2003). The fact that experts talked more when their expert status was known is consistent with a status characteristics perspective (e.g., Berger et al., 1977). When members knew who the expert was, they made adjustments to allow the expert more opportunities to contribute information to discussion. In this way, members used their expectations about which member was task competent to create opportunities for the presumed competent member to demonstrate his competence. Expectations about who was competent became self-fulfilled: Known experts gained higher status because of the discussion opportunities afforded to them.

Larson Jr. et al. (1996) explored differences between leaders and non-leader members in information mentioned and repeated. Although leaders tend to have higher status than non-leaders, the concept of leadership is more complex. Leaders also tend to have more power than non-leaders and may be more responsible for the group's outcome relative to others in the group. Nevertheless, higher status may be inferred from a member's assigned or acquired role as group leader. Larson Jr. et al. (1996) had three-person teams, composed of a resident, intern, and medical student, read information about a hypothetical diagnosis case and decide the correct diagnosis. The resident was the most experienced and knowledgeable member of the group and thus served as leader to the intern and medical student. Like the men in Wittenbaum's (1996) study, leaders repeated more total information compared to non-leader members. Botero and Wittenbaum (2003) reported a similar repetition effect for leaders. High-status members used their speaking time to emphasize information that had previously been mentioned.

Finally, informational centrality may be used as a status cue. Some group members know proportionally a lot of shared, relative to unshared, information compared to other members. Those with much-shared knowledge are known as cognitively central members (Kameda et al., 1997). Other members with little-shared knowledge and much unique knowledge are known as cognitively peripheral members. To the extent that a member holds shared knowledge with others, that member can more easily facilitate communication and form a common ground. Thus, cognitively central members are expected to hold the higher-status position and dominate discussion more than cognitively peripheral members. Sargis and Larson Jr.

(2002) tested this idea using three-person groups composed either of a target member who was central or one who was peripheral. They found that cognitively central members talked more than peripheral ones, largely because the latter members withdrew from talking. Talk in this case consisted of number of speaking turns, time-spent talking, and information-based comments. This finding is consistent with the notion that high-status members communicate more information than low-status members.

Regardless of whether status was defined by member sex, expertise, leadership, or cognitive centrality, being highly regarded in a heterogeneous status group was associated with greater participation and communication of information compared to being less well regarded. Sometimes the greater participation of high-status members was manifested as higher first mentions of information and sometimes as higher repetitions of information compared to low-status members. Both are examples of communicating information and thus support the development of the following proposition:

Proposition 1. In mixed-status, decision-making groups, high-status members will communicate more information than low-status members.

The Bias Toward Shared Information

Although the tendency for groups to favor shared information during discussion is robust, the pervasiveness of the discussion bias likely varies across members. High-status members should be less prone to favor shared over unshared information during discussion. Communicating unshared information can be viewed as a risky action for members (Wittenbaum & Park, 2001; Wittenbaum & Stasser, 1996). As no other member can verify unshared knowledge when it is mentioned, members must feel quite confident in the accuracy and relevance of that information to communicate it and particularly to repeat it. Also, members who are judged by others as competent may be afforded the opportunity and credibility necessary for emphasizing unshared information. High-status members are more likely than lower-status members to possess the confidence and credibility to manage unshared knowledge in decision-making groups. Evidence from several experiments supports this idea.

In two separate experiments, Wittenbaum (1998, 2000) composed four-person groups of two members with prior task experience and two without such experience. Groups chose between two hypothetical job candidates, a task that was similar to one that experienced members had completed prior to discussion. Results showed that group members' tendency to mention more shared than unshared information was evidenced only by inexperienced members. Experienced members mentioned shared and unshared information equally often. Even though most groups also tend to repeat more shared than unshared information, experienced members showed the opposite effect: They repeated more unshared than shared information (Wittenbaum, 1998). Experienced members embraced the high-status position in the group; they felt more task capable and were judged by others as more task competent compared to inexperienced members. These findings are consistent with the notion that unshared information is favored by members who have the status to risk emphasizing it, and shared information is favored more by low-status members.

Leaders of decision-making groups showed a similar pattern of behavior to experienced members. In medical decision-making teams, the team leader repeated unshared diagnosis information increasingly as discussion progressed (Larson Jr. et al., 1996, 1998a). During the later parts of discussion, leaders repeated more unshared knowledge compared to non-leaders. Directive, as opposed to participative leaders, were particularly likely to repeat unshared over shared information (Larson Jr. et al., 1998). Leaders adopted a role where they took responsibility for returning the group to previously mentioned unshared information, almost as if they did not want the group to miss this information.

In Savadori et al.'s (2001) experiment, judges in the Judge Advisory System functioned as group leaders. Judges were responsible for obtaining information from advisors in order to make the group's decision. Their control over the group outcome likely gave them greater status in the group relative to advisors. As such, judges emphasized unshared knowledge more than advisors. Advisors mentioned and repeated more shared than unshared information, the typical discussion bias. However, judges did not favor shared information when they mentioned or repeated their contributions. The high-status judges demonstrated a different pattern of information use than lower-status advisors, with the former using more unshared and less shared knowledge than the latter.

As Franz and Larson Jr. (2002) showed, known experts mentioned more information and manifested the higher-status position in the group relative to non-expert members. Whereas, their report did not include a test of whether experts mentioned or repeated more unshared information than non-expert members, the report of Thomas-Hunt and Burris (2003) did. In four-person teams, Thomas-Hunt and Burris had members rank 12 items in order of importance for survival in an Australian bushfire. One member of the team was given additional unique information that made that member an expert, and their expert status either was or was not acknowledged to other team members. During discussion, acknowledged experts contributed more unique information than unacknowledged experts. This study, like Franz and Larson's Jr. (2002), points to the importance of others' knowledge of one's expertise in order for expert members to fulfill the high-status position in the group.

Insight into the effect of member expertise also can be inferred from experiments that induced it at the group level. Stasser, Stewart, and Wittenbaum (1995), and Stewart and Stasser (1995) composed three-person groups of members who each held additional unshared knowledge about a particular decision alternative. Either all members knew the expert roles of one another or they did not. When members' expert roles were known, groups discussed more unshared information and solved a hidden profile task better than when members were not explicitly assigned such expertise. Although the data did not allow a direct comparison between the information sharing of known and unknown experts, we would expect that members widely recognized as experts would offer more unshared information during discussion, compared to members whose expertise is unknown by self and others.

In another study of group composition, Hollingshead (1996) provided one member in a three-person group with more critical, unshared information for solving a homicide investigation. In half of the groups, the member with the key, unshared information for solving the homicide investigation was low in status (i.e., a freshman from an introductory course), and in the other half of groups, the information-rich member was of equal status (i.e., an upper-level communication student like the others). The ability of the group to discover the best decision alternative in this hidden profile task was possible if the information-rich member contributed his/her critical, unshared information. The most informed member had more actual and perceived influence on the group decision (thus improving it) and contributed more critical information when of equal rather than low status. This study demonstrated the barrier that low status can be in getting critical, unshared information into the group discussion. However, Phillips, Mannix, Neale, and Gruenfeld (2004) suggested that when the information-rich member in a three-person group is a stranger and the other two, information-poor members are friends, the information-rich member's unshared information is repeated more than when she shares a friendship with one information-poor member. The authors reasoned that members expect strangers to contribute novel information but not friends; when friends violate that expectation, it distracts members from performing the task well. We wonder, then, whether information-rich, low-status members are especially unlikely to communicate unshared information when they share a friendship with another member.

The aforementioned studies suggest that the group discussion bias favoring shared over unshared information is less pervasive for higher-status members. Higher status in the group was associated with less bias toward shared over unshared information during discussion compared to lower-status members. This was the case for status characteristics such as task experience, leadership, and expertise. We offer the following proposition:

> **Proposition 2.** In mixed-status, decision-making groups, high-status members will be less prone to favor communicating shared over unshared information compared to low-status members.

The Valuing of Unshared Information

The fate of unshared information may depend on who communicates it. As unshared information cannot be verified by others as accurate, its importance may be augmented when a high-status member communicates it. If the speaker is considered task capable and credible, then unshared knowledge may be more readily accepted, remembered, and used by other members. Also, high-status members may be more convincing than low-status members when they mention their unshared information. For this reason, unshared information likely has greater impact and value when mentioned by a high rather than a low-status member.

Two experiments suggest that unshared information is better retained in the memory of recipients when mentioned by a high-status member. Wittenbaum (2000) gave group members an unexpected recognition task after discussion. Members were asked to identify whether each listed item of information was correct or incorrect. Half of the items were listed correctly as they originally appeared in the application materials for the hypothetical job candidates. The other half were foils, incorrect versions of similar information in the applications. Wittenbaum compared the recognition of unshared information by members with and without prior task experience. Results showed that inexperienced members correctly recognized the unshared information of experienced members better than experienced members recognized the unshared information of inexperienced members. This finding was not due to inexperienced members having overall better recognition performance than experienced members. This memory effect suggests that the unshared information of high status, experienced members had greater impact than that of lower status, inexperienced members.

A similar finding was reported by Stewart and Stasser (1995). They gave group members an unexpected post discussion recognition task similar to that used by Wittenbaum (2000). They compared the recognition performance of groups with and without known experts. Unshared information that was mentioned by known experts was better recognized after discussion, than that mentioned by members not recognized as experts. This finding, along with that of Wittenbaum (2000), suggests that unshared information is met with some skepticism and perhaps valued less when mentioned by a low-status member.

Another index of the extent to which group members value unshared information is whether it is repeated by those members who did not originally possess the information. Thomas-Hunt and Burris (2003) predicted that the unshared information of the lone expert in a four-person team would be emphasized by other members more when that expert's status was known rather than unknown. Indeed, they found that unique knowledge contributed by an acknowledged expert was repeated by others more than that of an unacknowledged expert. In ad hoc groups such as theirs, immediate recognition of a member's expertise solidifies that member's higher status early on and ensures that their unshared information is valued. We offer the following proposition:

> **Proposition 3.** In mixed-status, decision-making groups, unshared information communicated by high-status members will be remembered and repeated by others more than that communicated by low-status members.

The Implications for Communicating Information

The communication of information acquires additional importance when related to outcomes such as decision influence and member evaluations. In general, high-status members have greater impact on the group's decision than lower-status members. For example, Kirchler and Davis (1986) found that the decision preferences of high-status members were more likely adopted by the group, than those of lower-status members, when the task was judgmental (i.e., a matter of opinion). Likewise, the communication of information has implications for member influence and evaluations. Specifically, we argue that communicating much shared relative to unshared information can result in greater decisional influence and positive evaluations of member competence.

Managers create decision-making teams composed of members with heterogeneous expertise. The assumption underlying this strategy is that unshared knowledge is more valuable and important to communicate than shared information. If the group's only concern is task performance, this may be the case. When information is distributed as a hidden profile, discussing unshared information will help members overcome their initially incorrect preferences. Communicating shared information, however, yields benefits as well. Shared knowledge helps members create a common ground, which allows them to more easily and comfortably communicate and connect (Clark & Brennan, 1991). Shared information can also be socially validated (Festinger, 1954), others can confirm or disconfirm its accuracy and importance. According to Wittenbaum and Park (2001), the social validation benefits associated with mentioning shared information can yield evaluative advantages for communicators of such information.

Wittenbaum, Hubbell, and Zuckerman (1999) tested the evaluative benefits connected with mentioning shared knowledge. They assigned two-person groups (i.e., dyads) to discuss information about hypothetical job candidates. Both dyadic members read the same (i.e., shared) or different (i.e., unshared) information about the job candidates. When dyads discussed shared information, they rated each other after discussion as more task capable, compared to dyads that discussed unshared information. Wittenbaum et al. (1999) claimed that this *mutual enhancement* effect occurred because of a social validation process.

Wittenbaum and Bowman (2004) provided more direct evidence in support of a social validation explanation for mutual enhancement. Like Wittenbaum et al. (1999), they assigned dyads to discuss information that was either shared or unshared. During discussion, dyads recalled information about hypothetical job candidates with recall accuracy either emphasized or not. They found that mutual enhancement occurred for dyads that had a higher, rather than lower, concern for recall accuracy. Wittenbaum and Bowman argued that when accuracy demands were higher, members had a need to verify the legitimacy of information. In this case, shared information could be validated successfully by others, whereas, unshared information could not. Therefore, members who communicated information that could be verified as accurate (i.e., those who mentioned shared information) were judged as more competent than members who said nothing that could be verified as correct (i.e., those who mentioned unshared information). Thus, group members who communicate much shared information may reap positive social rewards, especially when members value informational accuracy. By mentioning shared information, members may increase their status in the eyes of other group members.

Members who are cognitively central possess proportionally more shared information and less unshared information compared to other members. As a result, central members are especially likely to communicate a lot of shared knowledge during discussion. Members who are cognitively central may benefit from the increased status that results from contributing much shared information to discussion. Kameda et al. (1997) tested this idea by having three-person groups discuss and decide which prisoner was more eligible for parole. They composed groups of two members who preferred the same decision alternative (i.e., the majority) and one who preferred a different alternative (i.e., the minority). Group members read a combination of shared and unshared information with the minority member receiving proportionally more (i.e., central) or less (i.e., peripheral) shared knowledge. Results showed that the minority member influenced the group decision more, when cognitively central than peripheral. The results of Kameda et al. (1997) support the idea that communicating shared knowledge increases one's status and influence in a decision-making group. In addition, cognitively peripheral members may have less decision influence because they engage in fewer speaking turns and offer less information than cognitively central members (Sargis & Larson Jr., 2002).

Given the apparent superiority of being cognitively central, the findings of Larson Jr., Sargis, Elstein, and Schwartz (2002) are surprising: Cognitively peripheral members were judged as more influential than cognitively central members. In that study, it is possible that members' high amount of expertise may have equalized the effects of cognitive centrality. As mentioned earlier, it is important to note that the benefits of communicating shared information likely vary by context. For example, when members have clear roles based on expertise, or when unshared information is more important or diagnostic for determining the better decision alternative, shared information may seem relatively less important to group members (e.g., Stasser et al., 1995). When members are known experts, others may expect them to communicate much unshared knowledge congruent with their expertise. Therefore, some factors may moderate the effects of cognitive centrality and communication of shared information on decision-making influence and member perceptions. In general, with no other salient status cues in newly formed groups of strangers, the following should hold:

Proposition 4. Increasing the proportion of shared, relative to unshared, information communicated augments the status and influence of a decision-making group member.

Strategic Acquisition of Status

If communicating proportionally much shared, relative to unshared, information increases a group member's status, then members, if aware of this fact, may deliberately share information to acquire status. Wittenbaum, Hollingshead, and Bowman (2003) proposed that members of decision-making groups strategically communicate information to satisfy group and personal goals. Although members of work groups often have task-related goals (e.g., to make a good group decision or influence the decision), they also hold social goals (e.g., to maintain cohesiveness or gain status). Historically, researchers who investigate information sharing in groups have been more preoccupied with members' task goals rather than social goals. Special focus has been on how collective information sharing influences group decision quality rather than member relations or social dynamics. Also, researchers have been interested more in how status affects collective information exchange rather than how communicating information affects members' status. Research on mutual enhancement (e.g., Wittenbaum & Bowman, 2004; Wittenbaum et al., 1999; Wittenbaum & Park, 2001) and cognitive centrality (e.g., Kameda et al., 1997; Sargis & Larson Jr., 2002) has demonstrated that, at least under some conditions, communicating shared knowledge elevates members' status and influence in decision-making groups. The next question is whether members intentionally manage information in order to gain status. To date, no research has investigated this question. However, recent research by Wittenbaum et al. (2003) demonstrated that members of decision-making groups strategically share information to influence the group decision.

Wittenbaum et al. (2003) distributed information about three hypothetical cholesterol reducing drugs to members of three-person groups. Information, and monetary incentives, given to the member made each prefer a different drug before discussion. Although members had an additional group level incentive to select the best drug to market, individual incentives to get their preferred drug adopted by the group largely influenced members' information sharing behavior. Members discussed information about the drugs while viewing sheets containing the information; they did not have to rely on memory to retrieve items for discussion. This procedure aided members' ability to selectively choose some items and not others for mentioning. Results from this experiment showed that members favored preference-consistent information during discussion and framed their communication of this information to make their preferred drug seem especially good (and others' preferred drugs seem especially bad). Members preferred to frame unshared information strategically over shared information, probably because other members could not verify the veracity of the information when communicated. The member who was most influential in the group was the one who engaged in more strategic framing of preference-consistent unshared information.

These results cannot be explained, as due to biased recall, because members had the information in front of them during the entire discussion. As they knew which information items were shared and unshared, members could deliberately select some items and not others to mention in order to satisfy their personal goal to influence the group (and gain a monetary reward). These findings suggest that group members are strategic in how they share information. A logical next step is to test whether members are equally strategic when their goal is a social one: To attain status in the group.

We expect that if members are aware that communicating shared knowledge elevates one's status, then members will deliberately select this information for mentioning, if possible, and bypass unshared knowledge in order to elevate their social standing. In this way, member status can emerge as an outcome of group information exchange. Similar to Proposition 4, we expect that members will bias communication toward shared information in order to increase their status under limiting conditions: When members are equal-status strangers in newly formed groups with no task experience or salient status cues such as known expertise. When members feel relatively uncertain about the group task and their roles vis-à-vis each other, communicating much shared knowledge may be a way to demonstrate that they are contributing truthful and relevant information. In addition, in order for members to bias their selection of information, they must have a sense of which items are shared and which are unshared. Under these conditions, if members have a motivation to co-operate with other members and attain respect from them, they may intentionally communicate shared knowledge. For these limiting conditions, the following proposition should hold:

> **Proposition 5.** Members of decision-making groups will intentionally select shared over unshared information to communicate in order to acquire status.

Summary

Two decades of research has identified a reliable effect: Decision-making groups discuss more shared than unshared information. Our review of the literature suggests that group member status can exacerbate this discussion bias. Low-status members are more prone to favor shared over unshared information during discussion than are higher-status members (Proposition 2). In fact, lower-status members may intentionally favor shared information while communicating (Proposition 5), because doing so increases their influence and status within the group (Proposition 4). If a low-status member does communicate unshared information, it will not be remembered and repeated to the extent of that communicated by higher-status members (Proposition 3).

Based on this logic, low-status group members may gain status and influence in the group by initially favoring shared information. Then, once credibility and greater status are established, the member may risk communicating unshared information that other members cannot verify as accurate. This strategy yields hope that an information-rich, low-status member can benefit the group's decision in a hidden profile task: By favoring shared information initially during discussion, the member may gain the status necessary to contribute unshared knowledge that subsequently improves the group decision quality.

As member status influences and potentially exacerbates the group discussion bias favoring shared information, it is important that any theoretical explanation for this discussion bias incorporate member status processes. The following section identifies three main theoretical explanations for the discussion bias and the ability of each to account for the member status effects proposed herein.

THEORETICAL EXPLANATIONS FOR THE DISCUSSION BIAS

Three major explanations have been offered for why groups favor shared over unshared information during discussion: (a) shared information has a higher probability for being recalled; (b) members evaluate information in the hidden profile paradigm in a preference-consistent manner; and (c) shared information provides members with social validation. Each explanation has strengths and limitations. We will review each explanation and identify the ability of each to account for processes related to member status as identified in the five propositions.

Collective Information Sampling Model

Stasser (1992) first explained the discussion bias in favor of shared information as due to probability. According to Stasser's information sampling model, information is randomly sampled for discussion from members' minds. The model presumes that group members will mention any piece of information that they recall. So, increasing the memorability of an item of information increases the likelihood of its being mentioned and therefore discussed by the group. In addition, increasing the number of group members who know a piece of information increases the likelihood that the information will be discussed. If information is randomly sampled from members' memories, then shared information is more likely than unshared to be discussed because there are more members' minds from which shared information can be sampled. As a result, shared information has a "sampling advantage" over unshared information. Following from Stasser's model, the process of group members discussing information became known as information "sampling." However, we prefer to use the terms "information sharing" or "information exchange" because we believe the process involves more than simple probability.

According to Stasser's (1992) model, the sampling advantage of shared information can be mathematically demonstrated when holding constant many factors that typically vary in natural groups. For example, the model assumes that all items of information are equally memorable and all members are equally likely to mention information. As a result, the collective information sampling model cannot account for differences between members in information sharing. Propositions 1 and 2 predict, respectively, that high-status members will communicate more information and be less prone to favor communicating shared over unshared information compared to low-status members. These propositions violate the model's assumption of equal participation among members. Therefore, Stasser's model is incapable of explaining why some members favor shared information more than others.

In addition, Stasser's (1992) model presumes that information sharing is an unbiased and cooperative process that involves communicating recalled information. Members' only presumed goal is to reach the best group decision, and they have no incentives to act in accord with personal interests. As members are assumed to randomly sample information from memory, the information sampling model does not allow for members to strategically mention some items of information in order to gain status (Proposition 5).

The model also focuses exclusively on whether information is mentioned or not, rather than the additional strategic frames that members may place on information when mentioned. To its credit, the purpose of the model is not to predict information discussion in natural group settings but rather to show that probability alone can explain the discussion bias under certain (albeit unnatural) conditions. Nevertheless, the model is unqualified to explain status processes in collective information sharing.

Preference-Consistent Evaluation of Information

Greitemeyer and Schulz-Hardt (2003) proposed that group members favor shared information during the discussion of a hidden profile because their pre-discussion preferences are associated with shared information. In a hidden profile task, shared information supports a sub-optimal alternative, whereas unshared information supports the best alternative. As a result, preferences for alternatives are confounded with information type (shared versus unshared). Greitemeyer and Schulz-Hardt demonstrated that group members evaluate preference-consistent (i.e., mostly shared) information more favorably than preference-inconsistent (i.e., mostly unshared) information. As shared information largely supports members' initial preferences, it is evaluated as more important and therefore more worthy of discussion than unshared information. Attempts to improve the quality of group decisions in a hidden profile task are difficult because members are driven to maintain their initial preferences. When they later encounter unshared information (e.g., during discussion) that counters their prevailing preference, members may devalue that information in order to preserve their initial preferences.

Greitemeyer and Schulz-Hardt (2003) claimed that the dominance of shared information during discussion and poor group performance on a hidden profile task can be explained solely as an individual level cognitive bias. Assuming a hidden profile task, their theory explains effects predicted by Proposition 4. As shared information is preference-consistent, it is judged as important and its communicators reap rewards of social status and influence. Despite this strength, their explanation has some limitations. First, it does not account for why shared information is favored during discussion over unshared for information distributions other than hidden profiles (e.g., when shared and unshared information both support members' initial preferences). Second, it cannot explain why some members favor shared information more than others and why some members, such as leaders, emphasize unshared information. The theory would need to be embellished to account for differences between members in motivation to support initial preferences. A strength of the model is its ability to explain why members strategically communicate some (i.e., preference-consistent, shared) information over other (i.e., preference-inconsistent, unshared) information. It could not, however, explain some effects consistent with Proposition 5, that members may favor preference-inconsistent information if that information supports status acquisition. The model of Greitemeyer and Schulz-Hardt can account for some, but not all status processes in collective information exchange. Their model needs additional elaboration to account for all of our proposed status processes.

Social Validation

A final explanation for the discussion bias relies on members' need for social validation, the desire to ascertain the accuracy and relevance of information (Festinger, 1954). In uncertain situations, such as while working on an unfamiliar task, group members may look to others to evaluate the relative importance of their information. When shared information is mentioned, others can attest to the importance and accuracy of that information, making members feel more certain of their own and others' task capabilities (Wittenbaum & Bowman, 2004; Wittenbaum et al., 1999; Wittenbaum & Park, 2001). Moreover, hearing that others possess the same information may make that information appear more valuable, important, and relevant. Research supports the notion that shared information is evaluated as more important, relevant, and accurate than unshared information (Postmes, Spears, & Cihangir, 2001; Wittenbaum et al., 1999). Encouragement and validation from others when shared information is mentioned may lead members to favor repeating such information. Therefore, the advantage of this explanation lies in its ability to account for the tendency of group members to repeat, rather than to mention, shared information.

This explanation can account for groups' tendency to mention more shared than unshared information if members know whether an item of information is shared or unshared before mentioning it. If a member mentions a shared piece of information and is reinforced for doing so, the member may select a different piece of shared information to mention in order to evoke the same response. In most information sharing experiments, however, members were not aware of which pieces of information were shared and unshared. Such insights would have only been apparent after information was mentioned and others could assert that they either knew it or did not. Therefore, this explanation is less parsimonious in explaining group members' greater likelihood of initially mentioning shared, over unshared, information compared to the models of Stasser (1992), and Greitemeyer and Schulz-Hardt (2003).

The social validation hypothesis grew out of an interest in explaining Wittenbaum's (1998, 2000) status effects in information exchange. The model does a good job of explaining Propositions 4 and 5. Members value shared information and those who contribute it because that information can be verified as correct, whereas, unshared information cannot. As members may aspire to increase their status, they may strategically favor shared information over unshared information in discussion. Low-status members, if aware of the status enhancing value of shared information, may favor communicating it over unshared information, more than high-status members, an effect predicted by Proposition 2. Without credibility to make others believe their unshared knowledge is accurate and relevant, low-status members' unshared contributions may be less valued than those of high-status members (Proposition 3). Of all models, the social validation approach does the best job of explaining: (a) the differential susceptibility of low- and high-status members to the discussion bias; (b) the differential impact of unshared information depending on the status of the communicator; (c) why communicators of much shared information attain status and influence; and (d) why members would strategically communicate shared information to gain status.

CONCLUSIONS AND FUTURE DIRECTIONS

The propositions advanced in this chapter organize and summarize existing theory and research regarding the relations between member status and information exchange in decision-making groups. Considerable research supports the notion that in mixed-status, decision-making groups, high-status members communicate more total information and are less prone to the discussion bias favoring shared information. The unique contributions of high-status members are valued more than those of lower-status members. Low-status members can gain status and influence by communicating shared knowledge and may deliberately select this information to increase their social standing. Although some research supports these propositions, additional scholarship is necessary to identify the limiting conditions under which they hold.

As an example, Thomas-Hunt et al. (2003) predicted the sole expert in a group of three to contribute more unique knowledge than non-expert members, consistent with Proposition 2. However, they found no differences in the tendency for experts and non-experts to repeat their own unshared information (although the means were in the expected direction). Instead, experts repeated others' unshared information and shared information more than non-experts. They suggested that experts may play the role of information managers by emphasizing others' information. This may be the case for group tasks where the unshared information is particularly salient or important. In Thomas-Hunt et al.'s study, unshared information was so much the focus during discussion that group members overall repeated more unshared than shared information, a repetition effect that counters that traditionally found in collective information sharing experiments. When all members contribute much unshared knowledge or when such information is particularly valuable, experts may adopt the role of managing all of the unshared knowledge that has already been mentioned.

Information technology is another factor that may moderate status effects in information exchange. Some researchers have argued that status effects are attenuated when group members interact via computer technology because cues on which status is based are less visible and members feel less inhibited given the anonymity (e.g., Dubrovsky, Kiesler, & Sethna, 1991; Sproull & Kiesler, 1986; Tan, Wei, & Watson, 1999). However, others claim that status differences persevere in group decision-making when computer technology is used (e.g., Scott & Easton, 1996; Weisband, Schneider, & Connolly, 1995). Two studies that examined member status and information exchange used groups whose members interacted via computer technology (i.e., Hollingshead, 1996; Thomas-Hunt & Burris, 2003). Both found evidence of status differences in information sharing despite the communication medium. Hollingshead (2001) argued that it is not the communication medium, per se, but rather whether the medium allows for anonymous communication that moderates member status effects in collective information sharing. Specifically, member status effects are attenuated when members' identities remain anonymous relative to when they can be identified. This argument suggests that any communication medium that makes members' identities anonymous will attenuate the likelihood of finding support for each of the five propositions.

The identification of moderating factors may suggest managerial interventions to facilitate the contribution and valuing of low-status members' unshared knowledge. At stake is the quality of group decisions: If the unshared knowledge of low-status members is unlikely to be mentioned or valued if communicated, then the group is deciding with insufficient information funds. Interventions may ameliorate an otherwise gloomy picture. For example, the unshared information of acknowledged experts is more likely to be mentioned and valued by others compared to that of unacknowledged experts (e.g., Franz & Larson Jr., 2002; Stewart & Stasser, 1995; Thomas-Hunt & Burris, 2003). Members who are low in status because of their diffuse status characteristics but have valuable expert knowledge, may benefit the group by having a manager point out their unique expertise to all other members. Managers also may capitalize on the fact that unshared information emerges during discussion at an increasing rate over time (Larson Jr. et al., 1994, 1996, 1998a, b). If low-status members gain status by mentioning shared information during the early part of interaction, they later may spend earned idiosyncrasy credits (e.g., Hollander, 1958) by mentioning unshared information. Managers may encourage groups to engage in lengthy discussions in the hopes that the unique knowledge of low-status members will emerge over time. These and other interventions may attenuate the informational disadvantage of low-status group members and improve group decision quality.

Most of the collective information sharing literature has used college students participating in ad hoc, cooperative decision-making groups in laboratory experiments. This body of literature limits the understanding of information sharing as it naturally occurs in organizational work groups (Wittenbaum et al., 2004). In organizational and political settings, group members experience mixed motives, wanting to aid group performance but also being pulled by personal and interpersonal incentives. Propositions 4 and 5 extend the literature by suggesting that not only does member status affect information exchange in decision-making groups, but information exchange also alters member status. Group members who are influenced by the power and politics in the workplace may strategically manage information in order to gain status and influence. We believe that studying collective information sharing, as it occurs in natural contexts, requires the examination of member motives, and in particular, the desire to increase one's social standing. Status is not a stable characteristic of members, but rather a quality that can change through information management and modifications in task and team composition (e.g., Thomas-Hunt & Phillips, 2003). Incorporating organizational dynamics into the study of group information exchange will result in a richer understanding of the effects of status diversity and the contribution of information use to status differentiation.

REFERENCES

Berger, J., Fisek, M. H., Norman, R. Z., & Zelditch, M., Jr. (1977). *Status characteristics and social interaction*. New York: Elsevier.

Berger, J., Rosenholtz, S. J., & Zelditch, M., Jr. (1980). Status organizing process. *Annual Review of Sociology, 6*, 479–508.

Botero, I. C., & Wittenbaum, G. M. (2003). *Effects of leadership and task demonstrability on information repetition in decision-making groups*. Unpublished manuscript.

Clark, H. H., & Brennan, S. E. (1991). Grounding in communication. In: L. B. Resnick, J. M. Levine & S. D. Teasley (Eds), *Perspectives on socially shared cognition* (pp. 127–149). Washington DC: American Psychological Association.

Cruz, M. G., Boster, F. J., & Rodriguez, J. I. (1997). The impact of group size and proportion of shared information on the exchange and integration of information in groups. *Communication Research, 24*, 291–313.

Dennis, A. R. (1996a). Information exchange and use in group decision making: You can lead a group to information, but you can't make it think. *MIS Quarterly, 20*, 433–457.

Dennis, A. R. (1996b). Information exchange and use in small group decision making. *Small Group Research, 27*, 532–550.

Devine, D. J. (1999). Effects of cognitive ability, task knowledge, information sharing, and conflict on group decision-making effectiveness. *Small Group Research, 30*, 608–634.

Devine, D. J., Clayton, L. D., Philips, J. L., Dunford, B. B., & Melner, S. B. (1999). Teams in organizations: Prevalence, characteristics, and effectiveness. *Small Group Research, 30*, 678–711.

Dovidio, J. F., Brown, C. E., Heltman, K., Ellyson, S. L., & Keating, C. F. (1988). Power displays between women and men in discussions of gender-linked tasks: A multi channel study. *Journal of Personality and Social Psychology, 55*, 580–587.

Dubrovsky, V. J., Kiesler, S., & Sethna, B. N. (1991). The equalization phenomenon: Status effects in computer-mediated and face-to-face decision-making groups. *Human-Computer Interaction, 6*, 119–146.

Eagly, A. H. (1983). Gender and social influence: A social psychological analysis. *American Psychologist, 38*, 971–981.

Festinger, L. (1954). A theory of social comparison processes. *Human Relations, 7*, 117–140.

Franz, T. M., & Larson, J. R., Jr. (2002). The impact of experts on information sharing during group discussion. *Small Group Research, 33*, 383–411.

Greitemeyer, T., & Schulz-Hardt, S. (2003). Preference-consistent evaluation of information in the hidden profile paradigm: Beyond group-level explanations for the dominance of shared information in group decisions. *Journal of Personality and Social Psychology, 84*, 322–339.

Hollander, E. P. (1958). Conformity, status, and idiosyncrasy credit. *Psychological Review, 65*, 117–127.

Hollingshead, A. B. (1996). Information suppression and status persistence in group decision making. *Human Communication Research, 23*, 193–219.

Hollingshead, A. B. (2001). Computer-mediated communication, the Internet, and group research. In: M. Hogg & R. S. Tindale (Eds), *Blackwell handbook of social psychology (Vol. 3) Group Processes* (pp. 557–573). Oxford, England: Blackwell.

Kameda, T., Ohtsubo, Y., & Takezawa, M. (1997). Centrality in sociocognitive networks and social influence: An illustration in a group decision-making context. *Journal of Personality and Social Psychology, 73*, 296–309.

Kelly, J. R., & Karau, S. J. (1999). Group decision making: The effects of initial preferences and time pressure. *Personality and Social Psychology Bulletin, 25*, 1342–1354.

Kelly, J., Wildman, H. E., & Urey, J. R. (1982). Gender and sex role differences in group decision-making social interactions: A behavioral analysis. *Journal of Applied Social Psychology, 12*, 112–127.

Kirchler, E., & Davis, J. H. (1986). The influence of member status differences and task type on group consensus and member position change. *Journal of Personality and Social Psychology, 51*, 83–91.

Lam, S. S. K., & Schaubroeck, J. (2000). Improving group decisions by better pooling information: A comparative advantage of group decision support systems. *Journal of Applied Psychology, 85*, 565–573.

Larson, J. R., Jr., Christensen, C., Abbot, A. S., & Franz, T. M. (1996). Diagnosing groups: Charting the flow of information in medical decision-making teams. *Journal of Personality and Social Psychology, 71*, 315–330.

Larson, J. R., Jr., Christensen, C., Abbot, A. S., & Franz, T. M. (1998a). Diagnosing groups: The pooling, management, and impact of shared and unshared case information in team-based medical decision making. *Journal of Personality and Social Psychology, 75*, 93–108.

Larson, J. R., Jr., Foster-Fishman, P. G., & Franz, T. M. (1998b). Leadership style and the discussion of shared and unshared information in decision-making groups. *Personality and Social Psychology Bulletin, 24*, 482–495.

Larson, J. R., Jr., Foster-Fishman, P. G., & Keys, C. B. (1994). The discussion of shared and unshared information in decision-making groups. *Journal of Personality and Social Psychology, 67*, 446–461.

Larson, J. R., Jr., Sargis, E. G., Elstein, A. S., & Schwartz, A. (2002). Holding shared versus unshared information: Its impact on perceived member influence in decision-making groups. *Basic and Applied Social Psychology, 24*, 145–155.

Lavery, T. A., Franz, T. M., Winquist, J. R., & Larson, J. R., Jr. (1999). The role of information exchange in predicting group accuracy on a multiple judgment task. *Basic and Applied Social Psychology, 21*, 281–289.

Parks, C. D., & Cowlin, R. (1995). Group discussion as affected by number of alternatives and by a time limit. *Organizational Behavior and Human Decision Processes, 62*, 267–275.

Phillips, K. W., Mannix, E. A., Neale, M. A., & Gruenfeld, D. H. (2004). Diverse groups and information sharing: The effects of congruent ties. *Journal of Experimental Social Psychology, 40*, 497–510.

Postmes, T., Spears, R., & Cihangir, S. (2001). Quality of decision making and group norms. *Journal of Personality and Social Psychology, 80*, 918–930.

Propp, K. M. (1995). An experimental examination of biological sex as a status cue in decision-making groups and its influence on information use. *Small Group Research, 26*, 451–474.

Ridgeway, C. L., & Diekema, D. (1992). Are gender differences status differences? In: C. L. Ridgeway (Ed.), *Gender, Interaction, and Inequality* (pp. 157–180). New York: Springer-Verlag.

Sargis, E. G., & Larson, J. R., Jr. (2002). Informational centrality and member participation during group decision making. *Group Processes and Intergroup Relations, 5*, 333–347.

Savadori, L., Van Swol, L. M., & Sniezek, J. A. (2001). Information sampling and confidence within groups and judge advisor systems. *Communication Research, 28*, 737–771.

Schittekatte, M., & Van Hiel, A. (1996). Effects of partially shared information and awareness of unshared information on information sampling. *Small Group Research, 27*, 431–449.

Scott, C. R., & Easton, A. C. (1996). Examining equality of influence in group decision support system interactions. *Small Group Research, 27*, 360–382.

Silver, S. D., Cohen, B. P., & Crutchfield, J. H. (1994). Status differentiation and information exchange in face-to-face and computer-mediated idea generation. *Social Psychology Quarterly, 57*, 108–123.

Sproull, L., & Kiesler, S. (1986). Reducing social context cues: Electronic mail in organizational communication. *Management Science, 32*, 1492–1512.

Stasser, G. (1992). Pooling of unshared information during group discussion. In: S. Worchel, W. Wood & J. Simpson (Eds), *Group process and productivity* (pp. 48–57). Newbury Park, CA: Sage.

Stasser, G., & Titus, W. (1985). Pooling of unshared information in group decision making: Biased information sampling during discussion. *Journal of Personality and Social Psychology, 48*, 1467–1478.

Stasser, G., & Titus, W. (1987). Effects of information load and percentage of shared information on the dissemination of unshared information during group discussion. *Journal of Personality and Social Psychology, 53*, 81–93.

Stasser, G., Stewart, D. D., & Wittenbaum, G. M. (1995). Expert roies and information exchange during discussion: The importance of knowing who knows what. *Journal of Experimental Social Psychology, 31*, 244–265.

Stasser, G., Taylor, L. A., & Hanna, C. (1989). Information sampling in structured and unstructured discussions of three- and six-person groups. *Journal of Personality and Social Psychology, 57*, 67–78.

Stasser, G., Vaughan, S. I., & Stewart, D. D. (2000). Pooling unshared information: The benefits of knowing how access to information is distributed among group members. *Organizational Behavior and Human Decision Processes, 82*, 102–116.

Stewart, D. D., & Stasser, G. (1995). Expert role assignment and information sampling during collective recall and decision making. *Journal of Personality and Social Psychology, 69*, 619–628.

Tan, B. C. Y., Wei, K. K., & Watson, R. T. (1999). The equalizing impact of a group support system on status differentials. *ACM Transactions on Information Systems, 17*, 77–100.

Thomas-Hunt, M. C., & Burris, E. R. (2003). *The effects of complex configurations of status on knowledge sharing and team performance*. (Unpublished manuscript).

Thomas-Hunt, M. C., & Phillips, K. W. (2003). Managing teams in the dynamic organization: The effects of revolving membership and changing task demands on expertise and status in groups. In: R. Peterson & E. A. Mannix (Eds), *Leadership in dynamic organizations*. New York: LEA, Inc.

Thomas-Hunt, M. C., Ogden, T. Y., & Neale, M. A. (2003). Who's really sharing? The context dependent effects of social and expert status on knowledge exchange within groups. *Management Science, 49*, 464–477.

Van Hiel, A., & Schittekatte, M. (1998). Information exchange in context: Effects of gender composition of group, accountability, and intergroup perception on group decision making. *Journal of Applied Social Psychology, 28*, 2049–2067.

Weisband, S. P., Schneider, S. K., & Connolly, T. (1995). Computer-mediated communication and social information: Status salience and status differences. *Academy of Management Journal, 38*, 1124–1151.

Winquist, J. R., & Larson, J. R. (1998). Information pooling: When it impacts group decision making. *Journal of Personality and Social Psychology, 74*, 371–377.

Wittenbaum, G. M. (1996). *Information sampling in mixed-sex decision-making groups: The impact of diffuse status and task relevant cues*. Miami University, Oxford, Ohio (Unpublished doctoral dissertation).

Wittenbaum, G. M. (1998). Information sampling in decision-making groups: The impact of members' task relevant status. *Small Group Research, 29*, 57–84.

Wittenbaum, G. M. (2000). The bias toward discussing shared information: Why are high status members immune? *Communication Research, 27*, 379–401.

Wittenbaum, G. M., & Bowman, J. M. (2004). A social validation explanation for mutual enhancement. *Journal of Experimental Social Psychology, 40*, 169–184.

Wittenbaum, G. M., & Park, E. S. (2001). The collective preference for shared information. *Current Directions in Psychological Science, 10*, 70–73.

Wittenbaum, G. M., & Stasser, G. (1996). Management of information in small groups. In: J. L. Nye & A. M. Brower (Eds), *What's social about social cognition? Research on socially shared cognition in small groups* (pp. 3–28). Thousand Oaks, CA: Sage.

Wittenbaum, G. M., Hollingshead, A. B., & Botero, I. C. (2004). From cooperative to motivated information sharing in groups: Moving beyond the hidden profile paradigm. *Communication Monographs, 71*, 286–310.

Wittenbaum, G. M., Hollingshead, A. B., & Bowman, J. M. (2003). *Strategic information sharing in decision-making groups* (Unpublished manuscript).

Wittenbaum, G. M., Hubbell, A. P., & Zuckerman, C. (1999). Mutual enhancement: Toward an understanding of the collective preference for shared information. *Journal of Personality and Social Psychology, 77*, 967–978.

INTERNAL STATUS SORTING IN GROUPS: THE PROBLEM OF TOO MANY STARS

Jennifer R. Overbeck, Joshua Correll and Bernadette Park

ABSTRACT

Social and task groups need a few high-status members who can be leaders and trend setters, and many more lower-status members who can follow and contribute work without challenging the group's direction (Caporael (1997). Personality and Social Psychology Review, 1, 276–298; Caporael & Baron (1997). In: J. Simpson, & D. Kenrick (Eds), Evolutionary social psychology (pp. 317–343). Hillsdale, NJ: Lawrence Erlbaum; Brewer (1997). In: C. McGarty, & S.A. Haslam (Eds), The message of social psychology: Perspectives on mind in society (pp. 54–62). Malden, MA: Blackwell). When groups come together without a priori status differentiation, a status hierarchy must be implemented; however, if the new members are too homogeneously status seeking, then it is not clear what will result. We argue that hierarchy will develop even in uniformly status-seeking groups, and that the social context and members' relational characteristics – specifically, the degree to which they are group oriented rather than self-serving – will predict which status seekers succeed in gaining status. We discuss why and how a "status sorting"

Status and Groups
Research on Managing Groups and Teams, Volume 7, 169–199

ISSN: 1534-0856/doi:10.1016/S1534-0856(05)07008-8

process will occur to award status to a few members and withhold it from most, and the consequences of this process for those who are sorted downward.

When people enter a new group, they carry expectations about the roles and status that they will occupy. In many cases, these prior expectations may be a problem. Specifically, when too many entering members all expect to have higher status in the group, then what happens? Can all the members simply form a super status "dream team," or will the group instead find a way of sorting the members so that there is a range of member statuses?

In many modern groups, new members have some sense of what their status will be, even as they first enter the group. For example, when a new player is drafted by a major league baseball team, cues such as salary and press coverage communicate quite clearly how the player ranks among his teammates, at least according to management and outside observers. These cues suggest that the best players will have the highest status. But we can also argue that status will be determined according to group needs, and as such the individual's status may look very different when observed from within the group. On the baseball team, we might find that there is an extremely competent hitter who lacks social skills and has low status because he is not seen as a good "team player." The players themselves may grant status to another person who is more congenial.[1]

In other groups, it is not clear upon entry how much status an individual member will have. Among newly recruited classes of first-year associates in law firms and consulting firms, and students in MBA programs and other graduate programs,[2] there are often no differences in titles or overt cues such as salary. Even though diagnostic differences will likely exist, they may be on a number of different dimensions (one student receives more fellowship support; another went to a more prestigious school; a third has the most personal income) and it may be harder to combine these into a clear, unidimensional ranking of status. Groups that are new or ad hoc may be likely to lack clarity in how status will be assigned and who will hold it within the group. In these settings, members must negotiate the rankings, implicitly or explicitly, in order to establish a status hierarchy.

This chapter is concerned with just such problems. When individuals, particularly those who seek or expect high status, join a group, the group must negotiate the internal process of assigning or withholding status. What happens in a group without a formal status-conferring mechanism when too many members are status seeking? In the following pages, we will lay out an argument that groups "sort" members into different status levels in order to achieve needed functional differentiation, and that this sorting process affects not only group effectiveness but also individual characteristics.

We are interested in both task-related and social status, because groups' internal status hierarchy may be based on either one, and we will not distinguish between these in the following discussion. However, we will focus on groups that are convened for the purpose of completing some task, rather than purely social groups. Further, we are interested in groups whose members have at least some degree of interdependence in completing their focal tasks. For this work to be relevant to groups and teams in work organizations, it is important to specify these characteristics.

WHAT IS STATUS?

Status characteristics theory (Berger, Cohen, & Zelditch, 1972; Berger, Ridgeway, Fisek, & Norman, 1998) holds that status is a marker of competence. That is, observers develop theories about characteristics that seem to correspond to competence, and as a result begin to confer status on individuals who have those characteristics, even in the absence of evidence of competence. This suggests that the highest status members of any group will be those who (a) display the most objective competence at valued tasks (also known as achieved status) or (b) have characteristics that seem associated with competence (also known as ascribed status). Such characteristics may often include being white, male, highly educated, from a privileged background, attractive, etc. As alluded to earlier, status (and, by extension, competence) could refer to either task or social aspects of the group. Hogan and Hogan (2002) point out that the highest status leaders must offer not only task competence, but also sociopolitical skill, suggesting that it might be difficult to disentangle how task and social competence might be proxies for high status.

An alternative view might equate status with referent power (French & Raven, 1959), which is the status holder's personal magnetism and attractiveness to others, such that others want to affiliate with the status holder and to emulate him or her. This view of status is descriptive and not as explanatory as status characteristics theory. However, it is a useful way to conceive of status and lends itself to clean operational definition. For purposes of this discussion, we accept the framework of status characteristics theory, but our use of "status" will refer more closely to others' desire to affiliate with, and assign leadership roles to, the status holder.

Our analysis of status in groups suggests that there must be differentiation within the group, at least on the status dimension (although the opening examples imply that status differences covary with other intragroup differences). This raises the issue of the role of heterogeneity within groups, which we will discuss next.

THE ROLE OF HOMOGENEITY AND HETEROGENEITY IN HUMAN GROUPS

A great number of column inches have been devoted to the question of how diversity affects group function. There is no clear answer; however, the bulk of evidence suggests that groups perform better on creative and performance tasks if there is substantial heterogeneity with respect to skills and functional backgrounds. If a work group consists of too many members with identical, limited skill sets, then the group cannot respond to situations that require different skills. On the other hand, homogeneity in affiliative qualities such as attitudes and demography (age, social background, ethnicity) lead to more harmonious, cohesive, satisfied groups (Jackson, 1982; O'Connor, Gruenfeld, & McGrath, 1993; O'Reilly, Williams, & Barsade, 1998).

In the current work, we are concerned with homogeneity and heterogeneity of *roles* and *status* within the group. *Roles* are informal positions associated with particular functions and responsibilities, and though they are conceptually distinct from status, in practical terms roles will tend to covary with status to such an extent that we will treat the two concepts as yoked for the following discussion.

Successful group functioning appears to require heterogeneity of intragroup roles. Caporael (1997), Caporael and Baron (1997), Brewer (1997), and Wilson (1997) have all argued that, throughout our evolutionary history, groups' structure and internal differentiation have been vital to basic survival as well as to higher-level coordinated activities. In order for needs to be met, there must be someone in the group who can handle any necessary function (historically: providing food, locating shelter, producing clothing, healing illness, raising children) and a reasonable chain of command for making decisions and resolving disputes. These requirements clearly point to the desirability of role heterogeneity. To return to the baseball team example, where would the New York Yankees be with a dugout full of star catchers who couldn't pitch, field, or bat? As implied by the need for a chain of command, heterogeneity itself might not be enough; the group probably needs at least a nominal hierarchy in order to best coordinate its activities.

IS HIERARCHY INEVITABLE?

Throughout human history and across all societies, social systems have tended to order groups according to differential status, providing unequal access to resources and rewards, and inevitably giving rise to both privileged, hegemonic groups and disadvantaged "negative reference groups" (Sidanius & Pratto, 1993). Social scientists have argued that such intergroup hierarchical organization is adaptive, or at least rational, because it can allow the protection of a successful group's resources (Allport, 1958; LeVine & Campbell, 1972; Sherif, 1958).

Somewhat less emphasized has been the likely fact that *within*-group hierarchy – by which we mean the differential valuing of individual members and the resulting ordinal ranking of these members along status lines – is also adaptive in its facilitation of individual coordination and mobilization. As Sidanius and Pratto (1993) point out, there are compelling reasons for hierarchy to be an adaptive feature of group development. Hierarchy can facilitate unequal distribution of resources, which by concentrating necessities in the hands of only a few, privileged members can maximize chances of group (though not individual) survival during times of scarcity. Those favored are likely to be group leaders, and others with valued skills. Paleolithic groups, for example, might have given priority resources to tribal leaders, shamans, and the most skilled hunters. On baseball teams, the highest salaries go to the players expected to contribute most to team wins. In all cases, these are people whose skills and positions are believed to be helpful to the larger survival of the group. Therefore, ensuring their survival may go further toward preserving the group (in some cases, even toward helping more individuals) than would assigning resources to lower-status members. Hierarchy can also preserve domestic tranquility by enforcing norms of obedience and subservience among low-status group members (Sidanius & Pratto, 1999). Finally, it can contribute to better military organization, which has been vital for the survival of living groups, as well as political and commercial groups in competitive environments.

For a group to succeed, individual members must be able to subjugate their own personal needs and desires to maximize the collective good (Hogan & Hogan, 2002). We believe that a "dream team" is unlikely to result when there are multiple status seekers. For one thing, the authors cannot generate a valid example of a flat, egalitarian group of homogeneously high-status members that does not develop hierarchy over time. More important, it seems probable that groups cannot accommodate too many status seekers because a substantial number of people are needed to follow, to carry out more menial tasks, and to serve the group without too much independent thought. A follower who is too self-starting might disrupt the coherent functioning of the group as a whole.

At the same time, groups do need some people to occupy top roles. High-status members of the group may set the agenda of the collective, so that the group does not flounder in the complete absence of guidance (Brewer, 1997). When coordination is critical, the role of the leader may actually necessitate the very characteristics of independent thought and self-direction that, when manifested in subordinates, interfere with group functioning.

All of this suggests that groups will have an interest in establishing and maintaining hierarchy, if only because members predisposed to want or expect high status will try to acquire it. They will do this partly because of their individual motivations, and partly because the group as a whole will begin to exert influence on members to differentiate and to coordinate effort, and these status seekers will find it most comfortable to have high-status positions that afford control and autonomy.

Having argued for inevitability, though, it must still be acknowledged that hierarchies may be more or less rigid and vertically differentiated. Organizations try to institute "flat" structures, and populations such as college undergraduates are particularly known for striving for social egalitarianism rather than stratification. Our arguments focus on status hierarchies with relatively strong vertical differentiation.

GROUP FEATURES THAT FACILITATE HIERARCHY DEVELOPMENT

We will argue that individual characteristics are important in determining how group members will strive for status within the group, and who succeeds in winning that status. Afterwards, we will present several ideas about how the sorting process might occur. First, however, we present characteristics of the group itself that may offer insight into which *groups* will establish the most vertically-differentiated hierarchies.

Social Integration

A group that is particularly "group-y" is said to have high social integration (Moreland, 1987). Groups can vary on this dimension, from loose assemblages of individuals who share physical proximity, but not identity or purpose (e.g., a crowd on a subway) to tightly woven groups such as families, fraternities, or even cults. The term *entitativity* (Campbell, 1958; Hamilton & Sherman, 1996) refers to a perceiver's sense of the group's social integration, and is determined by the degree of perceived similarity and common fate among members (Hamilton & Sherman, 1996; Lickel et al., 2000). A good metaphor for a highly integrated, or entitative, group is the individual human being, made up of multiple unique components (organs) that each provide a discrete function, but that are highly interdependent, and whose combination is so integrated and coherent as to present the face of a single entity.

To the extent that entitativity and social integration are simply actor observer perspectives on the same group quality, we might expect that groups made up of very similar individuals with a high degree of common fate will be the most integrated. However, to revisit our discussion of homogeneity, it is likely that such groups are similar on *affiliative* characteristics. The cohesiveness resulting from affiliative similarity will benefit certain aspects of group functioning, such as satisfaction and harmony. In order to function smoothly, the group will also need good coordination, and this will require clearer vertical differentiation on the status dimension.

We expect that groups with good social integration (affiliative similarity and a sense of common fate) will both need, and be able, to establish vertically differentiated status hierarchies more than less-integrated groups. This may seem counterintuitive because such groups' natural affiliation could be expected to lead to a more egalitarian system. However, in less-entitative groups, the group is not as tightly woven and members can be more independent; each can do his or her own thing. Though the group might benefit from hierarchical organization, the group is not in a position to enforce it. On the other hand, more entitative, "group-y" groups should be better able to exert influence on members. This influence should allow groups to ensure that members embody needed traits and skills and do not display harmful or superfluous qualities. As a result, highly entitative groups should be more able to ensure that they achieve proper intragroup differentiation with respect to status. This differentiation should, in turn, yield better group functioning and performance.

Tightness

It may appear paradoxical to suggest that homogeneity is related to greater intragroup hierarchy. However, evidence at the cultural level suggests that this may indeed be the case. The term *tightness* (Triandis, 1989) describes cultures in which stringent norms are imposed on individuals, and thus the range of acceptable behaviors is narrow. Tight cultures tend to be quite homogeneous, not only behaviorally but also demographically. A prototypical tight culture is Japan, a homogeneous country in which conformity is highly prized – as evidenced by the common saying, "The nail that stands up gets pounded down." Japan is also known as a strongly hierarchical country in which ranks are clearly identified and understood, and social mobility is low (Benedict, 1946; Triandis, 1989).

Whereas very tight cultures – Japan, Greece, and even rural America – are marked by high degrees of hierarchy and a clearly defined social order, in looser cultures – urban U.S., western Europe – the social structure tends to be (or appears to be) more egalitarian.[3] Thus, we might expect that tight *groups* may also develop more polarized hierarchies. Certainly, in order to achieve functional differentiation, it should be necessary for these groups to develop hierarchy. It is even possible, that this hierarchy may be more marked in homogeneous than heterogeneous groups, which contain preexisting diversity and have less need to sort out members on the status dimension.

The concepts of entitativity, tightness, and intragroup hierarchy converge to predict that groups may need to subordinate certain individual behaviors and expressions in order to provide the benefits on which members depend. If the prehistoric group was to facilitate members' survival – and if the modern group is to facilitate members' achieving group goals – then the individuals in the group must function as a coordinated entity. Hierarchy is important to the functioning of a group, and the ability to force members to occupy the various roles in the hierarchy is determined at least in part by the degree of entitativity in the group. Given that individual human beings are notoriously likely to have different traits, preferences, work styles, and priorities, group coordination cannot be taken for granted. However, as our continued presence on the planet attests, human beings have clearly developed adaptive systems that facilitated our coordination in group settings.[4]

WHO ARE THE STATUS SEEKERS?

The character of our prototypical status seeker consists of high levels of trait self-esteem and self-efficacy, and an internal locus of control. It is important to note the strong element of self-determination implied by these traits. The dimensions of internal locus of control (Rotter, 1966) and self-efficacy (Bandura, 1986) represent an individual's belief in his or her own potency, competence and ability to control outcomes. Self-esteem has been characterized as a two-factor construct, gauging (similar) feelings of efficacy on the one hand, and self-liking on the other (Tafarodi & Swann, 1995). There clearly exists a great deal of overlap between these constructs, both conceptually and empirically. Measures of the constructs generally correlate with one another (Sherer, 1982; Stanley & Murphy, 1997), and Judge, Erez, Bono, and Thoresen (2002) argue that these dimensions are described well by a single construct.

Collectively, these traits seem to predict a cluster of self-relevant behaviors (Judge et al., 2002). People with high self-esteem (HSE), high self-efficacy and a belief in internal control, for example, are all more likely than others to persevere on a given task (Shrauger & Sorman, 1977; McFarlin, Baumeister, & Blascovich, 1984; Bandura, 1992; Di Paula & Campbell, 2002), and both esteem and efficacy are negatively related to "behavioral plasticity," or a willingness to yield, in response to social pressure (Janis, 1954; Hjelle & Clouser, 1970; Brockner, 1979; Sandelands, Brockner, & Glynn, 1988). Individuals high in esteem or efficacy also tend to take credit for success and deny responsibility for failure, consistent with a belief in their virtue and ability (Bandura, 1992; Blaine & Crocker, 1993). The research, then, seems to converge to predict that self-esteem, self-efficacy, and internal locus of control should form a constellation of traits that indicate status seeking in an individual.

Higher levels of self-esteem, dominance, and self-efficacy not only predict emergent leadership (Atwater, Dionne, & Avolio, 1999; Smith & Foti, 1998; but see Chemers, Watson, & May, 2000), but are also associated with dissatisfaction when leadership is withheld (Elangovan & Xie, 1999). Elangovan and Xie report that people with high, but not low, self-esteem (and internal, but not external, locus of control) experienced stress and decreased motivation under the direction of a dominant supervisor.

In line with these findings, Sidanius and Pratto (1993) predict that status and trait self-esteem should be positively correlated. These authors speculate that the relationship emerges because downward social comparisons are more frequently available to high-status group members, but more simply, it is likely that status seekers (HSE individuals) pursue and gain high status more often than do others. Relatedly, both dominance theory (Barkow, 1980) and sociometer theory (Leary, Tambor, Terdal, & Downs, 1995) hold that state self-esteem functions as a monitoring system to give the individual feedback about his or her standing (in the one theory, on dominance dimensions; in the other, on sociability dimensions) in social groups. Those whose status begins to slip should experience a hit to their state self-esteem.

When a new group comes together, we would expect that members' self-esteem – and thus status seeking – should vary widely. But this is not always the case. For example, new classes of MBA students are specifically selected to consist of people who have been high achieving throughout their lives, and so this group probably has both higher self-esteem and less variable self-esteem than the average group. This is the situation of particular interest for this paper. When such a group of uniformly status-seeking members comes together, can they all end up having high status? If not what will determine who succeeds?

WHO ARE THE STATUS WINNERS?

Accounts for who will emerge with status commonly focus on individual qualities of status seekers. Status characteristics theory, for example, states that certain demographic characteristics become associated with status in the larger society (Berger et al., 1972). Being male, white, and wealthy all covary with control of valued resources, and thus signal competence; therefore, individuals who have these characteristics tend to be ascribed status. Other theories focus on personality traits, pointing to high extraversion and low neuroticism as predictors of emergent status (Anderson, John, Keltner, & Kring, 2001). Finally, individual qualities such as attractiveness may be associated with status (Dion, Berscheid, & Walster, 1972; Anderson et al., 2001).

Although these individual differences indeed tend to covary with status, these frameworks do not take into account the importance of the larger social context in determining who will emerge with status. For example, such frameworks do not seem to accommodate the possibility that *all* members of a group may have similar characteristics, and thus are unable to predict what will happen in a uniform group of status seekers. To find an explanation that goes beyond individual traits, it seems important to consider *relational* characteristics as an important determinant of status. That is, given that status is inherently a relational construct (it cannot exist in the absence of a group), then some status-relevant characteristics are probably embedded in intragroup relationships as well as in individuals' relational characteristics.

The prototypical status seeker's strong sense of self-determination is consistent with an independent self-construal (Singelis, 1994). People with independent self-construals generally do not define the self with respect to the social context; they emphasize their internal attributes and capacities, and set goals that involve their own desired outcomes. Within groups, their concern tends to be their own strategic position (Caporael, 1997). Those with interdependent self-construals, on the other hand, emphasize roles and relationships, and do not perceive the self as very separate from others. In groups, they tend to seek connectedness with others (Markus & Kitayama, 1991; Caporael, 1997). Individualistic Western cultures are associated both with higher levels of individual self-esteem and a stronger tendency toward independent self-construals, whereas collectivistic cultures tend toward low self-esteem and interdependence.[5] However, because self-esteem and self-construal are distinct concepts, they should be expected to vary independently.

We expect that HSE in general predicts status seeking. When that is paired with an independent self-construal, then a *self-promoting* style should result. In short, individuals will follow their own direction and pursue their own goals, scanning the environment for opportunities and pursuing those opportunities according to their own internal compass. On the other hand, when HSE is paired with an interdependent self-construal, then the status seeker's style should reflect a more *group-oriented* tendency toward leadership.

This dichotomy is well represented in literature on leadership, negotiation, and interpersonal behavior. Foa and Foa (1974) conceive of human interactions as a series of processes of social exchange involving not only tangible goods but also relational resources. Two primary exchangeable resources discussed by Foa and Foa are status and love (in our framework, *love* might refer to the primary focus of one's caring and concern, so that self-directed "love" reflects self-promotion and other-directed "love" reflects greater group orientation). Our self-promoting individual is one who withholds status and concern from others in order to hoard them for the self. A group-oriented individual, on the other hand, should be more willing to provide concern, and potentially even status, to others.

Dual concern theory (Pruitt & Rubin, 1999), designed to account for conflict styles and approaches to negotiation, echoes this perspective in positing that individuals typically approach encounters with others with two orthogonal targets of concern: the self and one's own outcomes, and the other and his or her outcomes. Concern for one's self is associated with resistance to yielding (De Dreu, Weingart, & Kwon, 2000). In a group setting, one of the things that members must do is yield to the collective, particularly when it comes time to coordinate efforts in order to accomplish some task. Members who resist yielding are likely to interfere with smooth functioning of the group and may be ostracized. However, it is also possible that these members become leaders as long as they pair their resistance to yielding with concern for others.

People who are high in self-esteem and independent self-construal are likely to be high in concern for the self, and those with HSE and an interdependent self-construal are likely to be high in concern for others. The distinction between these two kinds of orientations is captured in De Dreu's categories of *prosocial* (other-concerned) and *egoistic* (self- and not other-concerned) negotiators (De Dreu et al., 2000). De Dreu and his colleagues argue that "prosocial negotiators perceive the negotiation as a collaborative game in which collective welfare is important; egoistic negotiators conceive of negotiation as a competitive game in which power and personal success is key" (p. 902). To the extent that members of a newly formed group may be seen to be "negotiating" the way the group will function and the relationships among group members, this is a particularly apt theory to account for how individual predispositions may have to be altered in order to assure proper group functioning. In general, egoistic members will jockey for high-status positions and roles. If that is difficult – because, for example, there are many others also seeking status – then prosocial status seekers, with their more collaborative orientations, may have an easier time ascending than their more self-promoting peers.

Similarly, Hogan and Hogan (2002) analyze leadership as a process that combines *getting along* with others in one's social group and *getting ahead* in terms of the status hierarchy of that group. To be a leader, to have the highest status, one must combine the drive to get ahead with the ability to get along. Having the first capacity without the second results in ineffective leadership and less potential for gaining status. Our self-promoters, and De Dreu's egoistic negotiators, are primarily concerned with getting ahead. However, our group-oriented status seekers and De Dreu's prosocial negotiators temper this ambition with attention toward getting along with others in the group. It should not be surprising that other group members might be more willing to yield status to the person who values getting along.

Finally, from the standpoint of the individual predispositions to status that we have been discussing, it seems likely that an individual's ability to gain status will depend on the predispositions of others in the group. For example, the opportunities may differ for a self-promoter surrounded by other self-promoters, and for a self-promoter with others who are happy to yield status.

WHAT HAPPENS TO THE STATUS "LOSERS"?

The research suggests, quite logically, that individualists will tend to resist low-status positions. Status-seeking individuals are likely to balk when they are pressured to assume subordinate positions in a group. These individuals are likely to prefer to seek control, or at least autonomy, within the group context to avoid having to subordinate the self to group imperatives. For a group to overcome this resistance and establish internal differentiation, Caporael (1997) suggests that social structures pressure their members to change through a process of *downward causation* (Caporael & Baron, 1997; Caporael & Brewer, 1995). Pure individualism must give way to group-focused leadership for a few, and, for the rest, to lower status and at least a degree of compliance.

According to Caporael's (1997) theory of sociality, just as the characteristics of members help determine the nature of a group (upward causation), the group, once established, exerts a reciprocal influence over its members, reshaping their characteristics and interactions to facilitate collective goals (downward causation). By rewarding some behaviors and punishing others, members of the group, as a collective, gradually influence each other as individuals. Sociometer theory (Leary et al., 1995) provides tentative support for the principle of downward causation. Leary finds that a group member's state self-esteem (i.e., feelings of self-worth in the moment) tends to drop as he or she falls out of favor with comrades. He suggests that this drop in esteem serves as an intrapsychic warning to the individual, prompting changes in behavior in an effort to stave off possible exclusion and regain the acceptance of the group. The individual's desire to belong becomes, in essence, a tool for the group. The individual who fulfills his or her role within the group is rewarded with acceptance, and the deviant is ostracized. Although sociometer theory predicts that people will try to improve their standing, and thus their self-esteem, not everyone can succeed at doing so. Insofar as the sociometer works to *align* the member's position with feedback received from the group, it is largely consistent with the concept of downward causation. Drawing on Caporael, we suggest that an individual's long-term roles and relationships in the group, including status, will respond to group-based pressure.

Downward causation provides a means for groups to adapt to their environment. In spite of any inclination for independence among individual members, when cohesion and cooperation become critical, groups may exert pressure to establish internal structure, restrain would-be status grabbers, and maximize their chances for success. In a military squad on patrol, for example, there may be a few scouts, several rear guards, but only one leader. Subordinates who attempt to subvert the group structure, potentially compromising the mission as well as, here, the lives of the individual members, are likely to encounter severe pressure to conform. Later, we will address more specifically how this process might affect downward-sorted members.

First, we will present some empirical evidence to support ideas that we have laid out so far.

TOWARD A TEST OF THE FRAMEWORK

Overall, our framework yields the following general predictions:

1. In groups that come together without a priori status structure, individuals with HSE will have a predisposition to seek high status.
2. In general, these individuals are likely to be successful in achieving high status.
3. However, the ability of status seekers to achieve their goals will be moderated by the social context. Specifically, when too many status seekers are present within the group, sorting will occur, such that most will be pushed down into lower-status roles and positions.
4. Sorting will result in a more vertically-differentiated hierarchy in highly entitative and/or tight groups.
5. Those who succeed in gaining status in these groups are likely to be more interdependent, group oriented, and high in concern for others.

Most of the predictions in this framework must await testing in future research. However, we have begun to explore some of our hypotheses in a longitudinal study of naturally occurring groups in which group structure emerges over time (Correll, Overbeck, & Park, 2003). The organization whose members we surveyed for this study is a national public service group that we will call Beacon. Beacon volunteers serve for 1 year in exchange for a nominal stipend. During that year, they are based in a central location and are assigned to teams of roughly 10–14 members. Teams may be sent all across the country, from Alaska to Florida, for 6-week terms, during which they work on projects ranging from Special Olympics to constructing wooden fences. Between the 6-week terms, all teams return to the home base for organization-wide communications and exercises. Except for one early term, an individual can expect to spend the entire year of service with the same 10–14 people: working, eating, socializing, and living together in an intensely group-oriented environment.

At the start of data collection, group members had nearly zero acquaintance. They completed three waves of questionnaires; questionnaires included self-reported self-esteem (Rosenberg, 1965) and independent and interdependent self-construal (Singelis, 1994), as well as social networks items that assessed respondents' task and interpersonal contacts. Following our argument, the self-esteem measure represents individuals' tendency to seek status. Self-construal reflects one's degree of other-orientation. We assessed self-esteem and self-construal very early in the year; thus, these individual propensity measures assess personal characteristics before group influence could take hold. We assessed status at two times, first about 6 weeks (Time 2) into the service year, and next about 7 months later (Time 3), near the end of the service year. The first measure was thus a very early assessment of group status, taken when the groups had had only a small amount of prior interaction and time to establish a hierarchy. The second measure occurred after a great deal of time had passed, when the group's hierarchy should be well-established.

Social network data allow for various approaches to the calculation of status (Wasserman & Faust, 1994). To best capture status according to our questions of interest, we opted to create a new index from the social networks data, as shown in the following equation:

$$\text{Index} = I^* \frac{I}{O}$$

where I is the number of incoming ties and O is the number of outgoing ties.

For any focal individual, being listed by someone else constitutes an incoming tie, and listing others constitutes an outgoing tie.

Presumably, the greater the number of incoming ties, the more valued that focal person is by the group. Because we conceptualize status as esteem or regard by other group members, it is likely that a member who has more incoming than outgoing ties is more valued than one for whom both kinds of ties are equal. The proportion of incoming to outgoing ties (I/O) captures the individual's unreciprocated, or asymmetrical, esteem.

We expected that groups with too many status-seeking members would find it necessary to produce more followers by sorting members' status downward; this should yield a pattern whereby high group mean self-esteem, especially if the group members were tightly clustered around that mean, leads to greater downward changes in status. To assess this, we examined change in status from Time 2 to Time 3 as a function of members' individual predispositions and the resulting composition of groups at Time 1.

Consistent with our predictions, in the Beacon organization self-esteem was associated with greater increases in status. In groups with many status-seeking members (i.e., those with relatively high average self-esteem), members were only able to gain status if the group was relatively variable on self-esteem. That is, if status seeking was highly variable, then there was sufficient "room" for status seekers to achieve their desired high status. However, if *too many* members sought status, then on average members' status declined over time. This suggests that the group was sorting members downward, as implied by our framework.

Further, individual interdependence predicted whether individuals would emerge with status in their group. Among groups low in status seeking predispositions on average, individual interdependence had little effect on changes in status. Both independent and interdependent members of low self-esteem groups had equivalent (and very slight) increases in status over time.

However, in HSE groups, interdependence had important influence, and that influence depended on group composition. In heterogeneous groups (status seeking on average, but high in variability), the independent self-promoters were able to gain high status. It seems plausible that, in these groups, there is less imperative for the group to exert downward influence because it is already sufficiently differentiated in terms of status seeking; the self-promoters' pursuit of status gives them the necessary distinctiveness to succeed in obtaining it. On the other hand, in homogeneous status-seeking groups, only those members high in interdependence were able to gain status within the group. To revisit an earlier discussion, in the homogeneous groups all (or most) members are apparently concerned with obtaining high status. Unfortunately, not all of them can do so. The group must sort out members along the status dimension. To succeed, members must have not only the concern for self to prompt seeking high status, but also sufficient concern for others that the group will agree to yield status.

When groups are in a position of having too many individuals predisposed to seek high-status positions within the group, these groups respond by sorting members downward. They suppress the status of some members, relative to other members and to groups in which sorting does not need to occur. In these groups, the members who are sorted downward are more likely to be both status seeking (high in self-esteem) and low in orientation toward others in the group. This may be explained through the contrast between self-serving and group-oriented status seekers. If all in my group seek status, then probably only those who form alliances or otherwise enlist others' support will succeed. It may be that only a competitor whom I perceive as being concerned with my well-being can obtain my support in gaining status; one who is too self-serving will be a greater threat than one who gives something back for the status he or she gains.

HOW MIGHT STATUS SORTING OCCUR?

One question that arises when considering these findings is exactly how groups go about sorting members. The sorting process may be explicit and overt; on the other hand, it may be implicit and relatively automatic. Literature on hierarchy development suggests that the latter is more likely.

Explicit status sorting certainly does occur, but it seems more obviously associated with *suppression* rather than development of hierarchy. In Israeli kibbutzim, there is awareness that different work tasks carry different levels of associated status. Because the kibbutzim value egalitarianism and wish to avoid developing hierarchies, members are rotated among different task assignments whose status varies. In this way, no individual becomes permanently associated with the status carried by a certain assignment (Snarey & Lydens, 1990). In other organizations, such as the design firm IDEO, similar efforts to eliminate formal hierarchy are explicitly enacted (Crainer, 2001; Hargadon & Sutton, 2000). At IDEO, though individuals are hired into positions of differential rank, the actual work process mandates that ad hoc teams be brought together for each new project. On these teams, member rank is consciously manipulated such that high-ranking employees take the lead only on some projects, and are expected to be subordinate on others. (However, as Sutton points out, even within this flattening structure, an informal system of differential status develops based on performance on projects and degree of adherence to the group norms.)

Implicit status sorting could occur through organizational processes such as the presence or growth of an organizational culture. In addition, it has been thought that the emergence of status hierarchy might be determined by individual differences, that is, people with more valued status characteristics may be more likely to emerge as high status within a group (Anderson et al., 2001; Carli, 1991). However, for nascent groups such as those in Beacon, it seems more likely that intragroup *interactions* give rise to hierarchy (see Ridgeway, Boyle, Kuipers, & Robinson, 1998).

A substantial literature in psychology, sociology, communication, and organizational behavior outlines how status becomes enacted through interaction. Many of these accounts focus on the language and dialogue exchange within the group. For example, hierarchies may develop because of conversational dominance (monopolizing the conversational "floor," interrupting, taking disproportionate turns, making jokes; Robinson & Smith-Lovin, 2001; Ridgeway et al., 1998; Shelly & Troyer, 2001; Schmid Mast, 2001) or because the use of less polite, more direct language signals others that the speaker is higher in status (Brown & Levenson, 1987; Fragale,

Chapter 5, this volume; Ng & Bradac, 1993). In addition, studies of animals focus on hierarchy-developing processes such as asymmetrical gazing (McNelis & Boatright-Horowitz, 1998), dominance contests (Chase, 1980), and facial expressions (De Waal, 1998).

One likely status-sorting process involves interpersonal complementarity on dominance-related dimensions. Interpersonal circumplex researchers show that people tend to respond to dominance or submission in a complementary manner, whereas they respond to affiliative behaviors (agreeability or hostility) with like behaviors. Although much of social psychological theory on interpersonal attraction holds that people are attracted to those similar to themselves, circumplex theory states that a more important determinant of attraction is how well interaction partners facilitate our own goals, a criterion that necessitates complementarity in terms of dominance (Dryer & Horowitz, 1997; Tett & Murphy, 2002). Some work has shown that verbal patterns elicit complementary responding. For example, Dryer and Horowitz assigned undergraduates to work in pairs and coded the complementarity of their behavior. The majority of experimental dyads displayed complementarity in terms of verbal patterns such as advice giving or criticizing (dominance) and deferring or expressing self-doubt (submissiveness). However, this pattern was not exceptionally strong. More importantly, across two studies, Dryer and Horowitz showed that verbal responses that were complementary to one's own trait dominance or submission led to greater liking for the interaction partner and greater satisfaction with the interaction.

Perhaps more powerful and pervasive, yet less obtrusive, is complementarity in physical behaviors. Tiedens and Fragale (2003) posed confederates and, in one study, participants in dominant (physically expanded) and submissive (physically restricted) postures during interactions. Participants who were part of complementary interactions reported greater liking for their interaction partners and greater comfort in the interactions. When only confederates were posed, participants rather quickly and automatically assumed complementary postures. That is, paired with a physically expanded partner, participants constricted their posture and vice versa. Tiedens and Fragale suggest that status differences may arise very early in an encounter when one interactant adopts a dominant posture, whether due to strategy or serendipity, and that the complementary, submissive response of the partner may set the tone for subsequent interactions.

If so, this suggests that one route through which groups sort members' status may be the postural balance of members, perhaps established very early in the life of the group. Those who comply with the first physical response expected of them (as a function of a partner's posture) will be liked and prized, and those who resist will be shunned. This suggests a "first mover" advantage in which status goes to the one who most promptly claims it. In homogeneous status-seeking groups, perhaps early physical displays of dominance (much like in a primate band, in fact) contribute to the marginalization of "uppity" status-seeking members.

It should also be noted that Chartrand and Bargh (1999) demonstrated that behavioral *mimicry*, rather than complementarity, led to greater liking and satisfaction. However, the behaviors mimicked in their studies either were irrelevant to dominance or reflected affiliation: They included rubbing one's face, shaking one's foot, and smiling. As Chartrand and Bargh argue, mimicry in these cases may serve the adaptive function of helping to establish unity, membership, and belonging – in short, social integration – between the interaction partners.

Within the scope of the ideas presented here, it is likely that both complementarity in dominance behaviors and mimicry in affiliative and irrelevant behaviors serve the purpose of strengthening the group. Mimicry establishes a sense of coherence and entitativity, while complementarity creates internal stratification that allows functional differentiation and coordination. Both facilitate intragroup liking and satisfaction, as well as heightening members' sense of similarity to one another.

Finally, status sorting may occur as a function of information processing by group members. At the individual level, De Dreu and Boles (1998) found that negotiators who tended to be individualistic or competitive attended to information consistent with these orientations, and employed heuristics that implied consistent strategies. On the other hand, prosocial negotiators attended to more prosocial information and used prosocially oriented heuristics. This suggests that, upon entering the group, status-seeking members may selectively attend to information from other group members that supports their view of themselves as autonomous individuals, and disregard information – including influence efforts – from group members eager to establish a more prosocial or collectivist environment. As other group members participate in establishing a shared group meaning (e.g., Weick, 1996), these self-concerned status seekers may find themselves marginalized by clinging to rules of engagement not recognized by the rest of the group.

Cognitive processing at the *group* level can also effect sorting. Gruenfeld and Hollingshead (1993) found that groups socially construct a group-level cognition that is largely convergent in nature. That is, group cognition incorporates and builds upon the individual cognitions of members, combining these cognitions into a larger whole superordinate to any one member's thought. As individuals come together and work to reconcile and integrate differing perspectives, some may be more represented than others in the final group reality. Sorted status may either predict or result from the degree of correspondence of a given member's cognitive contributions and the final group cognition.

HOW DO SORTED INDIVIDUALS RESPOND?

Another important question involves how people respond to the pressure exerted on them by their groups. One possibility is that status seekers denied intragroup status simply resist being sorted – if given the opportunity to exit, literally or through inaction, perhaps they take it. But in some environments, like Beacon, it is not possible – or at least, not very feasible – for individual members either to depart the group or to sit on the sidelines refusing to participate.

In groups without an exit option, we propose that individuals will acquiesce to intragroup sorting. They will assume the lower status granted them by fellow group members and they will comply with the group's requirements for their behavior and contributions. If they do not do so, the group will have difficulty meeting its goals, and therefore any resistance is likely to be met with increased group pressure. Although it may seem as if people would want to resist the aversive aspects of having low status, we believe that the sorting process will create psychological changes in the individual that may lessen the aversive experience of being sorted downward.

SHIFTING FROM INDIVIDUAL- TO GROUP-BASED MODEL OF SELF

One potential benefit of status sorting is that it helps to reduce uncertainty for individuals as to their social regard and standing. Uncertainty reduction has been shown to be a powerful motivation for development of social identity (Hogg, 2000), and within-group status sorting is clearly a process that will enable group members to understand their "place" among their most frequent and important relationships. Although researchers have shown compellingly that the individual self-concept has motivational primacy – it is the most fundamental level of self-definition (Gaertner,

Sedikides, & Graetz, 1999; Gaertner, Sedikides, Vevea, & Iuzzini, 2002) – it is also true that collective self-concepts exist (Triandis, 1989). That is, the model one holds of the self can be situated within the boundary defined not only by one's own skin, but also by one's group memberships and social categories.

We suggested earlier that a highly entitative group echoes the organization and functional unity of an individual person. Once a person becomes part of such an entitative group, then it should be fairly easy for his or her self-concept to accommodate not only the self that is a single organism, but also the new entity of which the person has become an interdependent part. In fact, just such a phenomenon has been well-documented in the social psychology literatures on self-categorization theory and optimal distinctiveness (see Brewer, 1991; Turner, Hogg, Oakes, Reicher, & Wetherell, 1987). Although one's awareness of the individual self should only be substantially *lessened* in the context of a very *extreme* group – for example, the Jonestown, Guyana, cult in the 1970s – it is likely that awareness of the collective, or group-based, self will *increase* dramatically when the individual spends time as a member of a highly entitative group.

This shift should have a number of consequences. For one, individuals may begin to feel less imperative to identify or change their in-group status as they begin to see the superordinate group as a more basic level of organizing their own social experience. That is, instead of looking outward from their own eyes at fellow group members, they and others may begin to look outward from the group's perspective at external actors. Thus, they may simultaneously begin to ignore intragroup differentiation, and to become attuned to intergroup relations.

Some evidence for the former process is found in the interpersonal complementarity literature, which shows that dyads who adopt complementary dominance behaviors and speech patterns actually begin to see each other as more similar, even though their actions are objectively more distinct, relative to noncomplementary dyads. If this is true, then being sorted into a lower-status role may not be aversive, because the status distinction may lose its salience for the sorted members.

As to orienting toward other groups, Caporael and Baron (1997) argue that intergroup differentiation may encourage acceptance of within-group disadvantage by emphasizing the intergroup advantages (protection, resources, etc.) that can accrue to members. Similarly, Levin, Federico, Sidanius, and Rabinowitz (2002) posit that individuals constrained by group status hierarchies, and thus unable to indulge their desires for higher status, may turn their focus to intergroup relationships in order to satisfy those desires. Thus, again, status sorting may not be very aversive because the focal distinctions in the social environment are intergroup rather than intragroup.

Finally, an emerging area of research suggests an extreme, but very powerful, incentive for individuals to willingly subjugate themselves to the imperatives of their groups. Castano, Yzerbyt, Paladino, and Sacchi (2002) demonstrated that making salient participants' mortality led them to feel more strongly aligned with their groups, to judge their groups as more entitative, and to show more ingroup favoritism. In line with our argument that groups are adaptive, these findings suggest that a functional, well-organized, entitative group buffers individuals from the fear of death. One function of social organization for human beings, then, may involve easing our most basic existential fears; and for such a benefit, acquiescing to assigned low status may appear a small price to pay.

CONSEQUENCES FOR INDIVIDUAL ATTRIBUTES

Although not all groups will constitute as intense a collective experience for individualistic Americans as Beacon, membership in a strong group should have consequences for the individual's attributes – that is, true downward causation will occur, whereby the individual's enduring traits are changed after the group membership. These consequences should be particularly strong in more integrated groups. We discussed possible changes in the representation of the self-concept, above. In addition, persons from a highly individualistic culture who join a highly integrated group should experience other self-related changes.

Self-esteem

As most commonly measured in the U.S.A., self-esteem (cf., Rosenberg, 1965) is an individual-level construct. Thus, when people with HSE join groups consisting of mainly HSE members, it is likely that their individual-level self-esteem will decrease over time. (This is probably not true for those who did not face group sorting or for those members selected in their group to assume a leadership role, because their self-concept was not subject to change as a function of group membership.) On the other hand, group-based self-esteem will probably increase for these sorted individuals.

Self-construal

As a consequence of group membership, we expect that interdependent self-construals will increase, on average. In particular, HSE members who started out being independent and then were granted lower status should show substantial increases in interdependent self-construal. Such an individual would learn fairly quickly that he or she could not count on obtaining rewards and resources through his or her own capacities, given low standing in the group. Therefore, the individual's reliance on the group as a source of rewards would increase. This should be accompanied by an increased sense of common fate, which is a frequently-identified component of entitativity (see Hamilton & Sherman, 1996; Lickel et al., 2000), and therefore an enhanced sense of the group as figure rather than ground. The group would, as a consequence, be more central in the member's self-construal.

Attention

Members of a group should pay greater attention to stimuli of interest or importance to the group after spending time in and becoming acculturated to the group. This effect should be particularly strong for those who entered as self-promoters, whose attention was likely focused outward toward the environment, looking for opportunities for personal advancement. Two changes are likely to occur for these individuals. First, attention to intra-group affiliation should increase as the perceivers learn to tune in to interpersonal relationships within the group and contribute to smooth group interactions. Copeland (1994) showed that higher-status perceivers tended to focus attention on information that helped them evaluate others' competence for completing important tasks, whereas lower-status perceivers' attention was directed toward the self, and presenting the self as likable and attractive. Copeland's work suggests that individuals who are sorted downward will be less likely to direct attention outward toward opportunities for reward, and instead will begin to attend more to the impressions that they are making on higher-status group members.

Second, attention to intergroup status should increase as the perceivers shift from concern about their position within the group (and find that they do not achieve a high position) to concern about their group's standing with respect to other groups (which, presumably, may still be high).

Models of Agency

Morris, Menon, and Ames (2001) argue that individualistic cultures are associated with implicit theories of agency that emphasize the efficacy of individual action; agency theories in collectivistic cultures, on the other hand, emphasize group action. We believe that self-promoters generally like to rely on themselves to "get things done." As they are sorted downward by their groups, they will begin to see the group as the locus of agency. Only in concert with others can things "get done," and the individual effort may be frustrated.

Simultaneously, at the personal level, another agency-related shift may occur. Snibbe and Markus (2002) discovered that Americans of low socioeconomic status (SES) seem to hold models of personal agency that differ from those in the middle and upper classes. Specifically, whereas higher-SES individuals generally perceive the concept of agency as reflecting their ability to engage the external environment and elicit a specific, desired reaction from that environment, members of the lower classes conceive of agency as simply protecting the integrity of the self (see Higgins, 1996). Paradoxically, as self-promoters become more acculturated in the group and more interdependent in their self-construals in the group, they may also shift their conception of personal agency away from "getting things done" toward protecting and maintaining their personal selfhood within the group context.

CONSEQUENCES FOR GROUP FUNCTIONING AND SATISFACTION

Well-sorted groups, in our view, feature appropriate differentiation and specialization among members, paired with sufficient hierarchy to allow for effective coordination of effort. A group sorted in this way should function better than groups that are insufficiently differentiated or that have too diffuse a status/authority structure. We have argued that members who were too similar on status seeking were detrimental to group functioning; indeed, much work on diversity in groups and teams holds that too-homogeneous groups do not function well (Jackson, 1982; O'Connor et al., 1993; O'Reilly et al., 1998). Instead of similarity, we believe that the better metaphor for a successful group is the individual human being itself – composed of different, unique parts (whether physical or psychological) that nonetheless function in a unified, coherent manner. Such groups – and we predict that they will result from successful sorting of members – should enjoy the benefits of diversity in expertise and perspectives, as well as of homogeneity in concern for group welfare and cohesiveness.

Therefore, groups that are heterogeneous with respect to vertical status differentiation, either a priori or after sorting, should function better than more homogeneous groups. This may happen because the group has developed a sufficient chain of command to organize member activity; because the group's direction is more unified given that not too many individuals are tussling over setting that direction; or because the group's attention is focused outward to the external environment.

Along these lines, members of groups that have succeeded in sorting status aspirations should experience greater satisfaction on average, due to their similarity on affiliative dimensions, and perceived similarity as a result of complementarity on dominance dimensions. Further, being sufficiently differentiated on status should reduce uncertainty and give each group member a clearer sense of "place" in the group, both likely to lead to happiness and satisfaction. This should even extend to sorted down members, particularly, as we have argued, that their personal attributes and group orientations do change.

FINAL THOUGHTS

From a functional perspective, the ability to sort on status should serve groups well. We have argued that when there is heterogeneity in status-seeking tendencies, the establishment of vertical hierarchy within the groups is likely to proceed with ease. But when a group consists of a relatively homogeneous set of status seekers then a sorting process must ensue, sorting some group members upward in status and some down. Based on our data and theory we argue that under these circumstances, an interpersonal (as opposed to individualistic) orientation is likely to serve both the individual and the group well. A number of key psychological processes kick in to help the group member who is sorted downward adjust to and embrace his/her role in the group. As noted earlier, the majority of these postulates have yet to undergo rigorous empirical testing. But the data in hand support the critical argument that groups with a strong concentration of HSE members those who are relatively homogeneous in their self-esteem force group members to sort with respect to status. Moreover, group members with a stronger interpersonal orientation sort upwards, whereas those lower on this dimension sort downward.

Our view of the interplay between individuals – particularly, as we focus on the most headstrong, self-promoting individuals – and groups may strike some as a bit extreme. After all, most readers of this chapter are members of multiple groups, many that require a great deal of coordination from members who assume that we will each be a leader, a prized member, or at least a capable, autonomous unit. And most such readers probably feel that being "sorted downward" is an alien experience.

It is exactly the usual experience of ease in being an individualist in modern American society that prompts us to reexamine the importance of groups. Although most Americans can quite easily avoid joining any groups that refuse to grant us the status we feel we deserve, when we *do* find ourselves in such a compelling group environment, functionality should dictate that we respond adaptively by finding a way to structure the group that makes it maximally effective and efficient.

NOTES

1. These task and social dimensions will not always correspond to the same internal–external perspectives. For example, an engineering division may establish its internal status rankings around who has the best technical skills, whereas higher-level managers who observe the division may be influenced more by the political and social skills of department staffers, and assign a different objective hierarchy (enacted through pay and privileges) than the staff itself experiences.

2. In several of these examples, the new group members have likely arrived after an extended "tournament" (Rosenbaum, 1979) in which they competed at successively narrowing levels to advance to a higher-status group. Stanford MBA students, for example, may have found that they were stars in high school, then arrived at a selective college as only one of many "stars." In order to advance, they had to stand out at the undergraduate level and then go on to be part of the smaller group selected by a prestigious employer; finally, they were selected from this group to join the even smaller group of MBA students at an elite program. This tournament model is not necessary to produce an "all-star" group with undifferentiated status and the imperative for sorting, but it is an excellent example of how such a need might arise.

3. Similar ideas have been presented by Hofstede (Hofstede & Bond, 1984) in his work on *power distance*, which refers to consensual acceptance of unequal power relations across members of a group or culture. Power distance appears to be at least somewhat correlated with tightness, with tight cultures possessing high power distance (i.e., greater acceptance of inequality) and loose cultures possessing low power distance (i.e., greater egalitarianism). However, the constructs are theoretically distinct: *acceptance of inequality* is the main dimension on which cultures differ in theories of power distance, and *degree of adherence to norms* is the theoretical dimension underlying tightness.

4. It should be noted at this point that we have been focusing on groups that are interdependent with respect to group goals and objectives. There are certainly groups in which coherence and coordination of individual effort is not particularly necessary. For example, in brainstorming groups, it is quite effective for each individual member to work alone. At the end of the brainstorming period, individual products are simply pooled, and the greatest disjunctive set of brainstormed items constitutes the group product. This can be distinguished from a group with high task interdependence, in which not only outputs, but even inputs for a given individual are dependent on the work produced by another individual. Our arguments assume some degree of interdependence in the group.

5. The literature on independence and interdependence is both large and controversial. Many theorists (e.g., Triandis, 1989; Singelis, 1994) have argued that independence and interdependence are orthogonal constructs, so that any given individual—or the profile of any group or culture—may be high or low on both. However, for purposes of our discussion, we are interested in examining people who are independent *and not* interdependent, and those who are interdependent *and not* independent. For simplicity, we will refer to the former as "independent" and the latter as "interdependent." It is interesting to consider what may happen when a status-seeker is high on both of these dimensions; however, we will leave that question to be explored in future work.

REFERENCES

Allport, G. W. (1958). *The nature of prejudice*. Reading, MA: Addison-Wesley.

Anderson, C., John, O. P., Keltner, D., & Kring, A. M. (2001). Who attains social status? Effects of personality and physical attractiveness in social groups. *Journal of Personality and Social Psychology*, *81*, 116–132.

Atwater, L. E., Dionne, S. D., & Avolio, B. (1999). A longitudinal study of the leadership development process: Individual differences predicting leader effectiveness. *Human Relations*, *52*, 1543–1562.

Bandura, A. (1986). *Social foundations of thought and action: A social cognitive theory*. Englewood Cliffs, NJ: Prentice-Hall.

Bandura, A. (1992). *Perceived self-efficacy in cognitive development and functioning*. Address to the annual meeting of the American Education Research Association, San Francisco.

Barkow, J. H. (1980). Prestige and self-esteem: A biosocial interpretation. In: D. R. Omark, F. F. Strayer & D. G. Freedman (Eds), *Dominance relations* (pp. 319–332). New York: Garland.

Benedict, R. (1946). *The chrysanthemum and the sword: Patterns of Japanese culture*. Boston: Houghton Mifflin.

Berger, J., Cohen, B. P., & Zelditch, M., Jr. (1972). Status characteristics and social interaction. *American Sociological Review*, *63*, 379–405.

Berger, J., Ridgeway, C. L., Fisek, M. H., & Norman, R. Z. (1998). The legitimation and delegitimation of power and prestige orders. *American Sociological Review*, *63*, 379–405.

Blaine, B., & Crocker, J. (1993). Self-esteem and self-serving biases in reactions to positive and negative events: An integrative review. In: R. F. Baumeister (Ed.), *Self-esteem: The puzzle of low self-regard* (pp. 55–85). New York: Plenum Press.

Brewer, M. B. (1991). The social self: On being the same and different at the same time. *Personality and Social Psychology Bulletin, 17*, 475–482.

Brewer, M. B. (1997). On the social origins of human nature. In: C. McGarty & S. A. Haslam (Eds), *The message of social psychology: Perspectives on mind in society* (pp. 54–62). Malden, MA: Blackwell.

Brockner, J. (1979). The effects of self-esteem, success-failure, and self-consciousness on task performance. *Journal of Personality and Social Psychology, 37*, 1732–1741.

Brown, P., & Levenson, S. C. (1987). *Politeness: Some universals in language usage*. Cambridge: Cambridge University Press.

Campbell, D. T. (1958). Common fate, similarity, and other indices of the status of aggregates of persons as social entities. *Behavioral Science, 3*, 14–25.

Caporael, L. R. (1997). The evolution of truly social cognition: The core configurations model. *Personality and Social Psychology Review, 1*, 276–298.

Caporael, L. R., & Baron, R. M. (1997). Groups as the mind's natural environment. In: J. Simpson & D. Kenrick (Eds), *Evolutionary social psychology* (pp. 317–343). Hillsdale, NJ: Lawrence Erlbaum.

Caporael, L. R., & Brewer, M. B. (1995). Hierarchical evolutionary theory: There is an alternative, and it's not creationism. *Psychological Inquiry, 6*(1), 31–34.

Carli, L. (1991). Gender, status, and influence. In: E. Lawler, B. Markovsky, C. Ridgeway & H. Walker (Eds), *Advances in group processes*, (Vol. 8, pp. 89–113). Greenwich, CT: JAI Press Inc.

Castano, E., Yzerbyt, V., Paladino, M. P., & Sacchi, S. (2002). I belong, therefore I exist: Ingroup identification, ingroup entitativity, and ingroup bias. *Personality and Social Psychology Bulletin, 28*, 135–143.

Chartrand, T., & Bargh, J. (1999). The chameleon effect: The perception-behavior link and social interaction. *Journal of Personality and Social Psychology, 76*, 893–910.

Chase, I. D. (1980). Social process and hierarchy formation in small groups: A comparative perspective. *American Sociological Review, 45*, 905–924.

Chemers, M. M., Watson, C. B., & May, S. T. (2000). Dispositional affect and leadership effectiveness: A comparison of self-esteem, optimism, and efficacy. *Personality and Social Psychology Bulletin, 26*, 267–277.

Copeland, J. T. (1994). Prophecies of power: Motivational implications of social power for behavioral confirmation. *Journal of Personality and Social Psychology, 67*, 264–277.

Correll, J., Overbeck, J.R., & Park, B. (2003). *Reciprocal causation in a national service group*. University of Colorado at Boulder (Unpublished data).

Crainer, S. (2001). *A success in design minus the capital D*. From http://www.ideo.com/media/times.asp (accessed May 4, 2003).

De Dreu, C. K. W., & Boles, T. L. (1998). Share and share alike or winner take all? The influence of social value orientation upon choice and recall of negotiation heuristics. *Organizational Behavior and Human Decision Processes, 76*, 253–276.

De Dreu, C. K. W., Weingart, L. R., & Kwon, S. (2000). Influence of social motives on integrative negotiation: A meta-analytic review and test of two theories. *Journal of Personality and Social Psychology, 78*, 889–905.

De Waal, F. (1998). *Chimpanzee politics*. Baltimore, MD: Johns Hopkings University Press.

Dion, K., Berscheid, E., & Walster, E. (1972). What is beautiful is good. *Journal of Personality and Social Psychology, 24*, 285–290.

Di Paula, A., & Campbell, J. D. (2002). Self-esteem and persistence in the face of failure. *Journal of Personality and Social Psychology*, *83*, 711–724.

Dryer, D. C., & Horowitz, L. M. (1997). When do opposites attract? Interpersonal complementarity versus similarity. *Journal of Personality and Social Psychology*, *72*, 592–603.

Elangovan, A. R., & Xie, J. L. (1999). Effects of perceived power of supervisor on subordinate stress and motivation: The moderating role of subordinate characteristics. *Journal of Organizational Behavior*, *20*, 359–373.

French, J. R. P., Jr., & Raven, B. H. (1959). The bases of social power. In: D. Cartwright (Ed.), *Studies in social power* (pp. 150–167). Ann Arbor, MI: Institute for Social Research.

Foa, U. G., & Foa, E. B. (1974). *Societal structures of the mind*. Oxford: Charles C. Thomas.

Gaertner, L., Sedikides, C., & Graetz, K. (1999). In search of self-definition: Motivational primacy of the individual self, motivational primacy of the collective self, or contextual primacy. *Journal of Personality and Social Psychology*, *76*, 5–18.

Gaertner, L., Sedikides, C., Vevea, J. L., & Iuzzini, J. (2002). The "I," the "We," and the "When": A meta-analysis of motivational primacy in self-definition. *Journal of Personality and Social Psychology*, *83*, 574–591.

Gruenfeld, D. H., & Hollingshead, A. B. (1993). Sociocognition in work groups: The evolution of group integrative complexity and its relation to task performance. *Small Group Research*, *24*, 383–405.

Hamilton, D. L., & Sherman, S. J. (1996). Perceiving persons and groups. *Psychological Review*, *103*, 336–355.

Hargadon, A., & Sutton, R. I. (2000). Building an innovation factory. *Harvard Business Review*, May–June, pp. 157–166.

Higgins, E. T. (1996). Ideals, oughts, and regulatory focus: Affect and motivation from distinct pains and pleasures. In: P. M. Gollwitzer & J. A. Bargh (Eds), *The Psychology of Action: Linking Cognition and Motivation to Behavior* (pp. 91–114). New York: Guilford Press.

Hjelle, L. A., & Clouser, R. (1970). Susceptibility to attitude change as a function of internal–external control. *Psychological Record*, *20*, 305–310.

Hofstede, G., & Bond, M. (1984). Hofstede's culture dimensions: An independent validation using Rokeach's value survey. *Journal of Cross-Cultural Psychology*, *15*, 417–433.

Hogan, J., & Hogan, R. (2002). Leadership and sociopolitical intelligence. In: R. E. Riggio & S. E. Murphy, et al. (Eds), *Multiple intelligences and leadership* (pp. 75–88). Mahwah, NJ: Lawrence Erlbaum.

Hogg, M. A. (2000). Subjective uncertainty reduction through self-categorization: A motivational theory of social identity processes. *European Review of Social Psychology*, *11*, 223–253.

Jackson, S. (1982). *Diversity in the workplace: Human resources initiatives*. New York: Guilford Press.

Janis, I. L. (1954). Personality correlates of susceptibility to persuasion. *Journal of Personality*, *22*, 504–518.

Judge, T. A., Erez, A. E., Bono, J. E., & Thoresen, C. J. (2002). Are measures of self-esteem, neuroticism, locus of control, and generalized self-efficacy, indicators of a common core construct? *Journal of Personality and Social Psychology*, *83*, 693–710.

Leary, M. R., Tambor, E. S., Terdal, S. K., & Downs, D. L. (1995). Self-esteem as an interpersonal monitor: The sociometer hypothesis. *Journal of Personality and Social Psychology*, *68*(3), 518–530.

Levin, S., Federico, C. M., Sidanius, J., & Rabinowitz, J. L. (2002). Social dominance orientation and intergroup bias: The legitimation of favoritism for high-status groups. *Personality and Social Psychology Bulletin, 28*, 144–157.

LeVine, R. A., & Campbell, D. T. (1972). *Ethnocentrism: Theories of conflict, ethnic attitudes, and group behavior*. Oxford: John Wiley & Sons.

Lickel, B., Hamilton, D. L., Wieczorkowska, G., Lewis, A., Sherman, S. J., & Uhles, A. N. (2000). Varieties of groups and the perception of group entitativity. *Journal of Personality and Social Psychology, 78*, 223–246.

Markus, H. R., & Kitayama, S. (1991). Culture and the self: Implications for cognition, emotion, and motivation. *Psychological Review, 98*, 224–253.

McFarlin, D. B., Baumeister, R. F., & Blascovich, J. (1984). On knowing when to quit: Task failure, self-esteem, advice, and nonproductive persistence. *Journal of Personality, 52*, 138–155.

McNelis, N. L., & Boatright-Horowitz, S. L. (1998). Social monitoring in a primate group: The relationship between visual attention and hierarchical ranks. *Animal Cognition, 1*, 65–69.

Moreland, R. L. (1987). The formation of small groups. In: C. Hendrick (Ed.), *Review of personality and social psychology*, (Vol. 8, pp. 80–110). Newbury Park, CA: Sage.

Morris, M. W., Menon, T., & Ames, D. R. (2001). Culturally conferred conceptions of agency: A key to social perception of persons, groups, and other actors. *Personality and Social Psychology Review, 5*, 169–182.

Ng, S. H., & Bradac, J. J. (1993). *Power in language: Verbal communication and social influence*. Thousand Oaks, CA: Sage.

O'Connor, K. M., Gruenfeld, D. H., & McGrath, J. E. (1993). The experience and effects of conflict in continuing work groups. *Small Group Research, 24*, 362–382.

O'Reilly, C. A., Williams, K. Y., & Barsade, S. (1998). Group demography and innovation: Does diversity help? In: D. H. Gruenfeld, M. A. Neale & E. A. Mannix (Eds), *Research on managing groups and teams*, (Vol. 1, pp. 183–207). Stamford, CT: JAI Press Inc.

Pruitt, D., & Rubin, J. Z. (1999). Strategic choice. In: R. J. Lewicki & D. M. Saunders, et al. (Eds), *Negotiation: Readings, exercises, and cases*, (3rd ed.) (pp. 14–31). Boston: Mc Graw-Hill.

Ridgeway, C. L., Boyle, E. H., Kuipers, K. J., & Robinson, D. T. (1998). How do status beliefs develop? The role of resources and interactional experience. *American Sociological Review, 63*, 331–350.

Robinson, D. T., & Smith-Lovin, L. (2001). Getting a laugh: Gender, status, and humor in task discussions. *Social Forces, 80*, 123–158.

Rosenbaum, J. E. (1979). Tournament mobility: Career patterns in a corporation. *Administrative Science Quarterly, 24*, 220–241.

Rosenberg, M. (1965). *Society and the adolescent self-image*. Princeton, NJ: Princeton University Press.

Rotter, J. B. (1966). Generalized expectancies for internal versus external control of reinforcement. *Psychological Monographs: General and Applied, 80*, 1–28.

Sandelands, L. E., Brockner, J., & Glynn, M. A. (1988). If at first you don't succeed, try, try again: Effects of persistence/performance contingencies, ego involvement, and self-esteem on task persistence. *Journal of Applied Psychology, 73*, 208–216.

Schmid Mast, M. (2001). Gender differences and similarities in dominance hierarchies in same-gender groups based on speaking time. *Sex Roles, 44*, 537–556.

Shelly, R. K., & Troyer, L. (2001). Emergence and completion of structure in initially undefined and partially defined groups. *Social Psychology Quarterly*, *64*, 318–332.
Sherer, M. (1982). The self-efficacy scale: Construction and validation. *Psychological Reports*, *51*, 663–671.
Sherif, M. (1958). Superordinate goals in the reduction of intergroup conflict. *American Journal of Sociology*, *63*, 349–356.
Shrauger, J., & Sorman, P. B. (1977). Self-evaluations, initial success and failure, and improvement as determinants of persistence. *Journal of Consulting and Clinical Psychology*, *45*, 784–795.
Sidanius, J., & Pratto, F. (1993). The inevitability of oppression and the dynamics of social dominance. In: P. M. Sniderman & P. E. Tetlock (Eds), *Prejudice, politics, and the american Dilemma* (pp. 173–211). Stanford, CA: Stanford University Press.
Sidanius, J., & Pratto, F. (1999). *Social dominance: An intergroup theory of social hierarchy and oppression*. New York: Cambridge University Press.
Singelis, T. M. (1994). The measurement of independent and interdependent self-construals. *Personality and Social Psychology Bulletin*, *20*, 580–591.
Smith, J. A., & Foti, R. J. (1998). A pattern approach to the study of leader emergence. *Leadership Quarterly*, *9*(2), 147–160.
Snarey, J., & Lydens, L. (1990). Worker equality and adult development: The kibbutz as a developmental model. *Psychology and Aging*, *5*, 86–93.
Snibbe, A., & Markus, H. (2002). You can't always get what you want: Educational attainment, agency, and choice. Stanford University (Unpublished doctoral dissertation).
Stanley, K. D., & Murphy, M. R. (1997). A comparison of general self-efficacy with self-esteem. *Genetic, Social, and General Psychology Monographs*, *123*, 79–99.
Tafarodi, R. W., & Swann, W. B. (1995). Self-liking and self-competence as dimensions of global self-esteem: Initial validation of a measure. *Journal of Personality Assessment*, *65*, 322–342.
Tett, R. P., & Murphy, P. J. (2002). Personality and situations in co-worker preference: Similarity and complementarity in worker compatibility. *Journal of Business and Psychology*, *17*, 223–243.
Tiedens, L. Z., & Fragale, A. R. (2003). Power moves: Complementarity in dominant and submissive nonverbal behavior. *Journal of Personality and Social Psychology*, *84*, 558–568.
Triandis, H. C. (1989). The self and social behavior in differing cultural contexts. *Psychological Review*, *96*, 506–520.
Turner, J. C., Hogg, M. A., Oakes, P. J., Reicher, S. D., & Wetherell, M. S. (1987). *Rediscovering the social group: A self-categorization theory*. Cambridge, MA: Blackwell.
Wasserman, S., & Faust, K. (1994). *Social network analysis: Methods and applications*. Cambridge, MA: Cambridge University Press.
Weick, K. E. (1996). *Sensemaking in organizations*. Newbury Park, CA: Sage.
Wilson, D. S. (1997). Incorporating group selection into the adaptationist program: A case study involving human decision making. In: J. Simpson & D. Kenrick (Eds), *Evolutionary social psychology* (pp. 345–386). Mahwah, NJ: Erlbaum.

COSMOPOLITANS AND LOCALS: STATUS RIVALRIES, DEFERENCE, AND KNOWLEDGE IN INTERNATIONAL TEAMS

Martine R. Haas

ABSTRACT

Drawing on sociological role theory, this chapter introduces and explains the distinction between cosmopolitan and local role orientations as status categories in international teams. Qualitative data from a multimethod field study conducted at a leading international development agency illustrates that the high status of cosmopolitans and locals in this setting was based on expectations that these team members would enable their teams to more effectively interpret knowledge obtained from outside sources. The possible dynamics of status rivalry and deference in teams with cosmopolitan and local membership are explored, and their implications for team performance are addressed. Thus, status in groups is viewed as both contested and contingent on the situation.

Status and Groups
Research on Managing Groups and Teams, Volume 7, 201–227

ISSN: 1534-0856/doi:10.1016/S1534-0856(05)07009-X

INTRODUCTION

There is a growing body of research on the dynamics and performance of teams with members of different nationalities (e.g., Argote & McGrath, 1993; Jackson, May, & Whitney, 1995; Snow, Snell, Davison, & Hambrick, 1996; Lawrence, 1997; Adler, 2002). Much of this research on international teams focuses on the number of nationalities represented on a team or the cultural distances between team members' nationalities to capture levels of team diversity, assuming that nationalities are directly related to team members' values, schema, demeanor and language, and thus to their perceptions and behaviors (e.g., Cox, 1993; Watson, Kumar, & Michaelson, 1993; Hambrick, Davison, Snell, & Snow, 1998). Researchers also have examined sources of heterogeneity in nationally diverse teams that go beyond simple nationality attributes (Earley & Mosakowski, 2000). For example, international teams are often structurally, as well as nationally, diverse with members who are located in multiple countries (virtual teams), perform different functions (cross-functional teams), or report to different managers (matrix teams) (Cummings, 2004). Demographic diversity, in terms of gender, race, age, tenure, and education characteristics, is another important source of heterogeneity in international teams (cf., Bantel & Jackson, 1989; Eisenhardt & Schoonhoven, 1990; Keck & Tushman, 1993; Williams & O'Reilly, 1998). Research on international teams, however, has largely overlooked the antecedents and consequences of diversity in the status attributed to team members with different types of international experience and expertise.

Status diversity can have important implications for the dynamics and performance of international teams because status hierarchies in groups reflect expectations about the task-related competencies of group members, and thus serve to organize interactions within groups, influencing how people behave toward one another and how work is conducted in group settings (Berger, Cohen, & Zelditch Jr., 1972; Berger, Rosenholtz, & Zelditch Jr., 1980). Research has shown, for example, that lower status group members feel pressure to conform to the demands of higher-status members (Kirchmeyer, 1993), obtain less useful information and ask fewer questions than higher-status members (Alkire, Collum, & Kaswan, 1968); are less likely to contribute unique information (Wittenbaum, 1998); and are given less consideration by higher-status members in group discussions (Propp, 1995). In contrast, individuals who possess expertise and experience that is valued by their colleagues are more confident and willing to share divergent information and advocate for their own position (Stasser, Stewart, & Wittenbaum, 1995; Stewart &

Stasser, 1995; Wittenbaum, 1998), and their opinions are more likely to be sought and heeded (cf., Blau, 1966). Being seen as an expert thus increases an individual's influence over the group (cf., Horai, Naccari, & Fattoullah, 1974). Given the importance of status in groups, our understanding of international teams might be advanced by addressing the sources and effects of status diversity in such contexts.

In this chapter, I focus on two different bases for the attribution of status in international teams: Whether a team member is a "cosmopolitan" who has lived and worked in many countries, or a "local" who has lived and worked in the country in which the team operates. To establish that cosmopolitans and locals can be viewed as status categories, I identify their status characteristics and explain the expectations that are associated with those characteristics, focusing on work settings in which team members regularly engage in extensive boundary spanning in order to gather knowledge to accomplish their tasks (cf., Tushman, 1977; Ancona & Caldwell, 1992). Specifically, I propose that both cosmopolitans and locals may be viewed as high in status because each is expected to enable their team to interpret knowledge obtained from outside sources accurately and appropriately for the task, although their interpretations are likely to be very different.

Building on these foundations, I then consider the possible implications of status diversity in the form of cosmopolitan and local membership for the dynamics and performance of international teams. Existing research on status diversity in groups usually focuses on the relations between high- and low-status members in groups where the status hierarchy is clear. But how do the dynamics of participation and influence play out in teams where there is more than one member with high status? The research tends to assume, moreover, that where there are multiple high-status individuals in a team, these individuals will be similar to each other (e.g., Owens, Neale, & Sutton, 1997). Yet in most organizations, the criteria for status attributions are numerous and heterogeneous. Sometimes two team members with very different status characteristics, such as cosmopolitans and locals, both have high status in a team. While cosmopolitans may be considered clearly superior to locals in some organizational settings and locals may be viewed as clearly superior in others, I focus here on contexts in which the relative ranking of cosmopolitans and locals is ambiguous. In such contexts, status in groups is likely to be more contested and contingent than current theories and research might suggest.

I illustrate my arguments with examples from qualitative data collected during a multimethod field study that I conducted at an international development agency whose mission is to promote economic development and alleviate poverty in developing countries. As they designed development projects, team members at this organization continuously gathered, interpreted, and applied knowledge from sources outside the team, where knowledge is defined as an organized body of information, data, facts, intelligence, or advice (Huber, 1991). The sources of knowledge they consulted included colleagues, professional experts, statistical and analytical reports, and document libraries and archives, both inside and outside the organization. After describing the research setting and approach, I examine the status attributions and expectations associated with cosmopolitan and local team members in this setting, and then turn to consider the status dynamics in teams with such members and their implications for team performance.

RESEARCH SETTING

"Quorum" (a pseudonym) is a leading international development agency with over 10,000 employees and 100 international offices. The organization has a matrix structure, with operations spanning six geographic regions (Africa, East Asia and Pacific, Eastern Europe and Central Asia, Latin America and Caribbean, Middle East and North Africa, and South Asia) and four divisions focused on different development and poverty alleviation domains. Between 1999 and 2001, I studied Quorum teams that were engaged in preparing two types of projects: Financial assistance projects, which took the form of major social and economic development programs that were backed by loans to the client governments for their implementation, and technical assistance projects, which provided detailed analysis and advice to client governments on specific development issues.

Qualitative Data Collection

To develop an understanding of the organizational setting, the teams, and their tasks, and to generate questions for a survey (not analyzed here), I conducted 70 formal and semi-formal interviews lasting between one and three hours each. This research began with 20 interviews with managers and staff, including members of the units responsible for strategy and change management, knowledge management, project quality assessment, human resources, and the staff association, as listed in Table 1. I used these open-ended interviews to gain an overview of the organization's functions and

Table 1. Manager and Staff Interviews.

Responsibility	Number of Interviewees
Line management	2
Strategy/change	3
Project quality assessment	4
Human resources/staff association	5
Knowledge management	6
Total	20

operations from a staff perspective, rather than an operational one. Next, I conducted 18 semi-structured interviews with the leaders and members of multiple teams based at Quorum's U.S. headquarters, and seven further interviews in Russia, where I visited Quorum's Moscow office. The purpose of these interviews was to explore the conditions that might be important for a team's project performance and develop measures of the central constructs for inclusion in a survey. I usually asked the interviewees to describe a project on which they were currently working, probing for specific details about the composition of the team and how the members carried out the work. I listened for examples of how they collected and used knowledge from outside sources, the problems they encountered, and how these were resolved. In Russia, I also asked the interviewees about various aspects of working in a Quorum country office, to develop an understanding of work at Quorum from the perspective of team leaders and members who were located in the client countries rather than at headquarters. Table 2 provides a summary of the projects discussed in the team interviews. I then conducted another 25 interviews as part of detailed case studies of seven teams, which I undertook in order to gain a fuller understanding of how teams worked together at Quorum. These seven teams were selected for variation across regions and divisions, as my preliminary research had suggested that there might be significant differences in how work was done in different parts of the organization. As these teams' projects were underway at the time these teams were studied, the quality of their project outputs was not yet known. I interviewed the leader of each team, all the members who were currently engaged substantially in the team's work, unless they were traveling at the time, and specialists and consultants who were involved with the team on a more sporadic basis. In addition, I observed team meetings and read project materials that were generated as the teams worked. I later reviewed my tapes and notes to identify data that pertained to the team's use of knowledge

Table 2. Team Interviews.

Region	Project Focus	Project Type
Africa	Civil service reform	Research
Africa	Infrastructure sector	Investment
Africa	Macroeconomic restructuring	Investment
Africa	Private capital flows	Research
Africa	Social security reform	Research
Africa	Urban development strategy	Investment
Africa	Water transfer scheme	Investment
East Asia and Pacific	Macroeconomic restructuring	Research
East Asia and Pacific	Macroeconomic development	Research
Europe and Central Asia	Assorted (seven Russian interviews)	Assorted
Europe and Central Asia	Agriculture sector reform	Investment
Europe and Central Asia	Fiscal sustainability	Research
Europe and Central Asia	Public finance legal framework	Investment
Latin America and Caribbean	Environmental protection	Investment
Latin America and Caribbean	Poverty assessment	Research
Latin America and Caribbean	Urban slum upgrading	Investment
Middle East and North Africa	Agricultural policy	Research
Middle East and North Africa	Poverty assessment	Research
Middle East and North Africa	Public expenditure management	Investment
Total		25 interviews

from outside sources, the composition of the team, status attributions and dynamics, project quality, and the extent to which these constructs varied across teams. Table 3 summarizes the interviews conducted during these case studies, and these provide the primary data on which I draw to illustrate the arguments of this chapter.

I also gained insights into the organizational setting from three additional sources. First, my access to Quorum came about because I was brought in to help the organization conduct a major internal review of its knowledge management programs and structures. This review gave me a broad overview of the organization's aims and operations, as well as providing specific details on the challenges involved in obtaining and using knowledge at Quorum. Second, through observation and participation in a customized executive education program that had been set up to train top managers from Quorum and several organizations with which it regularly collaborated, I learned more about the objectives, attitudes and concerns of Quorum's employees, and the work of the organization and its teams. Finally, I consulted archival materials extensively throughout the field research, reading external documents about Quorum, internal organizational documents, and

Table 3. Case Study Interviews.

Region	Project Focus	Number of Team members	Number of Interviewees
Africa	Urban slums	10	4
Europe and Central Asia	Education	9	5
Europe and Central Asia	Social services	4	3
Latin America and Caribbean	Urban slums	6	4
Latin America and Caribbean	Environment	5	4
Middle East and North Africa	Cultural heritage	7	3
Middle East and North Africa	Housing	4	2
Total		45	25

project-related documents. Access to Quorum's Intranet site provided information on ongoing issues and events, as well as the opportunity to follow active online discussions. I also attended events including meetings, seminars, workshops, and speeches concerning a wide range of aspects of the work at Quorum.

Quorum Teams

Teams at Quorum ranged in size from 2 to 23 members (the average was 8.5 members), who allocated anywhere from 10% to 80% of their time to the project (the average was 30%). The team members moved on and off the team as needed over the duration of the project, which typically lasted about a year, though they ranged from 2 months to 4 years. Every Quorum team was interdisciplinary, and made up of experts who were brought together specifically for the purpose of a particular project and frequently had little prior or subsequent contact.

The team members were all highly trained, mostly with Ph.Ds and extensive experience in development. They included economists and other social scientists, engineers, technical specialists, procurement specialists, and lawyers, with wide-ranging specialties in areas, such as public finance, agriculture, housing, health, education, and gender issues. Yet even with all their expertise, obtaining knowledge from sources outside the team was critical to the work of every team member, because the projects inevitably demanded more knowledge than a team could possess. In recognition of the centrality of knowledge sharing to the work, Quorum had introduced a high profile "knowledge management strategy" that was widely acclaimed by independent business groups, and had made substantial investments in information technology, document databases, communities of practice, help desks, and directories of experts.

One team that was working on a slum-upgrading program for an impoverished West African country was typical of those at Quorum. The purpose of this project was to improve the living conditions of millions of slum dwellers in the main cities of this country. The team was charged with designing the program, which was then to be backed by a $50 million loan to the client government for its implementation. The team members included both Quorum employees and external consultants who were all international experts in specialized fields that included water and sanitation service provision, urban transport systems, coastal management, resettlement, and community participation. The amount of time the team members devoted to the project, which varied widely, was spent mostly on collecting, interpreting, analyzing, and integrating information and knowledge from other experts and sources outside the team, as well as on team meetings and on information gathering trips to the client country, including one visit to 13 cities to compare their slum conditions.

Like this West Africa team, approximately 80% of Quorum teams were based at the organization's U.S. headquarters, flying in and out of the client countries regularly during the course of their projects, while 20% were based in those client countries. Yet wherever the teams were based, they usually included team members with a range of national backgrounds. There were three main reasons for this. Quorum's hiring policy was explicitly built on national quotas, with the result that employees were drawn from every country in the world; Quorum tried to staff its project teams with those who had the greatest technical expertise in the domain of the project, and these experts were often people who previously had worked on similar projects in other countries; and Quorum was actively concerned about its teams "going local" – prioritizing the interests of domestic stakeholders over the best interests of the project – and believed that this was less likely to occur if the teams were staffed with non-nationals of the client country. Despite these concerns, however, there had been a movement in recent years to ensure that Quorum teams also included members with background and experience in the client country, in order to increase teams' sensitivity to local conditions and constraints. The result was that Quorum teams often included both cosmopolitan and local team members.

COSMOPOLITANS AND LOCALS AS STATUS CATEGORIES

The distinction between cosmopolitans and locals draws from sociological theories of role orientations that are rooted in Merton's (1957) distinction between types of influentials. In his work, locals were individuals whose interests were confined to the community in which they exerted influence, and cosmopolitans were individuals who were oriented to the world beyond the community in which they exerted influence and regarded themselves as part of that wider world. Gouldner (1957) developed this distinction in an organizational context, where he defined locals as those employees whose primary loyalty was to the employing organization, and cosmopolitans as those who were oriented more toward their professional community beyond the organization. The distinction between organizational and professional role orientations has proved fruitful for empirical research on commitment (e.g., Tuma & Grimes, 1981; Cornwall & Grimes, 1987; Becker & Billings, 1993). The concepts of cosmopolitan and local have also been adapted to apply to research on international management; however, there they are used to distinguish between individuals who have a global orientation because they operate across countries, and individuals who are oriented to a particular local environment because they are rooted in that country (e.g., Kanter, 1995; Tung, 1998). This application of the concepts to international organizations is the one that emerged as relevant to Quorum's teams.

At Quorum, some team members had lived and worked in many countries and spoke the languages of those countries. These individuals I call "cosmopolitans." An example was a team member who was a native of El Salvador, spoke Spanish, Portuguese and French, and had worked and lived in countries including Mozambique, Algeria, and Venezuela. Meanwhile, others had lived and worked in the client country and spoke the language of that country. I call these "locals." For example, one team member who worked on Russian projects had completed a Ph.D. on Russia's integration into the world economy and spent 11 years at the Russian Academy of Sciences before joining Quorum. It was rare, though not impossible, for one individual to possess the characteristics of both a cosmopolitan and a local, but it was common to be neither a cosmopolitan nor a local for the purposes of a given project.[1] At the group level, the composition of a Quorum team did not necessarily include members who were locals of the client country, since it was usual practice to assign nationals from one country to work on projects in a different country, though increasingly efforts were being made to include locals on the teams. Likewise, although most individuals worked on projects in many countries over the course of their tenure at Quorum, they did not necessarily spend time living in those countries, or learn the local languages, and so some teams did not include cosmopolitan members. Nevertheless, many teams did include at least one cosmopolitan and one local member.[2]

Status Attributions

The backgrounds of cosmopolitans and locals were important at Quorum because their different sets of characteristics each served as a basis for status attributions. According to status characteristics theory, status beliefs (widely shared evaluations that one state of a characteristic is more highly valued and desirable than another) lead to a process of status generalization, whereby actors attribute a specific ability or an overall competence to themselves and others based on the possession of particular status characteristics (Berger et al., 1972; Berger, Fisek, Norman, & Zelditch, 1977). These status characteristics, defined as any characteristics of any actor that influence his or her own and others' evaluations and beliefs about that actor, and that have at least two differentially evaluated states (Berger et al., 1972; Cohen & Zhou, 1991), range from demographics to personality attributes (Berger et al., 1980; Anderson, John, Keltner, & Kring, 2001). While some status characteristics are diffuse attributes from which assumptions that are generalizable to many situations are inferred, others are specific to particular organizational and task-related situations (Berger et al., 1972). In the Quorum context, diffuse characteristics related to where team members had lived and worked and their language abilities served as one basis for the conferral of status.

In the status hierarchy of Quorum teams, there were numerous other dimensions along which status varied, including age, tenure in the organization, academic credentials, and technical specialty. Other factors being equal however, both cosmopolitans and locals tended to be viewed as higher in status than team members who were neither cosmopolitans nor locals. This was apparent during many agonized conversations with team members about the discrepancy between the actual and the desired composition of their teams. For instance, a member of a team that was working on a housing project in French-speaking North Africa complained about the lack of locals on his team:

> ... it's been so difficult to put a team together. We need French speakers, who aren't easy to find. And the team leader knows about housing policy, but he's never worked in [this country] before. None of us have. The final team wasn't necessarily the preferred one.

In contrast, the leader of a social services project in an East–Central European country spoke proudly of a team member who was relatively young and junior in the organization, but had the status characteristics of a cosmopolitan:

> We've got a great team working on this ... One of the best things about it is that we managed to find [Leisa] and get her on board, she's Russian, but she's been all over the region, and really has a lot to offer.

Cosmopolitans and locals clearly were valued members of Quorum teams. This raises further questions, however: Why did cosmopolitan and local characteristics serve as important bases for attributions of high status to these team members, in addition to the numerous other bases for conferring status that existed at Quorum? What were the expectations associated with these status attributions? And what might be the possible implications of including cosmopolitan and local members on a team for that team's performance?

Status Expectations: Interpreting Knowledge

Status characteristics theory proposes that status hierarchies arise when it is widely believed that particular characteristics give individuals who possess them the potential to make valuable contributions to a task (Berger et al., 1972). At Quorum, cosmopolitans and locals were highly regarded because it was generally assumed that their backgrounds would enable them to help their international teams to address the critical challenge of "thinking globally, acting locally" (cf., Bartlett & Ghoshal, 1989; Snell, Snow, Davison, & Hambrick, 1998). Specifically, cosmopolitans and locals were expected to be able to guide the team in interpreting and applying the vast amounts of knowledge obtained from external sources in ways that were both accurate and appropriate for the task.

As people strive to understand their environments and function in them, they continually engage in a process of sense making (Weick, 2001). A team's use of knowledge from outside sources can be viewed as a specific form of interaction with its environment, involving an ongoing process of interpretation through which meaning is actively constructed by the team members. Such a view suggests that knowledge is not simply a "good" with an objective value; instead, there are many plausible interpretations of the environment (Smircich & Stubbart, 1985), and team members may select, manipulate, and even ignore information as they construct these interpretations (Pfeffer & Salancik, 1978). In an organizational context where knowledge is usually contested terrain rather than absolute fact, and often emerges from very specific local experiences, as at Quorum, controversies over interpretation and meaning are likely to be especially acute.

The difficulties at Quorum arose as teams struggled to arrive at interpretations that were as accurate and appropriate as possible for their projects. They had to interpret knowledge from the client country carefully, considering its potential flaws, assumptions, and relevance for the project at hand. And they also had to interpret knowledge from other countries with caution, taking into account the situations in those countries and evaluating how well these corresponded to the situation in the client country. The importance and challenges of interpreting knowledge accurately and appropriately were evident in the case of the Quorum team that was working on the housing project in North Africa. Most housing in this war-ravaged country was provided by the government, but ongoing fighting had pushed people from the countryside to the overcrowded cities, there were not enough rental housing units, and corruption ruled those that were available. The new housing program was intended to encourage a shift toward more private home ownership. There was no shortage of knowledge on this issue available within Quorum, in the client country, and in the international development community, but the problem lay in understanding the contexts in which this knowledge had been generated and how to adapt it for the present situation. As the team leader put it:

> There's a massive amount of information in report after report available on the housing sector in [our organization]. This can make it difficult because people have their own ways of doing things, but it's important to know what's been done in the past, what's happened in [the client country], experiences from elsewhere ... Take 'guided settlement', the idea is to allocate areas for squatters, knowing that later those areas will be provided with water, sewage services, etc. This is interesting and relevant, but it's not so much a matter of new ideas as of seeing which would work in the country.

Without careful interpretation, using such information from outside sources potentially could harm rather than improve a project. The sheer volume of available knowledge often created problems of information overload and competition for the limited attention of the team members (cf., Hansen & Haas, 2001). With inadequate insight into the contexts in which the knowledge they collected was generated, they could be tempted to substitute available solutions or "best practices" from other countries for their own independent thinking, or risk relying too much on superficial or partial impressions gained during a brief visit to the client country to guide their understanding of country-specific knowledge. Such problems plagued the

North African housing team, which found itself unable to design a housing program that would meet the standards of external evaluators. As a disillusioned team member noted:

> We circulated the project documents for comments last month, and got back two long sets of negative written comments, plus two brief positive verbal comments. The two people who don't like it know lots about [the country], and they think we've got some fundamental things wrong. The two people who do aren't really involved and don't know much about it.

This example illustrates the basis for the attributions of high status to cosmopolitan and local team members, and the associated expectations about their contributions to the team. Cosmopolitans were high in status because their wide-ranging exposure to different countries suggested that they could offer valuable insights into which lessons learned from previous projects and best practices developed in other countries were likely to hold across national contexts, and which were not. Sometimes they evaluated knowledge from the client country and weighed it against their experiences in other contexts, while at other times they drew on their international experiences to provide views on the relevance and applicability of knowledge from other countries. A team leader who was working on an environmental project in Latin America offered an example that illustrates how the attribution of status to a cosmopolitan team member was based on his potential contributions as an interpreter of external knowledge:

> [John] is essential to this team because he brings us back to reality when we're getting all excited about the latest ideas that economists are touting on how to impose charges for pollution ... He reminds us that there are places where this stuff should really have had a good chance of working, but it hasn't even got off the ground.

Locals were high in status, meanwhile, because their immersion in the client country suggested that they could provide critical input on how the specific demands and constraints of that country should shape the project. They could question or confirm interpretations of knowledge from other countries in light of their deep understanding of circumstances in the client country. One Quorum team member emphasized the importance of locals' credibility in generating respect from fellow team members when he criticized the composition of a team that was working on a project in Russia, yet included no Russian members:

> It's like if Russians were to do an analysis of the American education system without spending any significant time there – it's silly. When a person comes from D.C. for health reform and visits two hospitals for two hours each, it's not enough. And they stay in the national hotels and eat at the best restaurants ... But [another] team I'm working

> with is good because the core members have been working with Russia for seven years. They've visited more regions than many Russians, they know lots of people in the ministries ... they've traveled in trains and lived in dorms.

Relying on status categories like cosmopolitan or local to determine which team members are likely to be able to offer valuable contributions to a team is imperfect, yet frequently necessary because relevant experience and expertise is often difficult to identify directly in organizations (Einhorn, Hogarth, & Klempner, 1977; Yetton & Bottger, 1982). This is especially so when team members lack titles or roles that explicitly signal the depth of their experience (Olivera & Argote, 1999) and do not already know each other (Thomas-Hunt & Phillips, 2003). In such situations of uncertainty, status categories can provide a useful way for team members to understand their own and their colleagues' potential contributions to the task (cf., Podolny, 1993). At Quorum, it was an article of faith that all projects required extensive collection and application of knowledge that had been generated from past experiences in other countries, and also of relevant knowledge about the client country. Yet team members could not easily tell which of the various functional experts on a team really possessed the insight necessary to interpret such knowledge accurately and appropriately. Consequently, though they themselves did not often use the terms "cosmopolitan" or "local," they recognized the potentially valuable contributions of these team members by granting status to individuals with cosmopolitan and local characteristics. These status attributions were based on the expectation that these team members could provide accurate and appropriate interpretations of external knowledge. Such expectations are consistent with organizational theories that suggest that prior experience creates the cognitive frameworks needed to interpret new knowledge, thus increasing absorptive capacity (Cohen & Levinthal, 1990; Lane & Lubatkin, 1998). Following Swidler (1986), the cultural and cross-cultural understandings that cosmopolitan and local team members can offer may be viewed as providing teams with valuable cultural "tool kits" and the ability to wield these tools successfully.

In Quorum teams, a straightforward social exchange thus was expected, in which valuable help with the task would be received in exchange for the granting of status to team members with cosmopolitan and local characteristics (Blau, 1966). Cosmopolitans and locals were also valued both for their roles as team members with their own expertise, of course, and as boundary spanners who could access particular sources of knowledge. But these roles did not distinguish them from non-cosmopolitan or non-local team members, who were all experts in their own fields and all engaged in extensive boundary spanning activities. Rather, their high status was based primarily on their expected contributions as interpreters of external knowledge. While cosmopolitans and locals typically were regarded as higher in status than otherwise similar non-cosmopolitans or non-locals, considerable ambiguity surrounded the issue of whether cosmopolitans ranked higher in status than locals, or vice versa, as well as the issue of whether the views of cosmopolitans and locals were always or only sometimes superior to those of non-cosmopolitans or non-locals. Accordingly, status hierarchies in Quorum teams were contested and contingent on the situation. In the following section, I extrapolate from these findings to address the likely implications of cosmopolitan and local team membership for team performance.

STATUS RIVALRY AND STATUS DEFERENCE

In organizations like Quorum where there is ambiguity about the relative ranking of cosmopolitans and locals, and the usefulness of their contributions in particular situations, status rivalries may emerge and create problems for team performance. Such status rivalries are most likely to surface when one high-status member advocates a viewpoint that is then resisted by another high-status member with a different viewpoint. Due to their different orientations, cosmopolitans and locals will often differ substantially in their perspectives on important issues facing the team. Whereas cosmopolitans usually will emphasize the generalizability of lessons and insights from other countries, locals will usually emphasize the unique conditions that prevailed in the client country. For example, in a meeting at Quorum to discuss the progress of the West African slum-upgrading project, a local team member argued:

> NGOs [non-governmental organizations] that we've consulted tell us that the residents won't be able to pay for all these new water and sanitation services [that we're planning] ... we should really think through the possibility of creating a micro-credit program to help them finance their utility payments.

But a cosmopolitan who had worked on micro-credit schemes in other countries replied:

> Well, look at all the cases of schemes like that in [other countries]. What they show is basically that yes, we need to help residents pay for their services if the upgrading is going to succeed, but micro-credit is a very specialized area, it requires specific expertise and dedicated resources. It shouldn't just be added on as part of the upgrading, it needs to be done separately and properly.

While cosmopolitans and locals are likely to have different opinions, their relative abilities to influence their colleagues on the team may be unclear because their relative status within the team is ambiguous. Questioning of the opinion of one high-status member by another, therefore, may be viewed as a status challenge. If the group decides in favor of the advice offered by the local, then the status of the cosmopolitan as a source of valuable insight is undermined. Likewise, if the group favors the cosmopolitan, then the high status of the local is compromised. Individuals usually value the esteem of their colleagues and wish to retain high-status positions, and often harbor concerns that other high-status members might dilute their influence (cf., Owens, Mannix, & Neale, 1998). It is likely, therefore, that cosmopolitans and locals each will attempt to defend their views vigorously against perceived challenges from potential status rivals, causing status-based conflicts to flare. Status similarity thus can lead to an increase in contested influence in the team (cf., Owens & Sutton, 2002).

The implication of this jostling for influence among high-status team members is that cosmopolitan and locals may potentially impede the team's performance, rather than improve it, if they perceive different views as status challenges and react defensively by refusing to compromise or engage with alternative perspectives in an effort to assert their dominance in the team's status hierarchy. Since conflicts that result from status rivalries are likely to focus at least in part on interpersonal issues of relative standing in the status hierarchy, rather than exclusively on task-related issues, they may be dysfunctional rather than functional for the team (cf., Jehn, 1995, 1997). The team might be torn in different directions by competing cosmopolitan and local members who will not listen to each other, and thus fail to converge on a project solution that is internally coherent. Instead, different parts of the project may end up being tailored to the views of different constituencies. The team may end up settling for a solution that is coherent, but is also suboptimal, simply in order to assuage the tensions within the group and get the project completed. Or one or more of the team members may opt out of the team and refuse to pull their weight because they are unhappy with the team's dynamics, leaving the task short staffed and the other team members overburdened.

Dynamics of status rivalry are not confined, however, to teams that include both cosmopolitan and local members. Though probably less common, they also may surface in teams that have only cosmopolitan or local members. In such teams, the high-status cosmopolitans or locals again may find their views challenged, though this time by lower status members rather than by members of equal status. Skepticism or criticism from lower status team members who are neither cosmopolitans nor locals is somewhat less threatening than similar attacks from higher-status team members, but nevertheless might still be perceived as a status challenge, resulting in defensiveness and unwillingness to compromise on the part of the high-status members and increased conflict aimed at protecting standing in the status hierarchy.

The possibility of status rivalries thus suggests that cosmopolitan and local members can cause problems for their teams in organizational settings where they are accorded high status. Contrary to widely held status expectations, moreover, it is possible that these problems may even become so disruptive that teams that include such members actually perform less effectively than teams without them.

The problems caused by status rivalries are likely to be offset, however, to the extent that teams collect more external knowledge and therefore provide more opportunities for cosmopolitans and locals to play valid and useful roles as interpreters of such knowledge. As this is where their value lies for their teams, the benefits of having these individuals on the team may be greater in part because they truly have important contributions to offer, based on their cosmopolitan and local experiences and expertise. Not only may they contribute more to the team, but they also may be viewed by their fellow team members as contributing more. Since their status derives from expectations about their abilities to interpret external knowledge for the team, their colleagues are likely to consider their opinions and views more carefully when they are based on interpretations of external knowledge.

As the cosmopolitans and locals present their different perspectives, their colleagues' expectations about their potential contributions to the task will be fulfilled, and their high status perceived as well deserved. As a result, cosmopolitans and locals will be accorded respect not only by lower status team members, but also by each other. This status deference might be due in part to their objectively superior abilities to interpret that knowledge. But it also might be due to a tendency for higher-status individuals to be judged more competent at interpreting external knowledge than lower status individuals, even when no objective performance differences exist, as a result of double standards; because high-status members are expected to perform better, their contributions are evaluated against more lenient standards (Foschi, 2000). When teams use more external knowledge, therefore, cosmopolitans and locals may offer benefits that outweigh the potential problems caused by status rivalries; they are likely to contribute more, and to be viewed as contributing more by their colleagues, resulting in greater status deference and fewer status challenges.

These dynamics suggest that the more knowledge the team obtains from outside sources, the more valuable it will be to have cosmopolitan and local team members. The benefits of having both types of members are likely to outweigh the benefits of having either type of member alone, because a local can correct any tendency of a cosmopolitan to overlook the distinctive characteristics of the situation in the client country, while a cosmopolitan can correct any tendency of a local to assume that the situation in the client country was unique. The advantages of having both a cosmopolitan and a local member were apparent in the case of a Quorum team that was working on a cultural tourism project for another North African country. The team members collected large volumes of information from local consultants, ideas and insights from the client counterparts, and experiences from other countries where cultural heritage projects had been implemented in the past. As they did so, they heatedly discussed their views of this knowledge, each interpreting it within their own cognitive frameworks and then checking their assumptions and conclusions with each other, before arriving at a collective understanding of how to proceed. The two team members who were central to these processes of interpretation and integration were a cosmopolitan who had lived and worked in Jordan, Lebanon, Egypt and Morocco, and the team leader, who was very familiar with the client country, and although not born there, qualified as a local as she had lived and worked there, and spoke the language. As a third team member noted:

> People at [Quorum] mostly take a European approach to economics and management issues, but [this team leader] understands what will work well in [the country]. When she talks to [the cosmopolitan team member], you can see her figuring out which ideas make sense and which don't.

Although divergences in the opinions and views of cosmopolitan and local team members still can create conflict within teams like this one, this conflict is likely to be underpinned by deference to the expertise of these high-status team members, if their views are based on interpretations of external knowledge. The conflict thus is likely to focus on constructive engagement over substantive task-related concerns. Such task-related conflict between two high-status team members with different, but equally valuable, perspectives to offer is likely to benefit the team, resulting in improved performance (cf., Jehn, 1995, 1997). Indeed, this was the outcome of the West African team's discussion of micro-credit schemes, where the conflicting views of the local and cosmopolitan were based on interpretations and applications of external knowledge, and therefore resulted in a constructive debate that advanced the team's agenda rather than impeding it.

Teams that must interpret large quantities of external knowledge are likely to benefit most from having both cosmopolitan and local members, but having either cosmopolitans or locals alone also may help them to perform more effectively. While their contributions often will be useful for the team, the general tendency of lower status members to accord deference to the views of higher-status members may lead the team to accept the views of high-status cosmopolitans and locals too readily or uncritically, and problems of groupthink may result (cf., Janis, 1982). For example, if the cosmopolitan in the West African team had not challenged the view of the local, the team might have designed a micro-credit scheme that did not take into account the specific and dedicated resources that such a scheme required. Such an outcome is less likely in teams that include both cosmopolitans and locals, because the views of one high-status member are more likely to be subjected to close scrutiny by another equally influential high-status member.

The dynamics of status deference thus suggest that the problems of status rivalry are likely to be reduced or offset to the extent that cosmopolitans and locals have greater contributions to offer because the team uses knowledge from outside sources more extensively. Where the use of external knowledge is high, teams with only cosmopolitans or locals will perform better than teams with neither cosmopolitan nor local members, and teams with both will perform best. The more external knowledge a team uses, the greater will be the benefits of having high-status cosmopolitan and local team members.

DISCUSSION

The analysis of status in work groups presented in this chapter has argued that cosmopolitans and locals can be important status categorizations for the members of international teams, and suggested that the dynamics of status rivalry and deference that emerge within these teams may have significant implications for team performance. While status rivalries can result in dysfunctional conflict that harms team performance, these problems are likely to be offset by the benefits that cosmopolitans and locals can offer when they serve as interpreters of external knowledge.

International teams that need to interpret knowledge from outside sources rely on cosmopolitans and locals to perform this function in many organizational settings other than that exemplified by Quorum. Consider, for example, an international marketing team planning to launch a new cell phone in the Malaysian market. Or a management consulting team from

Europe that has been assigned to advise a new banking client in South Africa on corporate strategy. Or an international joint venture team that is developing a new line of Indian packaged foods for sale in U.S. supermarkets. These teams must draw extensively on knowledge from outsiders, including customers, competitors, and collaborators, if they are to carry out their tasks successfully. Accordingly, the Malaysian marketing team might benefit from the contributions of a member who has spent considerable time in Malaysia and knows the country well, and another member who can provide a more global comparative perspective on how conditions in Malaysia differ from conditions in other countries in which the company operated. The cosmopolitan might steer the team toward marketing approaches that had worked well in other countries and away from those that had failed, while the local might provide insights into the likely barriers to acceptance in Malaysia. Similarly, the composition of the South African banking team might usefully include locals who understand the particular opportunities and constraints of operating retail banks in that country, as well as cosmopolitans who can check the team's assumptions and ideas against realities that they have observed in other countries. The domains in which cosmopolitans and locals are likely to play important roles on international teams thus are wide ranging.

In developing arguments about status attributions, expectations, and implications in such teams, this chapter extends existing theory and research on status in groups in four main ways: by considering the role that status characteristics, attributions, and expectations play in the specific context of international teams; by examining the dynamics that evolve between high-status team members, as well as those between high- and low-status members; by taking an external perspective that considers the roles of team members as interpreters of knowledge from outside the team; and by addressing the implications of status categorizations and expectations for performance outcomes.

In analyzing status dynamics in international teams in particular, the chapter addresses gaps in both the status literature and the international management literature. Although race, gender, tenure, and other relatively well-studied status characteristics may create differential performance expectations in international teams, as they generally do in groups (cf., Berger et al., 1972, 1977), the status categories of cosmopolitans and locals and the performance expectations associated with them are particularly relevant to the domain of teams that operate across international borders. Indeed, given the likely cross-cultural differences in attributing high or low status to standard demographic categories such as male/female or white/black, status categorizations such as cosmopolitans and locals that traverse cross-cultural boundaries may be more salient and powerful in shaping group dynamics and outcomes because they are based on characteristics whose value is determined within organizations rather than by societies. Thus it is important for status researchers to analyze the distinctive context of international teams. Likewise, it is also important for international management research to consider the challenge of combining local differentiation with global integration not just from a structural perspective, by examining relations between subsidiaries and headquarters (e.g., Bartlett & Ghoshal, 1989; Nohria & Ghoshal, 1997), but also from a team composition perspective, by addressing the ways in which this challenge can be met through staffing teams with members who can contribute both local and global insights.

Focusing on the status dynamics between cosmopolitans and locals addresses another issue that has received relatively little attention in the literature on status in groups to date: how interactions between team members with high status for different reasons influence the team's work. For example, how does the division head interact with the Chief Financial Officer on a top management team? How does the Chief Executive Officer interact with the chairman on an executive board? How does the technical wizard interact with the marketing guru on a cross-functional product development team? Current status research that assumes that team members can be ranked quite easily from high to low status can offer only limited insights into such situations, but considering the contested nature of status hierarchies and the dynamics of status rivalry and deference offers opportunities to advance our understanding of the way these teams function and perform. One limitation of the present study that should be noted here, however, is that in studying cosmopolitan and local members of international teams at Quorum, I have developed arguments about status dynamics that are based on an organizational setting in which both cosmopolitans and locals are regarded as high-status team members. Clearly, this may not be the case in every organization, since sometimes cosmopolitans may be regarded as more valuable team members than locals, or vice versa, and the arguments therefore must be bounded accordingly.

Another way in which this chapter builds on the existing status literature is by taking an "external perspective" on teams that recognizes the importance of teams' interactions with external constituencies for their performance (cf., Ancona, 1987). Research from an external perspective has examined both the behavioral relations between teams and their environments, such as boundary spanning activities, scouting behaviors, and influence attempts (e.g., Tushman, 1977; Ancona & Caldwell, 1992; Gresov &

Stephens, 1993), and the structural relations between teams and their environments, such as task design and reward systems (e.g., Hackman, 1987; Wageman, 1995). Extending these concerns to the domain of status dynamics in international teams draws attention to how the contributions of cosmopolitans and locals to their teams depend on the extent to which teams are engaged in interpreting knowledge obtained from sources outside the team, and raises the question of whether and when teams' interactions with their external environments may hurt rather than help team performance (cf., Haas & Hansen, 2005).

The discussion of performance implications in this chapter also contributes to advancing the insights of prior research on status in work groups. Most of this research examines the effects of status on team members' participation levels and styles, but does not directly address the effects of these differential participation patterns on the team's eventual performance, or else focuses on laboratory-generated performance measures such as decision quality. Nevertheless, the question of how team performance is affected in real organizational settings, whether negatively, positively, or not at all, is clearly central to the issues raised by the status-based participation patterns that have been identified in prior studies. Here, I suggest that the performance implications of having cosmopolitan and local members may be contingent on the situation, depending on whether dynamics of status rivalry or deference dominate, which in turn depends on whether the team requires the services of these team members to interpret knowledge from sources outside the team.

The possibility that cosmopolitans and locals contribute to team performance in the ways suggested here raises some important questions for further investigation that are beyond the scope of this chapter. The argument proposed that team members with the status characteristics of cosmopolitans and locals are likely to offer and defend interpretations from different perspectives that have equal potential value to the team, and that a mix of these perspectives will benefit a team most when it uses external knowledge. This argument focuses on situations where a team includes at least one cosmopolitan and/or one local member, but there are other possible ways of analyzing a team's cosmopolitan and local membership. For example, the proportion of cosmopolitans and locals may matter more than the presence of at least one cosmopolitan and/or local on the team, since the status dynamics may be affected by the relative representation of the two status groups on the team (cf., Kanter, 1977; Allmendinger & Hackman, 1995). Alternatively, rather than the presence or number of team members who have the status characteristics of cosmopolitans or locals, it is possible that what matters is the overall level of "cosmopolitanism" or "localism" on a team, measured by indices that capture the total time that all the team members have spent living and working in the client country and in other countries, and the total number of languages they speak. These alternative specifications might suggest different causal arguments about how status dynamics affect team performance to those presented here, and they therefore are worthy of examination.

Extending these speculations, another avenue for future research is suggested by a more political perspective on organizations, which highlights the possibility that coalitions will form around different high-status members and engage in battles for dominance over the direction that the team will take (cf., Pettigrew, 1973; Bacharach & Lawler, 1980). As knowledge is usually socially constructed rather than absolute, teams can become contested terrain (cf., Edwards, 1979; Haas, 2003) in which the agendas and interests of external stakeholders are reflected and played out, to the possible detriment of the team's espoused goals. Since cosmopolitans and locals are likely to be oriented to different reference groups (cf., Merton, 1957) and to be subjected to pressures from different external stakeholders, they may have more at stake in a confrontation within the team than their own personal status; they may also see themselves as defending the status of the broader community with which they identify outside the team. This may result in attempts to organize potential supporters within the teams into coalitions that will actively defend the views and pursue the interests of those high-status members with whom they in turn identify themselves.

A final potential direction for future theory and research is the possibility that the concepts of cosmopolitan and local may offer insights into the functioning of teams that are not explicitly international, as well as those that are. In the original formulations of the concepts, cosmopolitans and locals were distinguished by their orientations to local versus wider communities (Merton, 1957) and to their employing organization versus their profession (Gouldner, 1957). Adapting these formulations, any team might be analyzed in terms of status hierarchies that distinguish, for example, those who prioritize the team and its task from those who prioritize their professional or wider community affiliations. For the more inclusive world of teams beyond those that operate across international borders, the concepts of cosmopolitans and locals might be more broadly defined in ways that offer intriguing avenues for further exploration.

In conclusion, the issues of status deference and status rivalry in teams are subtle but potentially powerful phenomena. As Geertz's (1973) seminal sociological analysis of the Balinese cockfight revealed, sometimes the way that interactions appear on the surface is really just a veneer that disguises the "deep play" of high stakes status games. Similarly, international teams that include cosmopolitan and local members might appear on the surface to be engaged in innocent information exchanges with no other purpose than to help the team to complete its task as successfully as possible, while underneath, status attributions, expectations, hierarchies, and contests shape their contributions in ways that sometimes may be less than helpful for the team.

NOTES

1. Of 550 team members who were surveyed for the quantitative part of this study, only 27 individuals met the criteria for being both a cosmopolitan and a local, 125 qualified as cosmopolitans, 75 qualified as locals, and 323 qualified as neither cosmopolitans nor locals.
2. Again drawing on the quantitative data to illustrate the prevalence of each of these configurations of team composition, of the 96 teams in my survey dataset, 24 included cosmopolitans but no local members, 9 included locals but no cosmopolitan members, and 21 included neither, while the remaining 42 teams included both cosmopolitan and local members.

REFERENCES

Adler, N. J. (2002). *International dimensions of organizational behavior*. Cincinnati, OH: South-Western.

Alkire, A. A., Collum, M. E., & Kaswan, J. (1968). Information exchange and accuracy of verbal communication under social power conditions. *Journal of Personality and Social Psychology*, *9*, 301–308.

Allmendinger, J., & Hackman, J. R. (1995). The more, the better? A four-nation study of the inclusion of women in symphony orchestras. *Social Forces*, *74*, 423–460.

Ancona, D. G. (1987). Groups in organizations: Extending laboratory models. In: C. Hendrick (Ed.), *Annual review of personality and social psychology: Group and intergroup processes* (pp. 207–231). Beverly Hills, CA: Sage.

Ancona, D. G., & Caldwell, D. F. (1992). Bridging the boundary: External activity and performance in organizational teams. *Administrative Science Quarterly*, *37*, 634–665.

Anderson, C., John, O. P., Keltner, D., & Kring, A. M. (2001). Who attains social status? Effects of personality and physical attractiveness in social groups. *Journal of Personality and Social Psychology*, *81*, 116–132.

Argote, L., & McGrath, J. E. (1993). Group processes in organizations: Continuity and change. In: C. L. Cooper & I. T. Robertson (Eds), *International review of industrial and organizational psychology* (pp. 222–289). Chichester, England: Wiley.

Bacharach, S. B., & Lawler, E. J. (1980). *Power and politics in organizations*. San Francisco, CA: Jossey-Bass.

Bantel, K., & Jackson, S. (1989). Top management and innovations in banking: Does the composition of the top team make a difference? *Strategic Management Journal, 10*, 107–124.

Bartlett, C. A., & Ghoshal, S. (1989). *Managing across borders: The transnational solution.* Boston, MA: Harvard Business School Press.

Becker, T. E., & Billings, R. S. (1993). Profiles of commitment: An empirical test. *Journal of Organizational Behavior, 14*, 177–190.

Berger, J., Cohen, B. P., & Zelditch, M., Jr. (1972). Status characteristics and social interaction. *American Sociological Review, 37*, 241–255.

Berger, J., Fisek, M. H., Norman, R. Z., & Zelditch, M., Jr. (1977). *Status characteristics and social interaction.* New York, NY: Elsevier.

Berger, J., Rosenholtz, S. J., & Zelditch, M., Jr. (1980). Status organizing processes. *Annual Review of Sociology, 6*, 479–508.

Blau, P. M. (1966). *The dynamics of bureaucracy: A study of interpersonal relations in two government agencies.* New York, NY: Wiley.

Cohen, B. P., & Zhou, X. (1991). Status processes in enduring work groups. *American Sociological Review, 56*, 179–188.

Cohen, W. M., & Levinthal, D. A. (1990). Absorptive capacity: A new perspective on learning and innovation. *Administrative Science Quarterly, 35*, 128–153.

Cornwall, J. R., & Grimes, A. J. (1987). Cosmopolitan-local: A cross-lagged correlation analysis of the relationship between professional role orientations and behaviors in an academic organization. *Human Relations, 40*(5), 281–298.

Cox, T. H. (1993). *Cultural diversity in organizations.* San Francisco, CA: Berrett Koehler.

Cummings, J. N. (2004). Work groups, structural diversity, and knowledge sharing in a global organization. *Management Science, 50*, 352–364.

Earley, P. C., & Mosakowski, E. (2000). Creating hybrid team cultures: An empirical test of transnational team functioning. *Academy of Management Journal, 43*(1), 26–49.

Edwards, R. (1979). *Contested terrain: The transformation of the workplace in the twentieth century.* New York, NY: Basic Books.

Einhorn, H. J., Hogarth, K. M., & Klempner, E. (1977). Quality of group judgment. *Psychological Bulletin, 84*, 158–172.

Eisenhardt, K. M., & Schoonhoven, C. (1990). Organizational growth: Linking team founding, strategy, environment, and growth among U.S. semiconductor ventures, 1978–88. *Administrative Science Quarterly, 35*(3), 504–529.

Foschi, M. (2000). Double standards for competence: Theory and research. *Annual Review of Sociology, 26*, 21–42.

Geertz, C. (1973). *The interpretation of cultures: Selected essays.* New York, NY: Basic Books.

Gouldner, A. W. (1957). Cosmopolitans and locals: Toward an analysis of latent social roles, I. *Administrative Science Quarterly, 2*, 281–306.

Gresov, C., & Stephens, C. (1993). The context of interunit influence attempts. *Administrative Science Quarterly, 38*, 252–276.

Haas, M. R. (2003). *The politics of knowledge sharing in organizations.* Working Paper, School of Industrial and Labor Relations, Cornell University. Ithaca, NY.

Haas, M. R., & Hansen, M. T. (2005). When using knowledge can hurt performance: The value of organizational capabilities in a management consulting company. *Strategic Management Journal, 26*, 1–24.

Hackman, J. R. (1987). The design of work teams. In: J. Lorsch (Ed.), *Handbook of organizational behavior*. Englewood Cliffs, NJ: Prentice-Hall.
Hambrick, D. C., Davison, S. C., Snell, S. A., & Snow, C. C. (1998). When groups consist of multiple nationalities: Towards a new understanding of the implications. *Organization Studies, 19*, 181–205.
Hansen, M. T., & Haas, M. R. (2001). Competing for attention in knowledge markets: Electronic document dissemination in a management consulting company. *Administrative Science Quarterly, 46*, 1–28.
Horai, J., Naccari, N., & Fattoullah, E. (1974). The effects of expertise and physical attractiveness on opinion agreement and liking. *Sociometry, 37*, 601–606.
Huber, G. P. (1991). Organizational learning: The contributing processes and the literatures. *Organization Science, 2*(1), 88–115.
Jackson, S. E., May, K. E., & Whitney, K. (1995). Understanding the dynamics of diversity in decision-making teams. In: S. Worchel, W. Wood & J. A. Simpson (Eds), *Group processes and productivity*. Newbury Park: Sage.
Janis, I. L. (1982). *Groupthink* (2nd ed). Boston, MA: Houghton Mifflin.
Jehn, K. A. (1995). A multimethod examination of the benefits and detriments of intragroup conflict. *Administrative Science Quarterly, 40*, 256–282.
Jehn, K. A. (1997). A qualitative analysis of conflict type and dimensions in organizational groups. *Administrative Science Quarterly, 42*, 530–558.
Kanter, R. M. (1977). *Men and women of the corporation*. New York: Basic Books.
Kanter, R. M. (1995). *World class: Thriving locally in the global economy*. New York, NY: Simon & Schuster.
Keck, S., & Tushman, M. (1993). Environmental and organizational context and executive team structure. *Academy of Management Journal, 36*(6), 1314–1344.
Kirchmeyer, C. (1993). Multicultural task groups: An account of the low contribution of minorities. *Small Group Research, 24*, 127–148.
Lane, P. J., & Lubatkin, M. (1998). Relative absorptive capacity and interorganizational learning. *Strategic Management Journal, 19*, 461–477.
Lawrence, B. S. (1997). Perspective: The black box of organizational demography. *Organization Science, 8*, 1–22.
Merton, R. K. (1957). *Social theory and social structure* (2nd ed). Glencoe, IL: Free Press.
Nohria, N., & Ghoshal, S. (1997). *The differentiated network: Organizing multinational corporations for value creation*. San Francisco, CA: Jossey-Bass.
Olivera, F., & Argote, L. A. (1999). Organizational learning and new product development: CORE processes. In: L. L. Thompson, J. M. Levine & D. Messick (Eds), *Shared cognition in organizations: The management of knowledge* (pp. 297–325). Mahwah, NJ: LEA.
Owens, D. A., Neale, M. A., & Sutton, R. I. (1997). *Status as a demographic variable*. Working Paper, Stanford, Palo Alto, CA.
Owens, D. A., Mannix, E. A., & Neale, M. A. (1998). Strategic formation of groups: Issues in task performance and team member selection. In: M. A. Neale, E. A. Mannix & D. H. Gruenfeld (Eds), *Research in managing groups and teams composition*, (Vol. 1, pp. 149–165). Greenwich, CT: JAI Press.
Owens, D. A., & Sutton, R. I. (2002). Status contests in meetings: Negotiating the informal order. In: M. E. Turner (Ed.), *Groups at work: Advances in theory and research*. Mahwah, NJ: Lawrence Erlbaum.
Pettigrew, A. M. (1973). *The politics of organizational decision-making*. London, UK: Tavistock.

Pfeffer, J., & Salancik, G. (1978). *The external control of organizations: A resource dependency perspective*. New York, NY: HarperCollins.
Podolny, J. (1993). A status-based model of market competition. *American Journal of Sociology, 98*, 829–872.
Propp, K. M. (1995). An experimental examination of biological sex as a status cue in decision-making groups and its influence on information use. *Small Group Research, 26*, 451–474.
Smircich, L., & Stubbart, C. (1985). Strategic management in an enacted world. *Academy of Management Review, 10*, 724–736.
Snell, S. A., Snow, C. C., Davison, S. C., & Hambrick, D. C. (1998). Designing and supporting transnational teams: The human resource agenda. *Human Resource Management, 37*(2), 147–158.
Snow, C. C., Snell, S. A., Davison, S. C., & Hambrick, D. C. (1996). Use transnational teams to globalize your company. *Organizational Dynamics, 32*(4), 20–32.
Stasser, G., Stewart, D. D., & Wittenbaum, G. M. (1995). Expert roles and information exchange during discussion: The importance of knowing who knows what. *Journal of Experimental Social Psychology, 31*, 244–265.
Stewart, D. D., & Stasser, G. (1995). Expert role assignment and information sampling during collective recall and decision making. *Journal of Personality and Social Psychology, 69*, 619–628.
Swidler, A. (1986). Culture in action: Symbols and strategies. *American Sociological Review, 51*, 273–286.
Thomas-Hunt, M. C., & Phillips, K. W. (2003). Managing teams in the dynamic organization: The effects of revolving membership and changing task demands on expertise and status in groups. In: R. Peterson & E. Mannix (Eds), *Leading and managing people in the dynamic organization* (pp. 115–134). Mahwah, NJ: Lawrence Erlbaum.
Tuma, N. B., & Grimes, A. J. (1981). A comparison of models of role orientations of professionals in a research-oriented university. *Administrative Science Quarterly, 26*, 187–206.
Tung, R. (1998). American expatriates abroad: From neophytes to cosmopolitans. *Journal of World Business, 33*(2), 125–144.
Tushman, M. L. (1977). Communication across organizational boundaries: Special boundary roles in the innovation process. *Administrative Science Quarterly, 22*, 581–606.
Wageman, R. (1995). Interdependence and group effectiveness. *Administrative Science Quarterly, 40*, 145–180.
Watson, W. E., Kumar, K., & Michaelson, L. K. (1993). Cultural diversity's impact on interaction process and performance: Comparing homogeneous and diverse task groups. *Academy of Management Journal, 36*, 590–602.
Weick, K. E. (2001). *Making sense of the organization*. Oxford: Blackwell Business.
Williams, K. Y., & O'Reilly, C. A. (1998). Demography and diversity in organizations. In: B. M. Staw & R. M. Sutton (Eds), *Research in organizational behavior*, (Vol. 20, pp. 77–140). Stamford, CT: JAI Press.
Wittenbaum, G. M. (1998). Information sampling in decision-making groups: The impact of members' task-relevant status. *Small Group Research, 29*, 57–84.
Yetton, P. W., & Bottger, P. C. (1982). Individual versus group problem solving: An empirical test of a best-member strategy. *Organizational Behavior and Human Decision Processes, 29*, 307–321.

HERE TODAY, GONE TOMORROW? EFFECTS OF NONSTANDARD WORK STATUS ON WORKGROUP PROCESSES AND OUTCOMES

Heather C. Vough, Joseph P. Broschak and Gregory B. Northcraft

ABSTRACT

Many workers today are employed under a variety of nonstandard work arrangements, such as contract work and agency temporary work. While prior research has shown that the use of nonstandard workers can be detrimental to standard workers' attitudes and behaviors, producing conflict between nonstandard and standard employees, that research has not shown how or why. We propose a model in which threat to status of, and accommodation by, standard workers cause negative reactions to nonstandard workers, contingent upon the competence of nonstandard workers. The model helps explain how subtle differences among seemingly similar nonstandard work arrangements can produce dramatically different challenges to work group effectiveness. Implications for the effective blending of work groups are discussed.

Status and Groups
Research on Managing Groups and Teams, Volume 7, 229–257

ISSN: 1534-0856/doi:10.1016/S1534-0856(05)07010-6

One of the distinguishing features of modern organizations is the diversity of work arrangements under which individuals can be employed. Historically, standard employment arrangements are those in which employees are compensated directly by employers for work performed on a preset schedule, and for an indefinite length of time at the employer's place of business while under the employer's control (Kalleberg, et al., 1997; Kalleberg, 2000). In contrast, today many workers are employed under a variety of nonstandard work arrangements, such as contract work, on-call temporary work, and agency temporary work. While precise estimates of the actual size of the nonstandard workforce vary, the percentage of U.S. workers employed in some form of nonstandard employment arrangement ranges between 10 and 30% (Kalleberg et al., 1997; Hipple, 2001). And the incidence of nonstandard work arrangements is rising. For instance, in the U.S.A. the number of people employed by temporary employment agencies grew by 10% between 1995 and 1997, considerably faster than the 2.8% by which traditional employment grew in that same time period (Cohany, 1998).

The pervasiveness of nonstandard work arrangements is not restricted to the U.S.A. (Cordova, 1986). In 1995, 11.5% of the workforce in European Union countries was employed as temporary workers, with temporary employment rates in individual countries varying from 5 to 30% (Delsen, 1999). In Japan in 1995, approximately 12% of the paid labor force worked as temporary workers (Houseman & Osawa, 1995).

The growing popularity of employing nonstandard workers has both positive and negative implications for managing organizations and work groups. Using nonstandard workers, such as temporary workers and contractors who have weak connections to the firms for whom they perform work (Pfeffer & Baron, 1988), can benefit organizations by creating the flexibility to readily expand and shrink the size of their workforce in response to fluctuating workload demands (Harrison & Kelly, 1993). Using nonstandard workers can also reduce overall labor rates, thus increasing firm profitability, by substituting lower paid contingent workers for a firm's standard workers (Davis-Blake & Uzzi, 1993) and by limiting the long-term financial commitments of organizations to workers in the form of health insurance, pensions, and other benefits (Segal & Sullivan, 1997). Finally, employing nonstandard workers allows firms access to unique functional skills and expertize for short periods of time (Matusik & Hill, 1998; Lepak & Snell, 1999), and the opportunity to preview individual workers' abilities and work habits before hiring them as part of their standard workforce (Segal & Sullivan, 1997; Davis-Blake & Broschak, 2000).

Unfortunately, using nonstandard workers also has potential drawbacks, particularly for managing work groups. The use of temporary workers and contractors often produces conflict between nonstandard and standard employees (Geary, 1992; Smith, 1994), and negatively affects the levels of organizational trust (Pearce, 1993), job satisfaction (Von Hippel, Mangum, Greenberger, Heneman, & Skoglind, 1997), and organizational commitment (Davis-Blake, Broschak, & George, 2003) among standard workers. These effects are particularly troubling considering that the fastest growing segments of nonstandard work are in professional, technical, and managerial jobs that can be critical to organizational functioning (Cohany, 1996; Segal & Sullivan, 1997; Kunda, Barley, & Evans, 2002). Given the increasing ubiquity of nonstandard work arrangements, understanding how and why the use of nonstandard workers negatively affects standard workers seems essential for designing and managing work groups for effective performance.

In this paper we explore the mechanisms by which standard workers are negatively affected by the presence of nonstandard coworkers. In the model we develop, the word "status" carries both formal and informal meanings. First, status *formally* refers to objective work arrangements (i.e., some workers are classified as full-time permanent members of the organization while others are not). There are two types of formal status to consider here. *Work status* refers to the characteristics of individuals' work arrangements. Thus, standard work, temporary work, and contract work are three distinctly different work statuses. *Employment status* refers to individuals' current state of employment with a focal organization. Across all types of work status, individual's employment status is one of two states: employed or unemployed. A second meaning of status is where it *informally* refers to the relative level of *prestige* (and self-esteem) that is wrapped up in and conveyed by these formal work arrangements (i.e., full-time permanent members of an organization like to think of themselves as having higher status than their nonstandard counterparts).

We begin by reviewing the relevant literature on nonstandard work arrangements, discussing important differences between the types of nonstandard work, how nonstandard workers are used in organizations, and the consequences of using them. We then propose that in work groups composed of individuals of diverse work status, standard workers' attitudes, perceptions, and behaviors will be influenced by a crucial characteristic of nonstandard workers, *level of competence*. When nonstandard worker competence is high, we expect standard workers to feel both their employment status and prestige threatened by the presence of nonstandard workers. When nonstandard worker competence is low we expect standard workers to resent the accommodations necessary to sustain group performance. We further propose that the magnitude of threats to formal and informal status, and the amount of accommodation will be influenced by two aspects of the structure of work: (1) the division of labor, that is, the degree of similarity and the amount of task interdependence between the nonstandard and standard employees' jobs, and (2) employment practices, that is, the duration of nonstandard workers employment and the amount of reward interdependence between nonstandard and standard workers (Broschak & Davis-Blake, 2006).

We integrate these ideas in a conceptual model that links nonstandard worker competence, threats to formal and informal status of, and accommodation by, standard workers, and the structure of work-to-work group relations and performance. Thus, we explore not just the negative effects of work status diversity in work groups, but the mechanisms that are triggered by diverse work status and the contextual factors that heighten or dampen the consequences of work status differences. We conclude by exploring the applications and implications of our model for structuring work to incorporate nonstandard work arrangements and discuss how to manage mixed work groups in ways that alleviate the tensions and conflict surrounding nonstandard work.

PAST RESEARCH ON NONSTANDARD WORK

There is a growing body of research looking at the use of nonstandard work arrangements in organizations. We review three prominent lines of inquiry that provide the backdrop for our conceptual model. First, we review research that illustrates differences between types of nonstandard work arrangements (Pfeffer & Baron, 1988; Kalleberg, 2000; Marler, Barringer, & Milkovich, 2002). Second, we discuss different ways that work groups can be structured to incorporate nonstandard workers. Finally, we review research on the impact of nonstandard work, with particular emphasis on standard workers' reactions to nonstandard workers (Geary, 1992; Smith, 1994; Davis-Blake et al., 2003).

WHAT ARE NONSTANDARD WORK ARRANGEMENTS?

Nonstandard work refers to a wide variety of employer/employee work relationships that provide alternatives to the traditional full-time organizational membership. Kalleberg (2000) and his colleagues (Kalleberg et al., 1997) define standard employment arrangements as those in which work is generally done full time, for an indefinite length of time, performed at the employer's place of business, and under the employer's control. All other types of arrangements – where there is temporal instability in the job, a distinction between the organization that employs the worker and the organization that has administrative control over the worker, or where work is performed at a location other than the employer's normal workplace – are nonstandard (Pfeffer & Baron, 1988; Kalleberg et al., 1997).

The defining characteristic of nonstandard work is a relatively weak connection (both psychologically and contractually) between nonstandard workers and the firms for whom nonstandard workers perform work. This weakened connection, or externalization from the focal organization, results from limiting the duration, location, or administrative control of employment (Pfeffer & Baron, 1988). As work externalization can occur by any one or a combination of these three mechanisms, nonstandard work is a heterogeneous category of varied structural arrangements (Davis-Blake & Uzzi, 1993; Uzzi & Barsness, 1998). For example, part-time workers are externalized through limits on the average number of hours worked per week, though they are typically under the direct administrative control of the focal organization (their employer) and perform their work at the employer's place of business. Contract workers, in comparison, often work full time at an employer's site, but are externalized through limits on the duration of their employment and because they are under the administrative control of a third party, their contractor organization.

The thrust of our argument here is that subtle differences among seemingly similar nonstandard work arrangements can present dramatically different challenges to work group effectiveness. We focus on the most common nonstandard work arrangements; specifically, situations where workers are *employed for limited durations*, are under the *administrative control of another organization* (e.g., a temp agency), and perform *work at the focal organization's normal location*. Previous empirical research suggests that nonstandard work arrangements with these characteristics have substantive effects on work group processes (Geary, 1992; Pearce, 1993; Smith, 1994; Davis-Blake et al., 2003). There are two prevalent types of nonstandard workers that share these characteristics: agency temporary workers and contract workers (Kalleberg, Reskin, & Hudson, 2000).

Both agency temporary workers and contract workers are hired by employers to perform work that lasts for a limited duration at the employer's premises. However, they differ in the extent to which they fall under the employer's direct supervision (Pfeffer & Baron, 1988; Kalleberg, 2000). Although agencies recruit and screen temporary workers and are the legal employers of record, responsible for administrative tasks including hiring and firing, and issuing compensation and benefits (Davis-Blake & Broschak, 2000; Kalleberg, 2000), the focal organization controls temporary workers' job-related activities. This triangular employment relationship (Cordova, 1986) is a distinguishing feature of agency temporary work arrangements. In contrast, the key feature of contract work arrangements is that the focal organization abdicates supervision and control of contract workers' job-related activities to the individual contract worker or the contracting organization (Kalleberg, 2000). Contract workers receive little formal supervision from focal organization managers beyond the specifications necessary to complete the work (Rebitzer, 1995).

Both temporary and contract workers typically receive little or no training from employers and instead are largely responsible for having or developing their skills. Employers refrain from training temporary and contract workers for two reasons. First, the limited duration of the employment arrangement makes it difficult to recoup any returns from investing in training. Second, employers can be held fiscally and legally liable as "co-employers" (Tansky & Veglahn, 1995) should they fail to differentiate between the treatment of standard and nonstandard workers; for example by offering training or other "employee" perks to these "non employees."

How much skill or competence a nonstandard worker brings to the job is the key moderator in our model. Since they are not supervised by the focal organization, contract workers generally must possess skills, knowledge, or expertise that is greater than, or complementary to, standard workers, including perhaps skills that are not internally available to the focal organization (Harrison & Kelley, 1993; Matusik & Hill, 1998; Kalleberg, 2000). In contrast, temporary workers tend to be assigned jobs where expertise is neither assumed nor expected.

HOW ARE NONSTANDARD WORKERS USED IN ORGANIZATIONS?

Organizations differ in their orientation toward using nonstandard workers. For instance, some organizations use nonstandard work arrangements to identify potential standard employees prior to making any kind of employment commitment (Cohen & Haberfeld, 1993). In other organizations there are relatively impermeable boundaries between standard and nonstandard work (Feldman, Doerpinghaus, & Turnley, 1995). The heterogeneous use of nonstandard work arrangements by focal organizations as a staffing strategy, combined with the heterogeneous individual preferences for nonstandard work (Belous, 1989; Tan & Tan, 2002), can make the intent of nonstandard work arrangements ambiguous to standard workers. How standard workers interpret the meaning of nonstandard workers' presence, specifically whether or not nonstandard workers are perceived as potential replacements, will affect how standard workers react to nonstandard workers.

When nonstandard workers are used, a key decision for the focal organizations' managers is how to deploy them in the organization. We see the use of nonstandard employees varying along two critical dimensions: amount of contact between standard and nonstandard workers, and comparability of tasks between standard and nonstandard workers.

Amount of Contact

There are two general ways to organize the nonstandard workforce. One way is by placing nonstandard workers in jobs where there is little contact with standard workers, where they are socially and physically isolated (Rogers, 1995). Wells, Kochan, and Smith (1991) noted that contract workers at petroleum and chemical plants were treated as a separate and distinct workforce, with supervisory and training responsibility for contract workers assigned to the contractor rather than the plant manager. Davis-Blake and Broschak (2000) described how an electronics manufacturer used temporary workers to staff a completely separate production line from standard workers to test a new direct shipping concept. Isolating nonstandard from standard workers may prevent the dispersion of organizational norms and practices to outsiders (Kalleberg, 2000), and can preclude disruptions to standard workers' routines by giving nonstandard workers separate jobs (Lautsch, 2002).

A more common approach to organizing contract and temporary workers is to incorporate them into ongoing work groups with standard workers (Pearce, 1993; Smith, 1994; Rousseau & Libuser, 1997; Matusik & Hill, 1998; Broschak & Davis-Blake, 2006). This structure arises because technology, organizational politics, or the need for technical skills often make it impossible to physically segregate standard and nonstandard workers (Lautsch, 2002). In these cases, standard workers can find themselves working side-by-side with nonstandard workers in blended work groups (Olsten, 1997; Davis-Blake et al., 2003). Employers often use various administrative tools to maintain distinctions between standard and nonstandard workers, such as issuing different identification badges and prohibiting nonstandard workers from attending employee meetings or organizationally sanctioned social gatherings (e.g., department lunches, employee recognition ceremonies). Whether or not standard workers work directly alongside nonstandard workers is important because the interaction between members of the two groups may influence work group outcomes.

Comparability of Tasks

A second decision concerning the organization of nonstandard work involves the division of labor. In some cases standard and nonstandard workers perform similar tasks and jobs (Lautsch, 2002; Broschak & Davis-Blake, 2006). This is likely in contexts where production processes are simple or continuous, and where the focal organizations' managers have few opportunities to redesign jobs to create separate roles for nonstandard workers (Lautsch, 2002).

In other cases, nonstandard workers are assigned tasks that are more specialized and simplistic than those assigned to standard workers. For instance, Smith (1994) described how the use of temporary workers created a "polarized division of labor" (p. 294), with standard workers performing more complex work, such as interactional and boundary spanning roles, while temporary workers performed routine, unskilled tasks. Similarly, Pearce (1993) reported how supervisors at an aerospace manufacturer assigned contract engineers simpler tasks that were easily monitored, reserving complex and interdependent tasks for standard engineers. Finally, Lautsch (2002) found in a customer service organization that nonstandard workers performed the same tasks as standard workers but on a more limited range of products, responsible for a subset of the total phone calls coming into the organization.

Thus, standard and nonstandard workers can work side-by-side or be isolated from one another, can perform similar or separate tasks, and can perform tasks that are discrete from each other's or tasks where there is a high degree of interdependence (Lautsch, 2002). Precisely how nonstandard workers are integrated into the organization of work is likely to have a significant impact on how their presence affects work group processes and outcomes.

WHAT ARE THE CONSEQUENCES OF USING NONSTANDARD WORKERS?

In general, organizational researchers depict nonstandard work arrangements as being beneficial for organizations, and in fact some have argued that nonstandard work arrangements should be an integral part of human resource strategy (Matusik & Hill, 1998; Lepak & Snell, 1999). However, a small body of research has documented that the introduction of nonstandard workers into work groups can lead to negative consequences for standard workers, group processes, and group outcomes. For instance, Smith (1994, p. 299) noted that by using nonstandard workers, "hidden hierarchies are created that produce new sources of tension and conflict within and across organizations," and that standard employees were forced to adjust their approach to work when nonstandard employees were introduced. Davis-Blake et al. (2003), and Broschak and Davis-Blake (2006) found that the presence of nonstandard workers negatively affected standard workers work attitudes and that the magnitude of the effects differed across types of nonstandard work arrangements. Below we discuss some of these findings in greater detail.

Work Group Relations

There is substantial evidence that standard employees become agitated when nonstandard workers are incorporated into their work lives (Gannon, 1974; Smith, 1994; Von Hippel et al., 1997; Lautsch, 2002). Geary (1992) noted that standard employees described nonstandard workers as "saucy" and "cheeky." In other studies, standard workers reported feeling that nonstandard workers were not worth getting to know because of the limited time they would be working for the organization (Rogers, 1995). Sometimes standard workers would not even make an effort to learn the names of nonstandard workers (Von Hippel et al., 1997) or resented that some nonstandard employees often did the same tasks as them, but for twice the pay (Kador, 2000).

In a case study of an electronics manufacturer, Geary (1992) found that the use of temporary production workers, working alongside standard workers, produced conflict and tension among workers within the work group. In response to these conflicts, management provided closer than normal supervision of manufacturing workers that ultimately bred mistrust and resentment directed at standard workers' supervisors. Similarly, Davis-Blake et al. (2003) analyzed a national sample of organizations and found that standard workers, working in organizations where temporary workers were employed in the same job as them, had poorer relations with their supervisors, were more likely to turnover, and reported less loyalty to the organization than standard workers without temporary coworkers. Standard workers with contract coworkers also reported poorer relations with their supervisors.

Smith (1994) noted that the presence of temporary workers heightened conflict and tension in work groups as standard workers saw temporary workers as an added responsibility and a liability to performance in certain situations. Pearce (1993) reported that engineers with contract engineering coworkers had lower trust in the organization than engineers without nonstandard coworkers. Finally, George (1996) found that having temporary workers in work groups negatively affected standard workers' affective commitment, perceptions of mobility opportunities, and perceptions of the psychological contract.

Incorporating nonstandard workers into work groups and organizations can also affect standard workers in unanticipated ways that may have indirect effects on work group relations. Barnett and Miner (1992) found that temporary workers affected the interorganizational mobility of standard workers. When nonstandard workers block career mobility opportunities of standard workers, this may have an affect on the work attitudes of standard workers. In sum, there are multiple negative reactions from standard workers brought on by the use of nonstandard work, though the cause of these negative reactions remains largely undetermined.

Work Group Performance

Several researchers have noted that nonstandard workers exhibit poorer performance (Kochan, Smith, Wells, & Rebitzer, 1994; Smith, 1994) and fewer extra-role behaviors (Van Dyne & Ang, 1998; Broschak & Davis-Blake, 2006) than standard workers. These observations are not particularly surprising since nonstandard workers tend to have a limited temporal attachment to employers and receive fewer inducements to prompt commitment or extra-role behaviors. What is perhaps more surprising is that a number of studies of nonstandard work in the U.S. have found no systematic differences between the commitment or extra-role behaviors of standard and nonstandard workers (Kidder, 1995; Pearce, 1993). Broschak,

Davis-Blake, and Block (2005) even found that among white-collar clerical and administrative workers, temporary workers were more productive compared to standard workers. Further, standard workers who had previously been employed as temporary workers for the employer were more productive than those who had not. These findings suggest that nonstandard workers may have an incentive to outperform their standard coworkers if they perceive nonstandard work arrangements as auditions for permanent employment. Geary (1992) and Smith (1994) similarly reported that nonstandard manufacturing workers were often as productive as standard manufacturing workers and that nonstandard workers rarely refused requests to work overtime or be flexible in their job assignments, perhaps over fear of the tenuous nature of their positions.

Geary (1992) suggested that having temporary coworkers inadvertently puts pressure on standard workers, causing them to work harder and longer than they normally would. This is consistent with the claim that nonstandard work can be used as a subtle reminder to low-level standard workers of the precarious nature of their job security (Geary, 1992; Davis-Blake & Broschak, 2000). However, there is no indication whether the increased effort by standard workers translated to increased group performance. Smith (1994) reported that using temporary workers sometimes freed standard workers from some of the more mundane requirements of their jobs, allowing them to subsequently develop additional sets of skills. Thus, a division of labor between standard and nonstandard workers can allow standard workers, under some circumstances, opportunities to develop skills that ultimately enhance group performance.

These studies suggest that although there can be advantages to a division of labor between standard and nonstandard workers, these advantages are balanced by the fact that using temporary and contract workers creates additional, uncompensated tasks for standard workers. Responsibility for orientation, training, and socialization typically falls on the shoulders of standard workers as supervisors in focal organizations seek to minimize the appearances of co-employment relationships (Davis-Blake & Broschak, 2000). Standard workers frequently find themselves in the position of supervising and correcting, as needed, the work of their temporary coworkers (Geary, 1992; Smith, 1994). These peer-to-peer responsibilities can tax the ability of standard workers to maintain their own level of performance, particularly when the turnover of temporary and contract workers is high (Davis-Blake & Broschak, 2000). Thus while using nonstandard workers may free standard workers to develop new skills that enhance group performance, it can also burden standard workers with new responsibilities that may counter any efficiency or skill gain.

ORIGINS OF CONFLICT: THREAT AND ACCOMMODATION

While the aforementioned negative consequences of having blended work groups is well documented, virtually no research has explored the causes of these effects. We know that standard workers are bothered when individuals of a different work status appear in their work groups, but not why. From the existing body of research on nonstandard workers we suggest two possible causes of these negative effects: (1) the presence of nonstandard workers creates threats to the formal (employment) status and informal (prestige) status of standard workers, and (2) standard workers must make accommodations to incorporate nonstandard workers into work groups. These two mechanisms, labeled here as *threat* and *accommodation*, represent two distinct driving forces that affect standard workers and relations between standard and nonstandard employees in blended work groups.

Threat

The presence of nonstandard workers can threaten both the formal and informal status of standard workers in work groups. We argue that status in work groups is a reflection both of the formal work arrangements individuals are employed under, as well as individuals' psychological reactions to differences in work arrangements. Below we consider, in turn, how a standard worker's formal (employment) and informal (prestige) status might be threatened by the presence of nonstandard workers.

Formal (Employment) Status

Employment status refers to the stability and security of individuals' employment relationships. Perceptions of the security of employment status differ between standard and nonstandard workers. Nonstandard workers know that the duration of their employment is limited, or at best tenuous, while standard workers have an expectation of continued employment with the employer. This expectation of continued employment is central to the psychological contract that develops between standard workers and employers (Rousseau, 1989, 1995). The psychological contract is the implicit agreement between employer and employee concerning each side's mutual obligations to the other (Rousseau, 1995). All else held equal, standard workers have an expectation that their jobs are secure as long as they abide by the terms of their implicit contract (Rousseau, 1989), specifically, if they continue to satisfactorily perform their jobs.

Changes to the organization of work may be perceived by standard workers as a threat to their psychological contract. When work roles are redefined, when employers increase their expectations of employee contributions to the organization, or when job security or opportunities for advancement become less certain, standard workers often perceive that their employers have violated the terms of the psychological contract. Perceived violations may have material effects, such as standard workers' withdrawing their contributions to the organization (Coyle-Shapiro & Kessler, 2002), or reducing their extra-role behaviors (Coyle-Shapiro & Kessler, 2002; Robinson & Morrison, 1995), or the effects may be more attitudinal, such as reduced job satisfaction (Robinson & Rousseau, 1994) and lower organizational trust (Robinson, 1996).

The introduction of nonstandard workers into work groups may be perceived by standard workers as a violation of their psychological contracts. For instance, standard workers may interpret nonstandard workers as being possible replacements at lower labor costs, or perceive that the hiring of nonstandard workers is the first link in a chain of changes that the focal organization will make toward reducing their commitment to standard workers. It is in this vein that Pfeffer and Baron (1988, p. 262) recommend that when standard workers are asked to train nonstandard workers, standard workers "must be assured that they are not merely training their own replacements."

If standard workers perceive, correctly or incorrectly, that nonstandard workers are being hired to replace them or that their presence signals decreased organizational commitment to standard work arrangements, they may begin to question their own futures with the organization (Gossett, 2001) and are likely to view nonstandard workers as undermining the psychological contract. Even though organizations may hire nonstandard workers as a buffer to protect standard workers' continued employment (Von Hippel et al., 1997), standard workers are likely to view the presence of nonstandard workers as a threat to their employment status (Gannon, 1974; Smith, 1994). The once stable and secure employment status of the standard workers may no longer seem as stable or secure when nonstandard workers enter the workplace.[1]

Informal (Prestige) Status

While formal status refers to whether or not an individual is employed, informal status refers to the prestige that accrues from being in a position of value and esteem within an organization (e.g., Shepherd & Brown, 1956; see also Wegener, 1992 for a review of the prestige literature). Whenever people are categorized along dimensions such as work status (e.g., standard vs. nonstandard), the resulting categories often differ in their level of prestige (Chattopadhyay & George, 2001) because some categories are more highly valued by the organization. Berger, Cohen, and Zelditch Jr (1972, p. 243) state, "When a task-oriented group is differentiated with respect to some external status characteristic, this status difference determines the observable power and prestige within the group, whether or not the external status characteristic is related to the group task." Nonstandard workers are generally accorded lower prestige than standard workers not simply because of their relative contributions to the group task but due to their partial membership in the employing organization (Rogers, 1995; Smith, 1994) and to the fact they are not an intrinsic part of the organization and are, by definition, expendable.

'Social identity theory tells us that individuals categorize themselves and others into groups (such as standard or nonstandard) in order to self-enhance (Tajfel & Turner, 1979, 1986). The basis of categorizing themselves as part of an in-group is usually some positive dimension that the out-group does not possess. In the case of blended work groups, work status, and the value and prestige it carries are strong, salient dimensions for categorization.

When categorizations vary in their prestige, individuals in higher prestige categories attempt to guard against associations with, or being seen as, members of the lower prestige group. When members of two groups have unequal status due to their social positions (e.g., standard vs. nonstandard), contact between members of the two groups in social settings is likely to threaten the social standing of the high-status members and evoke negative reactions toward the lower status members (Blalock, 1967). Accordingly, when lower prestige groups become more similar to the higher prestige groups, the categorical distinction becomes less clear and the informal status of high-prestige groups begins to be threatened. These threats to informal status may cause the high-prestige group to search for distinctiveness and may also lead to intergroup conflict.

In the case of standard and nonstandard workers, the high-prestige standard workers may perceive nonstandard workers as a threat to their informal status when nonstandard workers are hired into work groups to perform similar or complementary jobs. Standard workers develop the distinctive capability of having organization specific knowledge and abilities while nonstandard workers are essentially interchangeable in terms of their abilities and competence. When nonstandard workers are used in the same jobs as standard workers, the boundaries of distinctiveness between members of the two groups becomes blurred, resulting in intergroup conflict. The informal status of standard workers may also become threatened in cases where nonstandard workers do in fact have comparable knowledge or abilities, or where standard workers and nonstandard workers begin to be treated similarly by the focal organization. In these cases, standard workers may feel their distinctiveness, and thus their informal status, threatened.

This discussion suggests that even when standard workers do not perceive threats to their formal employment status, the presence of nonstandard workers may threaten their informal (prestige) status. Once lower prestige nonstandard workers are given roles similar to standard workers, standard workers may perceive their jobs are no longer as highly valued (Gossett, 2001; Wiens-Tuers, 2001). Working hand-in-hand with lower status nonstandard coworkers thus can cause standard workers to question their own informal status in the organization (Broschak & Davis-Blake, 2006).

In support of this argument, Lautsch (2002) found that, even in organizations with relatively good standard/nonstandard worker relationships, standard workers became angry when they felt that they were not accorded the prestige of their privileged work status. This anger can cause standard workers to act out against nonstandard workers by being unwilling to interact with them or to train them (Von Hippel et al., 1997), because they question whether they are as highly valued as they once were.

Accommodation

A second mechanism resulting from blending standard and nonstandard workers into work groups is accommodation. Accommodation occurs when the presence of nonstandard workers in a work group changes standard workers' task-related work roles. The term accommodation refers to both the new or different tasks that standard workers must perform, as well as the attitudinal reactions they have about working alongside nonstandard workers. For instance, standard workers may be required to monitor the work of their nonstandard counterparts, thus making accommodations by accepting more tasks. Simultaneously, standard workers may become annoyed at having to take on additional tasks or resentful of the time being spent monitoring others. Thus, accommodation has two important components, one functional (adaptation and monitoring) and one psychological (annoyance and resentment).

Adaptation and Monitoring

The introduction of nonstandard workers often precipitates two changes in the task assignments of standard workers (Pearce, 1993; Smith, 1994). One change we refer to as adaptation, the redistribution of tasks among standard and nonstandard workers. Compared to standard workers, nonstandard workers tend to lag in at least their familiarity with organizational practices (e.g., norms, standard operating procedures) and at worst in their technical competence. Therefore, task assignments must be engineered around the capabilities of workers. As nonstandard workers typically will have lower capabilities than standard workers, they are assigned simpler, more peripheral tasks. Standard workers, in turn, are assigned on average the more complex and critical tasks (Lautsch, 2002). Reorganizing work around the technical and social competencies of nonstandard workers can result in operational inefficiencies while standard workers adapt to their new tasks.

In addition to adaptation, introducing nonstandard employees into work groups also often results in additional monitoring tasks for standard workers, such as the training and supervision of their nonstandard coworkers. In many focal organizations, standard workers become implicitly or explicitly responsible for checking the quality of work of their nonstandard coworkers. Further, to limit the appearances of co-employment, focal organization managers often delegate responsibility for training and socializing nonstandard workers to standard coworkers. And because nonstandard workers' employment is limited in duration, the tasks of training and socializing recur every time new nonstandard workers enter the organization. So in addition to the disruption caused by adaptation, the introduction of nonstandard workers forces standard workers to take time away from their *own* work, in order to monitor, train, check, or assist nonstandard workers.

Annoyance and Resentment

The shifts in task responsibility due to adaptation and monitoring interferes with standard workers' ability to do their own jobs and imposes extra job demands for which they are typically not compensated. We expect these inconveniences to create annoyance and resentment on the part of standard workers.

Some research has suggested that the inconvenience experienced by standard workers having to monitor and accommodate nonstandard coworkers leads to poorer work group relations (Broschak & Davis-Blake, 2006). The animosity that develops is particularly strong when standard workers suspect that management is utilizing nonstandard workers who cannot perform tasks at even a basic level (Geary, 1992). In these cases, standard workers can become annoyed or resentful that they are asked to go above and beyond their job descriptions to compensate for poorly trained, unskilled nonstandard workers. These feelings of resentment, while likely directed at nonstandard coworkers, can also spread to manager–employee relations as well since managers make decisions to use nonstandard workers (Davis-Blake et al., 2003).

Overall, the costs of managing the conflict between nonstandard and standard workers – either from threats to employment status and prestige, or from the inconvenience of adaptation and monitoring – remains a largely unanticipated consequence of using nonstandard work (Davis-Blake & Broschak, 2000; Uzzi & Barsness, 1998). For instance, in one of Lautsch's (2002) cases, the incorporation of nonstandard employees into an organization was described as "disastrous" by all involved. The conflict was so extensive, standard workers refused to even talk to the nonstandard workers. In such situations, the organizational benefits of using nonstandard employment can be outweighed by the negative repercussions. Next we consider what variables might determine the extent to which the introduction of nonstandard workers is likely to be problematic in this way.

COMPETENCE: THE KEY MODERATOR

A crucial factor that affects the extent to which threat to formal and informal status and accommodation operate in blended work groups is nonstandard workers' competence in the tasks that they are asked to do by the organization. Traditionally, worker competence has been associated with specific types of nonstandard work arrangements. Temporary work is often depicted as low-skill, low-pay work while contract workers often have a great deal of experience and possess technical skills that are in high demand (Hunter, McGregor, MacInnes, & Sproull, 1993). However, there is considerable variance in task-related skill levels among types of nonstandard workers. For instance, while many contract workers are utilized precisely because they possess experience and technical skills, in other contexts, contract workers can be quite young with little education and little industry specific experience (Kochan et al., 1994). Similarly, while many temporary workers tend to possess basic skills, other temporary workers can be highly experienced, especially if they have worked in nonstandard positions for a long time. The emergence of staffing strategies that incorporate temporary work arrangements (Matusik & Hill, 1998; Lepak & Snell, 1999) and the proliferation of temporary help agencies have contributed to the rise of highly skilled professional, technical, and managerial jobs that are now staffed by both temporary workers and contractors (Cohany, 1996; Kunda et al., 2002; Marler et al., 2002). Thus, for the purposes of our model the distinction between temporary and contract workers is seen as consequential only in so far as it implies nonstandard worker competence, which in turn determines the extent to which the presence of nonstandard workers creates a problem of threat to the formal or informal status of, or accommodation by, standard workers.

We propose that the level of competence of nonstandard workers determines which of the two paths, threat or accommodation, primarily drives work group outcomes. With highly competent nonstandard workers, work group outcomes should be determined primarily through threats to formal and informal status of standard workers. With low-competence nonstandard workers, work group outcomes should be determined primarily through accommodation by standard workers.

When nonstandard workers are highly competent in the tasks they are hired to perform, they are more likely to be perceived as a threat to the employment status of standard workers. As these nonstandard workers are able to perform their jobs well and are willing to do so while receiving lower pay and fewer benefits, standard workers are likely to perceive that their employment status (job security) is in jeopardy. Standard workers might also interpret the introduction of highly skilled nonstandard workers as a shift in the priorities of the focal organization. Instead of emphasizing job stability and loyalty, standard workers may perceive that the organization is more concerned with flexibility and cost cutting. This shift in priorities violates the psychological contract that standard workers have developed. Lautsch (2002) found that the strongest negative reactions of standard workers to temporary workers was in those cases where temporary workers were placed in jobs very similar to standard workers and where they were perceived as being strong threats to replacing standard workers. Thus, with the introduction of highly skilled nonstandard workers into a work group the formal employment status that standard workers had taken for granted now becomes salient.

The use of high-competence nonstandard workers may also threaten the prestige of standard employees if they believe having nonstandard coworkers erodes the respect and value accorded their positions. When lower work status nonstandard workers are brought in and competently perform the same tasks as higher status standard workers, this tends to blur the value and distinctiveness of standard work arrangements and threaten the esteem of standard workers.

When nonstandard workers have low task-related competence, we expect standard workers to be less threatened by their presence. Instead, low competence among nonstandard workers will likely necessitate greater accommodation on the part of standard workers. Specifically, standard workers will be expected to adapt more when nonstandard worker skill levels are low and there is greater need for standard workers to monitor nonstandard workers (Pearce, 1993; Smith, 1994). As standard workers are forced to take attention away from their own tasks to make sure that inexperienced nonstandard workers are producing quality products or services, standard employees' own performance is likely to suffer. Furthermore, standard employees are typically asked to engage in adaptation and monitoring, tasks that typically do not appear in their job descriptions (e.g., train nonstandard coworkers), without any commensurate increase in compensation. All these factors suggest that standard employees will resent the presence of nonstandard workers who may not be able to complete their jobs without assistance.

In sum, the competence of nonstandard workers in blended work groups influences the reactions of standard workers. When nonstandard workers are highly skilled, threats to status will dominate any accommodation that may be required. On the other hand, when nonstandard workers arrive with low task-related competence, their presence, while perhaps somewhat threatening to the status of standard workers, will cause standard workers to react more to the necessary accommodations to their work assignments.

These hypothesized effects are captured in Fig. 1, which portrays a comprehensive model for understanding the negative reactions of standard employees to the presence of nonstandard coworkers. As noted in the model, nonstandard worker competence is the key determinant of whether the presence of nonstandard coworkers is most likely to create problems of threats to formal or informal status or accommodation. However, several other secondary moderators also play an important role in standard workers' reactions to their nonstandard coworkers.

MODERATORS OF THREAT

Similarity of Tasks

The degree to which standard workers perceive nonstandard workers as a threat to their employment status is moderated by the similarity between standard and nonstandard workers' tasks. When nonstandard and standard workers perform different tasks, as is often the case, threats to status will be lower than when they perform identical tasks. When they perform different tasks, standard workers are less likely to view nonstandard workers as possible replacements. Further, task differentiation will likely preserve standard workers confidence in their distinctive abilities in the organization. On the other hand, when nonstandard and standard workers perform similar or identical tasks, standard workers are more likely to perceive these nonstandard workers as highly threatening to both their employment status and their prestige.

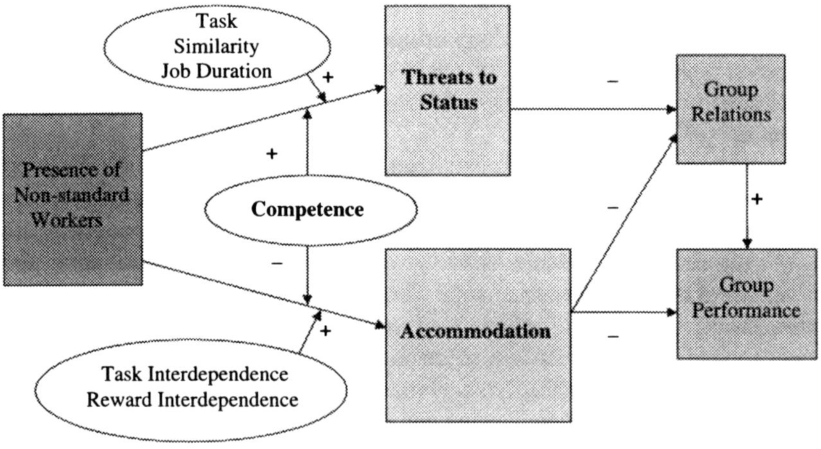

Fig. 1. The Reception of Nonstandard Workers by Standard Workers.

Duration of Employment

Threats to status are also likely to be moderated by the duration of nonstandard workers' employment in the organization. Nonstandard work arrangements vary in the amount of time individuals remain working with the focal organization, from only a few days, to assignments that can last for months or even years. Particularly, when used as part of ongoing work rather than specified projects, some nonstandard work arrangements last for undefined periods of time. If standard workers expect nonstandard workers to be present for short and defined periods of time, then nonstandard workers should be perceived as less of a threat to standard workers' employment status. They may also represent less of a threat to the prestige of standard workers when nonstandard workers are not employed long enough to gain the organization specific knowledge that standard workers have. On the other hand, when nonstandard workers are employed for long durations or indefinitely the standard/nonstandard employee distinction becomes ambiguous. In some cases, the only obvious difference between standard and nonstandard workers is the duration of an arrangement between the employee and the organization. Therefore, when this difference is no longer apparent, standard worker employment security and prestige could be highly threatened.

MODERATORS OF ACCOMMODATION

Task Interdependence

The adaptation and resentment experienced by standard workers because of the inconvenience of working with nonstandard workers will be moderated by the degree of task interdependence with nonstandard workers. When tasks are interdependent, task completion depends on all members of a group completing their jobs. The chain can be no stronger than its weakest link. As the tasks of standard and nonstandard workers become increasingly interdependent, the inconvenience, and hence annoyance and resentment, experienced by standard workers should increase. If any work group members, such as inexperienced nonstandard workers, cannot finish their tasks without assistance, other more experienced members must assist with or even perform the tasks of their less-competent coworkers. When tasks are more independent, there is less pressure for standard workers to assist nonstandard workers, and hence less accommodation that must occur.

Reward Interdependence

The structure of compensation can also compound the accommodation experienced by standard workers. If compensation or bonuses are based on group rather than individual performance, then rewards are contingent upon *all* members of the group successfully completing their tasks. In such cases, standard workers' compensation depends on whether nonstandard coworkers complete their tasks. Therefore, standard workers have strong motives to assist low-competence nonstandard workers when rewards are interdependent, simply so that the standard workers can be sufficiently compensated.

On the other hand, when rewards are based entirely on individual performance, standard workers who work with nonstandard workers have less reason to assist nonstandard workers. Their compensation does not depend on cooperation, nor on nonstandard workers' ability to complete their jobs. In fact, when rewards are independent, it may be to standard workers' advantage to not assist nonstandard workers. If nonstandard workers cannot complete their tasks, they probably are not suitable replacements for standard workers.

LINKS TO WORK GROUP RELATIONS AND PERFORMANCE

To this point, we have articulated a model of how standard workers are affected by the presence of nonstandard workers. The final piece of this model is the ultimate effect of standard worker reactions to nonstandard coworkers on work group relations and performance.

We expect that the effects of both threat and accommodation will be detrimental to work group relations. Whether from threat or accommodation, standard workers are likely to be hesitant to interact with nonstandard workers the way they do with other standard employees. As a consequence, standard workers are quite likely to marginalize nonstandard workers (Rogers, 1995), with this rift likely to have a subsequent negative impact on work group performance.

In addition, we propose that accommodation will directly diminish work group performance because the introduction of low-competence nonstandard workers has two immediate and direct consequences for work group performance. First and most obviously, the introduction of lower competence nonstandard workers lowers the average competence level of the work group, which translates into decreased ability to perform the group's tasks. Second, the increased effort that standard workers must put forth to train or assist these less-skilled nonstandard workers is likely to result in a decrease in their own performance. We do not propose a direct path from threats to status to work group performance; it is possible that the disruptive effects of nonstandard workers, due to the perceived threats they pose to standard workers, may be more than offset by the fact that these nonstandard workers possess skills and high competence. It is precisely this variation in the competence of nonstandard workers, as well as in the subsequent response from standard workers, that may explain the previous discrepant findings about the relationship between nonstandard work use and organizational performance (Matusik & Hill, 1998; Broschak, Davis-Blake, & Block, 2005).

IMPLICATIONS AND APPLICATIONS OF THE MODEL

Our model of the effects of nonstandard work use on standard workers suggests some apparent implications for managing the use of nonstandard workers more effectively. For example, when organizations hire low-competence nonstandard workers, managers who appreciate the potential disruption involved in introducing these workers into a work group could arrange for nonstandard workers to work independently of their standard counterparts to help minimize the negative impact of having standard and nonstandard employees working side-by-side. Similarly, when organizations hire highly skilled nonstandard workers, managers who understand the threat to standard workers' prestige could assign nonstandard workers dissimilar tasks from their standard counterparts to help diffuse threat by making any comparisons between standard and nonstandard workers, or their work, less immediate.

Unfortunately, such "easy" recommendations may fail to fully appreciate the contextual realities of the workplace outside of the simple relationship between standard and nonstandard coworkers. For example, managers may find that business necessity rather than managerial discretion dictates what tasks nonstandard workers are assigned. If standard workers leave and short-term help is needed, the vacancy is one that must be filled whether or not it threatens and/or disrupts standard workers. Even to the extent that circumstances allow task or compensation segregation of standard and nonstandard workers, either to minimize disruption or invidious comparisons, such segregation might not be in the organization's best interests. Segregation may decrease the potential for ill-will between standard and nonstandard workers but it also decreases the organization's performance potential. Contact between standard and nonstandard employees offers the promise of bringing nonstandard workers "up to speed" faster, so they make significant contributions to the organization more quickly. This is particularly true since for some tasks extensive technical experience and expertise cannot translate into immediate on-the-job competence. For that, adjustment to the specifics of the local environment and culture are required. That's where the social competence possessed by "old hands" (standard workers) can help. As a result, the lost personal productivity that standard workers endure, and even resent, may be more than made up for by the benefits achieved from getting their nonstandard counterparts effectively into the mix that much faster.

Furthermore, the same contact that helps nonstandard workers effectively adapt and adjust more rapidly can also increase organizational learning when standard workers are confronted with the differing perspectives that their "nonlocal" nonstandard co-workers bring to the discussion (Jehn, Northcraft & Neale, 1999). Thus, buffering an organization's core permanent employees from the threat and inconvenience of nonstandard coworkers may be neither possible nor desirable. Since organizations profit from organizational rather than individual performance, contact between standard and nonstandard workers (if not task and reward interdependence) should benefit both and therefore prove organizationally healthy in the long run, even if individually detrimental in the short run.

A missing dynamic in this picture relates to the central determining role of nonstandard workers' competence. In some cases, the ability to recruit and select nonstandard workers with high competence for specific organizational tasks may depend on the nature of the relationship between the focal organization and the staffing agency (Davis-Blake & Broschak, 2000). However, in many real life organizations, the choice between threatening and inconveniencing standard workers by hiring more competent and less-competent nonstandard workers carries an additional consideration – cost (e.g., hiring higher wage independent contractors versus low-wage temporary workers). If organizations feel that paying the additional cost to get highly competent nonstandard workers means they are damned if they do (threat), but also damned if they do not (accommodation and resentment), the rational choice would be not to spend the extra money. In fact, this would probably also be an obvious mistake. As noted in our model, while hiring highly competent nonstandard workers begs one problem (threat that indirectly can cause performance problems), hiring less-competent nonstandard workers really begs two (indirect performance problems via resentment and (direct performance problems via accommodation). Thus, managing threats to formal and informal status may represent a more tractable organizational problem than managing resentment.

Communication between management and standard workers may prove to be an important factor in managing threats to formal and informal status effectively. Two key pieces of information standard workers are unlikely to know without being told are the competence of nonstandard new hires and the organization's long-term intentions with respect to nonstandard workers. Certainly no organization would want their standard workers to think a highly competent nonstandard worker is incompetent if that belief drives an unnecessary wedge between coworkers by begging unwarranted resentment and expectations of inconvenience. And while some organizations may hire nonstandard workers with an eye toward using them to replace their standard workforce (Davis-Blake & Broschak, 2000), no organization without that intention would probably want to risk the damaging consequences of an inferred but false threat. Thus, at both ends of the competence spectrum, communication between management and standard workers could help better manage the psychological (threat and/or resentment) aspects of introducing nonstandard workers.

In the end, the psychological barriers to effectively integrating nonstandard workers into work groups seem most likely to be effectively managed by a more inclusive approach than just downward communication. The earlier standard workers are brought into the dialogue concerning the necessity of hiring nonstandard employees, and even given the chance to participate in the decision to hire nonstandard workers rather than trying to continue without them, the more likely standard employees will see their nonstandard counterparts as a solution rather than a problem. "Solutions" may take some effort to implement but they seem altogether less likely to be viewed as threatening or annoying.

CONCLUSIONS

The use of nonstandard employees and blended workforces seems to be more and more an accepted part of organizational life in today's organizations (Davis-Blake et al., 2003). It seems equally well accepted that the introduction of nonstandard workers into work groups is disruptive, both to work group morale and performance. This research adds to our understanding of *why* the introduction of workers with a different work status can be detrimental, not just that they are. Our proposed model clarifies the mechanisms responsible for those effects through threats to formal (employment) and informal (prestige) status, accommodation, and competence. Without understanding how the introduction of nonstandard employees is problematic, little progress can be made concerning how to effectively integrate nonstandard employees into a workplace. Armed with a better understanding of these effects, future research can focus on identifying ways to alleviate this tension and therefore smooth the transition for organizations into their apparently inevitably increasing use of nonstandard workers.

NOTES

1. Recent research has suggested that concern about job stability on the part of standard workers is often warranted. Studies have shown that standard jobs are no longer as secure as they once were (Osterman, 1996; Cappelli, 1999). Now, instead of job security through allegiances with certain organizations, job security is found in a worker's skills and abilities (Von Hippel et al., 1997).

REFERENCES

Barnett, W. P., & Miner, A. S. (1992). Standing on the shoulders of others: Career interdependence in job mobility. *Administrative Science Quarterly*, *37*(2), 262–282.

Belous, R. S. (1989). *The contingent economy: The growth of the temporary, part-time, and subcontracted workforce*. Washington, DC: National Planning Association.

Berger, J., Cohen, B. P., & Zelditch, M., Jr. (1972). Status characteristics and social interaction. *American Sociological Review*, *37*(3), 241–255.

Blalock, H. M. (1967). *Toward a theory of minority-group relations*. New York: Wiley.

Broschak, J. P., Davis-Blake, A., & Block, E. S. (2005). Nonstandard, not substandard: The relationship between work arrangements, work attitudes, and job performance. Working Paper, University of Illinois at Urbana-Champaign.

Broschak, J. P., & Davis-Blake, A. (2006). Mixing standard work and nonstandard deals: The consequences of heterogeneity in employment and relationships. *Academy of Management Journal*, Forthcoming.

Cappelli, P. (1999). *The new deal at work: Managing the market-driven workforce*. Boston: Harvard Business School Press.

Chattopadhyay, P., & George, E. (2001). Examining the effects of work externalization through the lens of social identity theory. *Journal of Applied Psychology*, 781–788.

Cohany, S. R. (1996). Workers in alternative employment arrangements. *Monthly Labor Review*, *119*(10), 31–45.

Cohany, S. R. (1998). Workers in alternative employment arrangements: A second look. *Monthly Labor Review*, *121*(11), 3–21.
Cohen, Y., & Haberfeld, Y. (1993). Temporary help service workers: Employment characteristics and wage determination. *Industrial Relations*, *32*(2), 272–287.
Cordova, E. (1986). From full-time wage employment: A major shift in the evolution of labour relations? *International Labour Review*, *125*, 641–657.
Coyle-Shapiro, J. A. M., & Kessler, I. (2002). Contingent and non-contingent working in local government: Contrasting psychological contracts. *Public Administration*, *80*(1), 77–101.
Davis-Blake, A., & Broschak, J. P. (2000). Speed bumps or stepping stones: The effects of labor market intermediaries on relational wealth. In: C. R. Leana & D. M. Rousseau (Eds), *Relational wealth: The advances of stability in a changing economy* (pp. 91–115). New York: Oxford University Press.
Davis-Blake, A., Broschak, J. P., & George, E. (2003). Happy together? How using nonstandard workers affects exit, voice and loyalty among standard employees. *Academy of Management Journal*, *46*, 475–485.
Davis-Blake, A., & Uzzi, B. (1993). Determinants of employment externalization: A study of temporary workers and independent contractors. *Administrative Science Quarterly*, *38*, 195–223.
Delsen, L. (1999). Changing work relations in the European Union. In: I. U. Zeytinoglu (Ed.), *Changing work relationships in industrialized economies*. Amsterdam, The Netherlands: John Benjamins Publishing Co.
Feldman, D. C., Doerpinghaus, H. I., & Turnley, W. H. (1995). Employee reactions to temporary jobs. *Journal of Managerial Issues*, *7*, 127–141.
Gannon, M.J. (1974). A profile of the temporary help industry and its workers. *Monthly Labor Review*, May, 44–49
Geary, J. F. (1992). Employment flexibility and human resource management: The case of three American electronics plants. *Work, Employment and Society*, *6*(2), 251–270.
George, E. (1996). The effects of external workers on internal workers' organizational commitment. Unpublished Ph.D. dissertation, University of Texas at Austin.
Gossett, L. M. (2001). The long-term impact of short-term workers. *Management Communication Quarterly*, *15*(1), 115–120.
Harrison, B., & Kelley, M. R. (1993). Outsourcing and the search for 'Flexibility'. *Work, Employment and Society*, *7*(2), 213–235.
Hipple, S. (2001). Contingent work in the late-1990s. *Monthly Labor Review*, *124*(3), 3–27.
Houseman, S., & Osawa, M. (1995). Part-time and temporary employment in Japan. *Monthly Labor Review*, *118*(10), 10–19.
Hunter, L., McGregor, A., MacInnes, J., & Sproull, A. (1993). The 'Flexible Firm': Strategy and segmentation. *British Journal of Industrial Relations*, *31*, 383–407.
Jehn, K. A., Northcraft, G. B., & Neale, M. A. (1999). Why some differences make a difference: A field study of diversity, conflict, and performance in work groups. *Administrative Science Quarterly*, *44*(4), 741–763.
Kador, John. (2000). The end of the world as we know it. *InfoWorld*, *22*(34).
Kalleberg, A. L. (2000). Nonstandard employment relations: Part-time, temporary, and contract work. *Annual Review of Sociology*, *26*, 341–365.
Kalleberg, A. L., Rasell, E., Hudson, K., Webster, D., Reskin, B. F., Cassirer, N., & Appelbaum, E. (1997). *Nonstandard work, substandard jobs*. Washington, DC: Economic Policy Institute.

Kalleberg, A. L., Reskin, B. F., & Hudson, K. (2000). Bad jobs in America: Standard and nonstandard employment relations and job quality in the United States. *American Sociological Review, 65*, 256–278.

Kidder, D.L. (1995). On-call or answering a calling? Temporary nurses and extra-role behaviors. Paper presented *at the annual meeting of the academy of management*, Vancouver.

Kochan, T. A., Smith, M., Wells, J. C., & Rebitzer, J. B. (1994). Human resource strategies and contingent workers: The case of safety and health in the petrochemical industry. *Human Resource Management, 33*, 55–77.

Kunda, G., Barley, S. R., & Evans, J. (2002). Why do contractors contract? The experience of highly skilled technical professionals in a contingent labor market. *Industrial and Labor Relations Review, 55*(2), 234–261.

Lautsch, B. A. (2002). Uncovering and explaining variance in the features and outcomes of contingent work. *Industrial Labor Relations Review, 56*(1), 23–43.

Lepak, D. P., & Snell, S. A. (1999). The human resource architecture: Toward a theory of human capital allocation and development. *Academy of Management Review, 24*, 31–48.

Marler, J. H., Barringer, M. W., & Milkovich, G. T. (2002). Boundaryless and traditional contingent employees: Worlds apart. *Journal of Organizational Behavior, 23*(4), 425–453.

Matusik, S. F., & Hill, C. W. (1998). The utilization of contingent work, knowledge creation, and competitive advantage. *Academy of Management Review, 23*(4), 680–697.

Olsten Corporation. (1997) *1996 research survey: Meeting business objectives with a blended workforce.* Melville, NY: William Olsten Center for Workforce Strategies.

Osterman, P. (1996). *Broken ladders: Managerial careers in the new economy.* New York: Oxford University Press.

Pearce, J. L. (1993). Toward an organizational behavior of contract laborers: Their psychological involvement and effects on employee co-workers. *Academy of Management Journal, 36*, 1082–1096.

Pfeffer, J., & Baron, J. N. (1988). Taking the workers back out: Recent trends in the structuring of employment. In: B. M. Staw & L. L. Cummings (Eds), *Research in organizational behavior 10* (pp. 257–302). Greenwich, CT: JAI Press.

Rebitzer, J. B. (1995). Job safety and contract workers in the petrochemical industry. *Industrial Relations, 34*(1), 40–57.

Robinson, S. L. (1996). Trust and breach of the psychological contract. *Administrative Science Quarterly, 41*, 574–599.

Robinson, S. L., & Morrison, E. W. (1995). Psychological contracts and OCB: The effect of unfulfilled obligations on civic virtue behavior. *Journal of Organizational Behavior, 16*(3), 289–299.

Robinson, S. L., & Rousseau, D. M. (1994). Violating the psychological contract: Not the exception but the norm. *Journal of Organizational Behavior, 15*(3), 245–260.

Rogers, J. K. (1995). Just a temp. *Work and Occupations, 22*(2), 137–167.

Rousseau, D. M. (1989). Psychological and implied contracts in organizations. *Employee Responsibilities and Rights Journal, 2*, 121–139.

Rousseau, D. M. (1995). *Psychological contracts in organizations: Understanding written and unwritten agreements.* Thousand Oaks, CA: Sage.

Rousseau, D. M., & Libuser, C. (1997). Contingent workers in high-risk environments. *California Management Review, 39*, 103–123.

Segal, L. M., & Sullivan, D. G. (1997). The growth of temporary services work. *Journal of Economic Perspectives, 11*(2), 117–137.

Shepherd, C., & Brown, P. (1956). Status, prestige, and esteem in a research organization. *Administrative Science Quarterly*, *1*, 340–359.
Smith, V. (1994). Institutionalizing flexibility in a service firm. *Work and Occupations*, *21*(3), 284–307.
Tajfel, H., & Turner, J. C. (1979). An integrative theory of intergroup conflict. In: W. G. Austin & S. Worchel (Eds), *The social psychology of intergroup relations* (pp. 33–47). Monterey, CA: Brooks-Cole.
Tajfel, H., & Turner, J. C. (1986). The social identity theory of intergroup behavior. In: S. Worchel & W. G. Austin (Eds), *The psychology of intergroup relations* (pp. 7–24). Chicago: Nelson-Hall.
Tan, H., & Tan, C. (2002). Temporary employees in Singapore: What drives them? *The Journal of Psychology*, *136*, 83–102.
Tansky, J. W., & Veglahn, P. A. (1995). Legal issues in co-employment. *Labor Law Journal*, *46*(5), 293–300.
Uzzi, B., & Barsness, Z. I. (1998). Contingent employment in British establishments: Organizational determinants and the use of fixed-term hires and part-time workers. *Social Forces*, *76*, 967–1007.
Van Dyne, L., & Ang, S. (1998). Organizational citizenship behavior of contingent workers in Singapore. *Academy of Management Journal*, *41*, 692–703.
Von Hippel, C., Mangum, S. L., Greenberger, D. B., Heneman, R. L., & Skoglind, J. D. (1997). Temporary employment: Can organizations and employees both win? *Academy of Management Executive*, *11*(2), 93–104.
Wegener, B. (1992). Concepts and measurement of prestige. *Annual Review of Sociology*, *18*, 253–280.
Wells, J.C., Kochan, T.A., & Smith, M. (1991). Managing workforce safety and help: The case of contract labor in the U.S. petrochemical industry. John Gray Institute.
Wiens-Tuers, B. A. (2001). Employee attachment and temporary workers. *Journal of Economic Issues*, *35*(1), 45–60.

THE CAMOUFLAGE EFFECT: SEPARATING ACHIEVED STATUS AND UNEARNED PRIVILEGE IN ORGANIZATIONS

Ashleigh Shelby Rosette and Leigh Thompson

ABSTRACT

In many organizational settings, status hierarchies result in the conferral of privileges that are based on achievement. However, in the same settings, status may result in the bestowal of privileges that are unearned. We argue that these unearned privileges are often awarded based on ascribed characteristics, but are perceived to be achieved. We further argue that these misattributions occur because acknowledging that one has benefited from unearned advantages that are awarded in a meritocracy can be threatening to a person's self-identity. We propose that by studying unearned privileges in organizational settings, a more accurate assessment of status hierarchies may result.

In 1997, the inaugural year of the University of Michigan's point system, two White applicants, filed a lawsuit which claimed that they were denied admission as undergraduates to the University of Michigan in favor of

Status and Groups
Research on Managing Groups and Teams, Volume 7, 259–281

ISSN: 1534-0856/doi:10.1016/S1534-0856(05)07011-8

less-qualified minority students (U.S. District Court, 1997). Under the point system, points were awarded to applicants based on merit-based categories, such as grade point average, Scholastic Assessment Test (SAT) scores, college preparatory classes, and rigorous curriculum. Points were also awarded to applicants based on non-merit-based categories, such as under-represented minorities (i.e., African American, Hispanic American, and Native American) and legacies (University of Michigan Archives, 2001). Of the non-merit-based categories that could have been chosen as the basis on which to challenge the legitimacy of the University of Michigan's point system, the category chosen by the plaintiffs was under-represented minorities (U.S. District Court, 1997). Legacies were not chosen as the basis for the lawsuit.

The key difference between under-represented minorities and legacies centers on status. When non-merit-based privileges are bestowed upon low-status individuals, such as the minorities who applied to the University of Michigan, the perception is that the benefits are unearned and, thus, not deserved. When non-merit-based privileges accrue to high-status individuals, such as legacies, challenges rarely occur because the benefits are perceived to be earned and therefore deserved. In both examples, the privilege was the same. In the former example, the privilege was rejected (i.e., challenged in the legal system), but in the latter example, the privilege was accepted (i.e., not challenged in the legal system).

The acceptance of accrued privilege to those with status in a meritorious organizational structure is not unique to the University of Michigan lawsuit example. In organizational settings, high status may result in the conferral of privileges that are often not merit-based and therefore unearned. The unearned nature of the privilege, however, is often not acknowledged by the organizational actor and others in the organization (Wildman, 1996) and may even be perceived as being earned. The conferral of unearned privileges to those people with high status is readily addressed by journalists in the popular press (Dorsey, 2003; Farrell, 2003; Sorkin, 2003; Strauss, 2003), but is not often considered by organizational behavior researchers who study status.

Much of the current research on status which is based on theories, such as expectation states theory (Berger, Cohen, & Zelditch Jr., 1972; Webster Jr. & Driskell Jr., 1978), status construction theory (Ridgeway, 1991, 2000, 2001), and status incongruence theory (Sampson, 1963), focuses on how status influences group interaction. This chapter builds on these existing theories and focuses on the privileges that accrue to people of high status and their tendency to categorize them as achieved as opposed to ascribed.

We begin with a definition of status in organizations, which includes two types of status relevant in organizational settings, ascribed status and achieved status. Next, we argue that privileges are often awarded based on ascribed characteristics, but are perceived to be based on achievement. We provide examples of types of privilege whereby this "camouflage" may occur. We then furnish several reasons why organizational actors with high status may be reluctant to acknowledge their unearned privilege. Finally, we demonstrate how current status theories may be applied to the study of unearned privilege and conclude with implications for organizational research.

STATUS DEFINED: THEORY AND RESEARCH

Within organizational behavior research, status has been a central focus. Max Weber's conception of status and social class (Gerth & Mills, 1970) serves as the foundation for much of this research. In Weber's model of social class, status is synonymous with honor or prestige and is expressed through lifestyle choices (Gerth & Mills, 1970). Expectations states theory (Berger et al., 1972; Webster & Driskell, 1978) builds on Weber's conceptualization of status, but streamlines the concept to specifically consider a person's social position. Our definition of status is taken from expectation states theory, which describes status as the position that someone occupies in a society or a social group and is not based on only one attribute; instead it is a generalized evaluation underlying a cluster of manifest attributes and positions (Anderson, Berger, Cohen, & Zelditch Jr., 1966; Berger et al., 1972). Status is divided into two types, ascribed status and achieved status. In U.S. organizations, achieved status is emphasized much more than ascribed status (Reskin, 2003).

Comparing Ascribed and Achieved Status

Ralph Linton (1936), in his seminal work, *The Study of Man*, first defined ascribed statuses as those which are assigned to individuals without referring to ability or innate difference and over which one has no control (e.g., gender, family lineage, skin color). He described achieved statuses as those which require special qualities and are left open to be filled through competition and individual effort (e.g., income, occupation, education). Where ascribed status is predominant, people are respected because of the family they are born into, their affiliations and group membership, and, later in life, because of their age and seniority. People are accorded status through inheritance or as a result of characteristics, such as social class, gender, or race. In ascribed societies, such as the caste society in India (Mencher, 1974; Deliege, 1992), it is accepted that social class and gender accrue more distinct advantages and rights.

In cultures where achieved status is prevalent, people are respected because of their personal and professional achievements. Achieved status is acquired by demonstrating merit. It is not assigned at birth and is expected to be attained through competition, merit, and ability. People attain power and influence by virtue of accomplishment and performance. In cultures in which status is based on achievement, status is earned and not merely a birthright. Children are encouraged at an early age to be self-reliant, independent, and ambitious.

Achieved Status in American Society

Both ascribed status and achieved status exist in many cultures; however, some cultures emphasize the importance of one over the other. In United States (U.S.) society, achieved status is emphasized whereby ascribed status is usually rebuffed (Griffin & Kalleberg, 1981). This can be seen in the admiration of "self-made" people, such as Oprah Winfrey and Bill Gates, and in the disdain for those who attain wealth by "mere" inheritance. The support of achieved status and the rejection of ascribed status in U.S. society is also reflected in governmental laws and policies. The Age Discrimination in Employment Act of 1967 was passed because people under the age of 40 years were treated more favorably than people over 40 years of age (Schuster & Miller, 1984). The American with Disabilities Act of 1990 was passed because people without disabilities were treated more favorably than people with disabilities (Wodatch, 1990). The Civil Rights Act of 1964 was enacted because Caucasian Americans and men were treated more favorably than African Americans and women (Edelman, 1992). So, generally in U.S. society, ascribed status is rejected and achieved status is embraced.

The societal emphasis of achieved status is mimicked in organizational settings in the U.S. According to Greenberg (1982), status in organizations is based on individual merit. U.S. and other western businesses and companies generally work within an organizational culture whereby status is earned, accomplished, or involves at least some effort or activity on the individual's part (Griffin & Kalleberg, 1981). Positions of power and influence are thought to be attained by achievements and performance (Greenberg, 1982). Thus, status is perceived to be earned.

Status in U.S. work settings is also perceived to be equitable. Greenberg's (1988) field study on equity, workspace, and workplace status found that for status to be maintained, it is important for organizational actors to believe that the status hierarchies they operate in are equitable. Greenberg used the assignment of workspace, a reward that reflects organizational status (Sundstrom, 1986), to investigate perceived equity in the workplace. Employees in a large insurance company were randomly assigned on a temporary basis to the offices of equal-, lower-, or higher-status workers while their own offices were being remodeled. Employees that were reassigned to offices of higher-status workers were more productive than those assigned to offices of equal status workers. Similarly, employees reassigned to offices of lower-status workers were less productive than those who were assigned to offices of equal status workers. The difference in productivity was found to be related to the status inconsistencies and the perceived equity in the reassigned offices.

Greenberg and Ornstein (1983) also found support for the relationship between status and perceived equity in a laboratory setting. Experimental participants who were "overpaid" by receiving an inappropriately high job title responded by increasing their job performance consistent with equity theory predictions.

There is wide agreement that status in U.S. organizations is *perceived* to be merit-based and equitable. However, we will argue that achieved status is more apparent than real in many organizations. Next, we consider how privileges that accrue to high-status individuals in U.S. settings are ascribed but often perceived to be achieved.

PRIVILEGE IN ORGANIZATIONS: THEORY AND RESEARCH

Sociologists have long acknowledged the relationship between status and accrued privileges. In his essay entitled *Class, Status, Party*, under the subheading *Status Privileges*, Max Weber wrote the following: "For all practical purposes, stratification by status goes hand in hand with a monopolization of ideal and material goods or opportunities, in a manner we have come to know as typical" (Gerth & Mills, 1970, p. 190). A discussion of inequitable resources and opportunity that result from status stratification is a cornerstone of sociology and serves as the foundation of much sociology research. Using Weber's concept of status privileges as a foundation, sociologists have conducted substantial research on inequalities in U.S. society that are based on achieved characteristics and the differences in privileges and rewards that are associated with ascribed characteristics. The relationship between privilege and status is not, however, at the forefront of organizational behavior research. Thus, one of the aims of this chapter is to consider the relationship between privilege and status, both achieved and ascribed, in the organizational context.

We define privilege as rewards and advantages that accrue to particular people or groups and are withheld from others. Sometimes the conferral of privilege is earned as is the case with achieved status. Sometimes, however, the conferral of privilege is not earned as is the case with ascribed status. We argue that in organizational settings, privilege is often awarded based on ascribed categories, but is perceived by the person with privilege to be based on achieved characteristics. Specifically, privileges are awarded based on categorical distinctions, such as demographic variables (i.e., race, sex, class), but the person with privilege perceives that the conferral occurs because of achieved elements, such as merit and ability. In this sense, the unearned nature of their advantage is "invisible" to them.

The Invisibility of Privilege

Invisibility implies that the person who has privilege is unable or unwilling to acknowledge that a portion or all of the privilege that is bestowed on him or her may have been awarded based on ascribed characteristics (McIntosh, 1988). Wildman (1996) who examined privilege from a legal perspective, wrote the following: "Privilege is not visible to its holder; it is merely there, a part of the world, a way of life, simply the way things are. Others have a lack, an absence, a deficiency" (Wildman, 1996, p. 17). She goes on to say that privilege is invisible because the characteristics of the privileged group usually determine the societal norm. As the social norm is the conferment of the unearned advantage, its [privilege] existence often goes unacknowledged, but those without it [privilege] have a lack, an absence, or a deficiency.

The evidence supporting the invisibility of unearned privilege and privilege as a social norm is largely subjective and consists of interviews with focus groups (Ancis & Szymanski, 2001), descriptions of personal experiences (McIntosh, 1988; Simpson, 1996), and descriptions of work environments (Wildman, 1996). With the exception of an unpublished manuscript which examined misattributions for performance in an organizational setting (DiTomaso, 2001), our literature review revealed no quantitative empirical investigations on the invisibility of unearned advantage in organizations. Thus, this assertion seems ripe for study in an organizational environment.

There are at least three reasons why organizational actors with high status, such as executives and managers, might be reluctant to acknowledge conferral of unearned privilege. One explanation derived from theories of motivated reasoning (Kunda, 1990) is that organizational actors are generally motivated to hold themselves in high regard and to maintain positive views of themselves (Dunning, Leuenberger, & Sherman, 1995). One of the most effective ways of maintaining high positive self-regard is to interpret one's own achievement and positive outcomes as a direct result of one's own effort and ability. This is known as an internal attribution (Miller & Ross, 1975; Zuckerman, 1979). Conversely, the recognition of privileges that are based on ascribed characteristics is inherently an external attribution (e.g., acceptance into law school is attributable to one's family connections versus intellectual ability). Thus, by invoking internal attributions organizational actors are able to maintain a positive view of their accomplishments.

A second, related mechanism derives from the just world hypothesis (Lerner, 1980), which states that people desire to believe that social systems are fair and just. One motivating force for the desire to believe that social systems are fair and just stems from the desire for individuals to have control over events (Jost & Banaji, 1994). Almost by definition, privileges that are based on ascribed characteristics are ones that offer little direct control and are determined by circumstance.

The just world hypothesis is consistent with the third explanation which is the socio-cultural milieu in the U.S. is largely achievement focused. It is counter to American culture and values to admit and acknowledge that the receipt of benefits may be because of their category of membership, as opposed to earned merit. The pressure to avoid the acknowledgement of privilege is great because in facing the presence of privilege, the holder must give up the myth of meritocracy (Wildman, 1996). It is important for people and organizational actors to believe that their achievements are based on individual merit, not on unearned advantages (Greenberg, 1988); at least in egalitarian cultures where society rewards success based on ability and effort (Schwartz, 1994) and sanctions unearned rewards based on group membership.

Headlines plucked from the most esteemed periodicals like the *Wall Street Journal* suggest that privileges which accrue to high status individuals are often unacknowledged in real world settings. The *Wall Street Journal* (Golden, 2003a) reported that in the mid-1990s a Harvard University alumnus gave his alma mater between $1 million and $5 million. In 1999, his son applied to and was accepted to attend Harvard. His son was ranked fourth in his class but had an SAT score of 1240. At the time of his son's admittance, three-fourths of Harvard students had SAT scores of 1380 or higher. The Harvard alum said that his donation to his alma mater had "absolutely nothing to do" with his son's acceptance. His son applied to one other college, Williams, which rejected him. It is possible that the son of the Harvard alumnus was accepted to Harvard entirely on his own merit, but the data does not support this. Harvard accepts more than 40% of its legacy applicants, but only has an 11% overall acceptance rate (Golden, 2003b).

In this situation, it is nearly irresistible to assume that an institution's desire to maintain lucrative and rewarding social relationships may have led to the acceptance of the student. Although Harvard admissions does not comment on its legacy policy, the *Wall Street Journal* reported that Harvard does extend certain courtesies to children of Harvard alumni, such as delayed admission for alumni children with borderline qualifications. Next, we consider the types of unearned privileges that may exist in an organizational setting.

Types of Privilege

We have argued that unearned privilege may be endowed upon people according to their socio-demographic categorizations. Although numerous privileges exist in our society, a review of the literature on unearned privilege which spans across numerous disciplines suggests that there are five types of privilege that are the most predominant in society: (1) class privilege, which is based on socio-economic variables (Marx & Engels, 1962; Marx, 1967); (2) gender privilege, which results from a gender-based hierarchy (Oseen, 1997); (3) race privilege, which is based on the supremacy of one race over another (McIntosh, 1988); (4) religious privilege, which benefits people with certain faith-based beliefs and affiliations (Schlosser, 2003); and (5) sexual orientation privilege, which advantages the shared sexual orientation of the majority (Simoni & Walters, 2001).

When we look into organizations, it is certainly reasonable to expect that the same five privilege categorizations pertain. We anticipate that these five privileges that mimic the existence of similar privileges in society at large to be the most relevant in an organizational setting. We concede that there are some organizational contexts in which the privileges based on these five ascribed characteristics may be relevant or justified. For example, if a health club solicits applications for a women's locker room attendant, one would argue that it would hardly be appropriate for the recruiter to accept and give thoughtful consideration to applications from men. Thus, our consideration of these privileges is not absolute in all organizational contexts.

Class Privilege

Class privilege is an advantage that derives from economic resources and is often associated with familial background and parents' occupation (Marx, 1967; Marsden, 1997). Parents' occupation does not directly cause their children's profession, but a family's social class determines children's opportunities (White & Lacy, 1997). For example, socio-economic standing is a principal determinant for access to higher education. Using two sets of longitudinal data published by the National Center for Education Statistics, Carnevale and Rose (2003) examined the characteristics of students who attended colleges and universities. They found that 74% of the entering students in 1995 at the most competitive, 146 four-year colleges came from families in the top-quarter of the nation's social and economic strata as determined by parental income, education, and occupation, whereas only 3% of the students came from families of modest or poor social and economic standing.

Marshall and Swift (1993) used data taken from a random sample of individuals from Britain and Goldthorpe's (1980) three class categories – service class, intermediate class, and working class – to demonstrate that class privilege influenced a person's opportunity to achieve or maintain an advantaged position in an organizational setting. They showed that among individuals having modest or no educational credentials, those from relatively privileged class backgrounds (i.e., service class) were less likely to end up with working class jobs than were similarly qualified men and women from disadvantaged class backgrounds (i.e., working class). Even when educational attainment was held constant, class background was the predominant factor that determined which of the three class categories a person would end up in. Thus, the more privileged social classes remain proportionately more successful in using their advantages to prevent downward mobility among their children.

Using data taken from a national random sample of individuals in the U.S., Jencks (1979) also showed that family background, which included father's occupation and income, and parent's education, was the most important characteristic that determined an individual's occupational prestige:

the esteem of a person's profession. A characteristic over which one has no control (family background) often determines an individual's potential for success in organizational settings.

Race Privilege

Although numerous privileges based on race may occur in an organizational setting, the most prevalent type of race privilege in an organizational setting is likely to be White privilege. Researchers have examined White privilege in an array of organizational settings including education (Henze, Lucas, & Scott, 1998; Arminio, 2001; Manglitz, 2003), counseling training (Ancis & Szymanski, 2001), and consulting (Butryn, 2002). According to McIntosh (1988), "White privilege is an invisible package of unearned assets which [one] can count on cashing in each day, but about which [one] was 'meant' to remain oblivious." McIntosh (1988) listed 46 advantages available to her as a White person that her African American coworkers, friends, and acquaintances could not count on. Some of these included: (a) being able to associate with people of her own race most of the time; (b) performing well in challenging situations without being called a credit to her race; (c) being able to go home from most meetings of organizations feeling somewhat tied-in, rather than isolated, outnumbered, out-of-place, or unheard; (d) thinking about social or professional options without asking whether a person of her race would be accepted or allowed to do it; (e) not asking whether each negative situation that is contributing to her bad week has racial overtones; and (f) engaging in behavior (e.g., talking with a full mouth or being late to a meeting) without it being attributed to race.

In addition to McIntosh's list of 46 privileges that are associated with being White in an organizational setting, statistics from the U.S. Department of Labor, the prevalence of race-based discrimination lawsuits, and current research also demonstrate that privileges may also be associated with being White in organizational settings. According to the Department of Labor Statistics (BLS), more than 88% of the executives and managers in the U.S. workforce in 2000 were White; however, according to the U.S. Census Bureau, only 69% of the U.S. population was White. In choosing to settle race-based discrimination cases out of court instead of engaging in a risky court trial, Coca-Cola Corporation and Texaco acknowledged that in their organizations, a White person was more likely to be promoted than an African American (Harrington, 2000; Winters, 2001). According to a study by Bertrand and Mullainathan (2003), applicants with White sounding names were 50% more likely to be called for interviews than were those with

Black sounding names. Thus, in an organizational setting certain privileges are attached to being White.

In addition, certain theories claim that in work organizations, the most advantaged group is White men. Split labor markets theory suggests that White men make up the primary or core labor market and that minorities and women are the secondary or peripheral labor market (Dressel, 1987, 1988). Miller (1986), utilizing split labor markets theory, proposed that White men, White women, minority men, and minority women form four different labor markets for work organizations and White men are the most advantaged labor market.

Gender Privilege

In addition to highlighting White privilege, split labor markets theory proposes that women and men constitute different and differently advantaged labor markets (Baron & Bielby, 1986; Miller, 1986; Tienda, Smith, & Ortiz, 1987) and as a result of the distinct labor markets, women are usually disadvantaged in an organizational setting whereas men are advantaged or privileged (Martin, 1991; Cleveland, Stockdale, & Murphy, 2000; Powell & Graves, 2003). Men dominate the echelons of top management, both numerically and positionally, and most women, even those in management positions receive lower pay, have limited opportunity positions, and exert only minimal power (Morrison & Von Glinow, 1990; Babcock & Laschever, 2003).

The statistics abound on the differences between men and women in an organizational setting. The statistics suggest that there is a privilege associated with being male in an organizational setting. Men far outnumber women in managerial jobs and high-prestige professions (Giele, 1988; Padavic & Reskin, 2002). In the labor force, women salaries are only 76% of men's salaries (DeNavas-Walt, Cleveland, Webster Jr., 2003). Even after determinants of wage differences and market influences are controlled, there is a substantial gender gap difference between women and men in the workforce (Nelson & Bridges, 2002). Both theory and empirical research suggest that men are privileged over women in an organizational setting.

Religious Privilege

Both theory and empirical research also suggest that there are privileges associated with being Christian (i.e., belief in Christ and the teachings of the Old and New Testaments) in U.S. society. Such privileges may include assurances that work or school will be closed on significant religious holidays, not worrying about the ramifications of disclosing a religious identity to others, and being fairly sure that some hate group whose primary goal is to eradicate your religious group does not exist (Schlosser, 2003). In organizational settings, privileges are awarded to people with Christian beliefs, especially people who adhere to the beliefs of the Protestant Establishment which is also known as liberal Protestant religion (i.e., Episcopalian, Presbyterian, and the United Church of Christ). Institutionalized policies and practices persist to propel people who adhere to the Protestant religion to the upper echelons of U.S. organizations so much so, that the Protestant ethic (Gerth & Mills, 1970) was built into the nation's economy, especially its devotion to work and discipline, and harsh attitudes toward people who do not work.

To explore the dominance of the Protestant Establishment in business organizations, Davidson and his colleagues (Davidson, 1994; Davidson, Pyle, & Reyes, 1995) divided the *Who's Who in America* listees from the 1930s and comparable listees from the 1990s into two broad categories, the power elites and the cultural elites. Power elites included occupations, such as bankers, businessmen/women, judges, lawyers, and politicians. Cultural elites included occupations, such as artists, authors, scientists, and engineers. The results showed that members of the liberal Protestant religion had 12.8 times as many leaders in business (and public policy) organizations as might be expected, based on their proportion of the total U.S. church membership. Their results showed that since the 1930s the Protestant Establishment's stronghold had given ground to Catholics (0.92 times as many leaders), Jews (5.17 times as many leaders), and conservative Protestants, such as Baptists, Lutherans, and Methodists (3.27 times as many leaders), and they still retained a pronounced dominance in business organizations. Although other theorists and researchers have promoted the ideal that the Protestant stronghold in corporate culture has dwindled (Christopher, 1989; Carroll & Roof, 1993), Davidson's longitudinal analysis provides credible evidence of religious privilege in organizational settings.

Davidson and his colleagues (Davidson, 1994; Davidson et al., 1995) suggested that a modified version of the fair shares theory may be the best theoretical explanation as to how the Protestant establishment has maintained their dominance in business organizations. According to their modified fair shares theory, the Protestant Establishment uses policies and standards, such as inheritance, legacy admissions, and appointment to high political offices to maintain their privilege (Davidson et al., 1995). Beaman's (2003) research on the prominence of the Protestant religion in the legal arena supports and perhaps adds another mechanism to Davidson's modified fair shares approach. She argued that the U.S. and Canadian legal systems support the dominance of Protestant religion in the U.S. and mainstream Christian-based religion in Canada and uses them as standards by which all other religions are compared. In addition, she provided poignant examples of how marginalized religions, such as Native American spirituality and Sikhs were denied equal opportunities in business organizations and how Muslims were subject to biased media reports. Thus, a biased legal system may also contribute to the religious privilege of Protestants and Christianity in business settings.

Sexual Orientation Privilege

In addition to class, race, gender, and religious privilege, heterosexual privilege may also abound in an organizational setting. Heterosexuals possess a privilege based on their sharing the sexual orientation of the majority that affords them unearned institutionalized entitlements and advantages (Simoni & Walters, 2001). The privileges associated with heterosexuality include tax and insurance benefits, anti-discrimination protection in employment, and benefits and protections in terms of military service (Gonsiorek, 1991).

There has been disparate work on privilege, but to our knowledge no research has collectively examined all these types of privilege and considered examining them in an organizational setting. Unearned privilege represents the "dark side" of the organization, an informal hierarchy that is a direct result of unearned advantage. The admittance of unearned rewards and benefits in an organizational setting violates the organizational assumptions of achieved status and meritocracy, and the societal sacred value of equality for all. If persons with unearned privileges are unwilling to recognize that benefits accrue to them because of their class, race, gender, religion, or sexual orientation, then they inherently assume equal opportunity for all and that everyone had the same opportunity to perform as well as they did. They assume that the status they have attained is entirely a result of individual merit. Our research demonstrates that such an assumption would be premature and incorrect. Thus, the study of unearned privilege that is perceived to be achieved may supplement the study of status in an organizational setting and bring the dark side or the less pronounced side of the organization to light.

The next question to be addressed is why are unearned privileges perceived to be earned by people with high status? We propose that the primary reason that this occurs is because acknowledging unearned privilege can be threatening to the organizational actors.

Acknowledging Privilege Is Threatening

People are often unwilling to acknowledge that their advantage may be unearned or undeserved because such an acknowledgment may be threatening to a person's self-identity (Jacques, 1997). Superior outcomes that are the result of unearned advantage may not be a source of positive social identity, but instead a source of negative social identity, because the accomplishments now instantiate their privileged state and highlight unjust rewards. Most people do not want to be recipients of unearned advantage. In an organizational culture that values meritocracy (Greenberg, 1982), unearned privilege may be particularly loathsome or disturbing.

The idea that unearned privilege is threatening is consistent with the self-serving egocentric bias (Pyszczynski & Greenberg, 1987). People generally take more credit than they deserve for their success, but dodge the blame when things go badly (Zuckerman, 1979). To acknowledge that success may have come about because of something external may be threatening to a person's identity and the accomplishments that are associated with that identity. For example, consider the high-status person in an organization. She can think that she earned her status through hard work, diligence, and effort or she can think that a portion of her achievements is a result of an unearned advantage. Which would she prefer? The more probable attribution for her success will be the former as opposed to the latter, because the former is consistent with a self-serving egocentric bias. To acknowledge that success may have occurred because of something external, such as an unearned advantage may be difficult because it places the person in an unflattering light. To acknowledge that status may have been attained based on something other than achievement may be threatening to an organizational actor's identity, because most organizations are based on the premise of meritocracy.

Even when, or if, unearned advantages are acknowledged by people with status, they may be threatened by the existence of the advantage and consequently use psychological defense mechanisms, such as cognitive rationalizations, to minimize the threat. A host of current theories supports this assertion. According to system justification theory, when group inequalities exist, the high-status group will stigmatize the low-status group to rationalize and justify their advantage (Jost & Banaji, 1994). Social dominance theory argues that promoting the superiority of one group over another is often legitimized to justify observed inequalities (Pratto, Sidanius, Stallworth, & Malle, 1994). The just world hypothesis argues that people are motivated to believe that they live in a world where everyone gets what he or she deserves; hence, the high-status group's superior rewards and performance is a reflection of effort and is therefore justified (Lerner, 1980). When and if unearned privilege is acknowledged (i.e., brought to the attention of an organizational actor with high status), those who enjoy privilege may be motivated to justify the advantage and rationalize that any benefits are deserved. In addition, these three theories also maintain that low-status group members often buy-in to the cognitive rationalizations used by high-status group members, such as stigmatization of low-status group members (Jost & Banaji, 1994), the superiority of others (Pratto et al., 1994), and the fairness of operating social systems (Lerner, 1980). Thus, the potential exists for low-status individuals to accept their lack of privilege, because they perceive the privilege of people with status to be earned or fair.

STATUS THEORIES AND UNEARNED PRIVILEGE

Current theories that address status in organizational settings, such as expectations states theory and status construction theory, focus on how status influences group interaction, but generally do not consider how unearned advantages accrue to people with high status and the attributions made for those advantages. Although these theories do not specifically consider the implication of unearned privilege on status, the theories may serve as a springboard for such research ideas.

Expectation States Theory

Expectation states theory (Berger et al., 1972; Webster & Driskell, 1978) argues that any diffuse status characteristic, such as gender, race, or class which is used to distinguish individuals will become salient to them in forming expectations about their performance in a given task. Unless they are certain that the diffuse status characteristic is not relevant to the given task, they will treat it as though it is relevant and form task-specific expectations consistent with the status characteristic. The interaction that occurs during the completion of the task is dependent on the relative expectations of the group members. Thus, status characteristics which are based on demographic variables are "loaded" with evaluation and performance overtones.

If we move the concept of status expectations theory to an organizational setting and consider unearned privileges, the theory may argue that those individuals who are rich, White, male, Protestant, and heterosexual are expected to contribute the most to organizational task accomplishment and are afforded high status; and thus, unearned privileges are awarded simply based on expectations of performance in the organization. The features of this status inequality as described by Webster and Driskell (1978) may include receiving and accepting chances to perform, positive performance evaluations, agreement, esteem, authority, and acceptance of influence. All of these artifacts of status inequality are awarded on expected traits of their diffuse characteristics. Therefore, any benefits and awards that accrue to those individuals with high status are a result of expectations, not proven merit and are partially or entirely unearned.

One may argue that the application of expectation states theory to our concept of unearned advantages accruing to high-status individuals is somewhat flawed because granting high status may lead to superior performance, and any awards and benefits are therefore justified and earned. This indeed may be the case and the expectations of the group may be fulfilled; however, we cannot negate the origins of the status. The status was awarded based on status characteristics that were determined outside the local task domain. The status is thus unearned in the current task domain and any awards that are accrued based on the status cannot be entirely attributed to merit or ability, but must also be attributed to ascriptions based on demographic variables, such as class, sex, race, religion, or sexual orientation.

Status Construction Theory

Status construction theory which draws from expectation states research could also serve as a launch pad to address the relationship between high status and unearned privileges in organizational settings. Status construction theory (Ridgeway, 1991, 2000, 2001) builds on Weber's (Gerth & Mills, 1970) claims about structural inequality and asserts that interaction spreads status beliefs through behavior, creating a diffusion process that makes widely shared beliefs possible. Ridgeway (2001, p. 262) makes the following statement with regards to status construction theory. "The implicit, often unconscious assumptions about the worthiness and competence of particular actors in an encounter can, under the right circumstances, provide the seeds out of which grow more general beliefs about the worthiness and competence of whole categories of actors." Group interactions that bolster the implicit assumptions are crucial encounters which begin the process that creates status beliefs. A primary assertion of status construction theory is that goal-oriented interactions between people who differ in both material resources and a random attribute (such as an ascribed status characteristic) create status beliefs which favor the affluent person's ascription (Ridgeway, Boyle, Kuipers, & Robinson, 1998). When we apply this primary assertion to unearned privileges and status, we propose that unearned benefits and advantages may accompany the favored status belief.

The application of expectation states theory and status construction theory to unearned privileges that accrue to those with status highlights the potential for a "multiplier effect." Status sorts people into categories and once people are sorted into high-status categories, unearned privileges accrue. We have discussed unearned privilege in somewhat of a static sense or a non-dynamic system, but in actuality, there exists an evolution of unearned privilege that compounds or multiplies. Those with high status are awarded benefits, their status is elevated or maintained and benefits are continuously awarded; however, the unearned aspect of the privilege becomes muffled by the achieved characteristics. For example, DiTomaso (2001) interviewed 246 U.S. White managers between the ages of 25 and 55 years in three areas of the country: New Jersey, Ohio, and Tennessee. She took a 2-h narrative history of their lives, at the end of which she asked them to identify the reasons for their successful job performance. Most of the participants' responses included sentiments like, "hard work," "sacrifice," "persistence," "motivation," and "competence." However, carefully tracing each life transition for the participants from high school to their then current occupations, the narrative revealed that their job career paths were spotted with unearned advantages, but that unearned advantage had become entangled with earned achievement (DiTomaso, 2001). By considering both privilege and status in an organizational setting, steps can be taken to address the dynamic evolution of privilege and how it may manifest itself in status.

CONCLUSION

The primary goal of this chapter was to highlight the ascribed nature of status in organizational settings and bring to light the unearned privileges that are associated with such ascriptions. We argued that the organizational actor may perceive the unearned privileges to be based on achieved characteristics of merits. One may counterargue that certain misattributions are perfectly acceptable because both ascribed status and achieved status are confounded with privilege in organizations, and a distinction between the privileges that are merit-based and the privileges that are not merit-based is irrelevant.

There are three reasons why the study of privileges that accrue to people with high status and their tendency to attribute them to achieved characteristics, as opposed to ascribed characteristics, should be considered in organizational behavior research generally and status research specifically: (1) a failure to do so stifles the accurate assessment of organizational hierarchies; (2) researchers and organizational actors may reach erroneous conclusions about the performance capabilities of those with low status; and (3) a failure to do so perpetuates the conditions of inequality in organizational settings.

The failure to examine the unearned privileges that are conferred upon people with high status, and the related misattributions made to the nature of the privilege, stifles the accurate assessment of organizations and their hierarchies. By ignoring the relationship between unearned privileges and status in organizations, one is only getting a partial assessment of the status hierarchies in organizational settings. By examining both privilege and status together, we are more likely to get a complete picture and better understanding of organizational experiences and organizational actors.

If we continue to downplay the role that unearned privilege plays in U.S. organizational settings, both researchers and organizational actors may make erroneous conclusions and attributions. As their categorically defined groups have a disproportionate number of senior positions in organizations, one may incorrectly conclude that rich people are superior to poor people, White people are superior to racial minorities, men are superior to women, Protestants are superior to Jews, and heterosexuals are superior to homosexuals.

Finally, by maintaining that individual merit is the principal determinant of opportunity and advancement in organizations, and that unearned privileges are only minimally relevant, conditions of inequality are allowed to perpetuate. Equalities cannot be achieved by asserting sameness and trying to rise above differences (Oseen, 1997). People in organizations are different. Just as the rich differ from the poor and women differ from men, legacies differ from under-represented minorities in the University of Michigan's point system. Instead of ignoring differences, organizational researchers and organizational actors should embrace differences, learn from them, and let them serve as the foundation for a more rich understanding of organizational hierarchies.

In the summer of 2003, the U.S. Supreme Court settled the University of Michigan case and struck down the constitutionality of their point system, but upheld the right to use race as a factor in college admissions (Supreme Court of the United States, 2003). Albeit counterintuitive, their decision perceptively acknowledged that low-status individuals are often undeservingly disadvantaged and correspondingly, unearned advantages sometimes accrue to people with high-status. Perhaps the resolution of the University of Michigan case can serve as impetus for understanding how unearned privileges interact with status hierarchies in organizational settings.

ACKNOWLEDGEMENT

This chapter was supported by a grant from The Kellogg Teams and Groups Center, Northwestern University.

REFERENCES

Ancis, J. R., & Szymanski, D. M. (2001). Awareness of White privilege among White counseling trainees. *The Counseling Psychologist*, *29*(4), 548–569.

Anderson, B., Berger, J., Cohen, B. P., & Zelditch, M., Jr. (1966). Status classes in organizations. *Administrative Science Quarterly*, *11*(2), 264–283.

Arminio, J. (2001). Exploring the nature of race-related guilt. *Multicultural Counseling and Development*, *29*, 239–252.

Babcock, L., & Laschever, S. (2003). *Women don't ask: Negotiation and the gender divide*. Princeton, NJ: Princeton University Press.

Baron, J. N., & Bielby, W. (1986). The proliferation of job titles in organizations. *Administrative Science Quarterly*, *31*, 561–586.

Beaman, L. G. (2003). The myth of pluralism, diversity, and vigor: The constitutional privilege of Protestantism in the United States and Canada. *Journal of the Scientific Study of Religion*, *42*(3), 311–325.

Berger, J., Cohen, B. P., & Zelditch, M., Jr. (1972). Status characteristics and social interaction. *American Sociological Review*, *37*(3), 241–255.

Bertrand, M., & Mullainathan, S. (2003). Are Emily and Greg more employable than Lakisha and Jamal? A field experiment on labor market discrimination. Working paper. University of Chicago Graduate School of Business, Chicago.

Butryn, T. M. (2002). Critically examining White racial identity and privilege in sport psychology consulting. *The Sport Psychologist*, *16*, 316–336.

Carnevale, A. P., & Rose, S. J. (2003). *Socio-economic status, race/ethnicity, and selective college admissions*. New York: The Century Foundation.

Carroll, J., & Roof, W. C. (1993). *Beyond establishment*. Louisville, KY: Knox/Westminster Press.

Christopher, R. (1989). *Crashing the gates*. New York: Simon and Schuster.

Cleveland, J. N., Stockdale, M., & Murphy, K. R. (2000). *Women and men in organizations: Sex and gender issues at work*. Mahwah, NJ: Erlbaum.

Davidson, J. D. (1994). Religion among America's elite: Persistence and change in the Protestant establishment. *Sociology of Religion, 55*(4), 419–440.
Davidson, J. D., Pyle, R. E., & Reyes, D. V. (1995). Persistence and change in the Protestant establishment, 1930–1992. *Social Forces, 74*(1), 157–175.
Deliege, R. (1992). Replication and consensus: Untouchability, caste, and ideology in India. *Man, 27*(1), 155–173.
DeNavas-Walt, C., Cleveland, R., & Webster, B. H., Jr. (2003). Income in the United States: 2002. In: *Current populations reports* (pp. 60–221). Washington, DC: U.S. Government Printing Office.
DiTomaso, N. (2001). The American non-dilemma: The reproduction of racial inequality without racism. Unpublished Working Paper. Rutgers University, New Jersey.
Dorsey, P. (2003, August 27). Executive perks pick shareholders' pockets. *Morningstar.com*. Retrieved September 7, 2003, from http://biz.yahoo.com/ms/030827/95728_2.html
Dressel, P. (1987). Patriarchy and social welfare work. *Social Problems, 34*, 294–309.
Dressel, P. (1988). Welfare workers as surplus population: A useful model. *Journal of Sociology and Social Welfare, 15*, 87–103.
Dunning, D., Leuenberger, A., & Sherman, D. A. (1995). A new look at motivated inference: Are self-serving theories of success a product of motivational forces. *Journal of Personality and Social Psychology, 69*, 58–68.
Edelman, L. B. (1992). Legal ambiguity and symbolic structures: Organizational mediation of civil rights law. *American Journal of Sociology, 97*(6), 1531–1576.
Farrell, G. (2003). More NYSE salaries to be disclosed. *USA Today*. Retrieved October 3, 2003, from http://story.news.yahoo.com/news?tmp/ = story&u = /usatoday/2003/003/bs_usatoday/1183463
Gerth, H. H., & Mills, C. W. (1970). *From Max Weber: Essays in sociology*. London: Routledge & Kegan Paul Ltd.
Giele, J. Z. (1988). Gender and sex roles. In: N. J. Smelser (Ed.), *Handbook of sociology* (pp. 291–323). Newbury Park: Sage Publications.
Golden, D. (2003a). A look at who got in where, shows preferences go beyond racial ones. *Wall Street Journal*, 1, April 25.
Golden, D. (2003b). Preference for alumni children in college admission draws fire. *Wall Street Journal*, 1, January 15.
Goldthorpe, J. H. (1980). *Social mobility and class structure in modern Britain*. Oxford: Clarendon Press.
Gonsiorek, J. C. (1991). The empirical basis for the demise of the illness model of homosexuality. In: J. C. Gonsiorek & J. D. Weinrich (Eds), *Homosexuality: Research implications for public policy* (pp. 115–136). Newbury Park, CA: Sage.
Greenberg, J. (1982). Approaching equity and avoiding inequity in groups and organizations. In: J. Greenberg & R. L. Cohen (Eds), *Equity and justice in social behavior* (pp. 389–435). New York: Academic Press.
Greenberg, J. (1988). Equity and workplace status: A field experiment. *Journal of Applied Psychology, 73*(4), 606–613.
Greenberg, J., & Ornstein, S. (1983). High status job title as compensation for underpayment: A test of equity theory. *Journal of Applied Psychology, 68*, 285–297.
Griffin, L. J., & Kalleberg, A. L. (1981). Stratification and meritocracy in the United States: Class and occupational recruitment patterns. *The British Journal of Sociology, 32*(1), 1–38.
Harrington, A. (2000). Coke denied ... prevention is the best defense. *Fortune, 142*(July 10), 188.

Henze, R., Lucas, T., & Scott, B. (1998). Dancing with the monster: Teachers discuss racism power, and White, privilege in education. *The Urban Review*, *30*(3), 187–210.

Jacques, R. (1997). The unbearable whiteness of being: Reflections of a pale, stale male. In: P. Prasad, A. J. Mills, M. Elmes & A. Prasad (Eds), *Managing the organizational melting pot* (pp. 80–106). London: Sage.

Jencks, C. (1979). *The determinants of economic success in America*. New York: Basic Books.

Jost, J. T., & Banaji, M. R. (1994). The role of stereotyping in system-justification and the production of false consciousness. *British Journal of Social Psychology*, *33*, 1–27.

Kunda, Z. (1990). The case for motivated reasoning. *Psychological Bulletin*, *108*, 480–498.

Lerner, M. J. (1980). *The belief in a just world: A fundamental delusion*. New York: Plenum.

Linton, R. (1936). *The study of man*. New York: D. Appleton-Century Company.

Manglitz, E. (2003). Challenging White privilege in adult education: A critical review of the literature. *Adult Education Quarterly*, *53*(2), 119–134.

Marsden, R. (1997). Class discipline: IR/HR and the normalization of the workforce. In: P. Prasad, A. J. Mills, M. Elmes & A. Prasad (Eds), *Managing the melting pot: Dilemmas of workplace diversity* (pp. 107–128). Thousand Oaks, CA: Sage.

Marshall, G., & Swift, A. (1993). Social class and social justice. *British Journal of Sociology*, *44*(2), 187–211.

Martin, P. Y. (1991). Feminism and management. In: E. Fagenson (Ed.), *Women in management: Trends, perspectives, and challenges*. Newbury Park, CT: Sage.

Marx, K. (1967). *Capital: The process of production as a whole*, Vol. 3. New York: International Publishers.

Marx, K., & Engels, F. (1962). *Manifesto of the Communist party, Karl Marx and Frederick Engels selected works*. Moscow: Foreign Languages Publishing House.

McIntosh, P. (1988). White privilege and male privilege: A personal account of coming to see correspondences through work in women's studies. Working Paper no. 189. Wellesley College Center for Research on Women.

Mencher, J. P. (1974). The caste system upside down, or the not-so-mysterious east. *Current Anthropology*, *15*(4), 469–493.

Miller, D. T., & Ross, M. (1975). Self-serving biases in the attribution causality: Fact or fiction. *Psychological Bulletin*, *82*, 213–225.

Miller, J. (1986). *Pathways in the workplace*. Cambridge & New York: Cambridge University Press.

Morrison, A. M., & Von Glinow, M. A. (1990). Women and minorities in management. *American Psychologist*, *45*, 200–208.

Nelson, R. L., & Bridges, W. P. (2002). *Legalizing gender inequality: Courts, markets, and unequal pay for women in America*. Cambridge: Cambridge University Press.

Oseen, C. (1997). The sexually specific subject and the dilemma of difference. In: P. Prasad, A. J. Mills, M. Elmes & A. Prasad (Eds), *Managing the organizational melting pot: Dilemmas of workplace diversity*. London: Sage.

Padavic, I., & Reskin, B. (2002). *Women and men at work* (2nd ed). Thousand Oaks, CA: Sage.

Powell, G. N., & Graves, L. M. (2003). *Women and men in management* (3rd ed). Thousand Oaks, CA: Sage.

Pratto, F., Sidanius, J., Stallworth, L. M., & Malle, B. F. (1994). Social dominance orientation: A personality variable predicting social and political attitudes. *Journal of Personality and Social Psychology*, *67*(4), 741–763.

Pyszczynski, T., & Greenberg, J. (1987). Toward an integration of cognitive and motivational perspectives on social inference: A biased hypothesis testing model. In: L. Berkowitz (Ed.), *Advances in experimental social psychology*, (Vol. 20, pp. 297–340). San Diego CA: Academic Press.

Reskin, B. F. (2003). Including mechanisms in our models of ascriptive inequality. *American Sociological Review*, *68*(February), 1–21.

Ridgeway, C. L. (1991). The social construction of status beliefs: Gender and other nominal characteristics. *Social Forces*, *70*, 367–386.

Ridgeway, C. L. (2000). The formation of status beliefs: Improving status construction theory. In: E. J. Lawler, M. Macy, S. R. Thye & H. A. Walker (Eds), *Advances in group processes*, (Vol. 17, pp. 77–102). Greenwich CT: JAI Press.

Ridgeway, C. L. (2001). The emergence of status beliefs. In: J. T. Jost & B. Major (Eds), *The psychology of legitimacy* (pp. 257–277). Cambridge: Cambridge University Press.

Ridgeway, C. L., Boyle, E. H., Kuipers, K. J., & Robinson, D. T. (1998). How do status beliefs develop? The role of resources and international experience. *American Sociological Review*, *63*(3), 331–350.

Sampson, E. E. (1963). Status congruence and cognitive consistency. *Sociometry*, *26*(2), 146–162.

Schlosser, L. Z. (2003). Christian privilege: Breaking a sacred taboo. *Journal of Multicultural Counseling and Development*, *31*, 44–51.

Schuster, M., & Miller, C. S. (1984). An empirical assessment of the Age Discrimination in Employment Act. *Industrial and Labor Relations Review*, *38*(1), 64–74.

Schwartz, S. (1994). Beyond individualism/collectivism: New cultural dimensions of values. In: U. Kim, H. C. Triandis & G. Yoon (Eds), *Individualism and collectivism*. London: Sage.

Simoni, J. M., & Walters, K. L. (2001). Heterosexuality identity and heterosexism: Recognizing privilege to reduce prejudice. *Journal of Homosexuality*, *41*(1), 157–172.

Simpson, J. (1996). Easy talk, white talk, back talk: Some reflections on the meanings of our words. *Journal of Contemporary Ethnography*, *25*(3), 372–389.

Sorkin, A. R. (2003). Attack and parry as Tyco arguments open. *New York Times*. Retrieved October 8, 2003, from http://www.nytimes.com/2003/10/08/business/08TYCO.html

Strauss, G. (2003, August 5). Pricey perk lets executives fly high. *USA Today*. Retrieved September 9, 2003, from http://www.usatoday.com/trave/news/2003/08/05-ceo-jets.htm

Sundstrom, E. (1986). *Work places*. New York: Cambridge University Press.

Supreme Court of the United States. (2003). *Grutter v. Bollinger* et al., Certiorari of the United States Court of Appeals for the Sixth Circuit (No. 02-241).

Tienda, M., Smith, S. S., & Ortiz, V. (1987). Industrial restructuring, gender, segregation, and sex differences in earnings. *American Sociological Review*, *52*, 195–210.

University of Michigan Archives. (2001). *Former undergraduate admissions policy: Excerpted from U-M 6th Circuit Brief of June 5, 2001*. Retrieved on March 3, 2004, from http://www.umich.edu/~urel/admissions/archivedocs/

U.S. District Court (1997). *Gratz & Hamacher v. Bollinger* et al., Civil action complaint (No. 97-75231).

Webster, M., Jr., & Driskell, J. E., Jr. (1978). Status generalization: A review and some new data. *American Sociological Review*, *43*, 220–236.

White, L., & Lacy, N. (1997). The effects of age at home leaving and pathways from home on educational attainment. *Journal of Marriage and Family*, *59*(4), 982–985.

Wildman, S. M. (1996). Privilege in the workplace: The missing element in antidiscrimination law. In: S. M. Wildman (Ed.), *Privilege revealed: How invisible preference undermines America*. New York: New York University Press.
Winters, G. (2001). Coca-cola still faces suits in race discrimination case. *New York Times*, July 7, Online.
Wodatch, J. (1990). The ADA: What it says. *Worklife*, *3*(3).
Zuckerman, M. (1979). Attribution of success and failure revisited, or the motivational bias is alive and well in attribution theory. *Journal of Personality*, *47*, 245–285.

FROM SYSTEM JUSTIFICATION TO SYSTEM CONDEMNATION: ANTECEDENTS OF ATTEMPTS TO CHANGE POWER HIERARCHIES

Paul V. Martorana, Adam D. Galinsky and Hayagreeva Rao

ABSTRACT

When will individuals accept or reject systems that subordinate them, when will they take actions that will challenge these status hierarchies, and when will such challenges be more intense, overt, and non-normative? Research suggests that individuals often justify and maintain systems that subordinate them, yet we suggest that there are certain boundary conditions that predict when individuals will no longer accept their place in such systems. We propose a model that examines how multiple factors: A sense of power, emotions associated with power, and perceptions of the system's legitimacy and stability – predict when those in low power will act against authority or when they will act to justify and maintain such systems. We also suggest that the level and type of action taken against a hierarchy changes as more of the elements (i.e., sense of power, emotions, perceptions of the status hierarchy) of our model are present. We predict

Status and Groups
Research on Managing Groups and Teams, Volume 7, 283–313

ISSN: 1534-0856/doi:10.1016/S1534-0856(05)07012-X

that the actions taken against hierarchies become more overt and non-normative as more of these factors are present.

Disobedience, in the eyes of anyone who has read history, is man's original virtue. It is through disobedience that progress has been made, through disobedience and through rebellion.
Oscar Wilde

I have learned through bitter experience the one supreme lesson to conserve my anger, and as heat conserved is transmuted into energy, even so our anger controlled can be transmuted into a power that can move the world.
Mahatma Gandhi

Many wish that the world could be hierarchy free, a land of true equality. There would be no subjugation, no reason for some to live in luxury and others to live in shackles. Against this ideal is evidence that hierarchies are inevitable, that no society exists without them (Sidanius, 1993). The existence of power hierarchies often translates directly into the oppression of lower power individuals. However, subordinated individuals do not always act to counter this oppression. This chapter seeks to understand the conditions under which individuals seek to change the hierarchies that oppress them. We propose a model that stipulates when group members will be most likely to act against authority to change a social hierarchy: when actors have a sense of power, particular emotions are salient, and actors perceive that the hierarchy is illegitimate and malleable.

A useful starting point in considering when individuals will act to change hierarchies is the growing literature on system justification in social psychology. A number of scholars have suggested those individuals who lack social power tend to accept their subordinated place (Jost & Banaji, 1994) and accept "hierarchy legitimizing myths" (Pratto, Sidanius, Stallworth, & Malle, 1994) that explain, situate, and normalize the hierarchy. System justification by both high- and low-power individuals reduces group-based conflict and provides social order. System justification theory holds that elites are producers of hierarchy legitimizing myths, and that low-power individuals are consumers of these myths, while elites and low-power individuals together complicitly maintain the hierarchy (Jost & Banaji, 1994; Sidanius, 1993; Sidanius, Pratto, Martin, & Stallworth, 1991). Although the system justification perspective usefully illuminates the psychological mechanisms underlying the maintenance of a hierarchy, it says little about when low-power individuals will act to change the hierarchy.

However, when members of a social system seek to change power hierarchies is an issue that cuts across disciplinary boundaries and is at the heart of the sociological literature on social movements. Since the work of Robert Park and his associates, collective action and social movements have been recognized as extra institutional sources of social change. In contrast to panics, riots, fads, and fashions that are evanescent forms of collective behavior with few structured roles, collective action refers to a broad range of purposive collective behavior, the most organized of which are social movements that occur over longer time stretches, are driven by long-term goals, and develop formal organizations. Social movement theorists emphasize that social change is possible when there are political opportunities, activists who frame grievances and provide solutions, and organizational vehicles to mobilize and channel individual dissatisfaction into organized challenges of the status quo (McAdam, McCarthy, & Zald, 1997; McAdam, Tarrow, & Tilly, 2001; Tarrow, 1994). Although the social movement literature usefully specifies the macro-structural conditions necessary for collective action, it overlooks the psychological processes that prompt individuals to act against a system.[1]

Social movement theory insists that protest is possible only when there are political opportunities, vehicles of mobilization, and framing activities by activists (McAdam et al., 1997). In this literature, political opportunity exists when the political system is open to expression of alternative views, the state has a low capacity and propensity to repress protest; relationships among members of the elites are unstable and can be exploited by challengers; and challengers have access to allies in the elite. Mobilizing structures include organizational vehicles ranging from informal networks to formal social movement organizations, and strategic framing consists of efforts by activists to assign blame to the system, and to proffer a solution that motivates action (Benford & Snow, 2000). Although the social movement perspective is very useful, it is more a theory of where collective action originates and it makes a distinction between special purpose activists and regular recruits, but says little about how the activist in all of us is aroused and awakened. A notable deficiency of the social movement literature is that it has glossed over how actors may be differentially involved (Stryker, 2000). Explaining how actors are differentially involved requires that we shed light on how political opportunity influences the cognitive beliefs of individuals with respect to alternatives; how it is not only objective power, but also a subjective sense of power that triggers action, and how cultural framings trigger perceptions of illegitimacy, and thereby, motivate individual action.

In this chapter we develop a typology that captures the range of actions that those in low-power positions might take in response to their subordination. To do so we propose that two orthogonal dimensions, how overt the action is and how non-normative it is, can provide a framework for understanding actions taken in response to subjugation. One distinction is between types of collective action, normative versus non-normative action (see Martin, 1986). Normative actions geared towards improving a group's (or individual's) station and position in a hierarchy functions within the confines of the current system; conversely, actions may be non-normative, existing outside the rules that govern the current social arrangements. The second distinction concerns whether the action taken is overt or covert. Overt actions are those in which the interests and the intentions behind the actions are known, and covert action occurs when those with power are unaware of the identities or intentions of the action taken (Morrill, Zald, & Rao, 2003).

In this chapter we develop a model of action against authority by presenting three lines of argument. We contend that when those who are subordinated by a hierarchy overtly and non-normatively act against that system, to try to reverse that hierarchy, three psychological conditions are involved. First, possessing a sense of power, despite one's subordinated position, may be an important precursor to perceiving one's lack of structural power as something that is not fixed but changeable. While those with more resources, as social movement theory holds, may have a greater sense of power, the sense of power can also be independent of objective factors, and so actors with a sense of power may still act against the system despite their lack of objective resources. Second, experiencing certain emotions often associated with high power (e.g., pride and anger) may lead individuals towards system condemnation and action. We propose that those with a high sense of power may be motivated emotionally to structurally reform the system, whereas those with a low sense of power may be consumed by negative emotion and may be more likely to act against the system through acts such as covert sabotage. That is, a sense of power and emotional states may interact to not only predict the amount or level of action, but also the type of action. Finally, drawing on social identity theory (Tajfel & Turner, 1986) we propose that seeing the hierarchy as illegitimate, unstable and impermeable to individual advancement appears to be an important precursor to taking action against systems. Thus, political opportunity and framing together might provide the macro-cultural pre-conditions, but it is individual perspectives concerning the legitimacy, stability, and impermeability of the hierarchy that induce individuals to opt for collective voice options rather than an individual exit option (Hirschman, 1970). We argue that when a sense of power, certain emotions, and beliefs about system illegitimacy and instability are present, individuals may use more overt forms of voice. If all or some of these factors are absent, then individuals will simply not act, or they will be more likely to resort to covert (as opposed to overt) forms of voice and attempt to alter the system by working within the logic of the system rather than against it.

This chapter extends the debate on when individuals act to change power hierarchies on the following counts. We complement the system justification perspective by identifying the boundary conditions of action rather than inaction and complicity. We extend the social movement literature by dimensionalizing the conditions under which people act, and thereby, shift attention from elite activists and mere followers who are recruited through networks, to the activist within all members. We also add to the interchange between social movement theory and social psychology by developing the scope conditions under which protest and voice become overt rather than covert.

Before examining the factors that lead individuals to maintain such systems, we must first delineate exactly what we consider to be power. For the purposes of this chapter we define power as the ability to control resources, own and others', without social interference (for related definitions see Keltner, Gruenfeld, & Anderson, 2003; Thibaut & Kelley, 1959; Weber, 1947). This definition of power includes two primary elements – personal, and social power. Personal power involves having control over one's own resources and having autonomy to take action on one's own. Social power involves having control over others' resources. Social power often involves the capacity to influence others (Emerson, 1962; Fiske, 1993; French & Raven, 1959). Since those who possess power depend less on the resources of others than vice versa, the powerful are more easily able to satisfy their own needs and desires.

In understanding when those in a subordinated position will act against their subordination, it is important to make a distinction between the sense of power and the possession of power. Although one's sense of power typically emerges from one's actual level of possessed power, an individual's sense of power can differ from the power that he or she actually possesses, and it can be more important in shaping thoughts, feelings, and behaviors than actual power (Anderson & Spataro, Chapter 4 of this volume). We define sense of power as the phenomenological, subjective experience of control over resources, own and others', combined with the belief that one is capable of influencing others and exerting control over the social environment.

In addition we need to clarify the level at which action is taken against a system. In thinking about how the powerless respond to their subordinated position, Wright, Taylor, and Moghaddam (1990) clarified the distinction between collective and individual action. They defined individual action as any attempt to improve one's personal condition, to move up the hierarchy individually. Collective action, on the other hand, is any activity that an individual undertakes to improve the condition of an entire group. As these actions are taken on behalf of the entire group, they can be undertaken by the collective, as in social movements, or they can be done individually. In this manner, an individual terrorist acting alone can still be seen as engaging in collective action because the action is taken on behalf of a collective.

WHY ACTIONS AGAINST AUTHORITY ARE SO RARE

Power hierarchies are often remarkably stable. Successful instances of revolt to upend oppressive systems are rare in comparison to the prevalence of such systems at the national, organizational, and group level. The powerful have a number of tools at their disposal that allow them to maintain their advantaged position. Since the powerful by definition have control over important resources, power can be maintained through procedures that retain that control. Furthermore, those with power can strategically provide these resources as a way of controlling the emotional states of those without power. By providing specific individuals with desirable resources (i.e., buying them out or co-opting them), those with power can alleviate specific grievances without having to alter the hierarchical arrangements. This control over resources can lead the powerless to accept being demeaned in order to acquire these desired resources; for example, De Cremer and Tyler (Chapter 1 of this volume) found that the desire to affiliate with powerful/high status, resource-rich groups will lead individuals to tolerate high levels of disrespect.

Moreover, the powerful have psychological devices at their disposal as well. The powerful proselytize hierarchy legitimizing myths – self-accepted truths that support discrimination and inequality (Pratto et al., 1994). Stereotyping is a related tool used frequently by those in power. Fiske (1993) points out that because stereotypes help to maintain one person's control over another, power promotes stereotyping, and stereotyping helps to maintain power. Self-fulfilling prophecies are another mechanism by which the powerful control the powerless. Self-fulfilling prophecies occur when a perceiver's false belief towards a target leads that belief to become reality and to be essentially fulfilled (Merton, 1948). This belief or expectancy shapes the way the perceiver acts towards the target and unintentionally elicits and solicits behavior that is consistent with the expectancy. In addition, not only do expectancies channel social interaction to confirm the original expectancy, but they also affect self-perception processes; the target of the expectancy oftentimes comes to see him/herself in terms of the very trait that the perceiver expected him or her to possess (Fazio, Effrein, & Falender, 1981). For example, prisoners often come to see themselves as being weak and lacking any control whatsoever over their circumstances, even to the degree that widespread abuses, and even torture, become accepted practices among prisoners (Haney, Banks, & Zimbardo, 1973; New York State Special Commission on Attica, 1972; Saenz, 1986; Zimbardo, Haney, Banks, & Jaffe, 1974). Thus, self-fulfilling prophecies are a method by which stereotypes are transferred from the powerful to the powerless, how the powerless come to see themselves as consistent with the stereotype.

System Justification Theory

The powerless maintain their subjugated status not only through the psychological processes of the powerful but also through their own devices. One might think that when confronted with oppression, that such oppression would be transparent, obvious, and abhorred and that one would react against it. Yet, the typical response is not only to endure such discrimination and degradation, but to not even see the oppression. In fact, low-status group members are less likely to attribute negative feedback to discrimination than are high-status group members (Ruggiero & Taylor, 1995); even though low-status individuals actually suffer discrimination to a greater degree, they are less likely to attribute negative feedback to it.

Beyond the invisibility of their subordination, the powerless also justify hierarchies that perpetuate their lack of power. System justification theory contends that low-power individuals justify, psychologically support, and maintain systems that subordinate them (Jost & Banaji, 1994). The system justification process occurs at multiple levels. The powerless justify systems by seeing their subordinated position as being legitimate and this justification develops through what Jost and Banaji (1994) refer to as false consciousness. Indeed the powerless belie what is thought to be a pervasive human phenomenon, ethnocentrism, and in-group favoritism. For example, individuals from low-status universities, ethnicities, and gender groups frequently exhibit out-group favoritism towards higher-status groups (Jost, Pelham, & Carvallo, 2002).

This manner of inadequately applying false consciousness is combined in system justification theory with stereotyping. Whereas stereotyping by the powerful helps to protect and maintain the individual or group interests of those with power, system justification describes maladaptive negative self-stereotyping in which the powerless accept and support categorizations that subordinate and oftentimes demean them. This justification process provides an explanation for why women recreate stereotypes for themselves as less competitive compared to men (Eagly, Makhijani, & Klonsky, 1992) and why some African-Americans come to value athletic ability at the expense of intellectual pursuits (Steele, 1992).

In addition, this system justifying false consciousness and self-stereotyping can create a psychological sense of superiority and self-righteousness concerning the benefits of one's subordinate position. Kay and Jost (2003) found that poor individuals self-righteously claimed that although they were less well-off economically, they were happier than the rich: The rich have money but lack the real contentedness that only the poor can find. The "poor but happy" and "rich but sad" stereotypes make existing social arrangements seem attractive and acceptable. This stereotype also relates to another psychological benefit that the powerless can get from their station: Stigma can provide people with a certain level of distinctiveness. Indeed when distinctiveness needs are particularly high, minority membership that is stigmatized is valued more than membership in a majority group (Brewer, Manzi, & Shaw, 1993).

All in all, social unrest and group-based conflict are minimized by a number of psychological reactions by the powerless. But there are other more fundamental psychological processes that help to maintain stability in hierarchies and prevent their disruption.

Power and the Activation of the Behavioral Approach and Inhibition Systems

Power transforms not only beliefs about existing hierarchies, but also alters basic cognitive and behavioral processes. Keltner et al. (2003) proposed an integrative account for how power and powerlessness influence and direct cognition and behavior. Specifically, they theorized that power activates the behavioral approach system and powerlessness activates the behavioral inhibition system. High power is associated with a range of approach-related cognitions and behaviors, including increased extraversion and impulsivity, reward sensitivity, and greater loquaciousness, whereas powerlessness is associated with neuroticism, shyness and anxiety, sensitivity to punishments, and general vigilance. In addition, both structural positions of power and the psychological sense of power lead directly to the taking of action whereas powerlessness leads to inaction (Galinsky, Gruenfeld, & Magee, 2003a). For example, Galinsky et al. (2003a) found that those without power were less likely to act against an obtrusive annoying stimulus that was placed in the environment; those in low-power did not take action to make their environment a better place to be. Thus, independent of any system justifying stereotypes or cognitions, those in low-power positions may maintain systems that denigrate them, because being in a low-power position activates the behavioral inhibition system, making all action, regardless of whether it is against a system, less likely to occur. The activation of the behavioral inhibition system and the tendency towards inaction help to explain why the powerless remain passively resigned and do not question their subordinate positions, nor take action to change their environment or the system in which they exist.

Power and Emotions

Connected to the activation of the behavioral approach and inhibition systems is the tendency for certain emotions to be associated with power and powerlessness. In addition to positive emotions such as desire, enthusiasm, and love (Anderson, John, Keltner, & Kring, 2001) and pride (Tiedens, Ellsworth, & Mesquita, 2000), power is also associated with aggressive emotions such as anger (Tiedens, 2001b). Powerlessness and subjugation, on the other hand, are associated with emotions such as sadness and guilt (Martin, 1993; Tiedens, 1999; Tiedens, 2001a). Indeed, the expression of certain emotions may be one mechanism by which individuals achieve status and power. Individuals who expressed sadness, whether they were political candidates, sitting presidents such as President Clinton, job candidates, or employees, were all perceived to be less competent and less likely to be conferred status, power, and leadership (Tiedens, 2001a).

Besides being associated with power, certain emotions are connected to action-oriented behaviors, whereas other emotions are associated with passivity and paralysis. In addition, different emotions are associated with different types of action readiness. Sadness, sorrow, and fear are associated with helplessness, avoidance and inhibition, or a general tendency to move away; on the other hand, anger, rage, and annoyance are all associated with moving against (Frijda, Kuipers, & Schure, 1989). Moving away refers to flight and withdrawal and moving against refers to opposition and attack. Therefore, the very emotions associated with power are associated with different types of action readiness. Correspondingly, anger leads to greater risk seeking, while fear produces a state of risk aversion (Lerner & Keltner, 2001). Another mechanism by which emotions produce different levels and types of action orientations is through attributional processes. Sadness leads to perceptions that situational forces produced an event, whereas the experience of anger leads individuals to perceive events to be caused by human agents and to see other individuals as responsible for the event (Keltner, Ellsworth, & Edwards, 1993).

In one example of how emotions and action are related, Woodzicka and LaFrance (2001) investigated reactions to real versus imagined instances of sexual harassment and discriminatory behavior in a job interview context. They found that, although women thought they would confront the harasser in some sort of direct way, either by refusing to answer one of the questions, leaving the interview, or even reporting the behavior to a supervisor, in actuality none of the women who actually experienced the harassment engaged in any of these responses. Predicted action and actual inaction were both driven by emotions. The women predicted that their dominant emotion would be anger in the face of sexually harassing questions, whereas for those who were actually faced with harassment, their most dominant emotion was fear and not anger.

These studies suggest that emotional states can play an integral role in preventing the oppressed from rising up against their oppressors. The work on the relationship between emotions and attributional thinking also suggests that emotions guide perceptions of the causes of social relationships. In the next section we turn to what system-based perceptions are necessary for individuals to feel compelled to act against a hierarchy that subordinates them.

Social Identity Theory

A basic motivational drive is to see the self in a positive light (Steele, 1988; Tajfel & Turner, 1986; Taylor & Brown, 1988; Tesser, 1988). According to social identity theory, an individual's self-esteem is affected by individuals' membership in social groups; that is, social identities are an important part of the self-concept (Tajfel & Turner, 1986). One, therefore, derives positive self-esteem from membership in consensually valued, high-status groups. Tajfel and Turner (1979) applied social identity theory to explain how individuals respond to their station in a social hierarchy. The strategies that low-status individuals use to achieve positive social identities depend on the nature of group boundaries (i.e., how easy it is to move up the status hierarchy as an individual) and beliefs about the legitimacy and stability of existing status arrangements. Whether low-power individuals attempt to change a social system that subordinates them depends on these three factors.

The first factor is *permeability* which refers to how easy it is for an individual to rise up the hierarchy while working within the system. For a low-power individual to act against a hierarchy there must be no possibility for that person to achieve higher status; the boundaries between the powerless and the powerful must be highly stratified or impermeable. Evidence concerning fraternal compared to egoistic relative deprivation also suggests that protest and collective action depends on the perception that one's entire group and not just oneself is being deprived (Walker & Mann, 1987). Given even mere tokenism, low-power individuals will seek to achieve positive social identities through individual advancement by attempting to individually climb up the hierarchy while working within the rules of the system. Wright et al. (1990) found that even a hint of permeability was enough to lead disadvantaged individuals to attempt to achieve individual advancement within the system rather than attempt disruptive forms of action. Therefore, for action to be taken against a system there must exist almost no possibility for the powerless to improve their position in the hierarchy while working within the norms that govern the social system.

Yet, even if the walls between the powerful and the powerless are impenetrable, other conditions must still be present for action to be taken against a system. The second governing factor according to social identity theory is the perceived *stability* of the current hierarchical arrangements. Essentially low-power individuals ask themselves: Will those in power remain in power regardless of any action I take? It should be noted that norms form quickly (Bettenhausen & Murnighan, 1985) within any social system and can lend an aura of stability even to arbitrarily determined social systems. Overcoming these perceptions of stability is necessary before effort is extended to change a system.

The third governing factor is the perceived *legitimacy* of the current hierarchical arrangements. Subordinated individuals who perceive the power hierarchy to be legitimate will not be motivated to change it. If those in power are perceived to have attained their positions in the system in a reasonable and legitimate way, then there would be no reason to attempt to change such a system. In addition, if the norms, rules, and parameters that regulate the current hierarchy are seen as having been legitimately established and fair, then no action against such a system will be deemed necessary. Indeed, fairness heuristic theory (Lind, 2001; Lind, Kulik, Ambrose, & de Vera Park, 1993) was developed from the group value model of justice to explain these attendant factors that produce individuals' obedience to authority. Fair procedures, such as being given a voice in decisions, indicate that the group respects them, whereas unfair procedures indicate that the group disregards them or is contemptuous of them (Lind & Tyler, 1988). Perceived level of procedural fairness can often be a more powerful predictor of implementation and system support than distributive outcomes. For example, perceived voice leads to a greater acceptance of defendants' verdicts whether they are for or against the defendant (Tyler, 1989). Accordingly, individuals often decide whether to obey the dictates of an authority based on their perceptions of that authority's general and historic legitimacy, and fairness.

Social identity theory stipulates that if any of these three conditions are present (permeability, stability, and legitimacy), then individuals will not act to change the system. These factors do in fact appear to be crucial for determining the psychological reactions to a subordinate position. Turner and Brown (1978) found that whenever a system was seen as legitimately established, those in low-status positions showed out-group favoritism, or a form of false consciousness that justified the existing social arrangements. Only when the system was seen as both unstable and illegitimate did low-status individuals show a significant amount of in-group favoritism. Although the three factors of permeability, stability, and legitimacy have been shown to be important determinants of identification with the subordinated group, no studies have formally manipulated all three factors to determine whether individuals will only attempt to change a power hierarchy if all of the factors are simultaneously absent (Ellemers, Wilke, & van Knippenberg, 1993; Ng & Cram, 1988; Wright et al., 1990). Perceptions of the justness and legitimacy of hierarchies and the rules that support them serve to maintain such systems. We contend that when a hierarchical system is seen as impenetrably stratified, unstable and illegitimate, the powerless will cease to justify the system, but instead condemn it.

ANTECEDENTS OF ACTIONS AGAINST POWER HIERARCHIES

The above review highlights why action against hierarchies is so rare. Over and above direct threats and fears of punishments and reprisals, there are a number of processes that lead the powerless away from action against the system, including the content of the powerless' thoughts (e.g., system justifying and hierarchy legitimizing beliefs), psychological processes (e.g., activation of the behavioral approach system), discrete emotions (e.g., sadness and fear), and system evaluations (e.g., it is legitimate, stable, and permeable). What factors lead the powerless to act against a social system, to try to disrupt a hierarchy that subordinates them? The above review provides some insight into when the powerless may be driven in the direction of taking action to change a system that derogates them. Particular perceptions about the nature of the hierarchy, certain emotions, and a sense of power may all be involved when the powerless make a call to arms.

Social Identity Mechanisms and Actions Against Authority

As previously mentioned, social identity theory predicts that for low-power individuals to act against a social hierarchy they must see that hierarchy as illegitimate and unstable with impermeable boundaries (Tajfel & Turner, 1986). Low-power individuals will only seek to overturn a social hierarchy and reshape it when they perceive the system is *impermeable* to individual advancement and that they will never be able to individually advance into a higher position (Wright et al., 1990). Collective action will not take place when individuals can defect from their low-power group and individually achieve a high-power position through their own effort. In addition, subordinate individuals must believe that the power hierarchy is *illegitimate.* For example, only when they perceive those in power to have arrived there by illegitimate means, or that the hierarchy itself is based on fraudulent criteria, will they be motivated to rebel against the system. Indeed, perceptions of organizational injustice are associated with increased lawsuits (Bies & Tyler, 1993), an increased likelihood to publicly denigrate one's own company (Bies & Tripp, 1996), and inducing sympathy for, and interest in, various forms of worker protest including strikes and sit-ins (Leung, Chiu, & Au, 1993). When authorities are perceived to be unjust and illegitimate, actions are more likely to be taken to change the power structure to repair the perceived imbalance. This is often likely to occur when those in power are seen as possessing unmerited privileges (Rosette & Thompson, Chapter 11 of this volume).

Yet, it is not sufficient to only perceive that a system is illegitimate. Individuals must also perceive that the system is *unstable* before they will be motivated to struggle to change the power structure. Subordinate groups must believe that a radical change in the social hierarchy is possible, that there is instability in the power relations between low- and high-power groups, before action will be taken against the hierarchy. Seeing a hierarchy as unstable and illegitimate can prevent system justifying beliefs and cognitions (Turner & Brown, 1978). It is when the oppressed perceive that their oppressor's grasp on power is tenuous that attempts will be made to wrench control and overthrow the powers that be.

Tajfel and Turner point out that these factors are the underlying and unifying factors that motivate rebellious acts to change power hierarchies and reshape the social structure; they thus apply to a range of situations, such as the civil rights movement in the United States, corporate sabotage, and even acts of terrorism. Research to date has not fully tested this model, although some partial support has been established. For example, Ng and Cram (1988) found that illegitimate and unstable power can lead to rebellion against mistreatment. A test of the necessity of all three component factors has yet to be completed. Moreover, research is needed to determine what conditions lead people to perceive a power hierarchy to be unstable, impermeable, and illegitimate. We consider this in the next section, where we describe how a sense of power and certain emotions may alter the powerless' perceptions of the hierarchy.

Sense of Power and Actions Against Authority

As previously discussed, Keltner et al. (2003) have suggested that power activates the behavioral approach system and that powerlessness activates the behavioral inhibition system. This dichotomous typology of action and inhibition orientations adds considerably to our understanding of power relations and individual's propensity to act or not. However, Horney (1939) suggested a third dimension on which power could affect behavior – rebelling or acting *against* others. Rather than simply acting or not acting, approaching or avoiding, sometimes individuals act against others. This acting against others may relate to power in a number of different ways. Those in power may act against those in low power when they feel their position of power is threatened in some way. Some evidence for this proposition comes from the finding that violence, although often suspected of being correlated with low self-esteem, is more often connected to high self-esteem (Baumeister, Smart, & Boden, 1996). Lashing out against others is most likely to occur when those with high self-esteem feel challenged in some way, when their inflated view of themselves has been disputed. But those in low power may also be driven to act against others. We contend that those in low power may feel the disposition to act against others when they have a sense of power and especially when that sense of power is in sharp contrast to actual levels of hierarchical power and control (Anderson & Spataro, Chapter 4 of this volume).

As previously discussed, individuals who possess a sense of power are more likely to take action in general (Galinsky et al., 2003a). Galinsky et al. found that simply having participants think about a time when they had power was enough to increase levels of action taken. Priming power, therefore, seems sufficient to increase one's sense of power. For this reason, we contend that individuals who are in a subordinated position in a hierarchy but who have been primed with power and thus have a sense of power, will be less likely to do the bidding of those in the high-power position in the hierarchy and more likely to take action to change their subordination. Supportive evidence for this notion comes from work on the locus of control; individuals with a greater sense of control over their situations are less likely to conform to authority (Rotter, 1966).

A recent study examining the effects of sense of power by Galinsky et al. (2003b) serendipitously found evidence that having a sense of power can lead people to defy authority. In the course of running their experiment, they noticed that a large number of participants refused to cooperate with one aspect of the experimental protocol. Their study was designed to explore whether a sense of power affected perspective taking. Participants were primed with a sense of power by recalling a previous experience with power and perspective taking was measured by the direction of a letter E that participants were asked to draw on their forehead. As it turned out, a number of participants refused to draw the E on their forehead and these refusals depended on whether participants had been primed with high power or not. Nearly a third of those primed with high power refused to draw the E despite being instructed to by the experimenter, who was in a structural position of power. Power primed can be authority resisted.

Moreover, we contend that small increases in resources may lead to even greater increases in one's sense of power. An activating sense of power may also arise when there are more resources at one's disposal. Resource mobilization theory proposes that the success of social movements depends on resources available to participants, such as funding, time, and members' organizational skills (McCarthy & Zald, 1977). We suggest that a sense of power may catalyze the effect of these resources on the success of social movements. Relatively well-funded movements, such as nuclear activism, may feel a greater sense of power compared to less well funded, non-specialized movements (Cook, 2001); this increased sense of power may arise despite the fact that they remain in a subordinated position relative to the Nuclear Regulatory Commission, Department of Energy, and other well-established organizations that decide nuclear policies.

The above analysis suggests that having a sense of power even while still in a subordinated position may be a necessary ingredient for the disposition to act against a system. How one feels about one's position may also be an important determinant of taking action against a system.

Emotions and Actions Against Authority

Emotions are often predictive of behavior and anger is one emotion that is predictive of acting against others. Anger is a negative emotional state that shows the same brain activity as other elements of the behavioral approach system (Harmon-Jones & Allen, 1998) and trait anger has been shown to be associated with assertiveness and competitiveness (Buss & Perry, 1992), with angry responses to failure leading to improved performance on subsequent tasks (Mikulincer, 1988). In addition to an association with power and the related disposition to take action, anger is also associated with an orientation to take action against those who demean and subjugate. Martin's (1993) and Woodzicka and LaFrance's (2001) work suggests that while emotions associated with low power such as fear inhibit action, emotions such as anger and pride are associated with taking action to change one's situation and rebel against those in positions of authority. Hochschild (1983) found that flight attendants needed to manage and control their anger in order to not take actions against rude first-class customers. Anger and pride may act as catalysts, providing the will to reverse the unwanted influence of cruel authorities. Understanding the current emotional state of the powerless may help us better predict when the powerless will act against a hierarchical system. In fact, researchers have begun to explore the importance of emotion in social movements (Horowitz, 2001), in particular, anger (Hercus, 1999; Gould, 2002).

Recent work has found that anger often plays an integral, contextualized role in catalyzing individuals to act against those with authority over them (Gould, 2001; Hercus, 1999; Martin, 1993). Gould's (2002) fieldwork found that members of the militant acquired immune deficiency syndrome (AIDS) activist movement ACT UP mobilized action by first transforming the gay communities' debilitating grief and fear into indignation and anger. Once this fear was turned into anger they used slogans such as "Turn Rage Into

Action" and "Angry? ACT UP" to marshal that anger into action against the health authorities. Anger can motivate and lead individuals towards action against authority.

Since anger and pride are associated with high power and sadness, and fear and appreciation are associated with low power (Tiedens et al., 2000), we hypothesize that when low-power individuals experience the emotions that are typically associated with high power they will also feel a greater sense of power. This affect-induced increase in a sense of power may occur because individuals use their moods as a source of information in understanding their place in the world (Schwarz, 1990).

This rage and anger is also often the result of perceived injustice within a system (Clayton, 1992). When individuals perceive that they have been unduly restricted from exercising expected rights or obtaining assumed privileges, they will become angry and attempt to correct their circumstances. Responses to injustice are often linked to the emotions associated with high power (Keltner et al., 1993). However, the relationship between perceived injustice and anger are non-recursive; anger also triggers perceptions of injustice (Miller, 2000; Solomon, 1995). Injustices make us angry and when we are angry we are more likely to perceive, label, and be incited to act against injustices. In the next section we turn to how the three antecedent factors (sense of power, emotions, and perceptions of the hierarchy) interact with each other to determine the type of action that individuals may take against authority.

MULTIPLE ANTECEDENTS FOR ACTIONS AGAINST AUTHORITY

Thus far we have discussed some of the variables that likely come into play when the powerless act against their position. But is there an order to the dynamics of acting against? Early sociologists proposed that riots were the result of irrational mobs, infectiously fueling each other with blind, uncoordinated anger (Le Bon, 1921). However, recent analysis suggests that there is order to the madness, that riots follow certain rules. Researchers have sought more complete, integrated models that consider contextual and social factors beyond the mere contagion of emotions (McPhail, 1991). It does appear that passionate emotions by themselves are not a sufficient condition to produce collective actions (Tilly, 1978/1990). Collective action requires the mobilization of many strategic, rational actors acting according to normatively accepted scripts for collective behavior called "repertoires of collective actions" (Tilly, 1986). The actions of rioters once an uprising has occurred are not driven by random events but are governed by a number of processes. Reicher (1984), in examining the St. Paul riots of 1980, concluded that crowd behavior is sophisticated and governed by social identity concerns.

This analysis, along with the other research on the sense of power and social identity described above, indicate that something other than simply feeling angry leads those in low power to take action. It appears that multiple factors coalesce to produce actions against authority and against systems that subjugate. We have discussed so far a number of factors, including perceptions of the hierarchy, the psychological sense of power, and particular emotions that might lead those without power to act against a system and hierarchy that subordinates them. We propose that actions taken by low-power individuals against those in authority are a function of the combined influence of an individual's sense of power, experience of emotions associated with high power, and perceptions of the hierarchy's illegitimacy, instability, and impermeability to individual advancement.

It has probably become clear that these elements may not exist independently of each other. Perceptions of legitimacy and stability, for example, are highly intertwined and naturally confounded in everyday life (Tajfel, 1981): Legitimate systems appear more stable and an unstable system can call into question its legitimacy. The model we propose encompasses these three primary antecedent conditions (sense of power, emotions, and perceptions of the hierarchy) which are often positively correlated with each other. As such, each element can act to abet and increase the experience of the other elements. These antecedent conditions can at times create a whirlpool of non-recursive interactions that can lead them all to be simultaneously present and produce an orientation to act against authority.

The experience of one element affects the experience of the other elements. As anger and power are associated with each other, a sense of power, even in the face of objective subordination, can inspire feelings of anger at one's subjugated position, but also feeling and expressing anger can sometimes increase one's sense of power. For example, ACT UP was able to turn anger into a sense of power. Though the Center for Disease control and Prevention (CDC) is an entrenched, stable organization, anger led ACT UP to believe that they had the power to force them to comply with their demands and revise the procedures for approving drugs. Their sense of power was exemplified in such slogans as "Turn the Power of the Quilt into Action."[2] Power and anger commingled to produce action to attempt to change the way in which drugs are approved and in this instance their efforts were successful. We are interested in this chapter in the factors that lead to such rebellions against systems, whether they are successful or not.

Similarly, perceptions of illegitimacy can inspire anger and anger can lead one to see a subordinating hierarchy as illegitimate. A hierarchy that is perceived to be impermeable to individual advancement will not only prevent individuals from satisfying their own individual needs, but may also produce anger and indignation on the part of low-power individuals. When access to high-power positions is proscribed by the nature of the system, anger and fury may be the result. Feelings of anger and pride, as opposed to sadness and fear, are more likely to reduce the clouded vision that prevents individuals from perceiving the injustices inflicted upon them. A proud and angry servant is more likely to realize that the emperor has no clothes, compared to the sad and fearful one.

Research concerning procedural justice seems to bear out this relationship between anger and perceptions of legitimacy, defendants in court hearings who feel that they have been given voice, perceive the process to be more fair, are less angry, and are less likely to take action in the form of seeking an appeal (Lind, Kanfer, & Earley, 1990; Tyler, 1989). The research on procedural justice generally suggests that perceptions of legitimacy can be controlled through regulations of affect. Giving people voice even when that voice produces no variations in distributive outcomes is enough to disperse anger and pacify the motivation to act against. Thus, when machinists are given more autonomy and control over their jobs, they are more satisfied and less angry at the system they toil under (Burawoy, 1979). Autonomy may also have affected perceptions of permeability, increasing the perception that individuals can advance through their own initiative.

Research on relative deprivation also suggests that when individuals perceive that a system prevents them from achieving outcomes they feel entitled to, they will become angry and will take action to change their situation (Crosby, 1976). Individuals will also seek retribution when they perceive that they are being denied some right or good, relative to what is provided to others (Greenberg, 1987). Collective actions require perceptions of relative deprivation, as well as a perception that sufficient resources exist (i.e., sense of power) to act against authority (Martin, 1986; Martin, Brickman, & Murray, 1984). A common belief holds that perceived injustices and the breaking of rules and norms merit acts of vengeance and retribution (Tyler & Smith, 1998). The perception of injustice does not result simply from objective inequality but requires attendant factors to be present as well.

Perceptions of illegitimacy can instill a sense of power that catalyzes individuals to take action to redress perceived injustices. Correspondingly, a sense of power influences and is affected by perceptions of stability and legitimacy of a power hierarchy. When people feel they have control over their environment, they may see a system that had shackled them, as being illegitimate. Furthermore, a sense of power may directly affect perceptions of stability, seeing the hierarchy as less fixed and reified. Moreover, an unstable hierarchy may allow people to feel a sense of power, so that they can reverse the hierarchy.

We suggest a model of action against authority that involves the joint, non-recursive influence of a sense of power, high-power emotions, and perceptions of the illegitimacy, instability, and impermeability of the social system all acting as a non-recursive whirlpool, with each abetting and increasing the other (see Fig. 1).

It should be noted that despite the non-recursive nature of these antecedent conditions for action against a hierarchy to take place, such action is rare and uncommon. How do we reconcile the positive relationships among the antecedent conditions with the infrequency of such actions? We contend that there must be a high level of one of the elements combined with a sufficient level of each of the other elements before they can start influencing each other in a positive feedback loop. These elements typically reinforce each other away from action, with sadness producing perceptions of stability and a sense of low power. But, at times, forces can increase each element independently and then they can "tip" (Gladwell, 2000) and increase each other in a non-recursive fashion.

Despite the fact that they can influence each other after this tipping point, not all of these elements will always be present. We claim that when all of these elements are present, full rebellion will be more likely to take place by those without power against a hierarchy. What happens when only some of the elements are present? We turn to this question next.

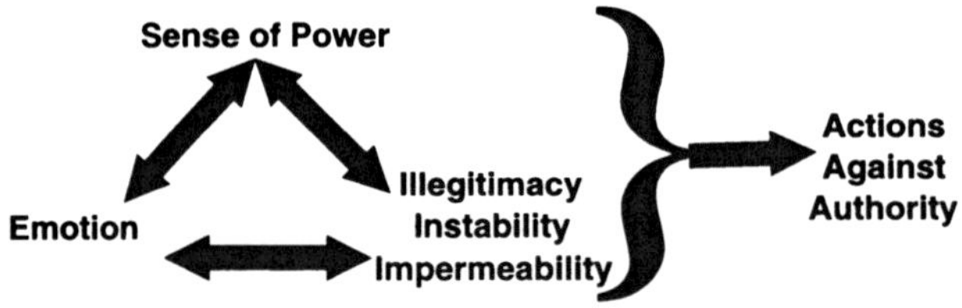

Fig. 1. Non-recursive Model of Against Orientation.

ACTION AGAINST AUTHORITY: THE ROLE OF OVERTNESS AND NORMATIVENESS

We propose that when the antecedent conditions are not simultaneously present (anger and pride, a sense of power, and perceptions of an unstable and illegitimate hierarchy that prevents individuals from rising up the ladder from the bottom rungs) then direct action to reverse or upend a hierarchy that subordinates someone will not be undertaken. The typical response will be no action. However, less extreme forms of action can occur if some of the factors are present.

Our model incorporates the distinction between two types of collective action, normative versus non-normative action (see Martin, 1986). Actions geared towards improving a group's (or individual's) station and position in a hierarchy oftentimes function within the confines of the current system; these actions conform to the norms that underlie the existing hierarchy and would be considered normative. Conversely, actions may be non-normative, existing outside the rules that govern the current social arrangements. Some civil libertarians contend that non-normative action is preferable when a system is unlikely to be uprooted. For example, Thoreau (1969) decried what he considered an illegitimate but stable and well-established social system; its stability necessitated non-violent action in the form of passive resistance to attempt small changes within the system.

Our model also incorporates the distinction between overt and covert action. "Two crucial aspects of social visibility are the degree to which elites comprehend (in some fashion) the political interests of those who oppose them and the degree to which the particular identities of those engaged in covert conflict are known" (Morrill et al., 2003). In overt politics, the identities of participants and their general political interests are relatively well known by elites and, more often than not, broader social audiences. In contrast, "for political conflict to be covert, it must avert the detection and direct engagement of various social audiences, especially elites and other authorities" (Morrill et al., 2003, p. 394). This is more likely to occur when authorities neither have knowledge of the political interests of actors nor the identities of actors.[3]

Full-fledged, overt, non-normative attempts to overturn a power structure through civil disobedience, such as the civil rights movement, are therefore differentiated from less overt aggression, for example corporate sabotage and work slowdowns. The Luddites rebelled in the late nineteenth century by sabotaging textile looms to slow the incursion of large manufacturers. However, we contend their low sense of power restricted their behavior to covert acts of subversion, as opposed to open attempts to overturn the power hierarchy. Another example of action that is not overt and non-normative is a situation in which employees covertly lower their quotas by working more slowly in response to wage rates that are matched to a standard level of output per hour (Roy, 1952). However, such quota restriction techniques only indicate that the employees are surreptitiously "working the system" instead of attempting to completely overturn the quota system. Lacking a sense of power to control one's situation, individuals often respond to frustration and injustice with sabotage (Giacalone, Riordan, & Rosenfeld, 1997) and organizational theft (Greenberg, 1993; Perlow & Latham, 1993). Organizational theft may be understood as an act of retributive justice in which employees attempt to rectify some grievance against the employer (Trevino, 1992).

Each of the antecedent factors may relate more to one factor than another. For example, anger may particularly relate to whether action is normative versus non-normative, with anger increasing the propensity to lash out in a non-normative way. Sense of power, on the other hand, may be a primary predictor of whether action is overt or covert; since power is disinhibiting (Keltner et al., 2003), a sense of power may reduce any fear of repercussions for actions taken against authority and thus, when members' sense of power increases they may be more likely to engage in overt action against elites. Indeed, empirical work is required to determine whether a sense of high power is a *necessary* factor for *overt* action to occur.

Not only will the antecedent conditions have direct effects on the type of emotion, but they should interact with each other to predict the type of action taken. We suggest that the level and type of action taken against hierarchies increases as more of the elements of our model are present (see Table 1). The most intense form of action involves overt, non-normative actions against authorities such as riots, terrorism, and revolutions. The next level of action involves non-normative actions that are covertly expressed such as covert forms of sabotage (e.g., spreading computer viruses). Next are actions that are normative and overtly expressed, such as legal strikes or formal demands made through proxy statements at annual board meetings. The lowest level of action against authority includes normative actions that are covertly expressed, such as normatively following directives to the letter in such a way that work is hampered and efficiency reduced.

We predict that the actions taken against hierarchies are more likely to become more overt and non-normative as more of the factors are present. Future research should examine the precise relationships of these antecedent

Table 1. Typology of Actions Against Authority.

	Overt	Covert
Non-normative	Terrorism Riots, revolutions Overt sabotage Wildcat strikes	Covert sabotage (computer viruses, defacing property) Sabotage by circumvention (work slow downs, social loafing, quota restriction, and goldbricking) Compensatory or justice-motivated theft Hidden transcripts (comedy, gossip, and hidden carnivals)
Normative	Proxy statements at annual shareholder meetings Strikes, protest rallies (normative as long as laws not broken)	Work-to-rule (obey rules to paralyze work)

factors (sense of power, emotions, and perceptions of the system) to the typology of action taken. Perhaps at the highest level of intensity, when a high sense of power, high-power emotions, and system illegitimacy and instability coexist, will members be most likely to engage in overt, non-normative action against the elite – action designed to overthrow the system and reverse or purge that hierarchy. At a reduced level of intensity, perhaps when anger and system illegitimacy coexist but without a sense of power, members will be likely to engage in covert, non-normative action against elites. Covert, normative action against elites, such as work to rule, may exist when a system is seen as illegitimate but stable, and the subordinated individuals lack a sense of pride. Finally, when none of the three conditions are present we predict that members are unlikely to act against authority and will accept the status quo.

A careful examination is necessary to understand the exact relationship between the antecedent factors and the types of actions taken. For instance, as more of the factors are present there may be an increase in the number of non-normative actions; however, this non-normative increase may actually be an inverted "U" shaped curve. For example, actions against authority may return to a more normative level again as a groups' sense of power increases. Normative actions such as proxy statements overtly directed at firms during annual shareholder meetings would be an example of this. This normative, overt form of action against authority would be more likely if the actors had an increased sense of power. In fact, lacking a sense of power is associated with impulsivity and actions that are detrimental to one's own well being in primates (Fairbanks, 2001). The more powerful one is, the more likely one is to define resources creatively and use existing institutional frameworks to his/her advantage. By contrast, the weaker one is (especially when one feels that the system is stable and closed, and yet feels angry) the more likely one is to use non-normative tactics. For example, federal and state enforcement of criminal penalties on anti-abortion demonstrators who blocked clinics led to a decline of peaceful clinic protests, even as some anti-abortion activists adopted more disruptive tactics (Meyer & Staggenborg, 1996).

It is important to note that some non-normative behaviors, such as revolutions, are designed to reverse the hierarchy and other times non-normative behaviors, such as riots, are simply an expression of anger – expressions that can unintentionally preserve disadvantage rather than reverse it. The riots that shook Los Angeles in 1991, after what was widely perceived to be an illegitimate verdict in the Rodney King trial, provide an example of such non-normative behavior. Angry rioters clearly perceived the system to be unjust and illegitimate. However, they also probably accepted that the system was firmly established, stable and not likely to be overturned. This may partly explain why most of the violence during these riots ended up being directed against the rioters' own communities, as opposed to the system of authority. A movement whose motto was "No Justice" scarcely took root after the riots, perhaps due to a sense of futility about the deeply entrenched and stable judicial and political system.

Finally, as a corollary to our model, future research could examine how these antecedent factors impact the psychology of the *powerful* and how they respond to the action and voice of the subordinated. The emotions, sense of power, and perceptions of the system that favors them, may predict when the advantaged will actively suppress revolts or when the demands of the subordinated will be acceded to. The defenders of power hierarchies are likely to fight more fiercely to maintain the status quo if they perceive it to be legitimate, stable, and open to social advancement by those lower in the hierarchy. For example, an archival analysis of the ACT UP's success in attaining changes in the process of drug approvals might indicate whether members of the CDC felt their sense of power, as well as self-perceived legitimacy, diminishing as the media and popular opinion swelled against them.

CONCLUSION

In this chapter, we have attempted to integrate divergent literatures and research including system justification theory, social identity theory, emotions, and the approach-inhibition theory of power into a model that predicts when and how those in low power will take action against authorities and systems that subordinate them. Our model also extends the literature on social movements by going beyond specifying the macro-structural conditions that promote collective action to explicate when the activist within the subordinated may be aroused. We have identified three antecedent psychological processes – a sense of power, emotions associated with power (e.g., anger and pride), and perceptions that the system is illegitimate, unstable, and impermeable to individual advancement – that we have proposed independently and interactively determine the type of action. These three antecedent conditions help to predict when the activist within the subordinated will be awakened and inspire system condemnation, and when the activist will remain dormant, a mere enabler and justifier of the current hierarchical relationships.

NOTES

1. When individuals take action to change power hierarchies also is an issue that has attracted the attention of political scientists. Much of political sociology draws on the social movement literature and so we do not review it independently. We note that rational choice political scientists treat the problem of changing the system as a collective goods problem in the tradition of Olson (1968), and suggest that individuals join collective effort when there are selective incentives. We acknowledge this literature, but develop an identity-based account of action rather than an incentive-based explanation.

2. The AIDS quilt was a powerful, unifying symbol connecting AIDS activists with the wider public. The quilt itself included thousands of hand-sewn designs representing those who had died of AIDS. ACT UP embarked on a highly popular cross-country tour to display the quilt, which successfully galvanized interest and activism by transforming grief into anger and activism (Gould, 2002).

3. Covert and overt actions can also be differentiated in terms of whether the identities of actors is known or not or whether the actions themselves are visible or not. We understand that covert and overt actions can be more broadly defined to include these distinctions. However, we restrict our definition to whether actors' interests are known or not. Examples of overt action would thus include Oaxacan insurgents who have press conferences while wearing ski masks; undisclosed, invisible undermining of financial markets by established anticapitalists; invisible computer-slowing viruses infecting abortion clinics sent within Right to Life campaign e-mails.

ACKNOWLEDGEMENTS

We thank Keith Murnighan for his extremely helpful comments and suggestions on this project. We also would like to thank Tom Tyler, Sam Fraidin, Elizabeth Mannix, and the participants at the Managing Groups and Teams Conference for their helpful suggestions on an earlier draft of this chapter. This research was supported by a grant from the Dispute Resolution Resource Center.

REFERENCES

Anderson, C., & Spataro, S. (this volume). Knowing your place: The sense of power in thought, feeling and action. In: M.C. Thomas-Hunt (Ed.), *Research in Managing Groups and Teams: Status and Groups.*

Anderson, C., John, O. P., Keltner, D., & Kring, A. M. (2001). Who attains social status? Effects of personality and physical attractiveness in social groups. *Journal of Personality and Social Psychology, 81*, 116–132.

Baumeister, R. F., Smart, L., & Boden, J. M. (1996). Relation of threatened egotism to violence and aggression: The dark side of high self-esteem. *Psychological Review, 103*, 5–33.

Benford, R. D., & Snow, D. A. (2000). Framing processes and social movements: An overview and assessment. *Annual Review of Sociology, 26*, 611–639.

Bettenhausen, K., & Murnighan, J. K. (1985). The emergence of norms in competitive decision-making groups. *Administrative Science Quarterly, 30*, 350–372.

Bies, R. J., & Tripp, T. M. (1996). Beyond distrust: "Getting even" and the need for revenge. In: R. M. Kramer & T. R. Tyler (Eds.), *Trust in organizations: Frontiers of theory and research.*

Bies, R. J., & Tyler, T. R. (1993). The "litigation mentality" in organizations: A test of alternative psychological explanations. *Organization Science, 4*, 352–366.

Brewer, M. B., Manzi, J. M., & Shaw, J. S. (1993). In-group identification as a function of depersonalization, distinctiveness, and status. *Psychological Science, 4*, 88–92.

Burawoy, M. (1979). *Manufacturing consent: Changes in the labor process under monopoly capitalism.* Chicago: University of Chicago Press.

Buss, A. H., & Perry, M. (1992). The aggression questionnaire. *Journal of Personality and Social Psychology, 63*, 452–459.

Clayton, S. D. (1992). The experience of injustice: Some characteristics and correlates. *Social Justice Research, 5*, 71–91.

Cook, S. (2001). Pressure groups hold a cosh over firms. *Management Today, 65*(May 31, 2001).

Crosby, F. (1976). A model of egoistical relative deprivation. *Psychological Review, 83*, 85–113.

De Cremer, D., & Tyler, T. (this volume). A matter of intragroup status: The importance of respect for the viability of groups. In: M. Thomas-Hunt (Ed.), *Research on Managing Groups and Teams: Status and Groups.*

Eagly, A. H., Makhijani, M. G., & Klonsky, B. G. (1992). Gender and the evaluation of leaders: A meta-analysis. *Psychological Bulletin, 111*, 3–22.

Ellemers, N., Wilke, H., & van Knippenberg, A. (1993). Effects of the legitimacy of low group or individual status on individual and collective status-enhancement strategies. *Journal of Personality and Social Psychology, 64*, 766–778.

Emerson, R. M. (1962). Power dependence relations. *American Journal of Sociology, 27*, 31–41.

Fairbanks, L. A. (2001). Individual differences in response to a stranger: Social impulsivity as a dimension of temperament in vervet monkeys (Cercopithecus aethiops sabaeus). *Journal of Comparative Psychology, 115*, 22–28.

Fazio, R. H., Effrein, E. A., & Falender, V. J. (1981). Self-perceptions following social interaction. *Journal of Personality and Social Psychology, 41*, 232–242.

Fiske, S. T. (1993). Controlling other people: The impact of power on stereotyping. *American Psychologist, 48*, 621–628.

French, J. P., & Raven, B. (1959). The bases of social power. In: D. Cartwright (Ed.), *Studies in social power* (pp. 150–167). Ann Arbor: University of Michigan Press.

Frijda, N. H., Kuipers, P., & Schure, E. (1989). Relations among emotion, appraisal, and emotional action readiness. *Journal of Personality and Social Psychology, 57*, 212–228.

Galinsky, A. D., Gruenfeld, D. H., & Magee, J. C. (2003a). From power to action. *Journal of Personality and Social Psychology, 85*, 453–466.

Galinsky, A. D., Magee, J. C., Gruenfeld, D. H., Whitson, J., Lilgenquist, K., & Cadena, B. (2003b). Power and the inattention to obstacles and social constraint: Implications for disobedience, conformity, and dissonance. Paper presented at the International Association of Conflict Management.

Giacalone, R. A., Riordan, C. A., & Rosenfeld, P. (1997). Employee sabotage: Toward a practitioner-scholar understanding. In: R. A. Giacalone & J. Greenberg (Eds), *Antisocial behavior in organizations* (pp. 109–129). Thousand Oaks, CA: Sage.

Gladwell, M. (2000). *The tipping point: How little things can make a big difference*. Boston: Little Brown.

Gould, D. (2001). Rock the boat, don't rock the boat, baby: Ambivalence and the emergence of militant AIDS activism. In: J. Goodwin, J. M. Jasper & F. Polletta (Eds), *Passionate politics: Emotions and social movements* (pp. 135–157). Chicago: University of Chicago Press.

Gould, D. B. (2002). Life during wartime: Emotions and the development of ACT UP. *Mobilization, 7*, 177–200.

Greenberg, J. (1987). A taxonomy of organizational justice theories. *Academy of Management Review, 12*, 9–22.

Greenberg, J. (1993). Stealing in the name of justice: Informational and interpersonal moderators of theft reactions to underpayment inequity. *Organizational Behavior & Human Decision Processes, 54*, 81–103.

Haney, C., Banks, C., & Zimbardo, P. (1973). Interpersonal dynamics in a simulated prison. *International Journal of Criminology & Penology, 1*, 69–97.

Harmon-Jones, E., & Allen, J. J. B. (1998). Anger and frontal brain activity: EEG asymmetry consistent with approach motivation despite negative affective valence. *Journal of Personality and Social Psychology, 74*, 1310–1316.

Hercus, C. (1999). Identity, emotion, and feminist collective action. *Gender & Society, 13*, 34–55.

Hirschman, A. O. (1970). *Exit, voice, and loyalty: Responses to decline in firms, organizations, and states*. Cambridge, MA: Harvard University Press.

Hochschild, A. R. (1983). Feeling management: From private to commercial uses. In: A. R. Hochschild (Ed.), *The managed heart: Commercialization of human feeling* (pp. 89–136). Berkeley, CA: University of California Press.

Horney, K. (1939). *New ways in psychoanalysis*. New York: W.W. Norton.

Horowitz, D. L. (2001). *The Deadly ethnic riot*. Berkeley, CA: University of California Press.

Jost, J. T., & Banaji, M. R. (1994). The role of stereotyping in system-justification and the production of false consciousness. *British Journal of Social Psychology, 33*, 1–27.

Jost, J. T., Pelham, B. W., & Carvallo, M. R. (2002). Non-conscious forms of system justification: Implicit and behavioral preferences for higher status groups. *Journal of Experimental Social Psychology, 38*, 586–602.

Kay, A. C., & Jost, J. T. (2003). Complementary justice: Effects of "poor but happy" and "poor but honest" stereotype exemplars on system justification and implicit activation of the justice motive. *Journal of Personality and Social Psychology, 85*, 823–837.

Keltner, D., Ellsworth, P. C., & Edwards, K. (1993). Beyond simple pessimism: Effects of sadness and anger on social perception. *Journal of Personality and Social Psychology, 64*, 740–752.

Keltner, D., Gruenfeld, D. H., & Anderson, C. A. (2003). Power, approach, and inhibition. *Psychological Review, 110*, 265–284.

Le Bon, G. (1921). *The crowd, a study of the popular mind.* London: T.F. Unwin.

Lerner, J. S., & Keltner, D. (2001). Fear, anger and risk. *Journal of Personality and Social Psychology, 81*, 146–159.

Leung, K., Chiu, W., & Au, Y. (1993). Sympathy and support for industrial actions: A justice analysis. *Journal of Applied Psychology, 78*, 781–787.

Lind, E. A. (2001). Fairness heuristic theory: Justice judgments as pivotal cognitions in organizational relations. In: J. Greenberg & R. Cropanzano (Eds), *Advances in organizational justice* (pp. 56–88). Palo Alto, CA: Stanford University Press.

Lind, E. A., & Tyler, T. (1988). *The social psychology of procedural justice*. New York: Plenum Press.

Lind, E. A., Kanfer, R., & Earley, P. C. (1990). Voice, control, and procedural justice: Instrumental and noninstrumental concerns in fairness judgments. *Journal of Personality and Social Psychology, 59*, 952–959.

Lind, E. A., Kulik, C. T., Ambrose, M., & de Vera Park, M. V. (1993). Individual and corporate dispute resolution: Using procedural fairness as a decision heuristic. *Administrative Science Quarterly, 38*, 224–251.

Martin, J. (1986). The tolerance of injustice. In: J. M. Olson, C. P. Herman & M. P. Zanna (Eds), *Relative Deprivation and Social Comparison: The Ontario Symposium*, (Vol. 4, pp. 217–242). Mahwah, NJ: Erlbaum.

Martin, J. (1993). Inequity, distributive justice, and organizational illegality. In: J. K. Murnighan (Ed.), *Social psychology in organizations: Advances in theory and research* (pp. 296–321). Englewood Cliffs, NJ: Prentice-Hall.

Martin, J., Brickman, P., & Murray, A. (1984). Moral outrage and pragmatism: Explanations for collective action. *Journal of Experimental Social Psychology, 20*, 484–496.

McAdam, D., McCarthy, J. D., & Zald, M. N. (1997). Introduction: Opportunities, mobilizing structures, and framing processes: Toward a synthetic, comparative perspective on social movements. In: D. McAdam, J. D. McCarthy & M. N. Zald (Eds), *Comparative perspectives on social movements: Political opportunities, mobilizing structures, and cultural framings* (pp. 1–20). Cambridge, England: Cambridge University Press.

McAdam, D., Tarrow, S. G., & Tilly, C. (2001). *Dynamics of contention.* New York: Cambridge University Press.
McCarthy, J. D., & Zald, M. N. (1977). Resource mobilization and social movements: A partial theory. *American Journal of Sociology, 82*, 1212–1241.
McPhail, C. (1991). *The myth of the madding crowd.* New York: Walter de Gruyter, Inc.
Merton, R. K. (1948). The self-fulfilling prophecy. *Antioch Review, 8*, 193–210.
Meyer, D. S., & Staggenborg, S. (1996). Movements, countermovements, and the structure of political opportunity. *American Journal of Sociology, 101*, 1628–1660.
Mikulincer, M. (1988). Reactance and helplessness following exposure to unsolvable problems: The effects of attributional style. *Journal of Personality and Social Psychology, 54*, 679–686.
Miller, D. T. (2000). Disrespect and the experience of injustice. *Annual Review of Psychology, 52*, 527–553.
Morrill, C., Zald, M. N., & Rao, H. (2003). Covert political conflict in organizations: Challenges from below. *Annual Review of Sociology, 29*, 391–415.
New York State Special Commission on Attica. (1972). *Attica: The official report of the New York State Special Commission on Attica.* New York: Praeger Publishers.
Ng, S. H., & Cram, F. (1988). Intergroup bias by defensive and offensive groups in majority and minority conditions. *Journal of Personality and Social Psychology, 55*, 749–757.
Perlow, R., & Latham, L. L. (1993). Relationship of client abuse with locus of control and gender: A longitudinal study in mental retardation facilities. *Journal of Applied Psychology, 78*, 831–834.
Pratto, F., Sidanius, J., Stallworth, L. M., & Malle, B. F. (1994). Social dominance orientation: A personality variable predicting social and political attitudes. *Journal of Personality and Social Psychology, 67*, 741–763.
Reicher, S. D. (1984). The St. Pauls' riot: An explanation of the limits of crowd action in terms of a social identity model. *European Journal of Social Psychology, 14*, 1–21.
Rosette, A. S., & Thompson, L. (this volume). The camouflage effect: Disentagling status and privilege. In: M. C. Thomas-Hunt (Ed.), *Research in Managing Groups and Teams: Status and Groups.*
Rotter, J. B. (1966). Generalized expectancies for internal versus external control of reinforcement. *Psychological Monographs, 80*, Whole No. 609.
Roy, D. (1952). Quota restriction and goldbricking in a machine shop. *American Journal of Sociology, 57*, 427–442.
Ruggiero, K. M., & Taylor, D. M. (1995). Coping with discrimination: How disadvantaged group members perceive the discrimination that confronts them. *Journal of Personality and Social Psychology, 68*, 826–838.
Saenz, A. (1986). *Politics of a prison riot: The 1980 New Mexico prison riot its causes and aftermath.* Corrales, NM: Rhombus.
Schwarz, N. (1990). Feelings as information: Informational and motivational functions of affective states. In: E. T. Higgins & R. M. Sorrentino (Eds), *Handbook of motivation and cognition.* New York: Guilford Press.
Sidanius, J. (1993). The psychology of group conflict and the dynamics of oppression: A social dominance perspective. In: S. Iyengar & W. J. McGuire (Eds), *Explorations in political psychology* (pp. 183–219). Durham, NC: Duke University Press.
Sidanius, J., Pratto, F., Martin, M., & Stallworth, L. M. (1991). Consensual racism and career track: Some implications of social dominance theory. *Political Psychology, 12*, 691–721.

Solomon, R. C. (1995). *A passion for justice: Emotions and the origins of the social contract*. Lanham, MD: Rowman & Littlefield.

Steele, C. M. (1988). The psychology of self-affirmation: Sustaining the integrity of the self. In: L. Berkowitz (Ed.), *Advances in experimental social psychology*, (Vol. 21, pp. 261–302). San Diego, CA: Academic Press.

Steele, C. M. (1992). Race and the schooling of black Americans. *The Atlantic Monthly, 269*, 68–78.

Stryker, S. (2000). Identity competition: Key to differential social movement participation? In: S. Sheldon, T. J. Owens & R. W. White (Eds), *Self, identity, and social movements* (pp. 21–40). Minneapolis: University of Minnesota Press.

Tajfel, H. (1981). *Human groups and social categories: Studies in social psychology*. Cambridge, UK: Cambridge University Press.

Tajfel, H., & Turner, J. C. (1979). An integrative theory of intergroup conflict. In: W. G. Austin & S. Worchel (Eds), *The social psychology of intergroup relations* (pp. 33–47). Monterey, CA: Brooks/Cole.

Tajfel, H., & Turner, J. C. (1986). The social identity theory of intergroup behavior. In: S. Worchel & W. G. Austin (Eds), *Psychology of intergroup relations* (2nd ed., pp. 7–24). Chicago: Nelson-Hall.

Tarrow, S. G. (1994). *Power in movement: Social movements, collective action, and politics*. New York: Cambridge University Press.

Taylor, S. E., & Brown, J. D. (1988). Illusion and well-being: A social psychological perspective on mental health. *Psychological Bulletin, 103*, 193–210.

Tesser, A. (1988). Toward a self-evaluation maintenance model of social behavior. In: L. Berkowitz (Ed.), *Advances in experimental social psychology*, (Vol. 21, pp. 181–227). San Diego, CA: Academic Press.

Thibaut, J. W., & Kelley, H. H. (1959). *The social psychology of groups*. New York: Wiley.

Thoreau, H. D. (1969). *Civil disobedience*. Boston, MA: D.R. Godine.

Tiedens, L. Z. (1999). *Feeling low and feeling high: Associations between social status and emotions*. Unpublished dissertation. University of Michigan, MI.

Tiedens, L. Z. (2001a). Anger and advancement versus sadness and subjugation: The effect of negative emotion expressions on social status conferral. *Journal of Personality and Social Psychology, 80*, 86–94.

Tiedens, L. Z. (2001b). The effect of anger on the hostile inferences of aggressive and non-aggressive people: Specific emotions, cognitive processing, and chronic accessibility. *Motivation & Emotion, 25*, 233–251.

Tiedens, L. Z., Ellsworth, P. C., & Mesquita, B. (2000). Stereotypes about sentiments and status: Emotional expectations for high- and low-status group members. *Personality & Social Psychology Bulletin, 26*, 560–574.

Tilly, C. (19781990). *From mobilization to revolution*. New York: McGraw-Hill.

Tilly, C. (1986). *The contentious French*. Cambridge, MA: Harvard University Press.

Trevino, L. K. (1992). The social effects of punishment in organizations: A justice perspective. *Academy of Management Review, 17*, 647–676.

Turner, J. C., & Brown, R. (1978). Social status, cognitive alternatives, and intergroup relations. In: H. Tajfel (Ed.), *Differentiation between social groups: Studies in the social psychology of intergroup relations* (pp. 202–234). New York: Academic Press.

Tyler, T. R. (1989). The psychology of procedural justice: A test of the group-value model. *Journal of Personality and Social Psychology, 57*, 830–838.

Tyler, T. R., & Smith, H. J. (1998). Social justice and social movements. In: D. T. Gilbert, S. T. Fiske & G. Lindzey (Eds), *The handbook of social psychology*, (Vol. 2, pp. 595–629). New York: McGraw-Hill.

Walker, I., & Mann, L. (1987). Unemployment, relative deprivation, and social protest. *Personality and Social Psychology Bulletin*, *13*, 275–283.

Weber, M. (1947). The theory of social and economic organization "reprinted section: Bureaucracy". In: O. Grusky & G. A. Miller (Eds), *The sociology of organizations: Basic studies*, (2nd ed.). New York: Macmillan.

Woodzicka, J. A., & LaFrance, M. (2001). Real versus imagined gender harassment. *Journal of Social Issues*, *57*, 15–30.

Wright, S. C., Taylor, D. M., & Moghaddam, F. M. (1990). Responding to membership in a disadvantaged group: From acceptance to collective protest. *Journal of Personality and Social Psychology*, *58*, 994–1003.

Zimbardo, P. G., Haney, C., Banks, C., & Jaffe, D. (1974). The psychology of imprisonment: Privation, power, and pathology. In: Z. Rubin (Ed.), *Doing unto others: Explorations in social behavior* (pp. 61–73). Englewood Cliffs, NJ: Prentice Hall.

ROLE OF STATUS IN GROUP PROCESSES

Edward J. Lawler

ABSTRACT

This chapter organizes the other chapters of the volume around a fundamental status-affirmation principle, namely, that status differentials generate corresponding differences in performance expectations which, in turn, produce behaviors that affirm performance expectations. The chapters in this volume elaborate that proposition by showing how information exchange, patterns of privilege, and the accuracy of power perceptions reflect or strengthen the status-affirmation process. Several chapters also suggest conditions that forestall or weaken this process such as claims to expertise and communication styles. Other chapters can be construed as offering applications of the status-affirmation principle to the performance of corporate project teams and to the relationships between standard and nonstandard employees in the workplace. Overall, the chapters reflect the strength and vitality of the tradition of work on group processes.

The importance of groups to human experience and interaction is undeniable and incontrovertible. People live their lives in groups, in the workplace, in families, among friends, in neighborhoods, and in communities. Groups or group affiliations are important sources of identity, cooperation, collaboration, and a sense of belonging. Such effects exemplify positive consequences of

Status and Groups
Research on Managing Groups and Teams, Volume 7, 315–325

ISSN: 1534-0856/doi:10.1016/S1534-0856(05)07013-1

group affiliations for individuals and organizations. Groups or group affiliations also are a source of negative consequences such as exclusion, injustice, discrimination, and violence. Still other group phenomena may have either positive or negative consequences in these terms. A conflict may promote collaborative relations and unity or discrimination and hostility, and the same can be said for a host of other phenomena. The upshot is that groups are a source of both order and disorder. On the one hand, group affiliations promote and organize social interactions, bringing together individuals with similar goals; on the other hand, groups generate divisions or differentiation that foster dissatisfaction, dissent, and conflict.

Status and status processes are fundamental to these "order producing" and "disorder producing" effects of group affiliations and relations. Status structures facilitate order by "expressing" or manifesting prevailing definitions of worth, value, and competence. Those of higher status are perceived (accurate or not) as higher on these dimensions. Status differentiation facilitates disorder by raising issues of justice/injustice, equal opportunity, and legitimacy. The chapters of this conference move the field of group processes forward by addressing these varied effects of status relations and processes.

The work here represents an important tradition of group process research that originated primarily in business schools over the last 20 or so years. I would term this the "management tradition." It draws heavily on theories from psychology (e.g., social identity theory) and, more recently, sociology (e.g., expectation states theory), but it is distinctive in at least three interrelated ways: The substantive focus is on problems and issues relevant to the workplace or work organizations; it is directed at addressing problems more than at building theory; and, it is more explicitly interdisciplinary than the group processes traditions found in psychology and sociology. These features of the "management tradition" are an important source of its research contributions to the "group processes" area as a whole. The workplace focus gives the tradition a theme, the problem focus around this theme gives it more explicit applied or practical value, and the interdisciplinary nature of the tradition gives it a refreshing intellectual openness and breadth. The chapters of this volume reflect these strengths quite well and suggest the vitality of this tradition.

BACKGROUND

Fundamental changes in the world suggest that a deep and subtle understanding of status processes in groups is increasingly important to most areas of human experience. Part of the reason is a general decline in hierarchy as a mechanism of control and for accomplishing collective or organizational goals. This is manifest in more collaborative work systems, an increase in the importance of negotiation and trust across groups within organizations, and so forth. In the workplace of today, collaborative relations linking actors in different geographic locations, from different social backgrounds, and with different experiences are critical parts of job responsibilities and essential for accomplishing organizational goals or objectives. These differences, however, have status implications. Similarly, changes in the family put more premium on shared responsibilities and the coordination and negotiation of tasks, most of which respond to and attempt to overcome gender status differentiation. Families have become more collaborative and less hierarchical, as have workplaces. Finally, the decline of formal memberships in organizations (e.g., the "bowling alone" phenomenon), the growing importance of networks of weak ties for professional success, and the changing nature of careers all point to the importance of groups as key social mechanisms. These give actors a sense of belonging that promotes career opportunities, constrains unethical behavior, and fosters commitments to larger social units shared by substantial populations of people. The most important aspects of group phenomena today are not necessarily the formal, highly structured features, but rather informal, ties, networks, and associations that "come and go" and have revolving memberships and ever-changing objectives. In this context, the informal processes by which status differentiation is created, enacted, and reproduced are even more central as research problems. This volume identifies and fleshes out several of these important informal aspects and dimensions of status in work settings.

Most all of the chapters in this volume conceive of status as involving social evaluations of worth or competence across individuals in a group or across groups within an organization. Such evaluations are the basis for ranking individuals, structuring responsibilities, and defining formal or informal positions. The evaluations can involve social categories (e.g., gender, age, race, ethnicity) that have cultural beliefs and expectations associated with them, group affiliations or memberships that bear on the perceptions of individual members (e.g., group identities), or particular performances that suggest relevant competence or expertise (e.g., education, prestige of school). Expectation States Theory in sociology (Berger, Fisek, Norman, & Zelditch Jr. 1977; Ridgeway & Walker, 1995) has distinguished "diffuse" status characteristics, which are based on cultural beliefs about worth (Ridgeway, Boyer, Kuipers, & Robinson, 1998), from specific status characteristics, which stem from demonstrated competence on some task. Status characteristics, whether diffuse or specific, promote patterns of deference, compliance, and conformity. The chapters of this volume suggest important elaborations of how and when status differentiation has positive or negative effects on group relations and success.

STATUS-AFFIRMATION PROCESS

A fundamental principle, that I will term "status affirmation," can serve as a backdrop for analyzing the implications of the work herein. The "principle of status affirmation" specifies and interconnects three "moments" in a status process:

(1) *Status differences (i.e., differences in social evaluation) create differential performance expectations.* Interpreted broadly, "performance expectations" include not only individual task performance, but also group performance (i.e., likelihood of being a good team member, contributing to the collective good, and giving priority to group over individual interests if necessary).
(2) *Performance expectations generate affirming behaviors on the part of a focal individual and others with whom they are interacting.* People act on differential performance expectations by behaving differentially toward those with different status (evaluations).
(3) *The affirming behaviors, in turn, strengthen and/or reproduce the social evaluations underlying the status differences.* I would argue that this "status-affirmation process" is one of the most well-founded principles found in the social sciences. It has been theorized carefully and researched substantially and could be construed as approximating a "basic law" of social interaction. The principle articulates in a simple way how and why status differences generate regular, predictable, and orderly patterns of interaction, how and why such differences are resilient, self-fulfilling prophecies, and why they may generate, under some conditions, a sense of injustice and behavioral efforts to change an existing status relationship.

Using the principle of status affirmation as a backdrop, the chapters of this volume can be grouped under three categories:

(1) those that elaborate the status-affirmation principle,
(2) those that offer strategies for mitigating status affirmation, and

(3) those that apply this principle to another group phenomenon.

Each of these categories is discussed, in turn, below.

ELABORATIONS

The Chen and Lo chapter emphasize the differential expectations embedded in individualist and collectivist cultures. Individualist cultures draw attention to intragroup differences and associated expectations, whereas collectivist cultures draw attention to intergroup expectations. Thus, "performances" around which expectations form are culturally grounded constellations that are embedded in the social context. This implies a broader conception or interpretation of "performance" and "performance expectations" than often found in the research literature on groups, especially by American Social Psychologists and Sociologists. What status-relevant information becomes salient (e.g., intragroup versus intergroup differences) in a given interaction or group setting is contingent on themes of the larger culture.

Rosette and Thompson provide a review and theoretical analysis of how privileges based on ascribed (unearned) statuses can become perceived as achieved (earned). This is termed a "camouflage effect." Privilege is defined as additional or ancillary "rewards and advantages" that are accorded to those in social categories or positions that yield status. The argument is that when high-status persons receive a privilege, it is viewed as earned, whereas when low-status persons are given a privilege it is viewed as unearned. An example is how the public responds to special consideration given to legacies versus under-represented minorities in college admissions. This chapter suggests that in work organizations, privilege is awarded on the basis of ascribed characteristics, but socially defined as achieved and deserved by those who receive such privileges. They interpret these effects as due to the threat to self-identity or self-esteem and the expectations associated with high-status positions (Berger et al., 1977). This chapter suggests that higher status, not only has "affirming effects" through expectations and related behavior, but also "status enhancing" effects that stem from adding privileges that enhance performance expectations.

Wittenbaum and Bowman offer several propositions about how status affects information exchange in groups. Status affects the patterns of information sharing, the nature of the information shared, and also the evaluation of the person doing the information sharing. They suggest that high-status members generally will communicate more information, shared and unshared; information that is unique will be valued more and remembered more if communicated by high-status members; and there is a general bias in favor of shared information because it is status enhancing, and this pattern is stronger for low-status persons. Patterns of information exchange tend to reflect and affirm status structures.

The chapter by Overbeck, Correll, and Park posits a sorting mechanism through which new, undifferentiated groups develop status hierarchies. Among heterogenous status seekers, hierarchy emerges rather easily, but among homogenous status seekers, a sorting mechanism moves some upward and others downward. Such conditions put a premium on interpersonal skills and sensitivity. Those that achieve more status in homogenous groups are likely to have a collective orientation and more concern for others, whereas in heterogeneous groups, an individualistic orientation is dominant. One implication is that there are evolutionary processes that generate hierarchy without the mediation of expectations. This chapter may help explain how positions with differentiated statuses develop initially and, therefore, unleash the process specified by the status-affirmation principle.

Two chapters build power into the analysis, though without explicit ties to status. Cameron, Spataro, and Galinsky develop the notion that the perception of power is as important as the actual power people have. A highly powerful person may not be perceived as having power and a person with low power may be perceived as having much more power than they in fact have. People develop a "sense of power" which is defined as the perception of one's capability of influencing another. Cameron et al. argue that having an accurate sense of one's power is important to effective use of power. Mortorana and Galinsky address the question of when lower power persons essentially respond in a subordinate way and reproduce conditions that disadvantage them. This entails a self-fulfilling prophecy that dovetails the status-affirmation principle. However, Mortorana and Galinsky put forth an emotional explanation for this behavior, that is, fear and sadness associated with low power positions generates inaction. Low power individuals resist and seek change when the power hierarchies are unstable, illegitimate, and allow mobility by individuals across levels. A sense of power helps transform fear into anger and related action to change the hierarchy. This also is a mechanism for changing the status structure.

To summarize, elaborations of the status-affirmation principle indicate that patterns of information sharing by low- and high-status persons tend to affirm the status order; individualist versus collectivist cultures make salient intragroup versus intergroup status differences, respectively; status differences are enhanced by patterns of privilege that add to the benefits and perceived worth of those in higher-status positions; and an accurate sense of power may enhance the degree that high-status persons strategically generate the status-affirmation process.

Reducing Status Affirmation

Three chapters suggest qualifications or ways to weaken or eliminate the status-affirmation process. Fraidin and Hollingshead suggest how gender stereotypes become "self-reinforcing" by virtue of what tasks are assigned to men and women. Task assignments tend to be shaped by gender stereotypes, that is, gender is perceived as entailing different competencies and thus differential status in particular task situations. Their research empirically demonstrates that "claims of expertise" are a mechanism for women to reduce the effects of gender stereotypes somewhat, and if these are validated by other information on the particular female's background, the claims have an even stronger effect. The important implication is that claims to expertise are a strategy for mitigating or eliminating the status-affirming process. Such claims involve a challenge to the existing status order.

The chapter by Fragale shows further that communication style, involving both verbal and nonverbal cues, is an important source of status if adjusted to the context. These effects occur by either conveying "interpersonal abilities" or "intellectual abilities." Fragale's research shows that in a finance department within a corporation, more assertive communication styles generate greater status and that this occurs because more assertive speakers are viewed as more competent. Interpersonal abilities play no role in status acquisition here. In a human resources department, however, assertive speech diminishes status because it is interpreted as implying poorer interpersonal abilities. A less assertive style conveys to others greater interpersonal abilities. In an organization with individualist values, persons will confer more status to persons with the more assertive communication styles, whereas within an organization with collaborative values, more status will be conferred upon persons with nonassertive communication styles. The implications are that, to be effective, the assertiveness with which "claims to expertise" are expressed need to fit the values and needs of the organizational context. Together, the Fragale chapter, along with the one by Fraidin and Hollingshead, suggest that those with lower status can acquire more status and influence in work groups and organizations, than their initial status position or ranking suggests, by adopting "appropriate" behavioral styles for the context and by making claims to expertise that will be perceived as valid and justifiable.

De Cremer and Tyler argue that "respect" from others in the group enhances the inclination of a member to contribute to the collective good. For instance, they indicate that when O conveys respect to S, S feels a greater sense of belonging and therefore is more willing to contribute to the group. Respecting behavior communicates a social evaluation that carries with it expectations for greater group contributions which S dutifully and willingly enacts. Respect is something that can be given by anybody to anybody, regardless of status position or evaluations. An interesting implication of this study is that mechanisms for generating behaviors that respect others in a group should mitigate the negative consequences of status differentiation with that group. Patterns of respect may not eliminate status differentiation around group tasks, but they presumably would encourage less deference to those with greater status, thereby weakening the status-affirmation process.

The status-affirmation process suggests a strong, inherent tendency for a status structure to be reproduced. The chapters by Fragale, Fraiden, and Hollingshead, and De Cremer and Tyler have implications for how the process can be counteracted by behavioral strategies and patterns. Claims to expertise and mutual patterns of respect are examples. The Wittenbaum and Bowman chapter suggests further that status effects are attenuated if the communication medium reduces the visibility of status cues and enhances the anonymity of individuals' identities.

Applications

Two chapters in the conference offer interesting applications of the status-affirmation process. Haas examines the performance of corporate project teams with an international composition. She argues that the distinction between "cosmopolitans" and "locals" on these teams generates status differences such that cosmopolitans participate more, are consulted more, and have greater influence than locals. Where such teams use more external knowledge, status evaluations are consensual, that is, cosmopolitans are perceived by group members as warranting more influence. When such teams use less external knowledge, status rivalry occurs between cosmopolitans and locals on the teams. Thus, the task determines whether a status characteristic, that is activated in the situation, has a positive or negative effect on group relations.

Vough, Broshak, and Northcraft interpret the relations between standard (regular) and nonstandard (contract) employees partially in status terms. The effects of nonstandard workers on group relations and performance depend on the competence (performance expectations) of the nonstandard workers. If highly competent nonstandard workers threaten the employment of standard workers status rivalry tends to occur, if standard workers perceive nonstandard workers as a burden, requiring more of their time, they represent a potential threat to the prestige of the work they do in the organization. These effects are stronger if standard and nonstandard employees work side-by-side and if they perform similar tasks. The Haas and Vough et al. chapters reveal distinct categories of employees that can be the basis for status rivalries. They identify conditions under which such rivalries are stronger or weaker, and some of these processes can be interpreted as status-affirmation effects.

CONCLUDING REMARKS

An implicit message of this volume is that status involves comparisons of general worth and these operate at multiple levels: (a) between individuals (person-to-person), (b) between persons and groups (person-to-group), and (c) between groups (group-to-group). Virtually all of the chapters in this volume incorporate multiple levels in some way. Some focus on one of these levels, but analyze it in the context of another, for example, examining the relation of person-to-person (intragroup) ties to person-to-group ties; others directly contrast conditions that make one level more salient than the other (e.g., intragroup versus intergroup statuses); and still others show how dynamics at one level affect processes at another. The notion that status should be interpreted as a multilevel phenomenon is not new, but the chapters of this volume add force and substance to this argument.

To illustrate, De Cremer and Tyler's chapter analyzes respect as an "intragroup" status, but shows its effect on person-to-group relations. Chen and Lo's chapter indicates that different types of culture shape whether intergroup and intragroup statuses are more salient, and Haas's use of the cosmopolitan–local distinction can be interpreted similarly. Fraidin and Hollingshead's and Rosette and Thompson's chapters have an intergroup focus involving different "groups" (gender, hierarchical status). A multilevel approach introduces more complexity in analyses of status and puts more demands on our theories. This volume suggests the need for multilevel theories of status that more explicitly and self-consciously bridge and interconnect the levels (see Markovsky, 1997, for discussion of multilevel theorizing). Only one chapter in this volume, Randel, Hoon, and Earley, moves in this direction. Randel et al. take notions of expectation states theory, which generally are focused on dyadic relations, and integrate these with the role identity theory of Sheldon Stryker (1980). Role identity theory can put the status characteristics in a structural context and offers a way of assessing how multiple identities with distinct status implications can vary in importance and salience to actors. Given people interact in the context of multiple identities or roles (i.e., group affiliations), the main argument is that identity salience and commitment determines the status characteristics most likely to become relevant in a given situation. This is a promising theoretical direction for future theorizing on status in the workplace.

As a sociologist, somewhat on the fringe of the "management tradition" of group processes, I see this volume as a reminder of the intellectual fragmentation within the group processes area. The lines of contact and communication among scholars in sociology, psychology, and management/OB fields are ad hoc and relatively unsystematic. Distinct collegial institutions within these fields have developed ways to promote intellectual exchange and collaboration around their own core set of problems. In psychology, this generally would be the yearly meetings of the Society of Experimental Social Psychology; in sociology, it would be the yearly Group Processes Conference organized at the meetings of the American Sociological Association, and the annual series, Advances in Group Processes. In the management/OB area, it is these yearly conferences and this annual series, Research on Managing Groups and Teams. It is noteworthy that within the same 15–20-year period, sociologists with an interest in group processes and those in business schools adopted similar strategies for building their areas (i.e., an annual volume and an annual conference). Each tradition has been strengthened and firmly established in their fields through these formal and informal associations. However, these strategies also tend to reduce incentives for or push toward stronger ties and collaborations across the sociologists and management/OB intellectual communities, in particular. Conferences that promote more cross-fertilization across these traditions would likely enrich each and bring more visibility and attention to the general area of group processes. The theoretical focus of the sociologic tradition and the problem focus of the management tradition are complementary and easy to bridge. Scholars in each of the traditions have much to learn from each other.

REFERENCES

Berger, J. M., Fisek, H., Norman, R. Z., & Zelditch, M., Jr. (1977). *Status characteristics and social interaction.* New York: Elsevier.

Markovsky, B. (1997). Building and testing multilevel theories. In: J. Szmatka, J. Skvoretz & J. Berger (Eds), *Status, network, and structure* (pp. 13–28). Stanford, CA: Stanford University Press.

Ridgeway, C. L., & Walker, H. A. (1995). Status structures. In: K. S. Cook, G. A. Fine & J. S. House (Eds), *Sociological perspectives on social psychology* (pp. 281–310). Needham Heights, MA: Allyn and Bacon.

Ridgeway, C. L., Boyer, E. H., Kuipers, K., & Robinson, D. T. (1998). How do status beliefs develop? The role of resources and interactional experience. *American Sociological Review*, *63*, 331–350.

Stryker, S. (1980). *Symbolic interaction: A social structural version*. Menlo Park, CA: Benjamin Cummins.

LaVergne, TN USA
04 October 2009
159836LV00006B/59/P

9 780762 312290